AN ECOLOGICAL THEOLOGY
OF LIBERATION

Ecology and Justice

An Orbis Series on Integral Ecology

The Orbis Series on Integral Ecology publishes books seeking to integrate an understanding of Earth's interconnected life systems with sustainable social, political, and economic systems that enhance the Earth community. Books in the series concentrate on ways to:

- reexamine human–Earth relations in light of contemporary cosmological and ecological science
- develop visions of common life marked by ecological integrity and social justice
- expand on the work of those exploring such fields as integral ecology, climate justice, Earth law, eco-feminism, and animal protection
- promote inclusive participatory strategies that enhance the struggle of Earth's poor and oppressed for ecological justice
- deepen appreciation for dialogue within and among religious traditions on issues of ecology and justice
- encourage spiritual discipline, social engagement, and the transformation of religion and society toward these ends.

Viewing the present moment as a time for fresh creativity and inspired by the encyclical *Laudato Si'*, the series seeks authors who speak to eco-justice concerns and who bring into this dialogue perspectives from the Christian communities, from the world's religions, from secular and scientific circles, or from new paradigms of thought and action.

AN ECOLOGICAL THEOLOGY OF LIBERATION

Salvation and Political Ecology

Daniel P. Castillo

ORBIS BOOKS
Maryknoll, New York 10545

ORBIS BOOKS
Maryknoll, New York 10545

Fathers and Brothers
MARYKNOLL

Founded in 1970, Orbis Books endeavors to publish works that enlighten the mind, nourish the spirit, and challenge the conscience. The publishing arm of the Maryknoll Fathers and Brothers, Orbis seeks to explore the global dimensions of the Christian faith and mission, to invite dialogue with diverse cultures and religious traditions, and to serve the cause of reconciliation and peace. The books published reflect the views of their authors and do not represent the official position of the Maryknoll Society. To learn more about Orbis Books, please visit our website at www.orbisbooks.org.

Chapter 2, "Integral Ecology: A Liberationist Concept," is a reworked version of the following published article: Daniel P. Castillo, "Integral Ecology as a Liberationist Concept," *Theological Studies* 77, no. 2 (June 2016): 355–76. Chapter 2 also contains material from the following published essay: "The Dynamism of Integral Liberation: Reconsidering Gutiérrez's Central Concept after the 'End of History,'" *Political Theology* 18, no. 1 (January 2017): 44–59

Chapter 3, "Reading Genesis Theologically in a Politico-Ecological Key," contains material from the following published essay: "Against the 'Unity' of Babel: Liberation Theology and the Language of Sustainable Development," in *Theology and Ecology across the Disciplines: On Care for Our Common Home*, ed. Celia Deane-Drummond and Rebecca Artinian-Kaiser (London: T&T Clark, 2018), reprinted with permission of T&T Clark, an imprint of Bloomsbury Publishing Plc.

Manufactured in the United States of America

Library of Congress Cataloging-in-Publication Data

Names: Castillo, Daniel Patrick, author.
Title: An ecological theology of liberation : salvation and political ecology / by Daniel P. Castillo.
Description: Maryknoll : Orbis Books, 2019. | Series: Ecology and justice, an Orbis series on integral ecology | Includes bibliographical references and index.
Identifiers: LCCN 2019020129 (print) | ISBN 9781626983212 (print)
Subjects: LCSH: Liberation theology. | Ecotheology. | Gutiérrez, Gustavo, 1928- Teología de la liberación. | Catholic Church. Pope (2013- : Francis). Laudato si'.
Classification: LCC BT83.57 .C365 2019 (print) | LCC BT83.57 (ebook) | DDC 230/.2—dc23
LC record available at https://lccn.loc.gov/2019020129
LC ebook record available at https://lccn.loc.gov/2019980668

To my children, Frances and Martin.

*Never would I wish your lives unmade
(to echo Wendell Berry).*

*May faith, hope, and love be your
enduring consolations.*

By your servants you have
mocked the Lord,
and you have said,
"With my many chariots
I have gone up the heights of the mountains,
to the far recesses of Lebanon;
I felled its tallest cedars,
its choicest cypresses;
I came to its remotest height,
its densest forest.
I dug wells and drank waters,
I dried up with the sole of my foot
all the streams of Egypt."

Isaiah 37:24–25

Contents

Acknowledgments

This book has benefited from the insights and generosity of many astute scholars and friends. I am grateful to Matthew Ashley for his wise direction of an earlier iteration of this argument, and for his friendship. I am likewise thankful to Jerry McKenny, Celia Deane-Drummond, and Omar Lizardo for their helpfully critical questions throughout that process. I am especially grateful to Gustavo Gutiérrez for his enthusiasm and encouragement throughout my work on this project, as well as for his work, which has greatly influenced my own.

I am deeply appreciative of those who have taken time to read through parts of this book and offer constructive feedback. In this regard, I am especially grateful to Richard Lennan who, since we met during the first semester of my master's program, has been steadfast in his generosity, unfailing in his encouragement, and productively critical of my written expression. I'm also grateful for the comments on the manuscript that I've received from Elizabeth Antus, Jim Buckley, David Carey, Christopher Carter, Lesley DiFrancisco, John Dougherty, John Fitzgerald, Steve Fowl, Brian Hamilton, Willis Jenkins, Kyle Lambelet, Kevin McCabe, Brandon Peterson, Trent Pomplun, Andrew Prevot, Nicole Reibe, Neto Valiente, and Matthew Whelan. I especially thank Roberto Goizueta, who took the time to read through the manuscript in its entirety.

I'm grateful to Jacqueline Hidalgo for inviting me to present part of Chapter 1 at the 2018 ACHTUS Colloquium and for the members of ACHTUS who took the time to read and comment on my work.

Additionally, countless persons have been generous with their time, allowing me to bounce my ideas off them and helping me refine my arguments over the course of several years. I am thankful for having so many great conversation partners, including Steve Battin, Fritz Bauerschmidt, Erin Lothes Biviano, William Brown, Brandon Bruning, Don Buggert, Peter Casarella, William Cavanaugh, Jessica Coblentz, Jeremy Cruz, Lorraine Cuddeback, Ilia Delio, Mary Doak, Heather DuBois, Denis Edwards, Rebekah Eklund, Julia Feder, Peter Fritz, Elizabeth Groppe, Mary Catherine Hilkert, Dan Horan, Natalia Imperatori-Lee, John Kiess, David Lantigua, Michael Lee, Tim Matovina, Ed McCormack, Claire Mathews McGinnis, Vince Miller, Kevin O'Brien, Pat Parachini. Margie Pfeil, Paul Scherz, Daniel Smith, Louis Vera, Tom Ward, Jeffrey Wickes, Tobias Winright, Raúl Zegarra, and Christiana Zenner. I am also grateful to the students I have taught throughout the years, for the ways in which their insights have sharpened my own.

I am thankful for the support of the GLOBES Program at the University of Notre Dame, Joanne Rodriguez and the Hispanic Theological Initiative, as well as Loyola University Maryland, all of whom have enabled and encouraged my research over the last decade, financially and otherwise.

I would not have been able to complete this project without the generous support of the Louisville Institute, from which I received a First Book Grant for Minority Scholars to help fund a year of research-leave while at Loyola University Maryland. I am grateful to Edward Aponte, Pam Collins, Keri Liechty, and Don Richter for their work in supporting Louisville's mission. I am also grateful to my cohort at Louisville's winter seminar—Randall Balmer, Candi Cann, Cheryl Townsend Gilkes, Leo Guardado, Nathan Jérémie-Brink, Melanie Jones, Andrew Krinks, A. G. Miller, and Courtney Bryant Prince—for the feedback that I received from them.

I am incredibly appreciative of the tireless staff at Orbis Books. I especially thank James Keane and Robert Ellsberg for seeing the promise of this project in its early stages, and Jill Brennan O'Brien for her patience, thoughtful feedback, and sharp editorial eye.

Finally, I thank Erika, who entered into marriage with me a week before I began my master's program. I am grateful for her friendship throughout my years of study, for her love of creation, her intelligence, and her sense of humor—thank you!

Abbreviations

Works by Gustavo Gutiérrez cited in this book

DoP   *Density of the Present: Selected Writings*, Eng. trans. Maryknoll,
           NY: Orbis Books, 1999.

GoL   *The God of Life.* Eng. trans. by Matthew J. O'Connell. Maryknoll,
           NY: Orbis Books, 1991.

LC   *Las Casas: In Search of the Poor of Jesus Christ.* Maryknoll,
           NY: Orbis Books, 1995.

OJ   *On Job: God-Talk and the Suffering of the Innocent.* Eng. trans.
           by Matthew J. O'Connell. Maryknoll, NY: Orbis Books, 1987.

PPH   *The Power of the Poor in History.* Maryknoll, NY: Orbis Books,
           1983.

TL   *A Theology of Liberation.* Eng. trans. Maryknoll, NY: Orbis
           Books, 1973.

TSMYF   *The Truth Shall Make You Free: Confrontations.* Eng. trans.
           Maryknoll, NY: Orbis Books, 1990.

WDFOOW   *We Drink from Our Own Wells: The Spiritual Journal of a People.*
           Eng. trans. Maryknoll, NY: Orbis Books, 1984.

Foreword

Gustavo Gutiérrez

The world today faces an ecological crisis. Especially the poor of the world face this crisis. It is a crisis that threatens the lives and livelihoods of so many and exerts even greater pressure on those already struggling with the crushing weight of injustice and exclusion. This poses a central question for an ecological theology of liberation: "How are salvation, liberation, and the care of creation related?" This question of the relationship of salvation, liberation, and the care of creation is one that the church, in solidarity with the world, must urgently wrestle with today. In his creative argument, Daniel Castillo gives us thought-provoking insights on how we can begin to answer this question, both in thought and action. There are three aspects of Castillo's text that I would like to highlight.

First, I find that Castillo captures well the meaning of the very important concept of integral liberation within the theology of liberation. He is correct in emphasizing the important roles that both spiritual poverty and the difficult goal of communion play in understanding liberation in its deepest sense. The fullness of human freedom is always directed toward the loving service of one's neighbor, even if that service requires, at times, confrontation. For Paul, Christians must be free, for "Jesus freed us" (Gal 5:1), but, he adds, they "serve each other out of love" (Gal 13). Castillo also makes important connections between the theology of liberation and the theology of Pope Francis in *Laudato Si'*. The book admirably shows how integral ecology can be thought of as a concept of liberation and rightly emphasizes the task of conversion to the earth and the poor as essential to the work of moving the world toward an integral ecology. It is certainly noteworthy that the concepts of "development" and "modernization," concepts that liberation theology was suspicious of from its beginning, now appear in the form of "sustainable development" and "ecological modernization." These terms, and the realities they represent, should be further examined.

Second, I value very much the interpretation of the scriptures in this book. The Bible always has been foundational to the life of the church—"The study of Sacred Scripture must be like the soul of Sacred Theology" (*Dei Verbum*,

24). Here Castillo provides an insightful reading of salvation history that demonstrates throughout the closest of relationships between salvation, liberation, and the care of creation. In particular, the symbol of the "gardener" gives us an important image for thinking about the human's relationship to God, neighbor, and earth, both in terms of the call to liberation and the call to communion. In a similar manner, Castillo's work in connecting Jesus's proclamation of God's reign to the Jubilee is extremely helpful at a time in which we must consider the "ecological debt" that the global north owes the global south. If, as Paul Ricoeur states, "the symbol gives rise to thought," then this text will help its readers think more fully about how they can incarnate the saving presence of God's love in a world where the preferential options for the earth and the poor are inseparable from each other.

Finally, this book establishes significant links between the concerns of Latin American liberation theology and those of black liberation theology in the United States and elsewhere. The terrible realities of racism and cultural degradation have always been essential issues to confront when thinking about the preferential option. The connections that Castillo draws out between the technocratic paradigm, market society, ecological debt, and racism are important. These connections deserve to continue to be analyzed.

With trenchant insight, this book recovers the language of liberation for the task of theology today, demonstrating how the church's response to God's call demands an urgent conversion to the earth and to the poor. In our current context, we must incarnate an "environmentalism of the poor" that, at the same time, learns to understand nature as a gift given freely by God—a God who desires that all of creation partake in the fullness of life. This is vital to the task of Christian discipleship.

Introduction

In December 1991, while he was working as chief economist of the World Bank, Lawrence Summers authorized an internal memorandum for distribution at the bank.[1] The memo advocated for the "migration of dirty industries" to the world's least developed countries. "The economic logic behind dumping a load of toxic waste in the lowest wage country is impeccable," the memo asserted, "and we should face up to that." It went on to single out sparsely populated countries in Africa as "*underpolluted*," and lamented the difficulty in efficiently transferring environmental costs to the African continent. Such transfers would be "world welfare enhancing," the memo asserted. Unsurprisingly, the Summers memorandum generated controversy and denunciations from observers who questioned the morality of externalizing toxic waste upon the people and lands of the world's poorest countries. For his part, Summers claimed that the memo had been "sardonic" in nature and not intended as a policy option.[2] However, as James Swaney points out, the document's recommendations are consistent with the economistic logic to which Summers subscribes.[3] Sarcastic or not, the memo discloses an insidious global dynamic.

Numerous and varied critiques can be leveled against the views expressed in the Summers memo. I surface three. First, the memo's recommendations exhibit dubious judgments with regard to the future. It attempts to justify the exportation of global waste to the least developed countries in the world on the assumption that trade in pollutants would financially benefit these countries. Presumably, the least developed countries would receive remuneration for housing the world's "dirty industries" within their borders. However, as Edith Brown Weiss argues, long-term environmental degradation can "affect the robustness of our ecosystems . . . and create a drag on future economic competitiveness."[4] From this perspective, the policies of the memo risk turning

---

[1]See Daniel M. Hausman and Michael S. McPherson, *Economic Analysis, Moral Philosophy, and Public Policy* (New York: Cambridge University Press, 2006), 12–13.

[2]See James A. Swaney, "So What's Wrong with Dumping on Africa?" *Journal of Economic Issues* 28, no. 2 (1994): 367.

[3]Ibid.

[4]Edith Brown Weiss, "Environmentally Sustainable Competitiveness: A Comment," *Yale Law Journal* 102, no. 8 (1993): 2126. Along similar lines, Swaney observes that the memo makes the assumption that the wealth accumulated by least developed countries would render the "legacy

the world's least developed countries (or at least regions within these countries) into environmental "sacrifice zones," regions whose health—both ecological and economic—is perpetually impaired.[5]

Second, if the arguments of the memo discount potential dangers in the future, they also discount the realities of the past. Specifically, the implicit recommendation that the "underpopulated" countries of Africa should receive a greater share of the world's pollution ignores the historical context out of which many of Africa's countries have come to be both "underdeveloped" and "underpopulated." This history is complex and, undoubtedly, cannot be reduced to any single source. Nonetheless, it is important to acknowledge that the relatively low populations and rates of economic growth in many modern African states likely have their roots in the colonial slave trade and the devastating effects that the mass-plunder of human beings had on African societies.[6] The slave trade radically destabilized much of the African continent in ways that have contributed to the formation of sparsely populated geographic regions throughout the continent in the twentieth century. Cast in this light, the recommendations of the Summers memo appear particularly odious. Carcinogens seem a poor form of reparation for the atrocities of colonial enslavement. The memo's blindness to the racist history of the colonial system renders the memo itself an artifact of neocolonialism. The "impeccable" economic logic of the Summers memo is enclosed within the logic of racist colonial exploitation.

Third, as Rob Nixon observes, the Summers memo is blind to the ways in which the world is made up of diverse cultures that possess "environmental practices and concerns of their own."[7] The recommendations of the memo require the imposition of a singular utilitarian logic upon the world, a logic

[handwritten margin note: environmental oppression]

---

of today's hazardous waste inconsequential." See Swaney, "So What's Wrong with Dumping on Africa?" 368. Arguments that make this assumption frequently point to the concept of the "environmental Kuznets curve" to claim that although economic growth creates initial environmental harm, that harm reverses as growth continues. The environmental Kuznets curve has proven to be a tenuous concept that is of dubious value when considering public policy options. On this, see Leigh Raymond, "Economic Growth and Environmental Policy? Reconsidering the Environmental Kuznets Curve," *Journal of Public Policy* 24, no. 3 (2004): 327–48. Swaney also notes that the recommendations of the memo, if enacted, would de-incentivize the development of "cleaner" technologies.

[5]I borrow the term "sacrifice zone" from Steve Lerner's book recounting the struggle for environmental justice among fenceline communities in the United States. Lerner notes that "the label 'sacrifice zones' comes from National Sacrifice Zones, an Orwellian term coined by government officials to designate areas previously contaminated as a result of the mining and processing of uranium into nuclear weapons." See Lerner, *Sacrifice Zones: The Front Lines of Toxic Chemical Exposure in the United States* (Cambridge, MA: MIT Press, 2010), 2.

[6]Herbert S. Klein, *The Atlantic Slave Trade*, 2nd ed. (Cambridge: Cambridge University Press, 2010), 128–130. See also Nathan Nunn, "Long-Term Effects of Africa's Slave Trades," *Quarterly Journal of Economics* (February 2008): 139–76.

[7]Rob Nixon, *Slow Violence and the Environmentalism of the Poor* (Cambridge, MA: Harvard University Press, 2011), 2.

that reduces the value of each element of creation to its instrumental value. For the memo's recommendations to appear reasonable, the logic that informs the memo must subjugate the complex and diverse value-systems of the world's cultures to itself. In this manner, "world-welfare enhancing" would come to be strictly identified with the optimization of economic growth. Like the builders of Babel, who seek to organize the world through the use of their one language, the Summers memo is dismissive of moral arguments and rationalities that do not conform to its own economistic rationality.[8]

In reality, the world today is far from monolithic. There exists a multitude of moral frameworks and worldviews that resist absolutizing instrumental reason. Nonetheless, it must be admitted that the logic informing the Summers memo occupies pride of place among "the builders" that order the structures and processes of the ongoing neoliberal globalization project. As Pope Francis writes in the encyclical *Laudato Si'*, the world has witnessed the globalization of a "technocratic paradigm" that reduces creation to an object that can be freely manipulated in the service of profit. This paradigm, and the world that it organizes in increasingly pervasive ways, should be interrogated.

THE CONTEMPORARY GLOBAL CONTEXT: PLANETARY EMERGENCY

Beyond its jarring rhetoric and dubious logic, the Summers memorandum does serve to highlight a basic truth about historical reality: human agency transforms not only social landscapes but also ecological landscapes through the distribution of both economic and environmental costs and goods. In recent centuries, human agency has structured the world's contemporary ecological and social contexts at the global level in significant ways.[9] Indeed, the memo presumes this ability on the part of human beings. However, in order to get a better sense of the ways in which human agency has shaped these settings, it is necessary to expand our horizon beyond the memo and consider the development of the emergencies of ecological degradation and economic inequity that presently characterize the world's historical reality.

---

[8]The memo reads, "The problem with the arguments against all of these proposals for more pollution in LDCs (intrinsic rights to certain goods, moral reasons, social concerns, lack of adequate markets, etc.) could be turned around and used more or less effectively against every Bank proposal for liberalization." See Hausman and McPherson, *Economic Analysis*, 13. On the reference to the project of the builders of Babel, see Gustavo Gutiérrez, "Theological Language: The Fullness of Silence," in *The Density of the Present: Selected Writings* (Maryknoll, NY: Orbis Books, 1999), esp. 194–98.

[9]See J. R. McNeil, *Something New under the Sun: An Environmental History of the Twentieth-Century World* (New York: W. W. Norton, 2000).

Ecological Emergencies

The biosphere of earth is an inherently unstable realm. The geological eras by which humans measure the planet's natural history have been constituted by radically different environments. Shifting continents, ice ages and thaws, the oxygenation of earth's atmosphere, mass extinctions, outbursts of speciation, plagues—all have reshaped the face of the planet dramatically in various instances, at times, rendering earth virtually unrecognizable from one epoch to another.

Viewed against this long backdrop of radical fluctuation and difference, the most recent geological era, the Holocene (beginning roughly 11,700 years ago), appears remarkably stable. The stability characterizing the Holocene has supported the emergence of complex human societies and the possibility for forms of human flourishing that previously had been untenable. It is noteworthy, then, that atmospheric scientists Paul Crutzen and Will Steffen find that the Holocene has been eclipsed by a new geological era they term the Anthropocene.[10] As the name suggests, this geological era is defined by the presence and activity of human beings on the earth. Within the Anthropocene, human beings have become the primary drivers of global ecological change.[11]

According to Crutzen and Steffen, the seeds of the Anthropocene germinated during the Industrial Revolution with the advent of the coal furnace, the steam engine, and a corresponding rise in economic productivity. However, this era truly came to fruition during the decades following the close of the Second World War. It was these decades that bore witness to a "great acceleration" in the growth of human impacts on the earth.[12] The great acceleration is observable across a multitude of categories and indicators, from the growth in the number of rivers dammed and the rise in fertilizer consumption to the amount of paper consumed and marine fish captured.[13]

To reflect on one impact of the great acceleration more closely, consider the historical levels of carbon dioxide (CO_2) in the atmosphere. For the first eleven millennia of the Holocene, atmospheric CO_2 concentrations remained relatively stable at around 220 parts per million (ppm). During roughly the two centuries after the onset of the Industrial Revolution, CO_2 density rose quickly from the

---

[10]Will Steffen, P. J. Crutzen, and J. R. McNeill, "The Anthropocene: Are Humans Now Overwhelming the Great Forces of Nature?" *Ambio* 36, no. 8 (December 2007): 614–21.

[11]Of course, in view of the radical economic disparity that characterizes the world, humans have contributed to this era in radically divergent manners—this is a point considered more fully in Chapter 5.

[12]Steffen, Crutzen, and McNeill, "Anthropocene." See also J. R. McNeil and Peter Engelke, *The Great Acceleration: An Environmental History of the Anthropocene since 1945* (Cambridge, MA: Belknap Press of Harvard University Press, 2014).

[13]See, for example, Steffen, Crutzen, and McNeill, "Anthropocene," 617, fig. 2.

pre-Industrial benchmark to 311 ppm by 1950. While this rise in atmospheric CO_2 levels is striking, it became even more pronounced in the decades following World War II. Over the last seventy years (roughly the time span of the great acceleration), CO_2 levels have skyrocketed to more than 406 ppm.[14] This bears emphasizing. After more than 11,000 years of relative stability, CO_2 concentrations have risen over 85 percent in the last three centuries with that increase growing exponentially in the last seventy years.[15]

As is well known, the sharp increase in atmospheric CO_2 concentrations threatens to upset the relative stability of the Holocene. According to Johan Rockström, for the earth's biosphere to maintain conditions similar to those of the Holocene, human societies must respect nine "planetary boundaries" (including a boundary referring to CO_2 concentrations).[16] Building off Rockström's analysis, John Bellamy Foster argues that these boundaries function as "tipping points." When they are surpassed, they can "lead to vast qualitative changes in the earth system that would threaten to destabilize the planet."[17] Thus, although public distress over the issue of climate change has focused attention on the planetary boundary associated with atmospheric carbon concentrations, *each of the nine boundaries represents a potential global ecological crisis.* For these reasons, many scientists worry that the Anthropocene portends an era of far greater instability within the biosphere than anything witnessed during the previous twelve millennia. This instability represents a grave threat not only to human life but to the myriad forms of life that have flourished in the Holocene. Already today, we are in the midst of the sixth mass extinction.[18] In the twenty-first century and beyond, the threats of climate change, increased drought, and ocean acidification (to name but three) figure to generate immense social and political upheaval, increasing the likelihood of war, mass social and geographical dislocation, and general human suffering on a global scale.[19]

[Margin annotation: Multiple issues that need to be addressed simultaneously]

---

[14]See NASA's graph, "The Relentless Rise of Carbon Dioxide," https://climate.nasa.gov.

[15]To be clear, that is "over 30 percent" from the already elevated level in the year 1950.

[16]Johan Rockström et al., "A Safe Operating Space for Humanity," *Nature* 461 (September 24, 2009): 472. Rockström delineates the nine boundaries as "climate change," "ocean acidification," "stratospheric ozone depletion," "nitrogen/phosphorous cycle," "biodiversity loss," "global freshwater use," "change in land use," "atmospheric aerosol loading," and "chemical pollution." Although Rockström has identified aerosol loading and chemical pollution as categories, he and his colleagues have not yet assigned these categories an empirical boundary. See also Jeffrey D. Sachs, *The Age of Sustainable Development* (New York: Columbia University Press, 2015), 181–217.

[17]This is a point made by the sociologist John Bellamy Foster and his colleagues. See John Bellamy Foster et al., *The Ecological Rift: Capitalism's War on the Earth* (New York: Monthly Review Press, 2010), 14

[18]See Elizabeth Kolbert, *The Sixth Extinction: An Unnatural History* (New York: Henry Holt, 2014).

[19]See Sachs, *Age of Sustainable Development*, 406–14; 459–74. On the link between climate change and war, see Solomon M. Hsiang et al., "Quantifying the Influence of Climate on Human Conflict," *Science* 341, no. 6151 (2013): 1190–1212.

Emergencies of Material Poverty and Economic Disparity

Within human societies, the period of the great acceleration also witnessed an acceleration of growth both in terms of economic wealth and disparity. Over the course of roughly the second half of the twentieth century, the gross world product (GWP) grew from approximately 9.2 trillion dollars to over 63 trillion dollars.[20] However, despite this explosion in economic wealth, by the end to the twentieth century the United Nations Research Institute for Social Development (UNRISD) estimated that the number of people living on less than $1 per day was over 1.2 billion. It is therefore unsurprising to find that the level of global economic disparity between the world's richest and poorest members broadened dramatically during that same time span. As the UNRISD reported in 2000, "The incidence of poverty has increased . . . not because the world as a whole is getting poorer, but because the benefits of growth have been unevenly spread. There has been a striking increase in inequality."[21] Indeed, it is remarkable to note that "the distance between the incomes of the richest and poorest country was about 3 to 1 in 1820, 35 to 1 in 1950, 44 to 1 in 1973 and 72 to 1 in 1992."[22] The global wealth gap described by the UNRISD led the United Nations to question the validity of a global market society predicated on an ideology of growth. In its 2000 report, the United Nations Development Programme (UNDP) states, "Economic growth cannot be accelerated enough to overcome the handicap of too much income directed to the rich. Income does not trickle down; it only circulates among elite groups."[23]

In recent years, however, there are signs that the acceleration in global inequality has slowed down, and is reversing altogether.[24] According to Jeffrey Sachs, this shift was to be expected. The reversal is due, at least in part, to the diffusion of technologies from economically wealthy countries to economically poorer ones. This diffusion allows for "catch-up" growth to occur rapidly in impoverished countries.[25] In the early twenty-first century, the combination of catch-up growth and the continued acceleration of GWP (which reached 108 trillion in 2015) has functioned to pull more than one billion people out of

is this growth sustainable?

---

[20] See "World GDP over the last two millennia," from "Our World in Data," Oxford Martin Programme on Global Development and the Leverhulme Center for Demographic Science at Nuffield College, https://ourworldindata.org.

[21] UNRISD, *Visible Hands: Taking Responsibility for Social Development* (Geneva: UNRISD, 2000), 11, www.unrisd.org.

[22] UNDP, *Human Rights and Human Development* (New York: UNDP, 2000), 6.

[23] UNDP, *UNDP Poverty Report, 2000: Overcoming Human Poverty* (New York: UNDP, 2000), 43.

[24] See, for example, Christoph Lakner's analysis of trends in global inequality. Christoph Lakner, "Global Inequality," in *After Piketty: The Agenda for Economics and Inequality*, ed. Heather Boushey et al. (Cambridge, MA: Harvard University Press, 2017), 259–79.

[25] Sachs, *Age of Sustainable Development*, 80–81.

how far can globalization go?

extreme poverty.[26] Moreover, there is hope that the trend toward convergence of economic wealth in rich and poor countries will continue in the twenty-first century.

Nonetheless, there are reasons both to continue to worry about the crisis of material poverty and to share the concerns expressed in the UNDP report. That more than one billion people remain in conditions of extreme poverty continues to demand urgent attention and action. Beyond this obvious point, economic disparity continues to present itself in pernicious and complicated ways within the contemporary global context. Most notably, the recent trend toward the overall reduction in global inequality has been accompanied by a countervailing trend in the increase in hyperwealth. A recent study by Oxfam finds that the world's eight richest persons (all men) control roughly the same amount of the world's economic wealth as the poorest half of the world.[27] Thus, while the gap between the average incomes in, for example, the United States and China may be shrinking, the gap between the wealth controlled by "the one percent" and the rest of the world continues to increase dramatically. Beyond the issue of hyperwealth, there is concern also as to whether rates of global economic growth can be sustained without exacerbating the ecological crisis to the point that it becomes an unmitigated disaster. If rates of growth cannot be sustained, then is it doubtful that levels of global economic disparity can continue to decrease. These are points to which I return in Chapter 5.

POLITICS, LEGITIMACY, AND THE TASK OF THEOLOGY

The foregoing observations regarding the Summers memorandum and the historical development of the ecological and economic emergencies suggest that these emergencies are rooted in politics. As Jedediah Purdy writes, "Both families of crisis . . . reflect the same predicament: if we want a self-sustaining world, both social and natural, we must build and preserve it." Purdy continues, "The only way to build a shared living place deliberately is through politics. Collective, binding decisions are how people can give the world a shape that we intend."[28] For Purdy, the world's socioeconomic and ecological formations, and the emergencies they harbor, demand political engagement and responsible praxis.

---

[26]Of course, this positive trend in economic disparity is accompanied by threats regarding politico-cultural imperialism. For a critique along these lines, see Vandana Shiva, *Earth Democracy: Justice, Sustainability, and Peace* (Boston: South End, 2005). Although critiques such as Shiva's are important, they should not be used simply to dismiss the effect that catch-up growth has had on reducing material poverty.

[27]For a summary of the OXFAM report, "An Economy for the 99%," see https://www.oxfamamerica.org.

[28]Jedediah Purdy, *After Nature: A Politics for the Anthropocene* (Cambridge, MA: Harvard University Press, 2015), 18–19.

It would be wrong, however, to separate the socioeconomic emergency from that of the ecological, as if one exists independent of the other. To make this separation would be to extend an error endemic in the modernist worldview of conceptually dividing nature from the realm of human life (be it "society," "history," or "culture"). The modernist worldview, with the separations it upheld, has never actually corresponded to any moment in history, modern or otherwise. As Bruno Latour argues, since the advent of human culture, nature has never existed wholly outside of culture. Nor has culture ever existed wholly apart from nature. Human social imaginaries have always negotiated the hybridized space of nature-culture.[29] For Latour, it is imperative that we recognize nature as a "marked category" that both shapes and is shaped by the dynamics of culture.[30]

The hybridization that Latour describes is also characteristic of the material processes that structure human society. This point is made apparent in the arguments of the Summers memo, since the exportation of "dirty industries" to impoverished countries would have significant effects on both nature and society. Likewise, the very notion of the Anthropocene presumes that the "humanization" of the world necessarily has an altering effect on the planet's physical environment. Reflecting on the material interconnections between nature and society, David Harvey writes: "All ecological projects (and arguments) are simultaneously political economic projects (and arguments) and vice versa."[31] The social crises of material poverty and inequality, then, are intricately and inextricably bound up with the multidimensional crisis of ecological degradation.[32]

In his prescient essay on environmental racism, James Cone recognizes the interconnected character of the social and ecological spheres. Decrying the tendency to divide these commitments, Cone writes, "The fight for justice cannot be segregated but must be integrated with the fight for life in all its forms."[33] Echoing Cone's sentiments, Pope Francis recognizes the necessity of understanding the connections between the ecological and the socioeconomic. Pope Francis writes, "We are faced not with two separate crises, one environmental and the other social, but rather with one complex crisis which is both social and environmental" (*Laudato Si'*, 139). The politics required for our present-day

---

[29]Bruno Latour, *We Have Never Been Modern* (Cambridge, MA: Harvard University Press, 1993), esp. 130–45.

[30]Bruno Latour, *The Politics of Nature: How to Bring Science into Democracy* (Cambridge, MA: Harvard University Press, 2004), 48–49.

[31]David Harvey, "The Nature of Environments: The Dialectics of Social and Environmental Change," in *Real Problems, False Solutions*, ed. Ralph Miliband and Leo Panitch (London: Merlin, 1993), 25.

[32]Indeed, this was intimated at different points in the initial analysis of the Summers Memorandum.

[33]James Cone, "Whose Earth Is It Anyway?" *Cross Currents* 50, no. 1–2 (2000): 36–46.

context, then, must be capable of integrating within its vision the ecological with the socioeconomic so as to discern a comprehensive way of responding to this complex planetary emergency.

To affirm that the global eco-social emergency is, at root, a emergency of politics, is to raise the question of legitimacy. If politics is fundamentally about organizing the world responsibly, then the eco-social emergency calls into question our politics. The realities of massive ecological degradation and economic disparity require us to interrogate the adequacy of our political structures and beliefs, and the ways that these structures and beliefs have formed the world. Do the global networks of power that constitute the contemporary globalization project respond rightly to the complex eco-social emergency? Are they, as Purdy would phrase it, "building a sustainable world?"

THEOLOGY AND THE NEED
FOR AN ECOLOGICAL THEOLOGY OF LIBERATION

The question of legitimacy also serves to turn us to the subject of Christian theology—the discipline out of which I advance my argument in this book. In a basic sense, theology can be understood as offering "a word about God," or "God-talk."[34] Christian theology is conditioned by the belief that speech about God is possible because God has graciously revealed Godself to the world.[35] Indeed, it is only because of God's revelatory self-disclosure that one can hope to speak rightly about the mystery of God with any sort of confidence.[36] However, in order to prevent this confidence from transgressing into hubris, theology must acknowledge that its discourse is always incomplete and fragmentary. The mystery of God is ultimately incomprehensible and cannot be exhausted by any limited human articulation. This is a basic tenet of any legitimate Christian speech about God.

The issue of limitation within theological discourse not only points to the infinitude of God but also to the contextual nature of the discourse itself. Human speech about God, which arises in response to God's self-disclosure, is speech that is always located in a particular time and place, always speech that comes from particular people. It is also speech marked by the particularity of *subjective, uses for an agenda*

[34]Both of these definitions reflect something of the etymology of the term itself: *Theos* meaning "God" and *logos* meaning "word."

[35]*Dei Verbum*, no. 1–6.

[36]A confidence which, as Gustavo Gutiérrez makes clear, can only hope to avoid hubris by affirming the ultimate ineffability of God and allowing its prophetic discourse about God to be interrupted by "the language of contemplation." On this point, see Gustavo Gutiérrez, *On Job: God-Talk and the Suffering of the Innocent*, Eng. trans. (Maryknoll, NY: Orbis Books, 1987), 51–103; Gustavo Gutiérrez, *The God of Life*, Eng. trans. (Maryknoll, NY: Orbis Books, 1991), 145–63; and Gutiérrez, *Density of the Present: Selected Writings*, 135–207.

the word of God can be misused

those contexts and people, rather than speech that is universal in its application.[37] Accordingly, theology attempts to elucidate something of the revealed mystery of God in a manner that is comprehensible within, and appropriate to, its given context. As Linell Cady writes, "The theologian . . . is engaged in extending a tradition, seeking to articulate its most appropriate interpretation for a particular time and place."[38] An essential task of theology is to make God's self-disclosure intelligible to the world (or at least a specific context within that world). Therefore, to speak legitimately about God, one must speak meaningfully about who God is and what God desires in relationship to the world.

This returns us, then, to the initial analysis advanced here. Today, the whole of humanity (from markedly differing social locations, to be sure) inhabits a world characterized by the complex and interrelated realities of ecological degradation and material poverty. This fact surfaces a number of theological questions: How do we speak of God in light of the eco-social crisis? How should we interpret revelation—our account of God's self-disclosure to the world—in the face of the complex perils of the Anthropocene? Or, in a slightly different key, how are we called to live responsibly before God within the world today? In responding to these questions, two directions of inquiry are required. On the one hand, it is necessary to interrogate our sources of God's self-disclosure so as to advance claims about who God is and what God desires in relationship to the planetary emergency engulfing the world. On the other hand, it is also vital to continue to "read the signs of the times," scrutinizing further the world and especially the manner in which the globalization project organizes the world. In carrying out these two tasks together, it is possible to begin to name more clearly (although always partially) the manner in which the dynamics of grace and sin are at work in the world today.

The guiding supposition of this book, one that has been anticipated in the preceding pages, is that the current global context demands the development of what I term "an ecological theology of liberation." Most basically, this theology can be understood as a mode of discourse that grounds the preferential options for both the earth and the poor in its confession of who God is and what God desires. This theology, likewise, seeks to elucidate and energize forms of praxis that make manifest these options in the world. The tasks of the subsequent chapters of this text are to clarify further the meaning of this theology and to articulate its foundations.

---

[37]This does not mean that speech emanating from each specific context will be incomprehensible to those in other contexts, but it will need to be "received" and "translated" into each new context.

[38]Linell Elizabeth Cady, "Identity, Feminist Theory, and Theology," in *Horizons in Feminist Theology: Identity, Tradition, and Norms*, ed. Rebecca S. Chopp and Sheila Greeve Daveney (Minneapolis: Fortress Press, 1977), 29.

THE STRUCTURE OF THE ARGUMENT

This book is divided into three interlocking parts, each composed of two chapters. Part I, "Structuring Eco-Liberationist Discourse," aims to elucidate a theological method and a grammar of salvation that are proper to eco-liberationist discourse. Chapter 1, "Toward an Ecological Theology of Liberation," develops a nuanced definitional understanding of the term "an ecological theology of liberation" and identifies the methodological commitments for advancing such a theology. To do so, the chapter retrieves Gustavo Gutiérrez's landmark work in liberation theology and soteriology, and analyzes how his insights might be broadened to respond comprehensively to a context characterized by politico-ecological emergency.

Chapter 2, "Integral Ecology: A Liberationist Concept," builds on the grammar of salvation outlined in Chapter 1. It does so by drawing on the integralist tradition of modern Catholic theology in order to clarify the relationship between salvation, liberation, and care for creation. Specifically, this chapter retrieves Gutiérrez's concept of integral liberation and Pope Francis's concept of integral ecology in order to demonstrate how human persons can witness to liberation from sin (which is salvation) through actively transforming the cultural/psychological and socio-structural dimensions of human life, so as to move humanity from alienation to communion with "the soil and all that comes from the soil."

Part II, "Interpreting the Word of God," develops the vision of salvation outlined in Part I narratively. To do so, it advances an eco-liberationist interpretation of salvation history. Chapter 3, "Reading Genesis Theologically in a Politico-Ecological Key," offers a theological reading of the book of Genesis. This reading surfaces a number of theological symbols key to eco-liberationist hermeneutics. Most notably, the chapter develops the symbolic vocation of the "gardener" (described in Gen 2:15), demonstrating that the praxis proper to this vocation is constituted by the threefold love of God, neighbor, and earth. In responding properly to the vocation of gardener, the human person abides within God's wisdom and cultivates communion with God, neighbor, and earth. Correspondingly, this chapter demonstrates that, in Genesis, sin impairs the human person's ability to love properly and thus disrupts the tripartite communion for which the person is created. The chapter then examines the manner in which this understanding of the human vocation and the dynamics of sin and grace operate throughout the subsequent narratives of Genesis.

Chapter 4, "The Jubilee of Liberation," interprets the key symbols and themes of salvation history through the triadic relational understanding of the human vocation developed in Chapter 3. The chapter argues that God liberates God's people from the disordered political ecology of Egypt so that this people might collectively reinhabit the vocation of gardener. Correspondingly, the promise of salvation and redemption comes to be symbolized by "city of the gardener"—a city whose political ecology is organized in accordance with the wisdom of God. The chapter then examines the function of the prophets in relation to the promise of salvation, and concludes by analyzing the manner in which Jesus is proclaimed as the fulfillment of both the human vocation and this promise.

Part III, "Christian Praxis in a Globalizing World," critically analyzes the structures and dynamics of what Pope Francis calls the present-day "global system" (*Laudato Si'*, 111). This final part reflects on the demands of Christian discipleship within this current situation. Chapter 5, "Making and Sustaining the Planetary Emergency," examines various dimensions of the global system referenced in *Laudato Si'*, focusing especially on how the technocratic paradigm, ecological debt, and consumer culture all play significant roles in shaping this system. Likewise, this chapter critically examines the manner in which the concepts of sustainable development and ecological modernization have been employed to justify the structuring and dynamisms of the globalization project, calling into question whether a form of sustainable development rooted in the prospect of "win-win" (environmental and economic) scenarios can adequately respond to the cries of the earth and the poor. The analysis focuses especially on the degree to which economic growth might be decoupled from ecological impact. Chapter 5 also raises doubt as to whether the neoliberal globalization project—which, for my purposes, is identifiable with the global system—can, in fact, produce long-term global equity. Instead, it argues that a more likely outcome of this project, as it is currently structured, is the longitudinal increase of global inequality and the rise of repressive politics aimed at protecting the interests of the hyperwealthy.

Chapter 6, "Bearing Witness to a Humane World," reflects critically on the globalization project (as it was discussed in Chapter 5) in light of the interpretation of the word of God advanced in Part II of the book. The chapter then moves to consider the possibilities for rightly ordered Christian praxis in view of these judgments. Finally, the chapter concludes by developing the contours of a Christian ecological spirituality of liberation, a spirituality that might animate and sustain Christian eco-liberationist praxis in the world today.

Part I

Structuring Eco-Liberationist Discourse

Part I delineates the basic methodological and theological commitments of a Christian ecological theology of liberation. It considers the role of Christian revelation, the question of anthropocentrism, and issues pertaining to ecological hermeneutics. The second half of Part I draws especially on the work of both Gustavo Gutiérrez and Pope Francis in order to conceptualize, within an integralist framework, the relationship between salvation, liberation, and care for creation.

Toward an Ecological Theology of Liberation

The aim of this book is to develop the foundations for a Christian ecological theology of liberation. As I noted in the introduction to this text, this theology is twofold in its orientation. First, it grounds the preferential options for both the earth and the poor in its confession of who God is and what God desires. Second, it elucidates and energizes forms of praxis that make manifest these options in the world. In service of the broad goal of developing the foundations for this theology, the task of Chapter 1 is to establish a general methodological approach for Christian eco-liberationist discourse and further clarify the definitional understanding of this theology.

In the first part of Chapter 1, I take up my stated task by clarifying three basic methodological commitments for a Christian eco-liberationist approach: (1) privileging the discourse of political ecology over that of ecological cosmology; (2) affirming a qualified form of anthropocentrism; and (3) prioritizing the "book of scripture" over the "book of nature" as a source of revelation. These three basic commitments, as I demonstrate below, disclose a fourth commitment, namely, that a Christian ecological theology of liberation must clarify the relationship between the options for the earth and poor, and the mystery of salvation in and through Jesus Christ. On establishing this fourth commitment, I turn, in the second part of Chapter 1, to examine the theology of Gustavo Gutiérrez, a key figure in early liberation theology. Gutiérrez's thought is explicitly concerned with the question of soteriology, and, as I argue, his own theological method can serve as the template for organizing an ecological theology of liberation. Thus, the chapter concludes with an analysis of Gutiérrez's soteriological argumentation, showing how his arguments might be retrieved and broadened to accommodate eco-liberationist concerns.

METHODOLOGICAL COMMITMENTS FOR A CHRISTIAN ECO-LIBERATIONIST DISCOURSE

the Anthropocene is not intrinsically evil

As I just noted, the argument of this book proceeds on the conviction that Christian eco-liberationist discourse should prioritize engagement with the discourse of political ecology (over that of ecological cosmology), affirm a qualified sense of anthropocentrism, and give pride of place to the book of scripture (over the book of nature) as a source of revelation. Since each of these moves is at least somewhat controversial, it is important to reflect on the reasoning behind making them. I begin by considering the discourses of political ecology and ecological cosmology, starting with a critical examination of the latter before turning to the former.

Privileging Political Ecology

The discourse and insights of ecological cosmology, especially within the Americas, have been significantly influenced by the work of the Jesuit paleontologist Pierre Teilhard de Chardin and Thomas Berry.[1] Of particular note for this study, the influence of Teilhard and Berry is evident in the work of both Leonardo Boff and Ivone Gebara, the two thinkers most closely associated with connecting liberationist concern for the poor to discussions of environmental ethics.[2] Broadly speaking, ecological cosmology refers to a mode of analysis that reflects on the history of cosmic evolution.[3] Within this framework, the discourse also examines the advent of life on the planet earth, and the ways in which life on earth has evolved over the course of billions of years. Thus, Boff's approach, in his widely regarded book *Cry of the Earth, Cry of the Poor*, is characteristic of the narratives of ecological cosmology. Boff tells the story of the evolving universe from "cosmogenesis" to the emergence of earth as a superorganism whose systems work not only to sustain the superorganism but to propel life *forward* so that novel and more complex forms of life can emerge.[4]

In narrating the story of the universe, the religious variations of ecologi-

purpose is to sustain life

progression of creation

---

[1] See Pierre Teilhard de Chardin, *The Divine Milieu* (Brighton: Sussex Academic, 2004). See also Thomas Berry and Brian Swimme, *The Universe Story: From the Primordial Flaring Forth to the Ecozoic Era—A Celebration of the Unfolding of the Cosmos* (New York: Harper Collins, 1992).

[2] See Leonardo Boff, *Cry of the Earth, Cry of the Poor* (Maryknoll, NY: Orbis Books, 1997); *Ecology and Liberation: A New Paradigm* (Maryknoll, NY: Orbis Books, 1995). See also Ivone Gebara, *Longing for Running Water: Ecofeminism and Liberation* (Minneapolis: Fortress, 1999).

[3] For an insightful critical appraisal of this discourse, see Lisa Sideris, *Consecrating Science: Wonder, Knowledge, and the Natural World* (Oakland: University of California Press, 2017), esp. 116–45.

[4] See Boff, *Cry of the Earth,* 1–63. Gebara makes similar appeals throughout *Longing for Running Water.* She is, however, suspicious of the progressivism that Boff embraces.

cal cosmology emphasize the spiritual dimension of evolution and the sacred character of the cosmos. From this perspective, all of life, indeed all of matter, is worthy of reverent wonder. Accordingly, both Boff and Gebara echo Teilhard in describing the universe as a "divine milieu."[5] The sacred character of this cosmic context elicits not only reverence from the human person for the universe and its composite parts; it also demands a transformation of praxis. Humans must adopt what Boff terms a "holistic ecological stance" to the patterning of human life.[6] The "omni-relatedness and connectedness of everything" within the divine milieu demands that humans move beyond narrow forms of anthropocentric self-concern and come to live in solidarity with earth and the universe.[7] Humanity must come to appreciate, as Gebara writes, that "at every instant, every being maintains its own uniqueness, and in this context every being is worthy to live the fullness of its own existence."[8] For Boff, this requires nothing less than an ethic of "unlimited responsibility for everything existing and alive."[9]

I am not opposed to many of the viewpoints that ecological cosmology endorses. Indeed, the argument of this book affirms the goodness of creation and seeks to counter any worldview that presumes the human person is the sole measure of the universe. With respect to forms of ecological cosmology articulated in an explicitly Christian register, this book likewise affirms the need for a sapiential Christology that helps buttress both a sacramental view of creation and a Christian theological cosmology.[10] Nonetheless, the discourse of ecological cosmology has significant limitations in its ability to support the aims of an ecological theology of liberation. These limitations crystallize around two general characteristics of the discourse.

First, ecological cosmology is ill equipped for adjudicating, or even surfacing, the complex and often conflictual relationships that constitute historical

---

[5]Boff, *Cry of the Earth*, 175; Gebara, *Longing for Running Water*, 124. Boff describes this milieu in explicit Christian theological terminology, whereas Gebara inclines toward a generalized account of panentheism, even when making explicit reference to the symbols of Christian theological discourse.

[6]Boff, *Cry of the Earth*, 34.

[7]Ibid. As Boff writes: "We are thereby in synergy with the entire universe and through us, it proclaims itself, advances, and remains open to new things that have never been attempted before, heading toward a Reality that is hidden behind the veils of the mystery located in the realm of what is impossible to humans."

[8]Gebara, *Longing for Running Water*, 129.

[9]Boff, *Cry of the Earth*, 136.

[10]Boff attempts such an articulation at the end of *Cry of the Earth*. See Boff, *Cry of the Earth*, 158–86. Gebara rejects such a proposition, suggesting that an articulation of the cosmic Christ is imperialist in character. For Gebara, it appears that the sacredness of the cosmos is found in interrelatedness as such. See Gebara, *Longing for Running Water*, 137–71. For examples of contemporary cosmic wisdom Christologies, see Celia Deane-Drummond, *Christ and Evolution: Wonder and Wisdom* (Minneapolis: Fortress, 2009); and Denis Edwards, *Jesus the Wisdom of God: An Ecological Theology* (Maryknoll, NY: Orbis Books, 1995).

Ignores the Western cul context

reality. As we have seen, ecological cosmology provides a grand unifying vision of the universe. The difficulty, however, as Mary Midgely writes, is that "once we have this new vision, there are many different interpretations that we can put on it, many different dramas that arise, many directions in which it can lead us. It is quite hard to distinguish among those directions and to map them in a way that lets us navigate reasonably among them."[11] Midgely points to the fact that, when taken by itself, ecological cosmology, rather dramatically, underdetermines ethics and praxis.[12] *two ideas stc?*

To affirm that the universe is a "divine milieu" and the earth a "sacred body" *may* have the effect of undercutting pernicious forms of anthropocentrism, but they do little more than that. To state it somewhat bluntly, while the oft-referenced observation that "everything is composed of stardust" may engender in the modern Western subject a greater sense of connectedness to the earth, it does nothing to clarify how this person should respond when faced with the prospect of history's gas chambers and bullwhips, the Ebola virus, nuclear weapons, and growing concentrations of atmospheric carbon dioxide. After all, each of these is also composed of that same solar dust. With this indeterminacy in view, Lisa Sideris finds that the narratives of ecological cosmology "encourage expressions of wonder that are powerless to critique or correct environmentally destructive attitudes and patterns of behavior."[13] Sideris's description of the ineffectual character of ecological cosmology is true not only for environmental ethics but also for social ethics and, most important, the complex ways in which the two relate. Thus, as Peter Scott observes, although the intention of ecological cosmology is to orient the human person toward the world, it "has sustained difficulties engaging with the world." Indeed, despite its intent, ecological cosmology "seems strangely *other*-worldly."[14] Ultimately, this otherworldliness has the unavoidable effect of muting the cries of the earth and the poor or otherwise rendering them unintelligible within the narrative framework of ecological cosmology.[15]

Even more problematic than the ethically underdetermined character of ecological cosmology is the manner in which this discourse tends to orient one

---

[11]Mary Midgley, *Science and Poetry* (New York: Routledge, 2001), 36.

[12]This is a point made by Willis Jenkins, who notes, "If all possibilities of action can write themselves into a story of nature, then that cosmology has little normative purchase for practical ethics." See Willis Jenkins, "Does Evolutionary Cosmology Matter for Ecological Ethics? The Case of Geoengineering," draft paper for Yale Living Cosmology conference, November 9, 2016.

[13]Sideris, *Consecrating Science*, 118.

[14]Peter Scott, *A Political Theology of Nature* (Cambridge: Cambridge University, 2003), 85.

[15]I am not suggesting that the narratives of ecological cosmology have not generated inspiring witnesses of solidarity with the earth; they undoubtedly have (see Sarah McFarland Taylor, *Green Sisters: A Spiritual Ecology* [Cambridge, MA: Harvard University Press, 2009]). Rather, my point is that these witnesses often connect strangely to the theoretical accounts that underwrite and energize them.

away from the preferential options for the earth and poor in an active manner.[16] In other words, to the extent that ecological cosmology is determinative of ethics, its recommendations actually cut against the commitments of an ecological theology of liberation. This is because ecological cosmology, too often, is informed by what Johann Baptist Metz describes as an "ersatz metaphysics" of evolutionary progress.[17] That is to say, "the universe story," as it is recounted in the discourses of ecological cosmology, is inclined to describe the unfolding cosmos as one in which complexification (of matter into life, and life into more intricate forms of life) is the inevitable and natural teleology of cosmic history. On this account, higher forms of being emerge inexorably through the evolutionary processes of the unfolding universe in a manner that justifies the dissolution of the "lower" forms of life that preceded them. Thus, with regard to life on earth, the sufferings and unspeakable tragedies experienced across the entire panoply of biotic existence—including even mass extinctions—are explained away by pointing to the ways in which these tragedies have given way to the emergence of higher forms of life.[18] In effect, this interpretation of cosmic history becomes a triumphalist account that celebrates the victors of history.[19]

Ironically, the problem that narratives of cosmic evolutionistic progress pose for eco-liberationist commitment is evidenced most strikingly in the arguments of Boff. As we have already noted, Boff draws heavily on the insights of ecologi-

---

[16]Sideris makes a similar observation, arguing that ecological cosmology's narrative frequently leads it to champion a Promethean account of human creativity and technological advancement. As such, Sideris finds that leading advocates of ecological cosmology are curiously sanguine in their views of the Anthropocene. See Sideris, *Consecrating Science*, 129–45.

[17]Johann Baptist Metz, *Faith in History and Society: Toward a Practical Fundamental Theology* (New York: Herder and Herder, 2007), 158.

[18]As J. Matthew Ashley writes, in raising concern over the presentation of cosmic history in Berry and Swimme's *The Universe Story,* "This narrative scheme allows Swimme and Berry to look with relative equanimity on, say, the Permian extinction—in which over 95 percent of marine species and 70 percent of terrestrial species became extinct. For them this mass extinction, as well as others, can and should be understood as setting the stage for a subsequent explosion of biological innovation. At an earlier point in the book, Swimme and Berry tell the story of how the self-assertion of the first cells supersaturated the earth's atmosphere with oxygen. This led to their demise, but it also forced the creative advance of a bacterium that could metabolize oxygen. If taken as a comprehensive narrative template, why might we not look at an ecological collapse in the coming centuries caused by human excess with equal equanimity? Might we not look with a little more serenity at the dangerous self-assertion of modern technological society?" See J. Matthew Ashley, "Reading the Universe Story Theologically: The Contribution of a Biblical Narrative Imagination," *Theological Studies* 71, no. 4 (2010): 887.

[19]Celia Deane-Drummond describes this presentation of cosmic history as an "epic." She contrasts the epic reading of cosmic history with that of the "theodramatic," drawing on Hans Urs von Balthasar. For Deane-Drummond, evolution requires a theodramatic reading of cosmic history, one that is more open to contingency and ambiguity. See Celia Deane-Drummond, *Christ and Evolution: Wonder and Wisdom* (Minneapolis: Fortress, 2009). Throughout her writing, Deane-Drummond emphasizes the importance of cultivating the virtue of wisdom for moral discernment amid nature's ambiguities. See, for example, Celia Deane-Drummond, *The Ethics of Nature* (Malden, MA: Blackwell, 2004), esp. 214–37.

cal cosmology in arguing for a connection between the concerns of liberation theology and ecological theology. However, Boff's desire to hear and respond to the "cries" of the earth and poor are undercut by his own argumentation. Reflecting on the destructive elements of cosmic evolution, Boff writes strikingly, "In the evolutionary process . . . there are falls, but they are falls on the way up. The emergence of chaos means the opportunity for more complex and rich forms of life to appear."[20] Here Boff justifies the myriad forms of destruction, death, and suffering that have characterized cosmic (and planetary) history as simply the means to the end of unceasing progressive complexification. But if this is the case, if every "fall" is simply a fall "on the way up," then why should anyone be concerned about the sixth great extinction, or for that matter, the annihilation of the human species (or, at least, the "least fit" elements of this species)? After all, on the view expressed by Boff, will not their destruction simply hasten the coming of more intensely realized forms of consciousness? From this perspective, the cries of the earth and the poor should not be met with care and concern but with either apathy or unabashed scorn.[21]

For the two reasons surfaced above, ecological cosmology does not lend itself to the articulation of an ecological theology of liberation (and certainly not in a foundational way). At least with regard to the first problem raised with respect to the arguments of ecological cosmology, a more helpful discourse is that of political ecology. As a mode of analysis, political ecology refers to the study of how the organization and exercise of power (be it discursive, political, economic, or metabolic) structures the symbiotic/hybrid relationship between a social system and the ecosystem(s) to which it relates. Moreover, this mode of analysis pays particular attention to social and ecological conflicts that underlie the formation and sustainment of any given pattern of eco-social structuring.[22] For example, Joan Martinez-Alier's groundbreaking work in political ecology analyzes the manner in which political and economic interests of multinational corporations and their governmental allies function to remake and often degrade the eco-social context of poor and marginalized communities within the global south. Likewise, Martinez-Alier's work highlights the ways in which "the environmentalism of the poor" seeks to contest these dominative forms of eco-social structuring.[23]

---

[20]Boff, *Cry of the Earth*, 83.

[21]Obviously, this is not Boff's desire. He is clear in his intention and often eloquent in his articulation of the need to hear and respond to the cries of the earth and the poor. Indeed, later chapters in *Cry of the Earth* (see esp. chapters 3–5) take a more politico-ecological turn that orient his argument toward his stated goal. My point here is that his intention is at odds with the way he appropriates ecological cosmology in a foundational manner.

[22]Political ecology resists any single definition or method. As Darcy Tetrault observes, political ecology can adopt materialist or constructivist modes of analysis, or develop a third mode that mediates between the first two. See Darcy Tetrault, "Three Forms of Political Ecology," *Ethics and the Environment* 22, no. 2 (2017): 1–23.

[23]See Joan Martinez-Alier, *The Environmentalism of the Poor: A Study of Ecological Conflicts*

For the task of developing an ecological theology of liberation, the discourse of political ecology is of far greater utility than that of ecological cosmology. This is because while political ecology remains open, in principle, to the pos- *[handwritten: double]* sibility of affirming the sanctity of the created order, <u>it is keenly interested in</u> *[handwritten: expand]* <u>exploring the messiness of historical reality</u>. In contrast to Scott's observation regarding ecological cosmology, the discourse of political ecology remains resolutely *this-worldly* in its orientation. In highlighting the conflictual character to the world's eco-social formations, the politico-ecological approach helps illuminate the concrete presence of or orientations toward the abuse of power within the world. Political ecology, then, provides a mode of analysis that can be of service to theology in naming the eco-social character of sin (or correspondingly the dialectical presence of God's saving grace) as it is made manifest within the world. Along these same lines, a politico-ecological mode of analysis is also necessary for specifying both the shape and content of the options for the poor and the earth within historical reality. The reader can note that this book's introduction began by describing the contemporary global context within a politico-ecological framework. However, I must note political ecology's own limitation. Although this discourse is vital for specifying how the options for the earth and poor can be made manifest, political ecology, in and of itself, does not provide the impetus for making these options.[24] The question of where this warrant might be located is an issue that I consider subsequently. However, before doing so, I must address the issue of anthropocentrism.

Affirming a Qualified Anthropocentrism

[handwritten: man has dominion of the earth]

Contemporary concern in religious environmental ethics over anthropocentrism, referenced briefly in the section above, finds its seminal expression in Lynn White Jr.'s essay, "The Historical Roots of Our Ecologic Crisis."[25] Published in 1967, the essay argues that the origin of the ongoing ecological crisis is located in the Judeo-Christian worldview. As White writes, "Christianity is the most anthropocentric religion the world has seen." Its religious ethos has "insisted that it is God's will that man exploit nature for his proper ends."[26] Accordingly, White finds that Christianity has desacralizd the natural world within the cultural imaginations that operate under Christian influence. This

[handwritten: made in the image of God; has God's powers?]

---

and Valuation (Northampton, MA: Edward Elgar, 2002).

[24]Political ecology, as a general discipline, is aimed at understanding the ways in which power shapes the webs of eco-social relationships that constitute the world. Its judgment on these relationships is not uniform. In other words, while political ecology can function as a tool to argue for an option for the earth and poor, it can also be used to justify the technological domination of the earth and the oppression of the poor.

[25]Lynn White Jr., "The Historical Roots of Our Ecologic Crisis," *Science* 155 (1967).

[26]Ibid., 1205. I have left the gendered language here without augment since the Christian worldview throughout much of its tradition has been androcentric as well.

desacralizing process, in turn, has sanctioned and catalyzed the exploitation and domination of nature, resulting in the contemporary ecological crisis.[27]

White's criticism has profoundly influenced Christian theology and environmental ethics over the last fifty years, as theologians have sought in varying ways to wrestle with his claims.[28] Here I do not enter into evaluative judgments regarding the theological or historical veracity of White's arguments.[29] Instead, I raise White's critique simply to point out that at its core lies a sharp criticism of anthropocentrism. This critique has set the agenda for a great deal of theological reflection post-White. In the wake of White's critique of the Judeo-Christian worldview, it has become somewhat fashionable within various strands of ecological theology and environmental ethics to level generalized condemnations of anthropocentrism in all of its forms.[30]

To be clear, insofar as the term "anthropocentrism" refers to a worldview in which only human persons are accorded innate value among creation, it must be wholly rejected. Likewise, it is vital to denounce the oft accompanying view that the proper vocation of the human person is to dominate nonhuman creation. (These are points that I affirmed in the section above.) Nonetheless, the wholesale uncritical dismissal of anthropocentrism is both impractical and otherwise problematic. For one, it is doubtful that simply de-centering the human within any given system of thought will necessarily render that system more conducive to hearing and responding to the cries of the earth and the poor. An omnicentric or earth-centered worldview is just as likely to embrace a technophilic epoch, one in which artificial intelligence and various technologically advanced machines replace any number of earth's organic life forms, as it is to affirm an ethic of biological conservation. After all, if the whole of matter is sacred, why give preference to the organic over the synthetic? Indeed,

---

[27]Ibid., 1203–7. "Contemporary" here should be understood loosely. Writing fifty years ago, White would not have understood the crisis in the manner scientists do today. Nor, for that matter, has the crisis remained static.

[28]For a critical assessment of White's theological legacy, see Willis Jenkins, "After Lynn White: Religious Ethics and Environmental Problems," *Journal of Religious Ethics* 37, no. 2 (2009): 283–309. Jenkins argues that White's critiques and subsequent responses have led the discourse to be overly determined by an emphasis on cosmology. In contrast, Jenkins argues for a pragmatic approach. My argument in this text seeks something of a middle way between Jenkins's recommendation and his object of critique. As it will become clear, I argue for the development of a praxic response to which cosmology is integral.

[29]For a helpful overview of the ways in which White's argument has been received, see Kevin Mongrain, "The Burden of Guilt and the Imperative of Reform: Pope Francis and Patriarch Bartholomew Take Up the Challenge of Re-Spiritualizing Christianity in the Anthropocene Age," *Horizons* 44 (2017): esp. 80–85.

[30]For a helpful critical summary of the anti-anthropocentric position that emerged within the field of environmental ethics in the second half of the twentieth century, see Richard Watson, "A Critique of Anti-Anthropocentric Biocentrism," *Environmental Ethics: An Interdisciplinary Journal Dedicated to the Philosophical Aspects of Environmental Problems* 5 (1983): 245–56.

as my foregoing analysis suggests, the inclination toward technophilia appears endemic to the holistic approach of ecological cosmology (or at least to some paradigmatic articulations of this discourse). *the choice not to do*

Even more problematic, however, is the tendency of anti-anthropocentric *any —* criticism to minimize the responsibility that the human person bears toward *why my* nonhuman creation. According to versions of the anti-anthropocentric line of *is* critique, it is arrogant to presume that the human can judge what is good for *still* the earth.[31] To be sure, there is value in this viewpoint insofar as it can act as *a* a hedge capable of interrupting the prideful surety of human valuations. The *choice* human person, after all, is not God. We would do well to be wary of the human capacity for hubris. Nonetheless, the danger of this line of criticism is that it can serve simply to relieve the human person of any sense of ethical responsibility. In alleviating the burden of responsibility for hearing and responding to the cries of the earth and the poor, anti-anthropocentrism arguments ironically open the way for the human person to lapse freely into unfettered narcissism. As J. Matthew Ashley writes,

> To state the matter polemically: Won't persons who are already weary of the high demands placed by the Enlightenment understandings of rationality and responsibility welcome the insight that humans are not really different from the rest of nature? Why not simply let the micro- or macro-subjects of history (genes, Gaia or "nature") take on the burden of history, while human beings seek what "niches" they can find to work out their individual destinies untroubled by broader questions of meaning and suffering in our common history?[32]

By minimizing the uniqueness of the human person's moral capacity, anti-anthropocentric arguments can simply give way to uncritical forms of self-concern and disordered self-love on the part of human beings.[33] This surrender

---

[31]As J. Matthew Ashley observes, this trend aligns with a broader cultural trend defined by a "postmodernism of the heart." Postmodernity, with its (often well-placed) emphasis on *difference*, attenuates the grounds for modernist appeals to solidaristic action. As a result, the contemporary milieu encourages a retreat by the human person into his or her more tightly defined "niche," where he or she can appear, somewhat ironically, to no longer bear responsibility for the other. See J. Matthew Ashley, "Environmental Concern and the New Political Theology," in *Missing God? Cultural Amnesia and Political Theology*, ed. John K. Downey et al. (Berlin: LitVerlag, 2006), esp. 141–48.

[32]Ibid., 148.

[33]Ashley's analysis, which follows closely the thought of Metz, is in many ways consonant with the critiques that David Harvey levels, in general, at the condition of postmodernity. Metz is concerned that, for all of its claims to the contrary, the projects of postmodernity have left intact the Enlightenment subject's propensity for self-assertion as the dominant force shaping reality. What postmodernity has undercut, however, with its exaltation of difference, is the prospect of commonality and, hence, solidarity with the other. Harvey takes a similar view, finding that the

feeds into a postmodern cultural milieu in which, as Ashley argues, "persons in general are increasingly numb to the sufferings of others and simply tired of appeals to the costly exercises of rational and moral accountability that come with being a subject in the modern sense."[34]

Anti-anthropocentric rhetoric, in attenuating or even rejecting the need for ethical responsibility on the part of the human person, fails to produce the requisite moral imperative for contesting the pernicious forms of anthropocentrism that are actively at work in the world today.[35] This rhetoric creates an inhospitable terrain for eco-liberationist concern. In light of this, Ashley writes, "At the risk of misunderstanding, I would say that our current problem is not too much anthropocentricity, but not enough, at least in the form that arises from an understanding of the subject formed by the Christian narratives and the praxis of discipleship."[36] Although the human person is not God, the person must stand responsible before God. To affirm James Gustafson's distinction, although human persons are not the *measure* of all things, they remain the *measurers* of all things.[37] Within a Christian theological framework, this is the qualified anthropocentrism that is required for hearing and responding to the cries of the earth and the poor. From an eco-liberationist perspective, then, it is vital for human communities, in cooperation with the Spirit, to refine their ability to name the realities of both sin and grace as they are at work in the world and to then act in accordance with such judgments. In order to contest the global networks of power that relentlessly exploit the world, an ecological theology of liberation must *center* its discourse on the human person and the person's capacity as a knower and doer of the Word—a subject who can confront reality and bear its weight, while working to transform that reality.[38]

---

condition of postmodernity is shaped by post-Fordist capitalism in a manner that attenuates the prospect of material solidarity. See David Harvey, *The Condition of Postmodernity: An Inquiry into the Origins of Cultural Change* (Malden, MA: Blackwell, 1990).

[34]Ashley, "Environmental Concern and the New Political Theology," 147.

[35]Thus, Metz's comment, which paraphrases Bertolt Brecht, remains an accurate descriptor of the cultural milieu promulgated by the globalization project: "When atrocities happen it's like when the rain falls. No one shouts 'stop it!' anymore." Metz, *Faith in History and Society*, 157. See also Bertolt Brecht, "When Evil-Doing Comes Like Falling Rain," in *Poems 1913–1956*, ed. John Willett and Ralph Manheim (New York: Routledge, 1987), 247.

[36]Ashley, "Environmental Concern and the New Political Theology," 148.

[37]James Gustafson, *Ethics from a Theocentric Perspective*, vol. 1: *Theology and Ethics* (Chicago: University of Chicago Press, 1981), 82. For Gustafson, the notion that humans are the measurers of all things is an unavoidable truth. Indeed, one must acknowledge that any argument that dismisses human judgment and agential capacity altogether falls into absurdity. The act of dismissal is, itself, a judgment that orients a certain form of praxis (though likely an unhelpful one).

[38]This terminology comes from Ignacio Ellacuría. For a helpful summary of Ellacuría's understanding of the human person's responsibility in relation to reality, see Michael Lee, *Bearing the Weight of Salvation: The Soteriology of Ignacio Ellacuría* (New York: Herder and Herder, 2009), 48–50.

The Two "Books" of Revelation: Reading the Signs of the Times in Light of the Word of God

In affirming the moral responsibility of the human person to know and shape the world, it is worth underscoring the point made by Ashley above. The type of human-centered discourse needed today, at least from a Christian eco-liberationist perspective, is one that works to form the person through the Christian narratives and the praxis of discipleship. In recalling this point, the presumption on my part is that the narratives shaping Christian identity can and should be interpreted in a manner that orients the human person toward hearing and responding to the cries of the earth and the poor. Here, though, another set of questions arises that requires consideration: What constitutes revelation? What shapes the narratives that, in turn, form the Christian person (and the Christian community) as a subject who is responsible before God? Moreover, how do we work to interpret God's self-disclosure so that human responsibility before God translates into a preferential option that responds to the needs of both the earth and the poor?

In responding to this set of questions, we can begin by noting that the Catholic Christian tradition long has affirmed the revelatory power of two "books"—the book of scripture and the book of nature. Here the book of scripture refers not only to the Bible but also to doctrine and the tradition through which the faith has been handed down.[39] The second of the two books, the book of nature, refers to creation. On this view, creation, in all of its wondrous complexity, is understood to communicate a "word" about the Creator, similar to the manner in which a text is capable of disclosing something about the character of its author.[40] Thus, as Pope Francis affirms in *Laudato Si'*, nature can be read like a book to gain insight into God.[41] Each of these two books, then, is partially constitutive of the Word of God—revealing something of who God is and what God desires, and offering testimony to Jesus Christ, the Word through whom all things were made. From this perspective, then, the books of scripture and nature together constitute revelation and in turn shape the narratives that form Christian identity.

The Christian tradition conventionally prioritizes the revelatory power of the book of scripture over that of the book of nature. In other words, the tradition

---

[39]On the connection between these sources of revelation, see *Dei Verbum*, 9–10. Note that the reference to a singular "book of scripture," should in no way be taken to suggest that these sources are univocal in nature. Both the Bible and the Christian tradition house within them a wide array of perspectives, perspectives that are often in tension with one another.

[40]For a helpful survey of the tradition's estimation of the revelatory capacity of nature, see Jame Schaefer, *Theological Foundations for Environmental Ethics: Reconstructing Patristic and Medieval Concepts* (Washington, DC: Georgetown University Press, 2009).

[41]*Laudato Si'*, 12 (hereinafter *LS*).

affirms that the former book gives us clearer and more far-reaching insight into God and God's will than the latter. On the traditional understanding, the book of nature should be read in light of and through the book of scripture. However, in the wake of White's critiques regarding Christianity, some contemporary strands of eco-theology and environmental ethics have come to view the book of scripture largely through a hermeneutic of suspicion.[42] As a result of this suspicion, there is a tendency within environmentally concerned theological discourse to reverse the traditional prioritization of the two books and thus grant pride of place to the book of nature. This reversal characterizes the thought of both Boff and Gebara, who, in varying ways, marginalize the book of scripture within their arguments.[43] This move, however, is problematic not only for the view it takes with regard to the book of scripture but also for the ways in which it construes nature.

Sideris observes that, in granting primacy to the book of nature, theologians and environmental ethicists frequently point to the discipline of ecology for warrant in making this decision. In appealing to this discipline, the discourses of eco-theology and environmental ethics typically foreground the notion of the "ecological *community*" as a way of highlighting the manner in which the various parts of nature fit together as a whole.[44] Eco-theology then emphasizes the ways in which this community is characterized by the interdependence, cooperation, and symbiosis of its members, in a manner that sustains the community as a whole. What emerges from this characterization of the natural order, Sideris notes, is a view in which nature appears largely benign and seems to produce the best of possible worlds.[45] From this perspective, the book of nature

---

[42]There is an irony here since traditionally the book of scripture is that which provides warrant for seeing nature as a book that reveals the goodness of God. At the very least, this should call into question a posture of uncritical suspicion with regard to the book of scripture (at least with respect to environmental concern).

[43]Boff makes this reversal explicit, arguing that although the two books cannot contradict each other, a "creation-centered theology requires the overhauling of all religious and ecclesial institutions. They must be at the service of cosmic revelation, which applies to all." See Boff, *Cry of the Earth*, 151. Gebara does not make explicit reference to the two books in *Longing for Running Water*. However, throughout her argument there, she adopts a position that is notably more anti-retrievalist than Boff's.

[44]Lisa Sideris, *Environmental Ethics, Ecological Theology, and Natural Selection* (New York: Columbia University Press, 2003) 5–6, 25–27. Also of note here is Zygmunt Bauman's analysis of the meaning of community and the sense of security that it engenders. Although Bauman's concern is societal and not ecological, his analysis helps explain the lure of the term "ecological community." See Zygmunt Bauman, *Seeking Safety in an Insecure World* (Malden, MA: Blackwell, 2001).

[45]Sideris, *Environmental Ethics*, 45–90. Although Sideris criticizes the tendency of eco-theology to romanticize nature, she also remains tepid toward the type of environmental ethics the book of scripture might underwrite. Instead, Sideris extols James Gustafson's "theocentric model" (a model that is minimally determined by the book of scripture) as a helpful proper framework for doing environmental ethics. Sideris's recommendation is helpful in leading environmental ethics toward a contemplative acceptance of nature as it is. Likewise, the model for which she calls

by solely relying upon the Book of Nature, the text the Christian (handwritten)

appears able to act as our guide in navigating and remediating the crises and *corpus* (handwritten) harms that afflict the world that humans inhabit. If not the "universe story," then the "earth story" can properly order the dispositions and praxis of the human person. The morally responsible subject need merely attune himself or herself to the ways of nature. The formation of Christian identity for which Ashley calls can be largely if not entirely naturalized—the narratives and praxis informing this identity are effectively disclosed by the book of nature.

The line of argumentation that I have just rehearsed, however, is built on faulty premises that, when recognized as such, ultimately delegitimize the exaltation of the book of nature. Privileging this book as the preeminent source of revelation creates a highly unstable foundation for constructing the preferential option for the earth and the poor. This is because nature is itself a far more ambiguous realm than is often admitted in the discourses of eco-theology and environmental ethics. Sideris herself is highly critical of the ways in which eco-theology tends to proffer romanticized views of nature. To this effect, she notes that although it is true that nature, in varying ways, is characterized by cooperation, interdependence, and mutualism, these characteristics do nothing to reduce the realities of scarcity, predation, suffering, waste, and competition that are also endemic in the natural world.[46] Even when taking the principles of ecology into account, the natural order continues to remain "red in claw and tooth." In other words, the Darwinian principle of "the survival of the fittest" and the tenets of natural selection endure as defining traits of the ecological community. Were nature to function as our sole or even primary ethical guide, *vital part of nature* (handwritten) there seems to be little to contravene the specter of social Darwinism.[47] This should be particularly concerning given, as we have already observed, the manner in which notions of evolutionistic progress can function to legitimize rather blithely the annihilation of a species or group.

Not only do appeals to the book of nature, within eco-theological discourse, tend to downplay the violence inherent in the natural order, they also frequently rely on outmoded scientific views that describe the natural world fundamentally

---

helps underscore the need to cultivate wonder at the complexity and mystery of nature. However, this model does not provide adequate warrant for making a preferential option for the poor or, for that matter, the earth. It does not sufficiently evoke the prophetic language of denouncement and announcement that calls for the transformation of the politico-ecological patterning of the world. The language of prophecy is a key element of the book of scripture and is vital to the task of clarifying and energizing the preferential options for the earth and poor. For this reason, Gustafson's theocentric model, by itself, is insufficient for eco-liberationist discourse.

[46]Sideris traces the ways in which the concept of "ecology" has been used (often inappropriately) in descriptions of nature as a way of attempting to counter the harsher elements of the natural order associated with evolution. See Sideris, *Environmental Ethics*, 21–31. See also her critique of Rosemary Radford Ruether, ibid., 45–60.

[47]After all, while interconnectedness is foundational for communities of mutual care, this characteristic is also essential to the predator/prey relationship.

in terms of equilibrium. From this perspective, nature inclines toward a definable stasis only to be driven from this point of balance by human interference. As David Lodge and Christopher Hamlin argue, this portrayal misrepresents the character of the natural order, which, in fact, exists in a state of constant change. For Lodge and Hamlin, it is more accurate to conceive of earth's ecology as an "ecology of flux"—one in which the myriad patterns of relationship within the biosphere are subject to ongoing transformation. As Lodge and Hamlin acknowledge, "This new ecology is terrifying because it exposes the inadequacy of our normative systems."[48] In other words, due to its constant flux, nature does not provide a clear "ought" with regard to social or even environmental ethics.[49]

In light of the opacity and constant flux of nature, Lodge and Hamlin find "it is not a matter then of doing things nature's way, but rather of deciding which of nature's ways or forms we want to establish, maintain, restore, or change."[50] Here nature provides neither unambiguous ethical norms nor a straightforward path on which orthopraxis might unfold. Most important for an ecological theology of liberation, neither the preferential option for the poor nor even the preferential option for the earth are inscribed in the book of nature. Rather nature presents any number of paths, each of which must be carefully observed and considered while discerning their ethical viability.

---

[48]David Lodge and Christopher Hamlin, eds., *Religion and the New Ecology: Environmental Responsibility in a World of Flux* (Notre Dame, IN: Notre Dame University, 2006), 9.

[49]Ibid., 4–9. Along these lines, Willis Jenkins writes that deriving a moral framework from "the practice of ecological science proves elusive. Researchers find it difficult to establish structuring principles of biotic communities, let alone the evaluative concepts of stability, integrity, beauty, or balance. Flux and chaos seem just as present in ecological systems, which makes it difficult to predict change and impossible to establish normative states of nature. In fact, scientists debate whether ecology can ever produce predictive laws about how ecosystems function. The science of ecology cannot supply moral foundations." Willis Jenkins, *The Future of Ethics: Sustainability, Social Justice, and Religious Creativity* (Washington, DC: Georgetown University, 2013), 151–52. Note that the consonant views of Lodge, Hamlin, and Jenkins need not preclude an affirmation of Pope Benedict and Pope Francis that nature has a "grammar" that humans ought to respect (see, for example, Benedict XVI's comment in *Caritas in Veritate*, 48). As Robert Schreiter argues, following the linguistic work of Noam Chomsky, grammars themselves are incomplete, somewhat indeterminate, and always evolving (see Robert Schreiter, *Constructing Local Theologies* [Maryknoll, NY: Orbis Books, 1985], 113–17). As such, the ecological and evolutionary patterns that compose nature's grammar remain in a state of flux, always evolving and subject to reformulation. Thus, one can affirm that nature maintains a grammar without suggesting that this grammar ultimately determines the foundation for ethical norms. To be clear, this characterization of grammar certainly applies as well to the grammars of faith that emerge from granting primacy to the book of scripture. My argument, then, is not that the book of scripture provides a self-evident or incontrovertible way forward in articulating an ecological theology of liberation. Rather, the view that I advance here is that the book of scripture (when compared with the book of nature) provides a relatively more well-defined and stable foundation for grounding and animating the preferential options for the earth and poor. This is because the book of scripture allows one to perceive nature as "creation" (i.e., nature in its relationship to God's creative and redemptive love).

[50]Lodge and Hamlin, *Religion and the New Ecology*, 7.

In light of nature's radical ambiguity, a Christian ecological theology of liberation should be wary of the move to privilege the book of nature over that of scripture. The argument of this text proceeds from the view that it is the book of scripture that presents the clearest warrant for the preferential options for the earth and the poor. Thus the book of scripture should be granted pride of place as the source of revelation that informs the narratives and praxis constituting Christian identity. This assertion may appear dubious to many environmentally concerned ethicists and theologians who have been conditioned over much of the late twentieth and early twenty-first centuries to approach the book of scripture with a hermeneutic of suspicion. To be clear, I am not suggesting that the book of scripture is without its own ambiguities. Even less am I proposing that the disclosure of this book can somehow be apprehended without an act of interpretation on the part of the person or community of faith. There is no perfectly stable or uncontestable foundation for an ecological theology of liberation. Nonetheless, the book of scripture is consistent in its affirmation that creation is a gift from a good God who, however inscrutably, works to redeem and save the world from the horrors of suffering and sin. In other words, the book of scripture allows one to conceive of the world within the drama of God's creative and redemptive love. Scripture articulates this view in a way that nature does not. This is vital because it is the trust and hope that one holds in the goodness and faithfulness of God that serve as the ultimate warrant for making a preferential option for the earth and the poor. Amid the whirlwind of creation, the book of nature could easily recommend the exaltation of the sword and spear over the plowshare and pruning hook. The book of scripture ultimately calls us to opt for the latter, trusting in the path of discipleship and the call to serve and not dominate. It is the task of Part II of this text to substantiate these claims more thoroughly. For now, I turn to consider an important ramification of the move to prioritize the book of scripture.

SALVATION: TURNING TO THE ORGANIZING THEME OF THE BOOK OF SCRIPTURE

In privileging the book of scripture, Christian eco-liberationist discourse should take the mystery of salvation in Jesus Christ as the central locus for its theological reflection. The reason for this is straightforward. Salvation in Christ is the fundamental mystery of the Christian faith. This mystery lies at the heart of the book of scripture, and all Christian theological discourse is ultimately predicated on and rendered intelligible by the good news of salvation. Pheme Perkins's claim about the resurrection (the climax of God's unsurpassable saving act in Christ) can be extended to the category of salvation in general: "It is the condition for the emergence of Christian speech itself."[51] Thus, the Christian character of God-talk requires an explicit grounding in soteriology. To extend the metaphor that I have been using, the mystery of salvation is not a page in the book of scripture, or even a chapter. Rather, it is the spine of the book to which all pages must adhere. Therefore, if eco-liberationist concerns for the "cries" of the earth and the poor are to be understood as central to Christian reflection and action, the relationship between these concerns and the mystery of salvation must be made evident.

The embrace of soteriology is controversial within the discourses of ecological theology and environmental ethics for many of the same reasons that the methodological commitments outlined above can be viewed as contentious. Eco-theology has often been ambivalent about the prospect of embracing soteriology in its talk of God. This hesitancy can be understood as part of the legacy of White's critique of Christianity's anthropocentric character. The critique of anthropocentrism creates at least two difficulties for eco-theological talk of salvation in particular that bear noting here. First, Christian soteriology is necessarily human-centered in character. Since, salvation is from sin, an act of which human persons are uniquely capable, soteriology focuses on the manner in which God works to save the human person from sin. Second, soteriology can be looked on skeptically by ecological theology because talk of salvation is often suggestive of the human person's otherworldly and suprahistorical experience of God. Thus, in valorizing that which is not of this world, talk of salvation can have the accompanying effect of degrading the things that are of this world and, by implication, deaden the possibility of ecological concern and commitment.

As a result of the difficulties that soteriology presents for ecological theology, Jenkins observes that the response of Christian eco-theology to the issue of salvation is often "garbled." Even while attempting to "follow patterns of grace or reach for symbols of redemption," eco-theology tends to underplay the significance of soteriological discourse.[52] However, as we just observed, the problem with the marginalization of soteriology within ecological theology is that it also diminishes the Christian character of eco-theology. This move actually provides a tacit endorsement of White's view that Christianity is inimical to ecological concern. One is left, it would seem, with the choice of embracing ecological concern on the one hand or Christian belief on the other.[53]

---

[51]Pheme Perkins, *The Resurrection: New Testament Witness and Contemporary Reflection* (New York: Doubleday, 1984), 18. On this point, see also Brian D. Robinette, *Grammars of Resurrection: A Christian Theology of Presence and Absence* (New York: Herder & Herder, 2009), introduction.

[52]Willis Jenkins, *Ecologies of Grace: Environmental Ethics and Christian Theology* (New York: Oxford University Press, 2008), 12.

[53]For his part, White believed that Christianity could be refashioned to embrace ecological

Jenkins, for one, is dissatisfied with this dichotomy and proposes an alternative approach. He writes, "Christian ethicists . . . know that no matter their position on White, whether they agree or not with his indictment of Christianity, they share in a common task: challenging bad legacies of salvation and revaluing nature. Why not do that by engaging soteriology?"[54] Rather than attempting to avoid the issue of soteriology, Jenkins advises that ecological theology confront the issue directly by retrieving or rehabilitating soteriological grammars that might allow one to locate ecological concern at the heart of the Christian faith.[55]

Ecological theology—including eco-liberationist discourse—might take its cue from early forms of Christian liberation theology, which also had to contend with "bad legacies of salvation." Like ecological theology, liberation theology was also confronted by the problem of otherworldly conceptions of salvation. Particularly problematic to liberationists was the manner in which such conceptions served to tranquilize the human person's capacity for liberating and transformative praxis by wholly deferring the hope for divine justice and salvation to the eschaton. However, when faced with these world-denying soteriologies, the tendency within liberationist discourse was not to marginalize the mystery of salvation in Christ from its speech about God. Rather, in a manner that aligns with Jenkins's recommendation, liberation theology sought to reconstruct Christian soteriology so as to place the historical struggles for justice at the center of their soteriological frameworks.[56] This move allowed liberationists to locate at the heart of Christian identity the commitment to a liberating praxis in history.

We can now begin to discern a way forward in the effort to articulate a

---

concern. However, other than pointing to St. Francis as an exemplar on which this reformation might be based, he does little to specify the constitutive elements of an ecologically sensitive Christian faith. The point I am stressing here, following Jenkins, is that the reinterpretation of the faith for which White calls must engage Christian soteriology robustly.

[54]Jenkins, *Ecologies of Grace*, 13.

[55]Ibid. In his more recent work, Jenkins moves away from his focus on the soteriology that characterizes *Ecologies of Grace* and instead advocates adopting a pragmatist framework for environmental ethics that assign significantly less importance to the value of worldviews (including a Christian worldview ordered around soteriology). He explains this shift, in part, due to his skepticism that orthopraxis emerges from orthodoxy in any direct manner. Nonetheless, even with this skepticism characterizing his later work, Jenkins acknowledges that worldviews, and the cultures they inform, do have the power to energize praxis and inform environmentally critical consciences. Thus, he does not fully dismiss the importance of *Ecologies*. See Willis Jenkins, *The Future of Ethics: Sustainability, Social Justice, and Religious Creativity* (Washington, DC: Georgetown University Press, 2013), see esp. chapters 3 and 4. In effect, the argument of my text seeks to chart a middle path between Jenkins's first and second books. It seeks to develop a praxically responsive theology that is informed by a soteriologically determined Christian worldview.

[56]Dean Brackley provides a helpful account of the manner in which liberationist thought on soteriology developed in relation to wider trends in twentieth-century Catholic theology. See Dean Brackley, *Divine Revolution: Salvation and Liberation in Catholic Thought* (Maryknoll, NY: Orbis Books, 1996).

theology that affirms both liberationist and ecological concern as integral to Christian faith. In constructing a Christian ecological theology of liberation, it is possible to begin by retrieving liberationist soteriology and then broadening the scope of that soteriological framework so as to include ecological concern within it. This, in effect, is to carry out Jenkins's recommendation (that ecological theology directly grapple with soteriology) through an engagement with liberation theology. Through this method it would be possible to locate the imperative to hear and respond to the cries of the earth and the poor at the heart of Christian belief and practice.

In this vein, a particularly promising avenue for advancing eco-liberationist discourse can be found by turning to the work of Gustavo Gutiérrez, one of the foremost expositors of Latin American liberation theology. The thought of Gutiérrez recommends itself here, not only for its paradigmatic character, but also because of the nuanced and penetrating manner in which it articulates a Christian theology of salvation. In short, a constructive retrieval of Gutiérrez's theology of liberation can serve as the basis for establishing the proper framework for a Christian ecological theology of liberation.[57]

In the remainder of this chapter, I survey Gutiérrez's thought in order to elucidate how he defines liberation theology and the way in which he conceives of the relationship between the historical process of liberation and the life of Christian faith, while also highlighting the soteriological implications of this relationship. Through this analysis, I surface a number of points that enable a fuller definition of "an ecological theology of liberation" to emerge. This allows us to conceive more clearly how to construct this theology along a soteriological axis. This examination of Gutiérrez's thought also considers the limitations of his soteriology with regard to ecological concern. I conclude by considering the manner in which Pope Francis's encyclical *Laudato Si': On Care for Our Common Home* might offer resources for attending to these limitations.

THE FOUNDATIONS AND CONTEXT OF LIBERATION THEOLOGY IN THE THOUGHT OF GUTIÉRREZ

In his groundbreaking text, *A Theology of Liberation*, Gutiérrez writes, "To speak of a theology of liberation is to ask: what relationship is there between salvation and the historical process of human liberation?"[58] Driving Gutiérrez's

---

[57]In turning to Gutiérrez's thought in the section below, I draw primarily on *A Theology of Liberation* (hereinafter *TL*). At the same time, my engagement with Gutiérrez is by no means confined to *TL*. Rather, I make use of Gutiérrez's subsequent works in order to clarify and further elaborate the fundamental soteriological argument that he sets out in his groundbreaking text.

[58]Gutiérrez, *TL*, 29.

embedding Christianity in a good way (handwritten)

query, of course, is his desire to demonstrate a positive relationship between salvation and human liberation. In order to establish this relationship, Gutiérrez makes three distinct moves: (1) he argues for the oneness of history; (2) he affirms the preferential option for the poor as constitutive of Christian praxis; (3) and he embraces the language of liberation (against the ideology of developmentalism) as the way of describing the praxis of Christian solidarity with the poor. Each of these moves requires further consideration.

resuming Himself argument/claims (handwritten)

History Is One

Gutiérrez operates out of the conviction that salvation history cannot be separated from the broad plane of human history.[59] The dynamics of sin and grace are woven into the fabric of all of human life: the political, the economic, the cultural, and the interior. "Sin is not only an impediment to salvation in the afterlife," writes Gutiérrez. "Insofar as it constitutes a break with God, sin is a historical reality, it is a breach of the communion of persons with each other, and it is a turning in of individuals on themselves which manifests itself in a multifaceted withdrawal from others."[60] Thus, the drama of salvation from sin and participation in the life of Christian faith does not orient one away from the world but rather toward it. It is, after all, in the world that one encounters God acting *pro nobis*.

In holding this view, Gutiérrez rejects what he terms the "*idealist* or *spiritualist*" approach to the life of faith.[61] This approach divorces the temporal, finite, and contingent realities of history from God. Within the spiritualist view, the struggles within history and the political character of human life are, at best, conceived of as tangential to salvation history, the life of sanctification, and love of God. According to the idealist or spiritualist line of thought, then, God's transcendence orients the one seeking God away from the world. This, Gutiérrez finds, is an impoverished understanding of divine transcendence with tragic consequences for both the life of faith and the world. He believes that this approach allows the human person and the ecclesial community to shirk their responsibility to God and neighbor. Indeed, Gutiérrez posits that although the spiritualist approach might appear as an apolitical construal of the life of faith, this construal, in fact, is thoroughly political. By endorsing a withdrawal from worldly politics, the spiritualist view functions to uphold the status quo. In the end, for Gutiérrez, the spiritualist and idealist approaches "are nothing but ways of evading a harsh and demanding reality"—they avoid confronting both the manner in which sin degrades the world and the ways God's grace might

---

[59]Ibid., 34–57.
[60]Ibid., 85.
[61]Ibid., 25.

call the ecclesial community to confront and denounce these degradations.[62]

In rejecting the spiritualist view of the life of Christian faith, Gutiérrez follows the fundamental orientations of the Second Vatican Council, which calls the ecclesial community to be a sacrament of salvation and a servant to the world (see *Ad Gentes*, 1, and *Gaudium et Spes*, 1). The council, in instructing the ecclesial community to take up these tasks, famously proclaims:

> "The joys and the hopes, the griefs and the anxieties of the women and men of this age, especially those who are poor or in any way afflicted, these are the joys and hopes, the griefs and anxieties of the followers of Christi. . . . This community [the followers of Christ] realizes that it is truly linked with humankind and its history by the deepest of bonds." (*GS*, 1)

From the perspective of the council, then, the life of faith requires that one face the world and commit to a praxis of solidarity with humankind.

Gutiérrez expresses the depth of the bond between the ecclesial community and the world in the strongest of terms. In describing the relationship between the love of God and the love of neighbor, he asserts that it is not enough to posit that the love of God and the love of neighbor are closely related. Instead, Gutiérrez finds that love of God is expressed *through* love of neighbor.[63] Within the unity of history, then, the human person—in responding to the movement of the Holy Spirit—enters more deeply into communion with God precisely through his or her life of loving solidarity with other human persons. These distinct, yet inextricably interlinked, forms of loving communion (with God and neighbor) constitute the experience of salvation within history.[64] For Gutiérrez, then, the responses of the people of God to the struggles and sufferings of the world are integral to the life of Christian faith and the history of salvation. "History," as Gutiérrez puts it, "is one."[65]

The Preferential Option for the Poor

If, within history, love of God is expressed through love of neighbor, then the question, "Who is my neighbor?" is of vital importance. Within Christian communities, this query is at least as old as the gospel of Luke in which a

---

[62]Ibid.

[63]Ibid., 114–15.

[64]For Gutiérrez, the love of God cannot be reduced to or wholly identified with the love of neighbor. However, neither can it be segregated from the love of neighbor.

[65]*TL*, 86. In this vein, Gutiérrez continues, "There are not two histories, one profane and one sacred, 'juxtaposed' or 'closely linked.' Rather there is only one human destiny, irreversibly assumed by Christ, the Lord of History. His redemptive work embraces all the dimensions of existence and brings them to their fullness. The history of salvation is the very heart of human history."

"scholar of the law" poses the question to Jesus. In Luke, Jesus responds by narrating the story of "the Good Samaritan" (Lk 10:29–37).[66] Here, I do not recount this well-known story but only point out that, in Jesus's response, the neighbor is revealed to be both the victim of a violent theft who is left to die on the side of the road and the culturally demonized Samaritan who helps restore him to life.[67] Thus, in Luke's gospel, Jesus intimates that one's neighbor is both the person who has been crushed by iniquity and the person who is despised and outcast because of the social imaginary that defines the outcast's reality. Jesus's response points to an underlying principle for Christian praxis. In discerning how love of neighbor is to be made manifest within the vagaries and ambiguities of history, the Christian community is called to exercise "a preferential option for the poor."

The concept of the preferential option for the poor is essential to Gutiérrez's thought.[68] Most basically, the concept affirms that the "cries" and "sufferings" (Ex 3:7) of those persons afflicted by death-dealing poverty—those who are materially impoverished or culturally marginalized—make a special claim on the lives of Christian communities.[69] Thus, Gutiérrez's affirmation that love of God is expressed through love of neighbor carries with it the qualitative dimension of Jesus's response to the scholar: our neighbors are principally those whom the powers of this world attempt to relegate to the status of "nonperson."[70] Although

---

[66]Gutiérrez references this biblical narrative in reflecting on the option for the poor. See Gustavo Gutiérrez, *The Power of the Poor in History* (Maryknoll, NY: Orbis Books, 1983), 44–48.

[67]In this story, the incapacitated victim is the object of the neighborly love demonstrated by the Samaritan. Given this, it is the vulnerable person who appears as the "neighbor" to be cared for. At the same time, it is the Samaritan, who was generally viewed with hostility in Jesus's culture, who acts neighborly. In casting the Samaritan as the protagonist of this narrative, Jesus challenges his listeners not only to identify the poor and vulnerable as neighbor but also the one conceived of as enemy. On another level, the story of the Good Samaritan also raises the vexed issue of the agency of the poor. As noted, the victim of theft in this story is incapacitated; the person is quite literally without agency. Discussions of the preferential option for the poor are sometimes criticized for not giving an adequate account of the agential capacity of the poor. Gutiérrez robustly affirms the agency of the poor, asserting that the poor are to be "agents of their own destiny" (in cooperation with God's liberating spirit). On this point, see *TL*, xxi, xxix, 91, and 155.

[68]The theme of the preferential option for the poor recurs throughout all of Gutiérrez's major works. For a prolonged and explicit engagement on this issue, see Gustavo Gutiérrez, "Option for the Poor," in *Mysterium Liberationis: Fundamental Concepts of Liberation Theology*, ed. Ignacio Ellacuría and Jon Sobrino (Maryknoll, NY: Orbis Books, 1993), 235–50.

[69]As Gutiérrez writes, "Our encounter with the Lord occurs in our encounter with others, especially in the encounter with those whose human features have been disfigured by oppression, despoliation, and alienation. . . . Our attitude towards them, or rather our commitment to them, will indicate whether or not we are directing our existence in conformity with the will of the Father. . . . This is what Christ reveals to us by identifying himself with the poor in the text of Matthew. A theology of the neighbor, which has yet to be worked out, would have to be structured on this basis." *TL*, 116.

[70]Gutiérrez describes "nonpersons" as "those who are not considered to be human beings with full rights, beginning with the right to life and to freedom in various spheres." See Gutiérrez, *TL*, xxix.

this captures perhaps the fundamental meaning of the concept of the option for the poor, it does not fully convey the richness of Gutiérrez's understanding of this option. In order to comprehend more fully Gutiérrez's construal of the option for the poor, it is necessary to consider both the manner in which this option is related to God and the conflictive character of the option.[71]

For Gutiérrez, the option for the poor is theocentric in character and rooted in the covenant.[72] YHWH, to whom the people of God are bound, is *Go'el*, the liberator and defender of the poor.[73] Thus, in binding themselves to YHWH, the people of God commit themselves to a praxis of care and liberation for the poor. Put another way, through the covenant, the people of God pledge themselves to the historical task of *imaging* God, the liberator: "I will place my law within them, and write it upon their hearts; I will be their God, and they shall be my people" (Jer 31:33).[74] The option for the poor, then, stems from a faithful affirmation of who God is and what God desires, and as Gutiérrez notes, citing Bartolomé de Las Casas, "God has a very vivid and recent memory of the smallest and the most forgotten."[75]

If the option for the poor is a theocentric option, for Gutiérrez, it is likewise a Christocentric option. In his dialogue with liberation theology, Ian McFarland notes that within the Christian imagination the preferential option for the poor

---

[71]To highlight the agonistic dimension of the preferential option for the poor is to take seriously the presence of sin in history. By no means, however, does this require that a liberationist construal of the option be rooted in an ontology of violence. With Augustine, one may still affirm that sin is fundamentally a privation.

[72]See Gustavo Gutiérrez, *The God of Life*, Eng. trans. by Matthew J. O'Connell (Maryknoll, NY: Orbis Books, 1991) (hereinafter *GoL*), esp. 33–47.

[73]Ibid.

[74]Gutiérrez's work has sometimes been accused of being Pelagian in character (see Brackley, *Divine Revolution*, 87–89). To be sure, there are passages of Gutiérrez's writing that can be interpreted in that direction. However, Gutiérrez rejects this characterization of his work, maintaining that he has always upheld the gratuitousness of God's saving work. To this point, Gutiérrez writes, "Salvation is God's unmerited action in history, which God leads beyond itself. It is God's gift of definitive life to God's children, given in a history in which we must build fellowship. Filiation and fellowship are both a grace and a task to be carried out; these two aspects must be distinguished without being separated, just as, in accordance with the faith of the church as definitively settled at the Council of Chalcedon, we distinguish in Christ a divine condition and a human condition, but we do not separate the two" (see Gutiérrez, *TL*, xxxix). Vital to Gutiérrez's thought is the notion of "spiritual poverty," a concept that dictates against attempts to locate his thought within a Pelagian framework. For Gutiérrez, spiritual poverty, which is at the heart of liberation, "is opposed to pride, to an attitude of self-sufficiency." Gutiérrez, *TL*, 169.

[75]Gustavo Gutiérrez, "Memory and Prophecy," in *The Option for the Poor in Christian Theology*, ed. Daniel G. Groody (Notre Dame, IN: Notre Dame University, 2007), 19. In Gutiérrez's later writings, he makes clear that we should always acknowledge the profound limitation of our knowledge of God. In this respect, the language of prophecy must always be held together with the language of contemplation. See Gustavo Gutiérrez, *On Job: God-Talk and the Suffering of the Innocent*, Eng. trans. by Matthew J. O'Connell (Maryknoll, NY: Orbis Books, 1987) (hereinafter *OJ*); and *Density of the Present: Selected Writings*, Eng. trans. (Maryknoll, NY: Orbis Books, 1999) (hereinafter *DoP*).

is ultimately "justified by reference to God's decision, definitively realized in the incarnation ... to encounter humanity as a whole in and through the poor."[76] For the Christian community, then, Christ reveals the fullness of God's character as *Go'el*. Jesus Christ, in proclaiming, enacting, and embodying the reign of God, offers good news to the poor and hope to those held captive by injustice and oppression. In Matthew's gospel, Jesus explicitly identifies himself with the poor and oppressed, telling his followers, "Whatever you did for one of these least brothers of mine, you did for me" (Mt 25:40).[77] Central to the challenge of Christian discipleship, then, is the task of witnessing to the good news of God's reign by responding positively to Christ's mission and presence in the world. Accordingly, Gutiérrez finds, "the option for the poor arises from faith in Christ."[78] *Part of Christian Praxis*

Gutiérrez also closely links the option for the poor to the experience of metanoia. For him, the option for the poor demands a deep and ongoing conversion—one which challenges and reorients the entirety of a person or a community's inherited life.[79] This emphasis on conversion should be underscored. Rohan Curnow observes that during the late-twentieth and early twenty-first century two divergent understandings of the option for the poor and its personal and social implications have emerged within Catholic Christian discourse. On the one hand, liberation theology consistently articulates a conception of the option for the poor that emphasizes the need for (often radical) transformation on the part of the people of God and the broader world. On the other hand, Curnow finds that the Vatican has tended to delineate a differing view of the option for the poor, one which places comparatively less emphasis on the need for conversion. This latter view, then, expresses a greater degree of comfort with the possibility of living out the option for the poor within the inherited frameworks of one's life and history.[80] For Gutiérrez, the transformational

---

[76]Ian McFarland, *The Divine Image: Envisioning the Invisible God* (Minneapolis: T&T Clark, 2005), 71.

[77]As Gutiérrez comments, "The proclamation of the kingdom begins with the promise made to the poor in spirit and ends with the gift of the kingdom to those who come to the aid of the materially poor. The disciples are said to be blessed because they give life by giving food to the hungry and drink to the thirsty, by clothing the naked and visiting prisoners, or, in other words, by concrete actions; in this way they proclaim the kingdom and enter into it." Gutiérrez, *GoL*, 132.

[78]Gustavo Gutiérrez, "The Option for the Poor Arises from Faith in Christ," *Theological Studies* 70, no. 2 (2009): 317–26.

[79]Brackley observes that Gutiérrez's theology has been profoundly influenced by the Augustinian dialectic between sin and grace (see Brackley, *Divine Revolution*, 71). It is this dialectic's manifestation in history that makes conversion necessary. For Gutiérrez, as for Augustine, sin is expressed through a destructive self-love that turns one against God and neighbor; conversely the love of God and the love of neighbor are manifestations of the graced experience of liberation from sin.

[80]See Rohan M. Curnow, "Which Preferential Option for the Poor? A History of the Doctrine's Bifurcation," *Modern Theology* 31 (2015): 27–59. It must be noted that Pope Francis (who is both Latin American and the bishop of Rome) operates out of the former conception, as is evidenced

and interruptive demands of the option for the poor are essential elements of the concept. There is an agonistic dimension to the preferential option for the poor: it requires a struggle against the myriad forces—psychological, political, cultural, economic—that orient one away from the marginalized and engender apathy for the plights of the so-called nonperson.

Although the preferential option for the poor requires metanoia, this conversion should not be construed in highly individualistic terms. For Gutiérrez, this is true on two accounts. First, and most basically, Gutiérrez presumes that the life of faith is one that is lived in communion with other believers. Accordingly, the Christian vocation to a life of holiness (understood here in terms of the option for the poor) is a "convocation."[81] The call to conversion is issued to the community, calling the community together to incarnate the preferential option for the poor as one body in Christ. Second, and relatedly, the task of incarnating the preferential option for the poor does not only entail practicing works of charity and mercy. Rather, this task also demands that the community of faith and those other communities to which it is allied work for the structural transformation of the world. In other words, for Gutiérrez, the community is called to confront and transform the socioeconomic, political, and cultural formations of the world that produce injustice, material poverty, and oppression. The option for the poor, then, is also made manifest through the labor to convert the social and cultural formations that attempt to reduce human beings to the status of nonpersons in history.[82]

In sum, for Gutiérrez, love of God is expressed especially through a preferential option for the poor. This option is a faithful response to God's liberating love, a love that is revealed most fully through the person of Jesus Christ. Moreover, requisite to the option for the poor is the demand of conversion. Gutiérrez's conception of the option for the poor, therefore, calls for the reorientation of one's life and community toward the service of transforming the world. This last point with regard to the preferential option for the poor, that of conversion, points us toward a key dimension of the language of liberation as it is employed by Gutiérrez.

The Language of Liberation as Ideology Critique and Imminent Expectation

Within contemporary theological discourse the term "liberation" can appear both ubiquitous and underdetermined. The term tends to be used broadly to refer

---

by the consistent emphasis that he places on the need for conversion. See my analysis of Francis's concept of "integral ecology" in chapter 2.

[81] *TL*, 45, 153.

[82] Of course, the human person's efforts to transform the structural and cultural formations presume a prior and ongoing conversion of heart on the part of the person, moving him or her from apathy to concern and solidarity with the sufferings of the world.

to any event or phenomenon that promotes human flourishing. Although such usages capture something of the character of liberation as it was employed by theologians such as Gutiérrez, they fail to capture its character fully. In order see why this is the case, as well as to gain a more complete understanding of the meaning of liberation as it was first employed by early Latin American liberationists, it is necessary to understand the language of liberation against the background of both the colonial and neocolonial projects of the last five centuries.

The complex legacy and often horrific realities of Western colonialism have profoundly shaped contemporary Latin America and, indeed, the modern world as a whole. Underlying perhaps all of the horrors endemic to the colonial project is the phenomenon of "plunder."[83] Through varying methods, the colonial powers of Europe appropriated the wealth and resources of the geographic regions at the periphery of the colonial system (i.e., the space of the colonized, including the region now known as Latin America) in order to secure and enhance their own economic and political status. The plunder of the global south, itself an inherently violent act, required multiple forms of violence to secure its continued existence. Violent repression and the domination of entire peoples were frequently concomitant to the phenomenon of plunder.[84] Moreover, the Western colonial project also relied on its ability to obfuscate or legitimize its violence. As Ignacio Ellacuría pointedly captures it, the global north's view of Latin America has been "characterized by the *covering up* of a fundamentally dominating and oppressive reality with a lovely ideological curtain that is only a mask."[85] The dominant powers of colonialism employed the ideological weapons of racism, misogyny, claims of cultural superiority, and the mythos of progress (all sanctioned in varying ways by appeals to the Christian theological imagination) in order both to underplay or justify the enormities of their project and thereby sustain the life of colonialism.[86]

It was only as the Second World War drew to a close, some four-and-a-half centuries after the colonial project began, that it was apparent that the project could no longer be sustained. Although colonialism's collapse was generally welcomed throughout the global south, its breakdown also opened up a period

---

[83]I borrow this term from Ta-Nehisi Coates, who, in a related context, notes that the wealth of white Americans in the United States has been procured chiefly through the plunder of black bodies. The dynamics of such plunder often require complex cultural and structural formations in order to be legitimized, secured, and sustained. See Ta-Nehisi Coates, "When Plunder Becomes a Form of Governance," in *The Atlantic*, https://www.theatlantic.com.

[84]See, for example, Gustavo Gutiérrez, *Las Casas: In Search of the Poor of Jesus Christ* (Maryknoll, NY: Orbis Books, 1995), esp. parts II, III, and IV (hereinafter *LC*).

[85]Ignacio Ellacuría, "The Latin American Quincentenary: Discovery or Cover-up?" in *Ignacio Ellacuria: Essays on History, Liberation, and Salvation*, ed. Michael E. Lee (Maryknoll, NY: Orbis Books, 2013), 29.

[86]On many of these points, see Willie James Jennings, *The Christian Imagination: Theology and the Origins of Race* (New Haven, CT: Yale University Press, 2011), esp. chap. 2.

of uncertainty. It was unclear what type of geopolitical project would emerge to structure the relationships between the global south and the global north. Clearly, the colonial project could no longer remain intact. The dramatically shifting context required a new paradigm. However, the exact contours of this paradigm needed to be defined and constructed.

Into the geopolitical vacuum created by the fracturing of the colonial project, US President Harry Truman, ushered in the era of developmentalism, calling for the United States to "embark on a bold new program for making the benefits of our scientific advances and industrial progress available for the improvement and growth of underdeveloped areas." The United States was to take a leading role in implementing Truman's vision:

> The United States is pre-eminent among nations in the development of industrial and scientific techniques. The material resources which we can afford to use for assistance of other peoples are limited. But our imponderable resources in technical knowledge are constantly growing and are inexhaustible. I believe that we should make available to peace loving peoples the benefits of our store of technical knowledge in order to help them realize their aspirations for a better life. And, in cooperation with other nations, we should foster capital investment in areas needing development.[87]

Truman's charge was soon echoed throughout the western nation-states of the global north with the United Nations proclaiming the 1960s "the decade of development."[88] Thus, the development project came into ascendance.

Importantly, as Truman's language suggests, the development project was portrayed throughout the world as a break with the colonial project—one that would redress the ills of colonialism, allowing those peoples who suffered the impoverishing effects of plunder and the oppressive political yoke of colonial rule to make gains in wealth and liberty. Early Latin American liberationists,

the Global south can pretty "conshruppn

---

[87]See Harry Truman, "Inaugural Address: January 20, 1949," American Presidency Project (http://www.presidency.ucsb.edu). Note that, as Truman's address also suggests, the development project's correctives to the colonial project would be realized primarily through the advancement and dispersal of technical knowledge, not through reparations or the redistribution of unjust concentrations of wealth accrued under colonialism. Thus, for the winners of the colonial project, the pivot to the project of development would be largely painless—economic and technological development and modernization would create a rising economic tide capable of lifting all boats on the global geopolitical landscape. Likewise, the development project sustained the thread of cultural imperialism that was endemic to colonialism. After all, within the development project, it was the values and technological sophistication of the Western powers that were exalted and deemed worthy of dissemination.

[88]See UN Intellectual History Project Briefing Note 7, "The UN and Development Policies" (2010), http://www.unhistory.org.

however, were deeply suspicious of the development project. For Gutiérrez, the project did not augur the eclipse of colonialism or the reversal of its effects. Instead, the project, through its various institutions and policies, was aimed at perpetuating the status quo with regard to global politico-economic power differentials. In other words, for liberationists, the development project ushered in a *neocolonial* era that continued the plunder of the global south by the north, thus sustaining the "situation of poverty" and repressive violence that had long plagued much of Latin America, while ensuring that this region would remain under the political hegemony of the global north (especially that of the United States).[89] leading to hyper wealth

While, as liberationists maintained, the inequity characterizing the development project's political economy was observable and verifiable, they also found that the concept of development (and, concomitantly, the concept of modernization) ultimately served to obfuscate the true nature of the development project. The language of development and modernization granted legitimacy to the project, suggesting that the project was, in fact, the antidote to the ills brought about by colonialism. Liberationists such as Gutiérrez, then, found that the concepts of "development" and "modernization" performed an ideological function. These concepts functioned to communicate an *inverted* construal of reality.[90] The development project, contrary to its claims, secured the continued "underdevelopment" of the global south.[91] Notions of developmentalism and

---

[89]In truth, liberationists had good reason to be suspicious of the promises attached to the language of development and modernization. Consider, for one, that just months before the "Four Points" address, George Kennan, Truman's Undersecretary of State, authored a classified document in which he describes the goal of US foreign policy in the following manner:

> We have about 50% of the world's wealth but only 6.3% of its population. This disparity is particularly great as between ourselves and the peoples of Asia. In this situation, we cannot fail to be the object of envy and resentment. *Our real task in the coming period is to devise a pattern of relationships which will permit us to maintain this position of disparity* without positive detriment to our national security. . . . We need not deceive ourselves that we can afford today the luxury of altruism and world-benefaction.

See Section VII in "Review of Current Trends in US Foreign Policy," in *Foreign Relations of the United States,* vol. 1 (Washington, DC: United States Government Printing Office, 1948), https://history.state.gov. Emphasis is mine. It should be noted that Kennan makes this statement with specific reference to US interests in Asia. Nonetheless, given that the statement concerns US global positioning and in light of the history of US interventionism in Latin America through the engineering of coups against democratically elected leaders and the support of dictatorships and oppressive military regimes, Kennan's statement is instructive for understanding the relationship between the United States and Latin America during the second half of the twentieth century.

[90]Karl Marx famously maintains that ideology functions as a *camera obscura* that misrepresents the reality it ostensibly describes, effectively turning reality on its head. This inversion is performed in the service of subordinating reality to the interests of the ruling class. See Karl Marx, with Friedrich Engels, *The German Ideology* (Amherst: Prometheus, 1998).

[91]This characterization of the socioeconomic context in Latin America is most closely associated with the long discredited theory of dependency postulated by André Gunder Frank. See André

modernization, therefore, functioned to perpetuate the "cover-up" requisite to sustaining the injustices of the neocolonial order.[92]

It is in contrast to the development project and its legitimization structures that the language of liberation can best be understood. According to Gutiérrez, "Only a radical break from the status quo," that is, a paradigm shift away of the structures of developmentalism, would effect the transformation needed for redressing the enormities of the colonial project. In Gutiérrez's view, the language of liberation best captures the urgency and dramatic nature of this break. As he explains, "Liberation in fact expresses the inescapable moment of radical change which is foreign to the ordinary use of the term development. Only in the context of such a process can a policy of development be effectively implemented, have any real meaning, and avoid misleading formulations."[93] Gutiérrez, therefore employs the language of liberation for two key related reasons. First, he does so in an effort to unveil the obfuscating and pacifying tendencies of the rhetoric of *development* and *modernization*, which legitimize a project "synonymous with timid measures, really ineffective in the long run and counterproductive to achieving a real transformation."[94] Second, he employs the language of liberation in an effort to call for a systemic conversion away from the sociopolitical and cultural structures of the development project.[95] With this

---

Gunder Frank, "The Development of Underdevelopment," *Monthly Review* 18 (September): 17–31. Subsequent liberationist discourse has tended to draw a distinction between the theory of dependency, which needs to be abandoned, and the fact of dependency, which continues to characterize the death-dealing situation of poverty in the global south. See, for example, Arthur F. McGovern, *Liberation Theology and Its Critics: Toward an Assessment* (Maryknoll, NY: Orbis Books, 1989) esp. 164–76. Moreover, it should be noted that although dependency theory, as it was originally formulated by Gunder Frank, has been rejected, there has been ongoing work in the field of sociology to rehabilitate the concept of dependency through more nuanced theorization. Indeed, Gunder Frank's final published work attempts such a rehabilitation in a manner that is also sensitive to environmental concern. See André Gunder Frank, "Entropy Generation and Displacement: The Nineteenth-Century Multilateral Network of World Trade," in *The World System and the Earth System: Global Socioenvironmental Change and Sustainability since the Neolithic*, ed. Alf Hornborg and Carole Crumley (Walnut Creek, CA: Left Coast Press, 2006).

[92]Of note here is Thomas Piketty's discussion of how Western powers promulgated the "Kuznets Curve" as an ideological weapon during the Cold War. In the mid-twentieth century, the economist Simon Kuznets theorized that in capitalist societies inequality would increase dramatically before flattening and then reversing (hence, when plotted on a graph, the level of inequality over time would appear as an "inverted U." Although Kuznets viewed his theory as tenuous, politicians and economists utilized it to explain and justify situations of inequality throughout the global south in the midst of the Cold War. Today, Piketty argues that the Kuznets curve appears more as a "fairy tale" than reality. See Thomas Piketty, *Capital in the Twenty-First Century* (Cambridge, MA: Belknap Press of Harvard University Press, 2014), 11–15.

[93]*TL*, 17.

[94]Ibid.

[95]It should be underscored that in calling for liberation, Gutiérrez was not opposed to the prospect of development. Rather, he was calling for the establishment of the condition for the possibility of development. At the same time, Gutiérrez argues that, endemic to this condition is a break from the imposition of the West's cultural values on the peoples of Latin America and

in view, I should emphasize that Gutiérrez's use of the term "liberation" also conveyed a sense of imminent expectation. The time for conversion could not be deferred to the distant future. Instead, the need for a dramatic transformation of the world was an urgent demand of the present.[96] Taken together, these points capture the nuance of the language of liberation.

The Limits and Promise of Gutiérrez's Vision for Eco-Liberationist Discourse

We are now in a position to summarize Gutiérrez's answer to the question of the relationship between salvation and liberation. First, for Gutiérrez, all of history possesses a soteriological density—one in which the dynamics of God's saving grace saturate the life of the world. Salvation is not simply an otherworldly reality; rather it is experienced as a constitutive element of history itself. Within the unity of history, communion with God and liberation from sin—which, for Gutiérrez, make manifest salvation—are realized proleptically through the experience of communion and solidarity with one's neighbor.

Second, for Gutiérrez the denominator "neighbor" implies especially the poor and the oppressed. Thus, a rightly ordered love of God is expressed especially through love for the "least of these." In this same vein, within history, communion with God is experienced especially through communion and solidarity with those whom the world would relegate to the status of nonperson. This is consonant with the view that the preferential option for the poor reflects God's own attentiveness, care for, and identification with the forgotten victims of history.

Third, for Gutiérrez, solidarity with the poor requires that the human person work to transform the cultural formations and social structures that produce the death-dealing realities of poverty and political repression. God's saving grace calls the community of believers to confront the cultural and structural realities of sin in the world, unveiling and denouncing the death-dealing character of these realities and announcing the advent of a new way of life for the world. It is the language of liberation, Gutiérrez posits, that best captures the character of the requisite sociocultural metanoia. Liberation from sin and communion with God require liberation from sinful structures and the obfuscations that are intrinsic to those structures so that the preferential option for the poor can be incarnated within history. It is in this way that Gutiérrez demonstrates the

---

the global south, so that differing peoples might be free to clarify the meaning of development within their own contexts. On this last point, his reflections on the Babel narrative are of interest. See *DoP*, 188–207.

[96] Consider this in relation to Catherine Keller's discussion of the concept of *kairos* in her recent work. See Catherine Keller, *A Political Theology of the Earth: Our Planetary Emergency and the Struggle for a New Public* (New York: Columbia University Press, 2018), 1–20.

manner in which the mystery of salvation in Christ is positively related to the task of liberation within history.

Before considering how Gutiérrez's thought might be reconstructed for the purpose of framing an ecological theology of liberation, it is worth noting Gutiérrez's own views regarding ecological concern. From the outset, it must be admitted that the interests that are central to environmental ethics are not at the foreground of Gutiérrez's arguments, especially the arguments of his early work. There are points where Gutiérrez's thought presents itself as inimical to the sensitivities of ecological theology. This is perhaps most apparent in *A Theology of Liberation*, where Gutiérrez takes the language of domination as normative when describing the human/earth relationship. He writes, for example, that a

> reason for the repudiation of the state of slavery and exploitation of the Jewish people in Egypt is that it goes against *the mandate of Genesis* (1:26; 2:15).[97] Humankind is created in the image and likeness of God and is destined to dominate the earth. Humankind fulfills itself only by trans-forming nature and thus entering into relationships with other persons.[98]

By affirming that the human vocation is to "dominate the earth," Gutiérrez embraces the very type of language that White condemns in his critique of the Judeo-Christian worldview.[99] Likewise, Gutiérrez's account suggests that the process of human liberation is realized through the uncritical and wanton exploitation of the earth. On this account, the options for the poor and earth appear to be set in opposition to each other.

Later in *A Theology of Liberation*, Gutiérrez acknowledges that creation

---

[97]Here Gutiérrez conflates "the mandate of Genesis" as it is found in 1:26 with that of 2:15, allowing the latter to be subsumed by the former. As we shall see in Chapters 2 and 3, this manner of conflation is problematic and should be resisted or even reversed.

[98]*TL*, 168 (italics are Gutiérrez's). Elsewhere, and in the same vein as the passage cited above, Gutiérrez writes: "The concept of political liberation—with economic roots—recalls the con-flictual aspects of the historical current of humanity. In this current there is not only an effort to know and dominate nature. There is also a situation—which both affects and is affected by this current—of misery and despoliation of the fruit of human work, the result of the exploitation of human beings; there is a confrontation between social classes and, therefore, a struggle for liberation from oppressive structures which hinder persons from living with dignity and assuming their own destiny," *TL*, 102. In the original Spanish, Gutiérrez employs the verb "dominar" when discussing the human vocation. See Gustavo Gutiérrez, *Teología de la Liberacion: Perspectivas* (Salamanca: Ediciones Sígueme, 1975), 374.

[99]To be fair to Gutiérrez, in the middle of the twentieth century he was hardly alone in constru-ing the human/earth relationship in these terms. Indeed, many of his sources, both theological and secular, adopted this type of language. See, for example, Marie-Dominique Chenu, *Theology of Work: An Exploration* (Chicago: H. Regnery, 1963); the encyclical *Populorum Progressio*; and Herbert Marcuse, *The One-Dimensional Man: Studies in the Ideology of Advanced Industrial Society* (Boston: Beacon, 1966).

itself is bound up in the drama of sin and grace within history. However, he immediately distances this concern from his own thesis: " 'Creation,' the cosmos, suffers from the consequences of sin. To cite Rom. 8 in this regard is interesting and does broaden our perspective, *but this passage is not directly related to the question at hand.*"[100] Within his soteriology, at least as he articulates it within *A Theology of Liberation*, Gutiérrez divides the question of the cry of the earth from the cry of the poor. This, of course, poses a difficulty for appropriating Gutiérrez in developing an ecological theology of liberation along soteriological lines—a difficulty compounded by Gutiérrez's description of the human/earth relationship cited above. It would appear, therefore, that his thought does not readily lend itself to the type of "traditioning" needed for the robust articulation of eco-liberationist discourse. Some may suggest that these elements of Gutiérrez's thought disqualify him from eco-liberationist appropriation.

In his subsequent work, however, Gutiérrez's views have shifted notably with regard to the human/earth relationship and, correspondingly, serve to reshape the breadth of his soteriology.[101] He indirectly repudiates his embrace of the language of domination found in *A Theology of Liberation*. This is evidenced in *On Job*, where Gutiérrez comments on Job's famous argument with God. Noting Job's inability to comprehend God's intention for creation, Gutiérrez asks: "Is everything that exists in the natural world really meant to be domesticated by human beings and subjected to their service?" He continues, asserting,

> God's speeches are a forceful rejection of a purely anthropocentric view of creation. Not everything that exists was made to be directly useful to human beings; therefore, they may not judge everything from their point of view. The world of nature expresses the freedom and delight of God in creation. It refuses to be limited to the narrow confines of the cause-effect relationship.[102]

Gutiérrez clearly rejects the instrumentalized account of creation that figures prominently in *A Theology of Liberation*.

Along these lines, in *God of Life*, Gutiérrez moves to acknowledge a greater connection between the cries of the earth and the poor within a soteriological matrix. Gutiérrez discusses at length the manner in which God opposes the myriad forms of oppression and injustice found in history and, in so doing, comes to liberate life. Gutiérrez writes:

---

[100]*TL*, 101. Italics are mine.

[101]One who has sought to underscore this development in Gutiérrez's thought is Douglas G. Lawrie; see his essay, "Gustavo Gutiérrez: From Gratuitousness to Community," in *Creation and Salvation*, vol. 2: *A Companion on Recent Theological Movements*, ed. Ernst Conradie (Zurich: LIT Verlag, 2012).

[102]*OJ*, 74.

When I speak of life, I mean all life. At the new beginning of creation that follows the flood, God says to Noah and his family that the covenant is "with you and your descendants after you and with every living creature that was with you. . . . This is the sign of the covenant I have established between me and all mortal creatures that are on earth" (Gen 9:9–10,17). The covenant is with the various forms of life, which all come from God. The important and pressing concern for ecology in our day finds in the Bible . . . a solid and fertile basis, provided that we set aside an exclusively anthropocentric interpretation of ecology. . . . Human beings, made as they are in "the image and likeness of God," occupy a privileged place among living things and are called to the grace of full communion with God. But Paul reminds us that the whole of creation waits for its liberation through the children of God. (Rom 8:21–22)[103]

While Gutiérrez rightly affirms the dignity of the human person in this passage, he also acknowledges the manner in which God's redeeming work is a covenantal activity that embraces all of creation. Likewise, he suggests that the liberation of the earth and the poor are intimately bound up with each other in a manner that indicates a shift away from his earlier desire to keep these issues separate. In *On Job* and *God of Life*, then, Gutiérrez signals a nascent turn to ecological concern. Although this concern remains underdeveloped within his theology, it can be advanced further precisely by allowing ecological concern to recalibrate the general movements of Gutiérrez's soteriology that we have surfaced above.

AN ECOLOGICAL THEOLOGY OF LIBERATION: STATING THE QUESTION, DEFINING THE TERMS

With Gutiérrez's theology in view, we can now more fully grasp what is meant by and required of a Christian ecological theology of liberation, while also describing a method for elucidating this theology. Of these two related issues, the first is straightforward. To speak of an ecological theology of liberation is to ask the question: What is the relationship of the mystery of salvation, liberation, and the care for creation?[104] Christian eco-liberationist discourse must demonstrate a positive relationship between the three terms in question.

---

[103] *GoL*, 81–82.

[104] The term "care for creation" will inevitably be viewed as suspect within some eco-theological circles. Nonetheless, the term is consonant with the view of human responsibility for which I argued above.

The phrasing of this controlling question is obviously patterned on that of Gutiérrez's key interrogative from *A Theology of Liberation*. Given this, it is reasonable to affirm that in seeking to elucidate a positive relationship between salvation, liberation, and the care for creation, we can proceed by following the contours of Gutiérrez's own argumentation while modifying the breadth of his argument appropriately. This tack would, then, follow the three basic moves outlined in the section above. First, an ecological theology of liberation must affirm not only that history is one but also that there exists an underlying unity between history and nature. This understanding of history as an eco-social phenomenon also presumes a fundamental revision in the liberationist conception of the human person. Liberation theology has traditionally understood the human person as a person-in-relation. This relational understanding of the human person underwrites the liberationist conception of social sin. Since the human person is constituted by his or her sociohistorical relationships, personal sin takes on a sociohistorical character. An eco-liberationist conception of the human person must affirm the human as person-in-relationship. However, in this case, the relational character of the human is broadened from a social matrix to an eco-social matrix. In other words, history and the human person alike are defined by their eco-social character. (As the reader should note, this conception of both history and the human person has been presumed since the opening pages of the introduction, affirmed in this chapter's call to advance politico-ecological analyses, and shall remain operative throughout the text.)

Second, Christian eco-liberationist discourse is required to delineate the manner in which the preferential options for the poor and the earth are interrelated and rooted in a faithful response to God's saving grace. It must demonstrate that these options arise from a faithful response to the God of Jesus Christ. Put another way, an ecological theology of liberation must establish how the Christian imagination can uphold the view that the love of God is expressed through the interrelated loves of neighbor and earth. This demonstration has important soteriological implications. Since the love of God orients us away from sin and toward communion with God (which is the experience of salvation), demonstrating that love of God is expressed through the loves of neighbor and earth allows us to affirm that the latter two loves bear an incarnational witness to, and proleptic experience of, God's saving work.

Third, it is incumbent on an ecological theology of liberation to establish the reasons for recovering the language of liberation within today's eco-social context. That is to say, it is necessary to give an account of why the use of liberationist rhetoric—with its appeals to apocalyptic and dialectical framings—is proper for describing precisely how the ecclesial community and human communities in general are called to manifest the preferential options for the earth and the poor in the world today. It is noteworthy that the terms "sustainable development" and "ecological modernization" are employed today to justify the contemporary globalization project—this terminology bears an obvious likeness to the terms "development" and "modernization," which Gutiérrez criticized in calling for liberation from the regime of developmentalism. The analysis in subsequent chapters, then, scrutinizes the globalization project and the function of the legitimizing terms "sustainable development" and "ecological modernization." It then considers the degree to which "a radical break" from this project is necessary.[105]

CONCLUSION

Gutiérrez's theology provides the outline for a way forward in articulating an ecological theology of liberation. At the same time, his thought requires a broadening and traditioning to actually advance along this path. For the task of traditioning, there are a number of interlocutors that can help us clarify the ways in which salvation, liberation, and care for creation are positively related to one another. In particular, the vision of Pope Francis, especially as it is articulated in his encyclical *Laudato Si'*, can prove helpful in framing and energizing the task at hand. While *Laudato Si'* has been frequently described in popular discourse as Francis's "environmental encyclical," this description actually fails to do justice to the pope's argument. As I have already observed in the introduction to this book, the encyclical should be understood as a reflection on the interrelated ecological and socioeconomic implications of caring for the world. The vision of *Laudato Si'* is notably politico-ecological in character.[106]

Francis not only points to the underlying unity between nature and society which must be the starting point for the development of an ecological theology of liberation; he also makes clear throughout the encyclical that a proper praxis of care for the world must be responsive to the cries of both the earth and the poor—a responsiveness which, as we will see, for Francis roots in faithfulness to God. Further still, the encyclical is similar to Gutiérrez's work in its affirmation of the pressing need for radical social and cultural conversion. *Laudato Si'*, then,

---

[105]Thus, the manner in which this book attempts to recover the language of liberation in the service of ecological concern evades a criticism proffered by Sideris. Sideris is critical of the vague manner in which ecological theology has sometimes called for the "liberation of life." She notes that this call is underdetermined, writing that " 'liberation' and 'oppression' are too often defined simply with reference to one another. . . . It is not clear in what sense life *as a whole* is in need of liberation from oppression." See Sideris, *Environmental Ethics*, 113 (italics are Sideris's). The present argument works to specify the manner in which "liberation" is appropriate for ecological concern by taking the globalization project as its object of inquiry and interrogating the language of sustainable development and ecological modernization, which serve to legitimize the project.

[106]The breadth of the concerns of *Laudato Si'* is subtly implied in the subtitle of the encyclical, "On Care for Our Common Home." As is frequently noted in both economic and ecological discussions, the Latin word for "home" is *oikos*, from which both the terms "ecology" and "economy" derive.

lends itself well to the task of expanding on Gutiérrez's thought for the purpose of articulating an ecological theology of liberation. This commensurability is especially true with respect to the manner in which the encyclical develops the modern Catholic theological tradition of integralism[107]—a tradition with which Gutiérrez also engaged in important ways—in accordance with its eco-social sensibilities. Thus, the argument of the next chapter turns to the integralist tradition—drawing robustly from both Gutiérrez and Francis—in order to clarify the relationship between salvation, liberation, and care for creation.

---

[107]Here I am referring to the integralist tradition that emerges with Jacques Maritain's concept of "integral humanism," which is subsequently utilized by Pope Paul VI and his papal successors. See Jacques Maritain, *Integral Humanism: Temporal and Spiritual Problems of a New Christendom*, trans. Joseph W. Evans (New York: Scribner, 1968); Paul VI, *Populorum Progressio*, http://w2.vatican.va. Generally speaking, Francis's conception of integralism seeks to respect the integrity of the secular political order while nonetheless attempting to unite the history of salvation with secular history. It must be contrasted, then, with earlier nineteenth- and twentieth-century forms of integralism which sought to reinstall Christendom and exhibited fascist tendencies.

Chapter 2

Integral Ecology

A Liberationist Concept

Drawing on the work of Gustavo Gutiérrez in Chapter 1, I posited that to speak of an ecological theology of liberation is to ask: What is the relationship between salvation, liberation, and care for creation? In considering how to respond to this query, I suggested that the respective thought of Gutiérrez and Pope Francis can be brought together to demonstrate a positive relationship between the three terms in question. The basic task of this chapter is to execute this dialogue, focusing on Gutiérrez's and Francis's respective concepts of integral liberation (vital to *A Theology of Liberation*) and integral ecology (central to *Laudato Si'*). Taken together, these concepts can establish a framework that elucidates the manner in which salvation, liberation, and care for creation are intimately related.

As we shall see, through the concept of integral ecology, Francis conceives of the dynamics of sin and grace in politico-ecological terms. That is to say, the concept presents the alienating effects of sin (and, correspondingly though implicitly, the saving and redeeming power of grace) in terms of the human person's relationship to God, neighbor, *and earth*. Moreover, these relationships are understood to be inextricably interlinked to one another. Likewise, the concept of integral ecology helps clarify how sin and grace are at work in the world, shaping the politico-ecological character of historical reality.[1] As I argue below, the concept of integral ecology can itself be understood as a liberationist concept—a concept that calls for the radical transformation of

---

[1] Thus, the concept of integral ecology presumes not only that history is one but that the earth's ecological formations are not separable from history.

the contemporary globalization project in accordance with God's saving will.

As the reader might assume at this point, Gutiérrez's conception of integral liberation, which predates *Laudato Si'* by some forty years, presents the dynamics of sin, grace, and history primarily in politico-economic terms (focusing on the human person's relationships to God and neighbor). Thus, integral ecology marks a broadening of the framework operative within integral liberation. It may appear tempting, then, simply to dispense with Gutiérrez's concept in order to embrace the concept of integral ecology as the sole starting point for developing Christian eco-liberationist discourse. However, it is inadvisable to take this tack. This is because for all of the attention that *Laudato Si'* gives to the concept of integral ecology, the encyclical neither straightforwardly defines the concept nor clearly delineates its structure and dynamism. Thus, integral ecology, which stands at the heart of Francis's encyclical, remains problematically opaque and vulnerable to both vague affirmations and outright misinterpretation. In light of this difficulty, Gutiérrez's concept of integral liberation can serve a vital role in the effort to grasp the complexity of the concept of integral ecology. We can analyze Gutiérrez's concept, which over the decades has become more clearly defined, in order to elucidate the "vertical" structure of integralism (what Gutiérrez's delineates as the three levels of integral liberation) as well as the dynamism at work within this structure. Grasping the structure and dynamism operative within Gutiérrez's concept allows for a nuanced understanding of how he conceives of the unity between history and salvation history. This, in turn, provides a helpful conceptual framework on which we can map Francis's politico-ecological construal of integralism. Whereas the concept of integral ecology broadens the focus of integralist discourse to include care for creation, Gutiérrez provides the means for comprehending the configuration and dynamism of Francis's concept.

In brief, then, this chapter proceeds by: (1) describing the three levels of liberation that constitute integral liberation; (2) elucidating the manner in which these levels are related to one another; (3) showing the ways in which Francis's concept of integral ecology maps onto the structure of integral liberation; and (4) demonstrating the manner in which Francis's concept of integral ecology aligns with Gutiérrez's in calling for a radical transformation of historical reality.

INTEGRAL LIBERATION

According to Gutiérrez, liberation is realized at three distinct yet "recipro-cally interpenetrating" levels or dimensions of human life.[2] I term these (1)

mutuality / relational

---

[2]Gustavo Gutiérrez, *A Theology of Liberation*, Eng. trans. (Maryknoll, NY: Orbis Books, 1973), 24 (hereinafter *TL*).

the socio-structural level, (2) the cultural/psychological level, and (3) the theo-logical level.[3] For Gutiérrez, the socio-structural level refers to the dimension of human life within which institutions and policies organize and structure society (especially the economic and material resources of society). Thus, the socio-structural dimension denotes the quantitative and empirically measur-able elements of society. Liberation at this level, then, is realized through the transformation of unjust social structures, oppressive political systems, and the institutions and laws that constitute and support injustice.[4]

Whereas the socio-structural level refers especially to the quantitative elements of society, the cultural/psychological level refers to a more qualita-tive dimension of human life. At this second level, it is the value systems, worldviews, and identities of human persons and their communities that are the particular objects of inquiry. Thus, liberation at the cultural/psychological level signifies the transformation of the imaginations of human persons and their communities away from dehumanizing and degrading self-understandings, imaginaries, and value systems.[5]

Finally, within Gutiérrez's schema, the experience of liberation finds its

---

[3] In *A Theology of Liberation*, Gutiérrez describes the second level as "the level of human becoming in history." However, this obscure denomination has led to a great deal of confusion as to precisely what the term connotes. Therefore, I have chosen to use the term "cultural/psy-chological" which more clearly describes the second dimension. See his discussion in *TL*, 17–22, 24–25. For helpful discussions of Gutiérrez's concept, see Miguel Manzanera, *Teología, salvación y liberación en la obra de Gustavo Gutiérrez: Exposición analítica, situación teórico-práctica y valoración crítica* (Bilbao: Universidad de Deusto: Mensajero, 1978); Dean Brackley, *Divine Revolution: Salvation and Liberation in Catholic Thought* (Eugene, OR: Wipf and Stock, 1996) esp. 72–77; and James Nickoloff, "Church of the Poor: The Ecclesiology of Gustavo Gutiérrez," *Theological Studies* 54 (1993): 512–35.

[4] To clarify what is connoted by the socio-structural level, it is possible to take a concrete example from the historical and present-day circumstances of the United States. Consider that from 1934 to 1968, the Federal Housing Administration (FHA) refused to back loans to black persons in the United States. This racist policy has had ongoing deleterious effects on black com-munities, who, for much of the twentieth century, were denied access to perhaps the most stable path to wealth accumulation available in the United States. The FHA's policy and its empirically demonstrable effects on society is an example of the socio-structural dimension of historical reality. With regard to this example, liberation and the establishment of justice would require not only an overturning of the policy but also reparations for the systemic plunder of wealth. For an astute and accessible argument to this effect, see Ta-Nehisi Coates, "The Case for Reparations," *Atlantic*, June 2014, https://www.theatlantic.com.

[5] To refer to the example used in note 4, consider that the racist policies of the FHA (and the ways in which this policy structured and continues to structure society) were bound up with a general cultural milieu of antiblack racism. With this example in view, then, the second level of liberation requires a break from the racist predispositions of this culture. Importantly, Gutiérrez emphasizes that those who are the object of cultural degradation can internalize this oppression and come to identify with it. In other words, human beings can internalize variations of the identity of nonperson. Thus, liberation at the second level can be required not only for privileged groups who perpetrate and benefit from sinfully degrading cultural valuation, but also for those persons and groups who are degraded by them.

deepest articulation at the theological level of reality. At this level, liberation denotes salvation: liberation from sin and communion with God and neighbor.[6] In order to understand the significance of this denotation, however, we must describe the theological level of reality more fully. For Gutiérrez, the theological level can be understood in a twofold sense. On the one hand, the theological dimension of reality encompasses the entirety of human experience (i.e., the socio-structural and cultural/psychological levels of reality). This is because, as I observed in Chapter 1, the whole of history is contained within and shaped by the dynamics of grace and sin. Liberation from sin (salvation) is realized precisely through the work of liberation at the socio-structural and cultural/psychological dimensions of life.[7] In a certain sense, liberation from sin might unfold in history anonymously.[8]

On the other hand, however, the theological dimension of human life also refers to the human person and faith community's explicit perception, language, and experience of God and God's relatedness to the world.[9] In this second sense, the theological dimension of human experience is disclosed thematically through the sources of Christian revelation and mediated through the narratives, symbols, prayers, and rituals of the ecclesial community.[10] Revelation elucidates

---

[6]As Gutiérrez writes, "Christ the Savior liberates from sin, which is the ultimate root of all disruption of friendship and of all injustice and oppression. Christ makes humankind truly free, that is to say, he enables us to live in communion with him; and this is the basis for all human brotherhood" (*TL*, 25).

[7]Along these lines, Gutiérrez writes, "Sin is evident in oppressive structures, in the exploitation of humans by humans, in the domination and slavery of peoples, races, and social classes. Sin appears, therefore, as the fundamental alienation, the root of a situation of injustice and exploitation. It cannot be encountered in itself, but only in concrete instances, in particular alienations" (*TL*, 103).

[8]Gutiérrez references, with somewhat ambivalent approval, the concept of "anonymous Christianity," a concept that is most closely associated with Karl Rahner (see *TL*, 45). While Rahner's concept remains controversial for a number of reasons, Francis J. Caponi offers a helpful way forward for critically appropriating this concept by arguing for the nonidentification of grace and categorical revelation, so that the dynamics of grace can be affirmed, at least potentially, as universally operative, whereas Christian identity remains bound up with categorical revelation. See Francis J. Caponi, "A Speechless Grace: Karl Rahner on Language," *International Journal of Systematic Theology* 9, no. 2 (2007): 200–221. The distinction for which Caponi advocates appears to be implicitly operative in the theological vision that Gutiérrez delineates in *TL*.

[9]Here, a point made by Roger Haight is helpful. He notes that the theological dimension of human experience "add[s] no new knowledge, in a strict sense of knowledge, about the world. But Christian symbols mediate an encounter with transcendence that transforms all our ordinary or scientific knowledge about finite reality." See Roger Haight, *Dynamics of Theology* (Maryknoll, NY: Orbis Books, 2001), 1–2. To continue with the example found in notes 4 and 5, the theological level allows us to name (and thus experience) the milieu of racism and racist policies as sinful. Likewise, it allows us to name the experience of liberation from racism and racist policies as an experience of God's saving grace.

[10]Thus, for example, Gutiérrez writes, "The first task of the Church is to celebrate with joy the gift of the salvific action of God in humanity, accomplished through the death and resurrection of Christ. This is the Eucharist: a memorial and a thanksgiving. It is a memorial of Christ which presupposes an ever-renewed acceptance of the meaning of his life—a total giving to others. It is

and makes manifest the grace, peace, and love of God, thereby drawing the person more closely into communion with God through the power and work of the Spirit.

Within this second sense of the theological dimension of reality, the experience of salvation is tightly bound with what Gutiérrez denotes as spiritual poverty. Spiritual poverty refers to the kenotic process through which human persons surrender themselves (and their sinfully disordered conceptions and desires) to God and become more deeply open to discerning and cooperating with God's will.[11] It is through this ongoing process that the person's imagination is more fully conformed to the mind of Christ (1 Cor 2:16)—the latter of which is most clearly revealed through Jesus's proclamation, enactment, and embodiment of God's reign, and discloses God's "very vivid and recent memory of . . . the most forgotten."[12] As Gutiérrez stresses, in opening the human person

---

a thanksgiving for the love of God which is revealed in these events" (*TL*, 148). Mary Catherine Hilkert's "experience interpreted by faith" provides an apt description of the function of the theological dimension within integral liberation. In effect, the theological dimension of integralism provides us with the language to *name* both sin and God's saving grace as we experience them in history. As Hilkert writes, "Human experience is interpreted. We do not have raw human experience apart from some framework for understanding or perceiving. We interpret our lives in the context of traditions. . . . We are given language; we do not create it. In speaking then of recognizing God or grace at the depths or limits of human experience, we are talking within the framework of a faith tradition which alerts us to a deeper dimension in our experience and gives us a language to name that dimension." See Mary Catherine Hilkert, "Naming Grace: A Theology of Proclamation," *Worship* 60, no. 5 (1986): 444.

[11]*TL*, 169–71; and Gustavo Gutiérrez, *We Drink from Our Own Wells: The Spiritual Journal of a People*, Eng. trans. (Maryknoll, NY: Orbis Books, 1984), 126–27 (hereinafter *WDFOOW*). Following Valerie Saiving's classic critique of the virtue of humility when it is employed uncritically, feminist theologians rightly have expressed suspicion with regard to concepts such as kenosis and spiritual poverty. After all, these concepts can be employed to direct subjugated peoples to accept their subjugation. Gutiérrez's retrieval of spiritual poverty, however, evades this concern. Indeed, his retrieval confronts and dismantles this perverse use of the concept. In retrieving the concept of spiritual poverty, one of Gutiérrez's fundamental concerns is the manner in which a marginalized person can internalize the identity of nonperson. In other words, when the world conveys to a person that he or she is less than fully human or that he or she is a "nonperson," there is the danger that he or she will believe these oppressive conveyances and internalize them within his or her own psyche. The internalization of oppression, in turn, promotes the acceptance of unjust situations ("If I am a nonperson, then I ought to be treated as such"). Surrender to God, then, entails the surrender of all life-negating identities, thereby, liberating one's imagination and agential capacity to resist and transform the various regimes of domination at work in the world. This is why Gutiérrez affirms the possibility of the poor becoming the agents of their own destiny. See *TL*, 14, 91; Gustavo Gutiérrez, *The Power of the Poor in History* (Maryknoll, NY: Orbis Books, 1983), 37 (hereinafter *PPH*).

[12]Gutiérrez is clear that while the graced encounter with the Lord is an encounter that allows one to enter into and conform to the mind of Christ, we can never penetrate the mystery of God. On this he is fond of quoting—and paraphrasing as here—Aquinas: "What we don't know about God is much greater than what we know." See Gustav Gutiérrez, *Density of the Present: Selected Writings*, Eng. trans. (Maryknoll, NY: Orbis Books, 1999), 145; and Gustavo Gutiérrez, "Memory and Prophecy," in *The Option for the Poor in Christian Theology*, ed. Daniel Groody (Notre Dame, IN: University of Notre Dame Press, 2007), 19.

more deeply to the will of God, the Spirit orients the person more fully to the work of liberation in history.[13] "To know God," he writes, "is to do justice."[14]

The Internal Dynamism of Integral Liberation

In introducing the concept of integral liberation, I observed that Gutiérrez describes the levels of integral liberation as "reciprocally interpenetrating." By describing the relationship between the levels in this manner, he indicates that liberation at one level of reality shapes and is shaped by liberation at the other two.[15] Accordingly, he describes integral liberation as a "single, complex process."[16] Indeed, as I just noted, there is a sense in which both the socio-structural and cultural/psychological dimensions of reality participate in the theological dimension. However, this description does not do full justice to the complexity of the relationship between the three levels of integral liberation. The nuances of this process often have been overlooked or misunderstood by interpreters of Gutiérrez. It is important, therefore, to give considered attention to the ways in which Gutiérrez conceives of the relationship between the three levels of liberation. In order to grasp better the dynamism of this process, I begin by considering briefly the relationship between the first and second levels of integral liberation.

It is commonly assumed that in their analysis of society, early liberationists adopted the Marxist position that culture is simply a superstructure of the socioeconomic. On this view, the socioeconomic formations at the first level of integralism are those which truly order the world, while the cultural formations at the second level are merely epiphenomenal. Or, as Peter Burke puts it in metaphorical terms, socioeconomic formations constitute the "cake" whereas cultural formations constitute the "frosting."[17] On this interpretation of reality, it follows that any meaningful and lasting social transformation occurs at the socioeconomic level of reality. Cultural transformation appears as a secondary or even inconsequential concern to the process of liberation.

Daniel Bell Jr. finds that theorists and scholars who adopt the classic Marxist conception of political economy problematically tend to reduce the practice of politics to "statecraft."[18] For these adherents of Marx, the struggle for political

---

[13] Along these lines, Gutiérrez writes, "Prayer to the God who liberates and does justice does not remove us from the historical process, but rather compels us to immerse ourselves in it so that we may responsibly exercise our solidarity with the poor and the oppressed." Gustavo Gutiérrez, *The God of Life*, Eng. trans. (Maryknoll, NY: Orbis Books, 1991), 47 (hereinafter *GoL*).

[14] Gutiérrez, *TL*, 110.

[15] Gutiérrez writes, "These different levels are profoundly linked; one does not occur without the others" (ibid., 137).

[16] Ibid., 25.

[17] Peter Burke, *History and Social Theory*, 2nd ed. (Ithaca, NY: Cornell University Press, 2005),

[18] Ibid., 116. Bell finds this is true of Gutiérrez's conception of politics. See his accounts of

liberation becomes wholly identified with the struggle to transform the social and economic structures of society through the use of coercive power (i.e., the legal power wielded by states and legal authorities). The problem with this, Bell argues, is that the classical Marxist construal of political economy and politics is misguided. Social structures are not produced and sustained merely through the use of coercive power. Instead, the order of the polis is also formed and legitimized through the exercise of "pastoral power"—a form of power that orders the values and desires of human persons and their communities.[19] This second form of power, Bell argues, is essential to the production and maintenance of the polis. Thus, he finds that liberationists who fail to account for the manner in which political power functions beyond the socio-structural dimension of reality impair their ability to conceive effectively of a liberating politics—a politics that could truly transform society.[20]

In light of Bell's critique of traditional Marxist interpretations of political economy (a critique that he derives from the thought of both Michel Foucault and Gilles Deleuze) it is important to note that Gutiérrez does not conceive of society in the traditional Marxist sense. For Gutiérrez, the formation of culture is not peripheral to either the socioeconomic formations of the world or, for that matter, to the process of liberation. Rather, according to him, the transformation of the socio-structural dimension of historical reality (liberation at the first level), is intimately bound up with the transformation of the cultural values and the reordering of human desire (liberation at the second level). Without the latter the former will always be problematically circumscribed. Gutiérrez provides a vivid elucidation of this assessment through his interpretation of the tribute narrative found in Matthew's gospel. According to this famous story, a group of Pharisees approach Jesus and ask whether it is lawful to pay the census tax to Caesar. Jesus, knowing that the Pharisees are attempting to trick him, replies: "Why are you testing me, you hypocrites? Show me the coin that pays the census tax. . . . Whose image is this and whose inscription?" The Pharisees respond that it is Caesar's, to which Jesus replies, "Then repay to Caesar what belongs to Caesar and to God what belongs to God" (Mt 22:15–22).

With respect to this passage, Gutiérrez comments,

Gutiérrez's thought in Daniel Bell Jr., *Liberation Theology after the End of History: The Refusal to Cease Suffering* (London: Routledge, 2001); and Daniel Bell Jr., " 'Men of Stone and Children of Struggle': Latin American Liberationists at the End of History," *Modern Theology* 14 (1998).

[19]Thus Bell writes, "Culture and politics . . . do not merely *reflect* economic realities; rather they produce and reproduce economics. Likewise, economic forces of production do not merely determine . . . cultural formations; rather economic forces of production *are* cultural and political forms" (Bell, "Men of Stone," 125). Emphasis is Bell's. Bell develops this view in *The Economy of Desire: Christianity and Capitalism in a Postmodern World* (Grand Rapids, MI: Baker Academic, 2012).

[20]As Bell writes, "It is precisely this commitment [to politics as statecraft] that, in the age of globalization, delivers liberationists to the capitalist order." Bell, "Men of Stone," 115.

The coin bears the image of its owner; the money belongs to the Roman oppressor and must be given back. The matter is important, because if the Pharisees' question suggests the possibility of not paying the tribute, it also suggests the possibility of keeping the money. Their vaunted nationalism did not go so far as to make them give up the money. Jesus goes to the root of the matter: all dependence on money must be rooted out. *It is not enough to throw off foreign political domination; one must also break away from the oppression that arises from attachment to money and the possibilities it creates of exploiting others.* Return the money to Caesar, Jesus is telling them, and you yourselves will be free of the power exercised by wealth, by mammon; then you will be able to worship the true God and give God what belongs to God.[21]

can't play by the oppressor's rules

Gutiérrez makes clear that liberation requires more than simply the ability to exercise coercive power. Instead, the experience of integral liberation also requires a pastoral power capable of transforming the desires and values that generate oppressive structures. Indeed, he articulates this view early in *A Theology of Liberation* when he laments that "the scope of liberation on the collective and historical level does not always and satisfactorily include psychological liberation."[22] After affirming that historical liberation cannot be placed in opposition to psychological liberation, he then approvingly cites David Cooper, who finds that a key failure of previous revolutions was their inability to hold together the concerns of the individual with those of class struggle. "If we are to talk of revolution today," Cooper concludes, "our talk will be meaningless unless we effect some union between the macro-social and the micro-social, and between 'inner reality' and 'outer reality.'"[23] Gutiérrez, then moves to connect the psychological transformation and interior liberation of the human person (the process of *concientización*) to his affirmation of the need for a "*permanent cultural revolution.*"[24]

Moving well beyond any reductive notion of politics-as-statecraft, Gutiérrez affirms that cultural/psychological liberation is important for the prospect of effecting socioeconomic liberation. After all, it is at the cultural/psychological level that human persons conceive of the values around which the world's socioeconomic and material structures can and should be organized. Liberation at the cultural/psychological level gives rise to the utopian imagination—an imagination that is capable of both denouncing the distorted value systems and

---

[21]*GoL,* 60, italics are mine.

[22]*TL,* 20.

[23]David Cooper, introduction to *To Free a Generation: The Dialectics of Liberation,* ed. David Cooper (New York: Collier, 1967), 9–10.

[24]Gutiérrez, *TL,* 21. Emphasis is Gutiérrez's. Here, contra Bell, Gutiérrez conceives of the second level of liberation as a form of political liberation.

formations of desire that produce and sustain oppressive social orders, and announcing new social imaginaries and valuations that can reorganize the world at both the socio-structural dimension of life and the cultural/psychological.[25] In this way, then, the cultural/psychological sphere of liberation penetrates and forms the socio-structural.

If liberation at the psychological/cultural level is intertwined with liberation at the socio-structural level, then the question becomes: What gives shape to the proper psychological/cultural formations of society and the human person? Or, put another way, what rightly orders the utopian imagination? Undoubtedly, Gutiérrez finds that any number of humanistic and socio-scientific sources are capable of contributing to a healthful and humane critical consciousness (with regard to Gutiérrez's own thought the works of Jose María Arguedas, Antonio Gramsci, and Frantz Fanon come to mind).[26] However, for Gutiérrez, the ordering of the utopian imagination finds its most vital source in Christian revelation proper to the theological level of his conception of integralism. As I observed above, it is the theological dimension of integral liberation that discloses the liberating valuations and politics of God's reign. Likewise, the theological level unveils the manner in which sin is at the root of humanity's experiences of alienation and oppression, both of which demand conversion. For Gutiérrez, then, the theological dimension of integralism, with its disclosure of God's love made manifest especially in the proclamation of God's reign, reveals a value system with the potential to challenge and transform the distorted valuations and desires operative at the cultural/psychological level of reality. Here, then, the theological sphere of integralism enters into the cultural/psychological sphere transforming the inherited valuations of persons and communities.

It is at this point that the role of the ecclesial community in the process of integral liberation comes into focus. For Gutiérrez, the church is the social body charged with the task of mediating the mind of Christ and disclosing the values of God's reign to both its members and the world.[27] As he writes, citing

guiding so little

---

[25]See *TL*, 135–40; and Gustavo Gutiérrez, *The Truth Shall Make You Free: Confrontations*, Eng. trans. (Maryknoll, NY: Orbis Books, 1990), 134–35 (hereinafter *TSMYF*). It must be acknowledged that the relationship between the first level and second level is fully reciprocal, so that the socioeconomic structures of the world actively work to transmit the value system intrinsic to their ordering to human persons and cultures.

[26]Each of these authors is cited by Gutiérrez in *A Theology of Liberation*.

[27]This view of Gutiérrez's, then, stands in contrast to John Milbank's, William Cavanaugh's, and Thomas Lewis's respective interpretations of Gutiérrez's thought. Milbank and Cavanaugh both worry that, with the concept of integral liberation, Gutiérrez "naturalizes the supernatural," thereby leaving the church vulnerable to being absorbed into the world. See John Milbank, *Theology and Social Theory: Beyond Secular Reason* (Malden, MA: Blackwell, 2006), 206–56; and William Cavanaugh, *Torture and the Eucharist: Theology, Politics, and the Body of Christ* (Oxford: Blackwell, 1998), 179. Drawing on the categories developed by Charles Taylor, Lewis characterizes Gutiérrez's thought as "expressivist." In so doing, Lewis argues that Gutiérrez's understanding of identity is defined primarily by action and only marginally by shared tradi-

Pierre Teilhard de Chardin to good effect, the ecclesial community is the "reflectively Christified portion of the world."[28] It is no accident, then, that when Gutiérrez comes to speak of the function of the church's liturgical prayer and the celebration of the Eucharist, he describes it precisely in terms of the acts of "denunciation" and "annunciation," which he also applies to the function of the utopian imagination in general.[29] For Gutiérrez, the narratives, symbols, prayers, and rituals of the visible ecclesial community provide the sacramental tools through which both the status quo can be collectively denounced and the community's utopian imagination can be more deeply conformed to the mind of God.[30] *The process of* concientización, *then, is fundamentally mystagogical.*[31] Likewise, the concept of integral liberation is not only Christocentric but also affirms the indispensability of the ecclesial community insofar as that community faithfully bears its vocation of being a sacrament of salvation.[32] Gutiérrez's concept enables us to conceive of a manner in which the theological (mediated through the ecclesial community) both informs and transforms the culture/psychological and socio-structural dimensions of historical reality. For Gutiérrez, Christian revelation and the ecclesial communities that proclaim and enact its good news are at the crux of the process of integral liberation.

However, a caution is in order. It is necessary to keep in mind that Gutiérrez understands the relationship between the theological level and the cultural/psychological level as truly reciprocal. In my argument thus far, I have highlighted the manner in which the impulse toward integral liberation emanates fundamentally from faith in the God disclosed by Christian revelation and mediated through the narratives, signs, sacraments, and practices of the com-

---

tion and narrative. In effect, Lewis's presentation of Gutiérrez's thought minimizes the latter's concern for "the Word of God." See Thomas A. Lewis, "Actions as the Tie that Binds: Love, Praxis, and Community in the Thought of Gustavo Gutiérrez," *Journal of Religious Ethics* 33, no. 3 (2005): 539–67.

[28]*TL*, 147.

[29]Ibid., 148–56; Gutiérrez, "Memory and Prophecy," 19–25.

[30]The possibility of knowing the mind of God is always highly qualified for Gutiérrez. Knowing something of the God who has revealed Godself to the world allows the community to speak prophetically. However, the "language of prophecy" must always be corrected by "the language of contemplation," which acknowledges the limitations of any speech about God. See Gustavo Gutiérrez, *On Job: God-Talk and the Suffering of the Innocent*, Eng. trans. by Matthew J. O'Connell. (Maryknoll, NY: Orbis Books, 1987) (hereinafter *OJ*). For a helpful treatment of the language of contemplation in Gutiérrez's thought, see Gaspar Martinez, *Confronting the Mystery of God: Political, Liberation, and Public Theologies* (New York: Continuum, 2002), 139–50.

[31]Cavanaugh worries that Gutiérrez's conception of *concientización* is tightly bound to secularization. However, when this process is considered in its relationship to spiritual poverty, this is not the case. See William Cavanaugh, "The Ecclesiologies of Medellín and the Lessons of the Base Communities," *Cross Currents* 44, no. 1 (1994): 72–73.

[32]Thus, within Gutiérrez's conception of integral liberation, the church is not absorbed into the world. Rather, insofar as the church fulfills its vocation, it bears witness against the sinful formations of the world.

munity of faith. This is a fair but incomplete presentation of the dynamic. Since the cultural/psychological and theological levels are reciprocating, it is not the case that the latter simply corrects the former. Instead, the valuations transmitted through the theological dimension can also be challenged and corrected by valuations proper to the cultural/psychological dimension of society. This is important to keep in mind because the ecclesial community cannot be identified with God's reign. Indeed, as Willie Jennings and others have argued in recent years, the life of Christian faith has been informed throughout modernity by "a diseased social imagination."[33]

not in accordance with the rule of life

Since the Christian imagination, in its historical concreteness, is diseased, it requires therapy and transformation as well. Part of the therapy should undoubtedly come from without. It is vital that critical thought from any number of sources outside the bounds of the strictly "theological" be employed to challenge the *scotosis* that is historically constitutive of the body of Christ and the imagination that animates it. At the same time, the Christian imagination also offers its own resources for diagnosis and therapy, so that the "depth structure" of Christian life can be transmitted in a manner that is both prophetic and faithful to the gospel. The therapy, thus, requires a turn to the cultural/psychological dimension of reality and a (re)turn to the theological dimension so as to reappropriate and reinterpret the disclosures of Christian revelation.[34]

Integral Liberation and Integral Communion

Before turning to Francis's concept of integral ecology, it is necessary to consider a critique made by Stanley Hauerwas of Gutiérrez's thought. By considering and rebutting Hauerwas's critique, it is possible to provide a final and important clarification to Gutiérrez's conceptual framework. This clarification, then, will allow for the concept of integral ecology to be received with greater nuance.

---

[33]Willie James Jennings, *The Christian Imagination: Theology and the Origins of Race* (New Haven, CT: Yale University Press, 2010), 9. Jennings's specific concern is the manner in which the Christian imagination has contributed to the construction of a racist colonial imagination. The validity of Jennings's analysis points to the need to complexify the example I refer to in notes 4, 5, and 9. The *scotosis* of the theological dimension can be corrected by the insights of a differing/broader cultural imagination. The theological dimension of human life is by no means free from the effects of sin. The church's talk of God and the imagination and praxis with which it is entangled also require exorcism and conversion. Along these lines, one might acknowledge that the modern Christian social imagination has also suffered from a disease conception of creation. Finally, although Jennings focuses on the Christian imagination in Western modernity, we can, with a nod toward patriarchy, acknowledge that distortions in the Christian imagination predate modernity.

[34]The twofold character of the dynamic at play here might be thought of as analogous to Ian McFarland's recommendation that communities of faith specify their conception of *imago Dei* through a tensive appeal to both the community of saints and the option for the poor. See Ian McFarland, *The Divine Image: Envisioning the Invisible God* (Minneapolis: T&T Clark, 2005), 51–74.

Hauerwas, a prominent Christian ethicist and contemporary of Gutiérrez's, is highly critical of the concept of integral liberation. Hauerwas avers that the concept underwrites "an account of liberation that is profoundly anti-Christian."[35] According to Hauerwas, Gutiérrez's understanding of liberation (and the manner in which it is employed within the concept of integral liberation) reverberates with the Kantian ideal of emancipation from every form of servitude and tutelage. Hauerwas, therefore, worries that the human person that emerges from the process of integral liberation is one who is bound to neither God nor neighbor.[36] The person liberated in this manner, according to Hauerwas, is not one who "freely suffers or freely serves," but, to the contrary, is simply free to lord power over others.[37] Thus, Hauerwas suggests that the form of freedom connoted by "total liberation" (a term which Gutiérrez uses interchangeably with "integral liberation") is such that it more closely approximates the character of Lucifer than it does Christ.[38]

The root of the problem with Gutiérrez's concept, Hauerwas continues, is that it fails to uphold the biblical distinction, articulated by Paul, of "freedom from" and "freedom for" (Gal 5:1, 13–15).[39] Accordingly, as Hauerwas would have it, Gutiérrez's failure to develop this distinction in his own thought results in a situation in which a distorted concept of "liberation" is left to stand alone as the sole metaphor for salvation.[40] On Hauerwas's reading, therefore, the concept of integral liberation does not demonstrate a positive relationship between human liberation and the Christian mystery of salvation as much as it imports a perverted understanding of freedom into the Christian imagination.[41]

To state the matter bluntly, Hauerwas dramatically misreads Gutiérrez. For one, Gutiérrez's emphasis on the importance of spiritual poverty to the process of liberation immediately undercuts Hauerwas's claim. Gutiérrez does not

---

[35]Stanley Hauerwas, "Some Theological Reflections on Gutiérrez's Use of 'Liberation' as a Theological Concept," *Modern Theology* 3, no. 1 (1986): 69.

[36]Ibid.

[37]Ibid.

[38]Ibid., 70. To be fair, Hauerwas claims that he is not trying to make this comparison. However, his protestation is at odds with both his rhetoric and his argument.

[39]Ibid., 75. A variation of this distinction is, of course, deeply embedded in the virtue ethics tradition with its distinction between the "freedom of indifference" and the "freedom for excellence."

[40]Ibid., 71.

[41]David Kamitsuka helpfully sums up Hauerwas's complaint against Gutiérrez: "Without a properly biblical understanding of [liberation], there is a risk that liberation will be understood not as a means to serve, but as a means to dominate." See David Kamitsuka, *Theology and Contemporary Culture: Liberation, Post-Liberal, and Revisionary Perspectives* (Cambridge: Cambridge University Press, 1999), 164. For his part, Kamitsuka is unpersuaded by Hauerwas's criticism of Gutiérrez. Kamitsuka finds that Hauerwas fails to account for the fact that Gutiérrez's primary addressee is the nonperson whose agency and dignity has been suppressed systemically. While Kamitsuka's point is certainly important, we shall see that Hauerwas's critique of Gutiérrez is flawed at an even more fundamental level than Kamitsuka acknowledges.

endorse a view of liberation in which the human person is no longer bound to any form of servitude or tutelage. Instead, Gutiérrez's elucidation of spiritual poverty makes clear that, in a fundamental manner, liberation connotes a deeper openness to God and God's will. It is *precisely* freedom for service to God and neighbor (especially the poor).

Hauerwas's claims regarding Gutiérrez's conception of liberation are even more strongly controverted by Gutiérrez's straightforward argument that liberation is precisely for the sake of communion (a point that I have noted throughout this book). Indeed, Gutiérrez makes the exact distinction between "freedom from" and "freedom for" that Hauerwas finds lacking. Simply put, Gutiérrez affirms throughout his writings that salvation is liberation *from* sin, *for* communion with God and neighbor (especially the poor).[42] This is perhaps most clearly articulated early in *A Theology of Liberation*, where Gutiérrez writes, in clear contrast to Hauerwas's characterization of him, "The freedom to which we are called presupposes the going out of oneself, the breaking down of our selfishness and of all the structures that support our selfishness." Gutiérrez continues, "The fullness of liberation—a free gift from Christ—is communion with God and with other human beings."[43] Indeed, "total liberation," the term that functions as the focal point of Hauerwas's ire, finds a perfect semantic counterpart in Gutiérrez's description of salvation as "total communion" with God and with other human persons.[44] The concept of integral liberation, then, cannot be understood apart from the end and hope of communion. The process

---

[42]Indeed, in the first edition of *TL*, Gutiérrez directly refers to the concept of communion in more than forty instances. This point has been drawn out by Joyce Murray, whose work has sought to elucidate the close relationship between liberation and communion in Gutiérrez's theology of salvation. Murray encapsulates Gutiérrez's view of this relationship: "Christ came to set us free and to give us life in its fullness (John 10:10), but the ultimate purpose of this liberation and life is communion in love. These different dimensions are simultaneously present, partially in this life and fully in the eschaton." See Joyce Murray, "Liberation for Communion in the Soteriology of Gustavo Gutiérrez," *Theological Studies* 59 (1998): 54.

[43]*TL*, 24. Gutiérrez makes this argument even more strongly in *We Drink from Our Own Wells*, his most comprehensive statement on Christian spirituality. Gutiérrez devotes the last third of this book to elucidating the manner in which encountering Christ and living according to the Spirit liberates human persons in history for the possibility of expressing the self-giving love revealed by Christ through his own life, death, and Resurrection. Indeed, within the final part of *Wells*, titled "Freedom to Love," Gutiérrez states explicitly that Paul's proclamation "Though I am free from all men, I have made myself a slave to all" (1 Cor. 9:19) clarifies "the full meaning of the process of liberation." See Gutiérrez, *WDFOOW*, part 3: "Freedom to Love." The liberation and service are two sides of the same coin.

[44]*TL*, 155. Gutiérrez's use of "communion" does not connote "reconciliation," at least not in the way the latter is sometimes appealed to prematurely as a sign of Christian love. Instead, "communion" should be understood as consonant with the "intimacy" for which Jennings calls. Still, the fundamental point remains, for Gutiérrez, that liberation is always ultimately meant to be in service of deepening and enriching the possibility of love and deepening the bonds of solidarity. See Jennings, *Christian Imagination*, 9–10.

of integral liberation necessarily orients the human person toward loving intimacy with God and neighbor through the vocation of service.[45]

Integral Liberation: A Dynamic Process Rooted in the Word of God

We are now in a position to summarize the character and dynamism of
Gutiérrez's integralism. For Gutiérrez, the concept of integral liberation is vital
to comprehending history's unity and the manner in which historical liberation
is positively related to the Christian mystery of salvation. More specifically,
the concept allows the community of faith to understand how the dynamics of
sin and grace (disclosed within the theological dimension of historical reality)
are operative within the socio-structural and cultural/psychological dimensions
of human life.

Within Gutiérrez's thought, the process of integral liberation is grounded
in an encounter with God. For the one who encounters God—at least for the
Christian who encounters God—this encounter catalyzes an ongoing process of
mystagogy and conscientization. Through this mystagogical and concientizing
process, which describes the experience of liberation at the cultural/psycho-
logical and theological levels, the Spirit works to form a critical consciousness
within the human person while also reshaping the desires of the person. This
consciousness is both attuned to the Gospel and the discernment of God's will,
and capable of denouncing disordered cultural valuations and announcing new
ways of conceiving of and acting within history. In turn, the transformation
of the human person's imagination also induces the person to commit to the
solidaristic work of transforming the oppressive and death-dealing elements
of reality at the socio-structural level. In all of this, we find that the experience
of God's liberating grace commits the person to the task of liberation within
history. Further, this lived commitment functions as an incarnational testimony
to God's saving love so that Gutiérrez finds salvation is expressed, partially
and proleptically, through liberation in history.

Moreover, the proper end of the process of integral liberation is communion
with God and neighbor. Integral liberation cannot be separated from the process of integral communion. Rather, these terms ultimately point to the same

---

[45]An important caveat must be added here. Within Gutiérrez's thought, liberation and justice
exercise a priority over communion. The possibility of Christian communion and intimacy can
be established only on the genuine freedom and recognition of those called to communion. For
example, Gutiérrez writes, "Being an 'artisan of peace' not only does not dispense from presence in these conflicts [of politics], it demands that one take part in them, in order to pull them
up by the roots. There is no peace without justice. This is a hard, uncomfortable truth for those
who prefer not to see these conflictual situations, or who, if they see them prefer palliatives to
remedies. It is equally hard for those who, with all the good will in the world, confuse universal
love with a fictitious harmony" (Gutiérrez, *PPH*, 48).

dynamic process—one that is rooted in and constantly returning to the word of God. It is on this understanding of the concept of integral liberation that we can map Pope Frances's concept of integral ecology. Thus, we can uphold the structure, dynamism, and ecclesial characteristic of Gutiérrez's integralism while broadening its framework from love of God and neighbor to love of God, neighbor, and nonhuman creation.

THE MEANING OF THE CONCEPT OF INTEGRAL ECOLOGY

As I observed in both Chapter 1 and the outset of this chapter, Pope Francis advances a worldview in *Laudato Si'* that affirms the underlying unity between history/society and nature. The pope attests to this unity through his definition of "ecology," which he uses to signify the broad complex of politico-ecological relationships that order historical reality, as well as with his recognition that "we are faced not with two separate crises, one environmental and the other social, but rather with one complex crisis which is both social and environmental" (no. 139). For Francis, there is no possibility of bracketing "the human world" from "the natural world." Instead, we must affirm that within history everything is connected (no. 16).

Francis develops the concept of integral ecology in accordance with his understanding of the unified character of historical reality. With this concept, Francis's discourse moves from descriptive to prescriptive. That is to say, the pope employs the concept of integral ecology in order to elaborate a vision of the *right* ordering of the world's political ecology so that it might best serve the common good (nos. 23–26, 156–58). For Francis, an integral ecology must manifest a preferential option for both the earth and the poor, while also recognizing the interconnectedness of these two options. Furthermore, the pope repeatedly asserts that the integral ecology for which he calls requires a personal and societal embrace of limitation, restraint, and humility (nos. 11, 105, 177, 193, 204, 208, 223, 224).

In the argument set forth in *Laudato Si'*, Francis makes clear that, for the Christian, the preferential options for the earth and the poor, as well as the requisite dispositions for making these options, can arise from a faithful response to the God of Christian revelation.[46] Moreover, within Francis's construal this response to God exercises a transformative effect on both the cultural/psychological and socio-structural dimensions of historical reality. As we shall see, Francis's conception of integral ecology helps elucidate the manner in which communities of faith are called to bear witness to the Christian mystery of salvation by responding to the cries of the earth and the poor within the complex

---

[46]See Pope Francis, *Laudato Si'*, chap. 2, "The Gospel of Creation" (hereinafter *LS*).

unity of historical reality. The vertical structure of Francis's concept can be mapped onto that of the concept of integral liberation (while also presuming the same basic dynamism at work between the levels of integralism) in order to demonstrate the unity between salvation, human liberation, and care for creation.

It is important to note that Francis does not advance his conception of integral ecology in the abstract; rather he does so in view of what he terms the contemporary "global system" (nos. 56, 111). Correspondingly, through his reading of the signs of the times, Francis finds that the realization of an integral ecology demands a paradigm shift away from the politics, economics, and cultural formations that now structure the global system.[47] According to the pope, the global system is ordered by a "false or superficial ecology which bolsters complacency and a cheerful recklessness" (no. 59) on the part of humanity. Thus, in examining the three levels at which the process of integral ecology operates, we find that while Francis's discussion of the theological level of integral ecology functions normatively, his descriptions of the socio-structural and cultural/psychological dimensions of integral ecology are largely framed within the language of critique. In other words, Francis consistently denounces the ways in which the global system is structured in opposition to God's desires for the world. In examining the vertical structure of the concept of integral ecology, I begin by considering its theological dimension.

The Theological Level of Integral Ecology

At the theological level, Francis emphasizes two elements of a Christian theological worldview that he believes are essential in shaping the life of the community of faith: the discernment of the sacramental character of creation and the human vocation to "'till and keep' the garden of the world" (no. 67). These two elements are interconnected. It is precisely because creation is a good gift from God—a gift that reveals something of God's own goodness—that the human person is called to respond to the garden of the world with a praxis of care rather than, say, a utilitarian ethic of optimal exploitation. Moreover, these two facets of Francis's theological worldview correspond to the contemplative and active dimensions of Christian life. Christian communities are called to contemplate the goodness of God's creation and respond accordingly through a praxis properly attuned to this contemplative discernment.

In learning to read the book of creation properly and in contemplating creation-as-gift, Francis finds that a proper dispositional response of the human

---

[47]In characterizing Francis's argument in this way, I am aligning the pope's position with a Latin American view of the option for the poor that emphasizes conversion. On this point, see Rohan M. Curnow, "Which Preferential Option for the Poor? A History of the Doctrine's Bifurcation," *Modern Theology* 31 (2015): 27–59.

person is that of gratitude to the God of life. The pope makes this point clear in his reflection on the way in which Saint Francis—an exemplar of holiness within *Laudato Si'*—understood creation. As the pope observes, "Saint Francis, faithful to Scripture, invites us to see nature as a magnificent book in which God speaks to us and grants us a glimpse of his infinite beauty and goodness" (no. 11). The pope continues, noting the saint's loving openness to the whole of creation: "His response to the world around him was so much more than intellectual appreciation or economic calculus, for to him each and every creature was a sister united to him by bonds of affection" (no. 11). Pope Francis's reflections on his canonized namesake echo Sallie McFague's exhortation that humanity must recover a way of seeing that recognizes nonhuman creation as a "thou" as opposed to an "it."[48]

Pope Francis locates this manner of perceiving creation not only in his namesake's way of seeing but also in "the gaze of Jesus" (nos. 96–100). As Francis observes, "In talking with his disciples, Jesus would invite them to recognize the paternal relationship God has with all his creatures. With moving tenderness he would remind them that each one of them is important in God's eyes" (no. 96). Pope Francis continues along these lines, observing, "The Lord was able to invite others to be attentive to the beauty that there is in the world because he himself was in constant touch with nature, lending it an attention full of fondness and wonder" (no. 97). For Francis, then, the process of contemplating the goodness of creation, discerning creation's intrinsic worth, and cultivating gratitude to God for the gift of creation are constitutive elements of Christian discipleship and *imitatio Christi.* Openness to the will of God opens one to the beauty of creation.[49]

As noted above, Francis affirms that the ways in which human persons perceive creation, at least in part, inform their praxis. "If we approach nature and the environment without this openness to awe and wonder, if we no longer speak the language of fraternity and beauty in our relationship with the world," the

---

[48]See Sallie McFague, *Super, Natural Christians: How We Should Love Nature* (Minneapolis: Augsburg Fortress, 1997), 91–117. On the topic of perceiving creation correctly, see also Norman Wirzba, "Christian *Theoria Physike*: On Learning to See Creation," *Modern Theology* 32, no. 2 (2016): 211–30; Vincent Miller, "Integral Ecology: Francis's Spiritual and Moral Vision of Interconnectedness," in *The Theological and Ecological Vision of* Laudato Si': *Everything Is Connected*, ed. Vincent Miller (New York: Bloomsbury, 2017), 14–18; and Michael J. Himes and Kenneth R. Himes, *The Fullness of Faith: The Public Significance of Theology* (New York: Paulist Press, 1993), 112–14.

[49]In learning to perceive nature as creation, the danger of romanticizing nature remains a constant presence. Indeed, this is a point on which Celia Deane-Drummond critiques *Laudato Si'*. See Celia Deane-Drummond, "*Laudato Si'* and the Natural Sciences: An Assessment of the Possibilities and Limits," *Theological Studies* 77, no. 2 (June 2016): 392–415, esp. 411–14. To address this danger, the hermeneutic operative in the encyclical might be complicated with the discourses on nature in the book of Job. Along these lines, see Elizabeth A. Johnson, *Ask the Beasts: Darwin and the God of Love* (New York: Bloomsbury, 2014), esp. chap. 7.

pope writes, "our attitude will be that of masters, consumers, ruthless exploiters, unable to set limits on their immediate needs. By contrast, if we feel intimately united with all that exists, then sobriety and care will well up spontaneously" (no. 11). These differing modes of perceiving creation (including the human person) correspond to two biblical descriptions of praxis. These descriptions are vital to the argument developed in this chapter and the subsequent chapters of this book, and so deserve careful attention here.

Early in the second chapter of *Laudato Si'*—"The Gospel of Creation"—Francis acknowledges that the term "dominion" (Gen 1:28), found in the first creation story of Genesis, has sometimes been used to encourage "the unbridled exploitation of nature" (no. 67).[50] The pontiff strongly rejects this understanding of dominion. As Francis writes, "This is not a correct interpretation of the Bible as understood by the Church. . . . We must forcefully reject the notion that our being created in God's image and given dominion over the earth justifies absolute domination over other creatures" (no. 67). In offering a vision to counter the distorted claims too often attached to dominion, the pope turns immediately to a key verse in Genesis's second story of creation.[51] There Francis finds that the human vocation "to 'till and keep' the garden of the world (cf. Gen. 2:15)" more appropriately captures the character of the relationship that God desires for humanity to have with the earth. As the pope observes, while "tilling" refers to "cultivating," the term "keeping" suggests "caring, protecting, overseeing and preserving" (no. 67). It is an ethic of care that properly characterizes the manner in which the human person is to act with regard to creation and allows for a proper conception of "dominion" to emerge.

On Francis's reading of Genesis, God creates the human person to live in a threefold relationship of communion—with God, neighbor, and earth. Accordingly, God calls humanity to preserve this threefold sense of communion through the work of cultivation and care—a praxis that emerges from seeing God and God's creation rightly. The human person's refusal to cultivate and care results in the disordering of communion with God, neighbor, and earth. These three sets of relationships are so inextricably linked that the distortion of one echoes in the other two. Francis describes this dynamic in his interpretation of the narrative of Cain and Abel:

---

[50]There have been a number of attempts at clarifying this symbol with regard to ecological concern. For a thoroughgoing defense of Genesis 1:28, see Ellen Davis, "Seeing with God: Israel's Poem of Creation," in *Scripture, Culture, Agriculture* (Cambridge: Cambridge University Press, 2009). For a slightly more critical interpretation of the language of Genesis 1, see Richard Bauckham, "Stewardship in Question," in *The Bible and Ecology: Rediscovering the Community of Creation* (Waco, TX: Baylor University Press, 2010), esp. 16–20.

[51]Claus Westermann maintains that Genesis 2:15 "is a decisive verse for the whole understanding of Gen 2–3." See Claus Westermann, *Genesis 1–11*, trans. John J. Scullion (Minneapolis: Augsburg, 1985), 220.

In the story of Cain and Abel, we see how envy led Cain to commit the ultimate injustice against his brother, which in turn ruptured the relationship between Cain and God, and between Cain and the earth from which he was banished. This is seen clearly in the dramatic exchange between God and Cain. God asks: "Where is Abel your brother?" Cain answers that he does not know, and God persists: "What have you done? The voice of your brother's blood is crying to me from the ground. And now you are cursed from the ground" (Gen 4:9–11). *Disregard for the duty to cultivate and maintain a proper relationship with my neighbor, for whose care and custody I am responsible, ruins my relationship with my own self, with others, with God and with the earth.* When all these relationships are neglected, when justice no longer dwells in the land, the Bible tells us that life itself is endangered. (no. 70, italics are mine)

According to Francis, the praxis of domination (which is often associated with idea of dominion) does not flow from the human vocation properly understood. Rather, this praxis results from the human person's *rejection* of that vocation, which results in the person's estrangement from God, neighbor, and earth.

It is possible, now, to observe two key points that emerge at the theological level of the concept of integral ecology. First, for Francis, the interlinked preferential options for the earth and the poor arise from faith in the biblical God—the one who calls humanity to cultivate and care for the garden of the world. Second, and even more theologically important, Francis's interpretation of Genesis presents us with a basic framework for conceiving, in an eco-liberationist key, the manner in which sin and grace are enacted within historical reality. As we just observed, in his reading of Cain and Abel, the pope emphasizes the manner in which sin distorts not only the human/divine and human/neighbor relationships, but also the human/earth relationship—all of which are interlinked. Here sin is not simply a historical-social phenomenon. Rather, it is a politico-ecological phenomenon, one that disorders the human person's proper threefold relationship of communion.

This construal of sin, of course, has important soteriological implications. Since salvation, fundamentally, is salvation from sin, the work of God's saving grace in history must likewise be a politico-ecological phenomenon. The Spirit labors in history to liberate humanity from sin and restore the threefold sense of communion that sin has warped. Likewise, the human person cooperates with the work of the Spirit in history through returning to the work of cultivating and caring for the garden of the world. Thus, the process of kenosis—the process of opening the human person more deeply to the will of God—will orient the person to solidarity, not only with the poor, but with the earth as well. In view of Francis's interpretation of the narrative of Cain and Abel, salvation can be defined as liberation from sin and communion with God, neighbor, and earth.

I elaborate upon this theological anthropology and its broader biblical-narrative implications in Part II of this text. For now it is sufficient to observe that the theological dimension of integral ecology, as elucidated by Francis, offers communities of faith a way of understanding the unity between salvation history and the eco-social character of historical reality. In other words, Francis's brief reading of Genesis provides a framework through which one can discern and name the dynamics of both sin and grace as they are made manifest at the socio-structural and cultural/psychological levels of history. Indeed, the "false and superficial" ecology of the global system, mentioned above, can be termed a sinful political ecology (a sinful patterning of the world's politico-ecological relationships) when read in light of the disclosure of Christian revelation. As we shall see, for Francis, the global system is, in large part, reflective of the character of Cain in both its proclivity toward domination and its refusal to see creation properly.

The Socio-Structural Level of Integral Ecology

With regard to the socio-structural dimension of human life, Francis is most concerned with the ways in which the globalized political economy has been ordered to privilege the maximization of short-term economic growth above all other considerations. As the pope laments, "The earth's resources are . . . being plundered because of short-sighted approaches to the economy, commerce and production" (no. 32). Later, he writes along similar lines: "The economy accepts every advance in technology with a view to profit, without concern for its potentially negative impact on human beings. Finance overwhelms the real economy. The lessons of the global financial crisis have not been assimilated, and we are learning all too slowly the lessons of environmental deterioration" (no. 109).

That the lessons of the global financial crisis have not been assimilated, speaks in part to the manner in which national and international political institutions, ostensibly charged with serving the common good, have been attenuated or captured by "the interests of a deified market, which become the only rule" (no. 56).[52] Against this backdrop, Francis decries the failure of the world's states and institutions to respond meaningfully to the ecological emergency. Lamenting the weak international responses and failures of global summits to address the planetary emergency, the pope observes, "There are

---

[52]In his classic essay on the future of the state in the era of globalization, Peter Evans argues that the state is unlikely to be eclipsed by transnational corporations. Nation-states will continue to exist, argues Evans; however, they will be placed increasingly at the service of corporate interests and less oriented toward safeguarding public goods. Evan's prescient analysis certainly appears to capture the character of the still unfolding neoliberal era. See Peter Evans, "The Eclipse of the State? Reflections on Stateness in an Era of Globalization," *World Politics* 50, no. 1 (1997): 62–87.

too many special interests, and economic interests easily end up trumping the common good and manipulating information so that their own plans will not be affected" (no. 54). Continuing his criticism with rhetoric that recalls Gutiérrez's lamentation at the "timid" and "ineffective" measures of reformism under the developmentalist paradigm,[53] the pope writes, "Consequently the most one can expect is superficial rhetoric, sporadic acts of philanthropy and perfunctory expressions of concern for the environment, whereas any genuine attempt by groups within society to introduce change is viewed as a nuisance based on romantic illusions or an obstacle to be circumvented" (no. 54).

The patchwork and superficial responses that Francis identifies cannot attend adequately to the eco-social emergency. Moreover, according to Francis, they also fail specifically to redress the ecological debt that the global north owes the global south. As Francis writes, "A true 'ecological debt' exists . . . connected to commercial imbalances with effects on the environment, and the disproportionate use of natural resources by certain countries over long periods of time" (no. 51). On this point Francis's analysis aligns with that of sociologist Andrew Jorgenson, who argues, "Throughout human history, more powerful societies and nation-states have utilized their geopolitical-economic power to create and maintain ecologically unequal exchanges with less powerful and less developed societies and countries."[54]

Jorgenson finds that the peripheral regions of the world are consistently coerced into functioning as both "environmental taps and sinks" for the powerful regions of the world. Thus, he finds that the globalization of trade, finance, and production has brought with them "the broadening and intensification of environmental destruction, *a form of ecological polarization in which the former colonies of the core absorb the environmental costs of natural resource extraction and consumption, many of which are spatially fixed.*"[55] As the pope asserts, this politico-ecological polarization requires redress—a point to which I return in Chapter 5.

In short, for Francis, the socioeconomic structures of the contemporary globalization project have failed to respond adequately to the complex eco-social crisis facing the world. Moreover, they appear ordered toward intensifying the problem. The structures of the globalization project must be transformed. However, as I have already observed in examining the dynamics of Gutiérrez's concept of integral liberation, the socioeconomic formations of historical reality are deeply interlinked with the cultural/psychological formations of that same reality. Thus, the transformation of one dimension is necessarily intertwined

[53]See Chapter 1 of this text.
[54]Andrew K. Jorgenson, "Social Change, Natural Resource Consumption, and Environmental Degradation," in *Global Social Change: Historical and Comparative Perspectives*, ed. Christopher Chase-Dunn and Salvatore J. Babones (Baltimore: Johns Hopkins University Press, 2006), 190.
[55]Ibid. The italics are mine.

with the transformation of the other. Unsurprisingly, then, Francis finds that the realization of an integral ecology requires metanoia at the cultural/psychological dimension of the global system.

The Cultural/Ideological Level of Integral Ecology

Early on in *Laudato Si'*, Francis rejects two extreme positions as starting points for possible paths forward in responding to the global eco-social emergency (no. 60). The first position maintains that, by itself, technological advancement in the service of economic growth is capable of redressing this emergency. The second, and opposite, view holds that all human invention and intervention is irredeemably corrupt and only capable of worsening the emergency. While the latter position is certainly problematic, it is the former view that captures Francis's full attention. This is because the pope finds that the first of these two extremes has actually become the ideology through which the globalization project has come to be structured. This is the ideology that informs what Francis refers to as "the technocratic paradigm."[56]

Central to this ideology is the belief "that every increase in power means 'an increase of "progress" itself' . . . as if reality, goodness and truth automatically flow from technological and economic power as such" (no. 105). From this perspective, technological advancement in the service of economic growth is viewed as an end unto itself, inexorably producing the best of all possible worlds. Within this mind-set, rationality is reduced to a form of instrumental reason that is solely intent on generating advancement and growth as intensely and quickly as possible.[57] Questions of social and environmental justice can be ignored because one assumes that technology and growth ultimately provide the proper answers. As a result, as Francis laments, "Our capacity to make decisions, a more genuine freedom and the space for each one's alternative creativity are diminished" (no. 108).[58]

The pope also maintains that within the ideology of the technocratic paradigm, the earth is viewed in desacralized terms. Nature is simply a mechanistic collection of atoms that exists to be rearranged and exploited in ever more efficient and productive ways. "This has made it easy to accept the idea of infinite or unlimited growth," Francis writes, "which proves so attractive to

---

[56] On this issue see broadly, *LS*, chap. 3, "The Human Roots of the Ecological Crisis."

[57] As Pope Francis writes, "The technocratic paradigm also tends to dominate economic and political life. The economy accepts every advance in technology with a view to profit, without concern for its potentially negative impact on human beings" (*LS*, no. 109).

[58] Here, then, Francis's analysis recalls the Frankfurt School's concept of the "dialectic of the Enlightenment." See Max Horkheimer and Theodor Adorno, *Dialectic of Enlightenment: Philosophical Fragments*, ed. Gunzelin Schmid Noerr, trans. Edmund Jephcott (Redwood City, CA: Stanford University Press, 2007). See also Tim Jackson, *Prosperity without Growth: Economics for a Finite Planet* (London: Earthscan, 2009), chap. 6, "The 'Iron Cage' of Consumerism."

economists, financiers and experts in technology. It is based on the lie that there is an infinite supply of the earth's goods, and this leads to the planet being squeezed dry beyond every limit" (no. 106). The ideology of the technocratic paradigm rejects the possibility of limits and instead embraces a Promethean view of technological development aimed at "a lordship over all" (no. 108).

Closely allied with the ideology of the technocratic paradigm is the globalized culture of consumerism, which as Francis writes, "prioritizes short-term gain and private interest" (no. 184). The pope states, "Compulsive consumerism is an example of how the techno-economic paradigm affects individuals" (no. 203). If the technological paradigm leads the human person to fail to attend to the cries of the earth and the poor by enclosing him or her within the iron cage of capitalism, then the culture of consumerism reinforces these attitudes by inducing indifference to these interrelated cries (no. 232). What emerges, then, is "an unethical consumerism bereft of social or ecological awareness" (no. 219).

In order to understand why the culture of consumerism promotes indifference to the eco-social crisis, it is fruitful to consider Francis's position in view of the macro-social theory of Leslie Sklair. According to Sklair, the dramatic growth in advertising and communication technologies over the last century has allowed transnational corporations to create and promulgate the fictive persona of the consumer as the ideal person.[59] In describing this persona, Sklair writes, "The culture-ideology of consumerism proclaims, literally, that the meaning of life is to be found in the things that we possess. To consume, therefore, is to be fully alive, and to remain fully alive we must consume."[60] One can discern why the culture of consumerism dampens any inclination toward a preferential option for the poor or the earth. Within the culture of consumerism, it is not concern for neighbor or care for creation that leads to a meaningful life but instead the incessant act of satisfying one's own (often artificial) needs. The culture of consumerism, then, unrelentingly shapes the desires of the human person toward a disordered form of self-love. As a result, as Francis observes, "People can easily get caught up in a whirlwind of needless buying and spending" (no. 203).[61]

Sklair's analysis is also helpful in conceptualizing the reciprocal relationship between the structural and cultural dimensions of society. Sklair observes that the ideal of person-as-consumer is essential to the life of global capitalism. This is because the functioning of the system is predicated on continuous economic growth and it is the act of consumption that drives the process of accumulation: "Without consumerism, the rationale for continuous capitalist accumulation

---

[59]Leslie Sklair, *Sociology of the Global System* (Baltimore: Johns Hopkins University Press, 1995), 47–48.

[60]Ibid., 48.

[61]Francis is especially concerned with the manner in which consumerism tends to debase and destabilize traditional cultural identity. See *LS*, nos. 143–46.

dissolves."[62] The culture of consumerism, then, is the "glue" that holds the structure of the system intact.

I return to Sklair's conception of the global system in Chapter 5 of this text. Here, however, one can begin to grasp the immensity of the task of conversion to which Francis calls the world. Transforming the social structures of the globalization project is not just a matter of institutional or policy reform, it also requires a transformation of the normative value systems of the globalization project. Likewise, in attempting a conversion away from the ideology of the technocratic paradigm or the culture of consumerism, the person or community must contend with powerful political-economic agents that unceasingly endeavor to inculcate and reinscribe those very cultures and ideologies into the collective heart of the world. Despite these difficulties, Francis finds, "An authentic humanity, calling for a new synthesis, seems to dwell in the midst of our technological culture, almost unnoticed, like a mist seeping gently beneath a closed door. Will the promise last, in spite of everything, with all that is authentic rising up in stubborn resistance?" (no. 112). Francis believes that there is indeed hope for an enduring conversion.

According to the pope, the culture appropriate to an integral ecology "cannot be reduced to a series of urgent and partial responses to the immediate problems of pollution, environmental decay and the depletion of natural resources." Instead, something more comprehensive is required. "There needs to be a distinctive way of looking at things . . . a lifestyle and a spirituality which together generate resistance to the assault of the technocratic paradigm. Otherwise, even the best ecological initiatives can find themselves caught up in the same globalized logic" (no. 111).

The Dynamism of Integral Ecology

Francis's call to cultivate a spirituality of resistance to the assaults of technocracy and consumerism returns us once more to the theological dimension of integral ecology. This is because, for Francis, the content of the Christian faith can serve as the foundation for the spirituality needed to contest these assaults. As is the case with Gutiérrez's concept of integral liberation, with the concept of integral ecology Francis finds that the book of scripture—operating at the theological level and inclusive of the symbols, narratives, and sacraments of the life of faith—can catalyze the construction of valuations and imaginaries that counter the disordered psychological/cultural formations of the global system. This constructive engagement with the Christian tradition—lived out through the practices of the faith—provides the grounds from which the ecclesial community

---

[62]Leslie Sklair, *Globalization: Capitalism and Its Alternatives* (Oxford: Oxford University Press, 2002), 116.

not only can denounce the distorted cultural/psychological, and socio-structural formations of historical reality, but also proclaim and enact a new way of life grounded in an alternative value system that itself is rooted in the word of God.

The disclosure at the theological dimension of integral ecology, when it is integrated into the life of the faith community, transforms the cultural/psychological life of the community, and allows for a liberating and transformative spirituality and way of seeing to emerge. Moreover, since, the cultural/psychological dimension of historical reality exists in a reciprocally interpenetrating relationship with the socio-structural dimension, the conversion of the community of faith at the cultural/psychological level necessarily calls the community to the task of transforming the disordered socio-structural dimensions of historical reality. In short, Christian revelation—when read in accordance with the Spirit—serves as the foundation and catalyst for the task of incarnating a fully integral ecology in the world.

I stated above that, according to Francis, the false and superficial ecology of the global system is reflective of the sinful character of Cain. By the same account, then, Francis's call to transform the socio-structural and cultural/psychological dynamics of the global system is a call to conversion away from sin. Indeed, the call to incarnate an integral ecology is the call to bear witness to salvation through ordering our eco-social relationships in accordance with fundamental dispositions of service and care whose end is communion with God, neighbor, and earth. The concept of integral ecology, therefore, parallels that of integral liberation: both of these concepts affirm that communion is the proper end of liberation from sin.

Moreover, integral ecology should be understood as a liberationist concept. In *Laudato Si'*, Pope Francis calls for the radical transformation of the globalization project. The encyclical unmasks and denounces the manner in which the socio-structural and cultural-psychological formations of this contemporary globalization project have failed to respond to the cries of the earth and the poor. The realization of an integral ecology within the context of the global system demands a liberation that very much reflects the early liberationist usage of the term. Integral ecology, then, elucidates the manner in which salvation, liberation, and care for creation are intertwined within the contemporary global context. The possibility of liberation from sin and communion with God, neighbor, and earth demands "an ecological conversion" (nos. 216–21) of the structures of the global system.

CONCLUSION

As the concept of integral ecology makes clear, love of God is expressed through love of neighbor and earth, making manifest in history the preferential options for the earth and the poor. Pope Francis roots this view, as we have observed, most fundamentally in his interpretation of Genesis 2–4. In *Laudato Si'*, these texts from Genesis emerge as the ground from which one can cultivate a Christian theological imagination capable of naming the politico-ecological dimensions of sin and grace. Indeed, within the theological imagination organized around Francis's reading of Genesis 2–4, the praxis of liberation and care for creation appears as nothing less than a participative witness to God's saving and redeeming work. Thus, for the community of faith, this imagination is vital to contesting and transforming the sinfully destructive cultural/psychological and socio-structural formations of the contemporary global system.

Nonetheless, the encyclical's engagement with scripture remains somewhat inchoate. This is true on two accounts. First, although Genesis 2–4 is clearly vital to the vision of *Laudato Si'*, the theological (and specifically soteriological) significance of these narratives, in and of themselves, can be explicated more fully than the encyclical does. Second, in specifying the politico-ecological dimensions of sin and grace, *Laudato Si'* leaves Genesis 2–4 to stand largely alone among the biblical witness. Thus, these narratives are made to bear a great deal of argumentative weight while appearing disconnected from the broader contours of salvation history as it is narrated through the canon.

The second point raises an important question: How might a politico-ecological reading of Genesis 2–4 (and the theology it outlines) serve to reframe an interpretation of the narratives of salvation history? How, for example, might this interpretation reshape the ecclesial community's understanding of God's liberating acts in the biblical accounts of the exodus? How might it help illuminate the significance of the law and the witness of the prophets? Most important, from a Christian perspective, how might such an interpretation of Genesis 2–4 help surface the politico-ecological dimensions of both Jesus's inauguration of God's reign and the resurrection? Responding to these queries is helpful, if not vital, for these responses can contribute to a more fully formed Christian politico-ecological imagination—a theological imagination capable of judging the eco-social formations of historical reality and both envisioning and animating a Christian praxis in accordance with these judgments. Part II of this book, then, continues the dialogue between Gutiérrez and Francis in a more implicit fashion. It appropriates and develops Francis's politico-ecological hermeneutic, employing it to interpret the themes of scripture that have been vital to Gutiérrez's own articulation of salvation history.

Part II

Interpreting the Word of God

The argument of this book proceeds from the view that Christian eco-liberationist discourse must locate its practical commitments at the heart of the Christian faith. Accordingly, the guiding question of this text asks: What is the relationship between the mystery of salvation, liberation, and care for creation? In Chapter 2, I began to elucidate the positive relationship between the three terms in question by drawing on the integralist thought of Gustavo Gutiérrez and Pope Francis. In so doing, I demonstrated that God's saving work in history calls humanity to cooperate with the Spirit in transforming the sinfully disordered cultural/psychological and socioeconomic dimensions of the world's political ecology, so that the world might hear and mercifully respond to the cries of the earth and the poor. Further, I pointed to Genesis 2–4, following Francis's reading in *Laudato Si'*, as the passage that helps ground this worldview in Christian revelation.

In Part II, I develop Francis's reading of Genesis 2–4 at length. I do so in two ways. First, I expand on *Laudato Si'*'s interpretation of the text itself, nuancing and drawing out the theological implications of these passages in Genesis. Second, and even more important, I contextualize Genesis 2–4 by placing the passage within the broad sweep of salvation history mediated through scripture. Thus, Part II both explores the ways in which Genesis 2–4 symbolically conveys a theological anthropology that unites the loves of God, neighbor, and earth, and examines how the fulfillment of these interrelated loves is an integral and recurring theme of the story of salvation.

Through a canonical reading of the biblical story of salvation, Part II sets forth a narrative response to the orienting question of the book.[1] The theological

---

[1] Whereas the content of Part I of this book most closely parallels Gutiérrez's arguments in *A Theology of Liberation*, the content of Part II most closely approximates his argument in *God of Life*, in which Gutiérrez offers a wide-ranging interpretation of salvation history.

interpretation of salvation history that I advance here is fundamentally concerned with the ecclesial task of reading scripture in a manner that orients and energizes communities of faith to the tasks of discipleship within the contemporary historical moment. Thus, the reading of scripture in Part II is organized around the dual concerns of interpreting salvation history in a manner that is responsible to the dynamic and stabilizing Christian tradition, and in a manner that is generative for communities of faith seeking to bear witness to the good news of God's reign within a context of politico-ecological emergency.

Chapter 3

Reading Genesis Theologically
in a Politico-Ecological Key

In his influential commentary on Genesis,[1] Gerhard von Rad argues that
the first book of the Bible cannot be read as a coherent text in itself. Instead,
Genesis functions as a prologue to the subsequent books of the canon. It is
only in light of these later books, argues von Rad, that one can make sense
of the themes and narratives introduced in Genesis. Undoubtedly, von Rad is
correct that the themes and symbols that constitute the book of Genesis are
interwoven throughout the biblical canon. The textual world of Genesis can, for
example, illuminate those of the prophetic literature and vice versa. Nonetheless, in recent decades a number of scholars have taken issue with von Rad's
doubtfulness regarding the internal coherency of Genesis. In contrast to von
Rad, for example, Bruce Dahlberg argues that Genesis "offers itself as a unified
work of literary art . . . thematically developed and integrated from beginning
to end—and of course its art is in service to its theological affirmations."[2] Accordingly, Dahlberg finds that the themes introduced in Genesis's primordial
history (Gen 1–11) culminate, at least proleptically, in the book's concluding
chapters—especially the Joseph narrative (Gen 37–50).

Affirming Dahlberg's basic intuition, this chapter explores the narrative arcs
and theological claims of Genesis. More specifically, taking the vocation of
Genesis 2:15 ("to cultivate and care" for the garden) as its hermeneutical key,
the argument I advance here elucidates a politico-ecological theology that runs
throughout the first book of the Bible. Fundamentally, this theology claims (in
a manner that coheres with the views of *Laudato Si'*) that God creates the hu-

---

[1]Gerhard von Rad, *Genesis: A Commentary* (Louisville, KY: Westminster Press, 1961).
[2]Bruce T. Dahlberg, "On Recognizing the Unity of Genesis," *Theology Digest* 24 (1976): 361.

to wil God is to luc the earth and neighbor

man person to live in communion with God, neighbor, and earth, and that the human person's corresponding love of God, neighbor, and earth exist as distinct but interrelated realities. This reading of Genesis grounds the eco-liberationist interpretation of the broader history of salvation developed in Chapter 4.

I begin this chapter by exploring the theological worldviews presented in the first narrative cycle of Genesis's primordial history (Gen 1–4), highlighting the theological symbols of gardener, city-builder, and city and analyzing their relationship to the wisdom of God. From there, I move to consider the manner in which these symbols continue to be developed in both the second narrative cycle of the primordial history (Gen 5–11) and the initial stories of the "patriarchs" (Gen 12–36). Finally, I demonstrate the manner in which the politico-ecological theology of Genesis is brought to its culmination in the story of Joseph. To anticipate the conclusion, I find that Joseph functions as an anti-type of Adam. Whereas Adam's disobedience fractures the tripartite communion for which the human is created, Joseph's obedience to God restores, at least partially, this threefold sense of intimacy.

Here, Genesis 2:15 functions as the interpretive key to understanding the theological vision of Genesis as a whole. However, instead of beginning this analysis with 2:15 and then working backwards to Genesis 1 and beyond, I start with a brief consideration of the first creation account of Genesis (1:1–2:3). This consideration anticipates and coheres with the subsequent analysis of the second creation account of Genesis. The choice to begin with Genesis 1:1–2:3 serves to maximize the fluidity of this chapter's argument, allowing the analysis to follow the sequence of Genesis itself, rather than jumping back and forth between narratives.

CREATION, VOCATION, FALL, CITY: GENESIS 1–4

creation is peaceful
creation is love

Perhaps the most striking feature of the first creation account of Genesis is the peaceful character that it ascribes to God's creative action. It was common for the creation narratives of the ancient Near East to depict the creation of the cosmos in violent agonistic terms. For example, in the Babylonian account of creation within the *Enuma Elish,* the god Marduk forms the world out of the murdered body of the mother-goddess Tiamat and human persons out of the blood of the treacherous god Kingu. Thus, in the *Enuma Elish*, violence is constitutive of creation in an essential manner.[3] By way of contrast, in Genesis, God calls creation into existence peaceably. Facing the chaotic nothingness "in the beginning," God brings creation into being, not through a primordial act of

---

[3]See Walter Wink's discussion of the Babylonian creation narrative, *Engaging the Powers: Discernment and Resistance in a World of Domination* (Minneapolis: Fortress, 1992), 13–17.

God's love

violence, but through the gratuitous and generative power of God's "word" and "spirit" (as they would come to be understood by the early Christian church).[4] Creating the cosmos in this manner, God delimits the elements of the world, organizing them in accordance with God's wisdom. Thus, the first creation account of Genesis, as it has been understood within the Christian tradition, intimates an ontology of peace.[5]

The striking tone of Genesis's first account of creation is underscored by God's own perception of the world. In *calling* creation into being, God judges *past tense verb* it as "good." According to Ellen Davis, the divine affirmation of creation's goodness—repeated seven times in the course of the first chapter of Genesis—functions as something of a thematic refrain to the narrative, inviting one to pause and contemplate the goodness of the created order.[6] Delight is God's fundamental response to the gift of God's good work.[7] Thus, it is not only in light of Genesis 2:15 that the commands for humans to "have dominion" and "subdue the earth" must be understood, but also in view of both God's peaceable manner of creating and God's delight in the goodness and beauty of creation itself. *not controlling*

In interpreting the meaning of "to have dominion" (*radah*), Davis argues that the verb is best understood in terms of "firmness rather than harshness."[8] *similar* On this point, she cites Ludwig Koehler and Walter Baumgartner, who write of *radah*: "The basic meaning of the verb is not to rule; the word actually denotes the travelling around of a shepherd with his flock."[9] This view is consonant with that of Walter Brueggemann, who argues that human dominion among earth's living creatures "is that of a shepherd who cares for, tends, and feeds the animals. Or, if transferred to the political arena, the image is that of a shepherd king (cf. Ezek. 34)." The call to have dominion, therefore, does not sanction exploitation. To the contrary, "It has to do with securing the well-being of every

human's responsibility

---

[4] Irenaeus, *Against the Heresies* (London: Aeterna, 2016), 4.20.1.

[5] For a theological discussion of creation *ex nihilo* and its relationship to peaceableness, see Brian Robinette, "The Difference Nothing Makes: *Creatio Ex Nihilo*, Resurrection, and Divine Gratuity," *Theological Studies* 72, no. 3 (2011): 525–57. The reading of scripture that I advance runs counter to the hermeneutic developed by Catherine Keller, who argues that the doctrine of *creatio ex nihilo* and much of the Christian tradition exhibits a pervasive "tehomophobia" (fear of the chaotic deep) that underlies the patriarchal will to dominate creation. See, for example, Keller's "No More Sea," in *Christianity and Ecology: Seeking the Well-Being of Earth and Human*, ed. Dieter T. Hessel and Rosemary Radford Ruether (Cambridge, MA: Harvard University Press, 2000), 183–84; Catherine Keller, *God and Power: Counter-Apocalyptic Journeys* (Minneapolis: Fortress, 2005), 143–49. In my view, the symbol of chaos in scripture should be linked more closely to imperial domination. I hasten to add that these two interpretations can be read as mutual correctives.

[6] See Ellen Davis, *Scripture, Culture, Agriculture* (Cambridge: Cambridge University Press, 2009), 44–47.

[7] See the discussion of *Laudato Si'* (*LS*) in Chapter 2 of this book.

[8] Davis, *Scripture, Culture, Agriculture*, 55.

[9] Ibid.

other creature and bringing the promise of each to full fruition." Perhaps most tellingly, Brueggemann interprets dominion in light of Christ, writing that "a Christian understanding of dominion must be discerned in the way of Jesus of Nazareth (cf. Mk 10:43–44). The one who rules is the one who serves. Lordship means servanthood."[10] This final point of Brueggemann's, as we shall see in more detail below, coheres well with the ethos of Genesis 2:15.

In many ways, the verb "subdue" (*kabas*) is more troubling than that of "having dominion." It frequently connotes a harshness that resonates with notions of domination.[11] However, as Norbert Lohfink argues, within the context of Genesis 1:28, *kabas* is best understood as "to take possession."[12] For Lohfink, then, human beings are called by God to take possession of the earth. In more contemporary parlance, this can be understood as a divine call for the "humanization" of the world. While this call is undoubtedly anthropocentric, it is so in a qualified sense. The human person is to be the measurer of creation, not the measure. Within the context of Genesis 1, the process of humanization is meant to ensure the flourishing of God's good creation as a whole.[13] Moreover, the call to take possession of the land is further qualified by the underlying presumption that the land belongs to God and that human possession of the land is vouchsafed through obedience to God.[14]

At this point, we must also consider the significance of Genesis's pronounce-

---

[10]Walter Brueggemann, *Genesis* (Atlanta: John Knox, 1982), 33.

[11]See Theodore Hiebert, "The Human Vocation: Origins and Transformations in Christian Traditions," in *Christianity and Ecology: Seeking the Well-Being of the Earth and Humans*, ed. Dieter T. Hessel and Rosemary Radford Ruether (Cambridge, MA: Harvard University Press, 2000).

[12]Lohfink argues that within the *Priestly* source's (*P*'s) original context, "take possession of the land" likely refers to possessing the land of Canaan and the covenantal promise. See Norbert Lohfink, *Theology of the Pentateuch: Themes of the Priestly Narrative and Deuteronomy* (Minneapolis: Fortress, 1994), 7–11. Davis takes this line of interpretation further. Placing *P* within the context of the Babylonian captivity, Davis interprets *kabas* as a call to return from exile. It functions, therefore, primarily as a call to maintain hope for a people in the midst of catastrophe—Babylon will not author the final word in history. Furthermore, Davis suggests that the call to "conquer" the land should be understood within the broader context of the theology of *P*, which ties possession of the land and the land's fruitfulness to Israel's faithfulness to God. Davis, thus, reads *kabas* as an ironic call to repent and return to God even amid the catastrophe of exile. See Davis, *Scripture, Culture, Agriculture*, 59–63.

[13]Both J. Richard Middleton and J. Gordon McConville connect *kabas* with the notion of "organizing" or delimiting the elements of the created order. In taking possession of the earth, the human person is to continue that process of organizing that God began by separating, for example, the waters from the land. See J. Richard Middleton, *The Liberating Image: The Imago Dei in Genesis 1* (Grand Rapids, MI: Brazos, 2005), 89; J. Gordon McConville, *Being Human in God's World: An Old Testament Theology of Humanity* (Grand Rapids, MI: Baker, 2016), 22. This reading is particularly noteworthy in light of an unrelated essay by Joseph Blenkinsopp, who finds within the delimiting character of the law a biblical foundation for a Judeo-Christian environmental ethic. See Joseph Blenkinsopp, *Treasures Old and New: Essays in the Theology of the Pentateuch* (Grand Rapids, MI: W. B. Eerdmans, 2004), 36–52.

[14]See Davis, *Scripture, Culture, Agriculture*, 60.

ment that the human person is created in "the image and likeness of God" (Gen 1:27), which is frequently linked to the commands to "have dominion" and "take possession." In light of my argument in Chapter 1, the symbol of *imago Dei* poses no inherent problem for developing an ecological theology of liberation. The symbol, at least in part, affirms the human person as a culpable subject before God. As such, the human must discern good from evil and bear responsibility for the life of the world. Moreover, it is likely Genesis's affirmation that the human person is created in *imago Dei* is not intended primarily as a reflection of the human's status in relation to nonhuman creation but, rather, stands as a reflection of the human's status in relation to monarchical power. According to Richard Middleton, in Genesis the symbol of *imago Dei* subverts the notion, common in the ancient Near East, that it was the political ruler alone who existed in the image of god (consider the observation above that in the *Enuma Elish* the human, formed from the blood of traitorous Kingu, is created as a slave). Thus, the affirmation of the human as *imago Dei* serves to defend the dignity of the human person against the tyranny of power while also affirming the political agency of humanity in general.[15] *autonomy?*

The affirmation of the human person as *imago Dei* is not intended primarily as a statement of the human person's relationship to nonhuman creation as such. Nonetheless, it is important to acknowledge that the understanding of the human person proper to the first account of Genesis remains significant with regard to humanity's status in relation to the broader created order. After all, it is by virtue of the fact that human persons are created in the image of God that they are called to shepherd and humanize the earth. The key point here is *ma* not that the human is called to humanize the earth but that *all human persons* *just* (or better, all human communities) are called to participate in this process. In *"when"* applying *imago Dei* to all of humanity, Genesis 1:27 undercuts any attempt to absolutize a particular mode of organization. Just as no single ruler can define the right ordering of the world, no one culture or political regime can dictate, in a totalizing manner, the proper ways of relating to earth. In making this claim, I am not proposing a radical relativism that rejects the possibility of formal criteria for conceiving of a "right relationship" between human persons and nonhuman creation. Humans are called by God to distinguish between good and evil and to act accordingly in light of these judgments. My point, rather, is that Genesis 1:27 subverts any tyrannical or colonial impulse that would subjugate all peoples to a single political-ecological project.[16]

relationship back to the Babylon man aslu

---

[15]Middleton, *Liberating Image*, 204–28.

[16]Here, I wish to affirm Willie James Jennings's criticism of the European-Christian colonial project, which reduces *imago Dei* to the image of the European colonizer. Jennings writes that, as a result, "rather than the emergence of spaces of communion that announce the healing of the nations through the story of Israel bound up in Jesus, spaces situated anywhere and everywhere the disciples of Jesus live together, we are now the inheritors and perpetrators of a global process of

In Genesis's first account of creation, what emerges is an understanding of the created order as that which God perceives as good and beautiful, and, correspondingly, delights in. Accordingly, God calls all of humanity to continue the task of organizing creation so that the world, as a whole, might flourish. Further, in creating humanity in God's image and likeness, God undercuts the presumptions of any regime of imperialist power that might reify its own programs of politico-ecological organization. Along these lines, the first creation account in Genesis finds its narrative apex on the final day of creation, when God rests. Here, God invites all of creation into the peace of sabbath rest, an invitation that, as we will see, stands in stark contrast to the fallen political ecologies described in scripture. These conceptions of both creation and the human/earth relationship cohere well with the ethos of care that is championed in *Laudato Si'*. As I have observed, the encyclical connects this ethos most prominently to Genesis 2:15 and the vocation "to cultivate and care" found in the second account of creation in Genesis. It is to this account that I now turn so as to better illuminate the significance of this key verse.

[handwritten margin note: all humans are in God's image]

God, Gardener, and the Image of God: Genesis 2:4–25

The vocation that God gives to the human person in Genesis 2:15 may be understood against the backdrop of the garden's "geo-ethical landscape," to use William Brown's term. After first forming the human person out of the "fertile soil,"[17] God plants a garden in Eden, causing beautiful and healthful vegetation to grow within its boundaries (2:7–9). It is significant that God is the one who plants the garden. As William Brown observes, this depiction places God in the role of landowner; the human is but a tenant upon God's land.[18] The earth, then, is God's (Ps 24:1), to whom humans are responsible. The most notable element of the garden's geography, however, is the presence within it of "the tree of life" and the "tree of knowledge of good and evil." In planting the garden, God locates the tree of life at its center, with the tree of knowledge apparently close in proximity (Gen 2:9).[19] Here I focus on the significance of

---

spatial commodification and social fragmentation. These processes are performed within the class and economic calculations of global real estate. They force local communities to reflect global networks of exchange in regard to private property that echo colonialism's racial hierarchies and division." See Willie James Jennings, *The Christian Imagination: Theology and the Origins of Race* (New Haven, CT: Yale University Press, 2010), 293.

[17]Theodore Hiebert, *The Yahwist's Landscape: Nature and Religion in Early Israel* (Minneapolis: Augsburg Fortress, 2008), 34–35.

[18]William P. Brown, *The Ethos of the Cosmos: The Genesis of Moral Imagination in the Bible* (Grand Rapids, MI: Wm. B. Eerdmans, 1999), 138.

[19]The verse is notoriously difficult to translate. The Anchor Bible translates it as "with the tree of life in the middle of the garden and the tree of knowledge of good and bad." See *Genesis*, vol. 1, trans., intro., and commentary by E. A. Speiser (New York: Doubleday, 1964), 14.

the tree of life before considering the meaning of the tree of knowledge below.

Read canonically, the tree of life symbolizes the wisdom of God. Proverbs affirms that wisdom "is a tree of life to those who grasp her, and those who hold her fast are happy" (Prov 3:18). This identification is prevalent within early Christian exegesis. On this point, Augustine's discussion of the tree is illuminative. According to him, the tree of life serves as a sacrament within the garden: "On this interpretation the tree of life in the material paradise is analogous to the wisdom of God in the spiritual or intelligible paradise; for Scripture says of wisdom, 'It is the tree of life to those who embrace it.'"[20] Augustine continues with a distinctly Christian reading, observing that, as God's wisdom, the tree of life "must be Christ himself."[21]

In light of the identification of the tree of life with Christ, it is particularly noteworthy that the tree is located at the center of the garden. In Genesis 2, the garden itself is organized around and in accordance with the wisdom of God. As with the first creation account of Genesis, the second account indicates symbolically the way in which God's wisdom rightly and beautifully orders creation. Moreover, given Augustine's identification of the tree of life with Christ, there is also a resonance between the symbolic organization of the garden and the cosmic Christological claim found in the hymn of Colossians: "In him all things hold together" (Col 1:17). The order of the garden coheres in and according to God's wisdom. The garden of Eden, then, appears as the reign of God in its protological form. If Christ is *autobasilea*—the reign of God realized in a self—and the garden is organized in accordance with Christ, then it follows that the garden as a whole reflects the character of God's reign.

Having organized the garden in this manner, God sets the human person to the task of "cultivating and caring" for the garden (Gen 2:15). In effect, God calls the human to cooperate with God's wisdom, giving the person the symbolic vocation of "gardener." God creates the human as *homo hortulanus*. In reflecting on this vocation, Theodore Hiebert argues that the primary object of the human's care is the soil.[22] However, this claim is too constrictive. It is better to understand "the garden" as referring not simply to "the soil" but also to "all that comes from the soil." Thus, to cultivate and care for the garden is to cultivate and care for the soil and all that comes from the soil.[23] This is significant because within the narrative imagination of Genesis 2, God forms the animals of the earth, the birds of the air, and, perhaps most notably, the human person, from the garden's rich soil. The intimacy of the relationship between the human and the soil is reinforced etymologically: God creates the human,

---

[20]Augustine, *City of God*, 13.20.

[21]Ibid., 13.21.

[22]Hiebert, "Human Vocation," 140.

[23]See Brown, *Ethos of the Cosmos*, 141.

"Adam" (*'ādām*), out of the earth (*'ădāmâ*).[24] Here, then, both love of earth and love of neighbor are constitutive of the vocation of gardener.[25] Moreover, since the love of earth and neighbor are understood as the proper response to God's call to the human, the love of God is also intrinsic to the vocation of gardener. The human person responds positively to God (thereby exhibiting a love of God) by cultivating and caring for the soil and all that comes from the soil. Formulated another way, Genesis 2:15 intimates that the love of God is expressed *through* the interrelated loves of neighbor and earth.

The polyvalence of the two Hebrew verbs, *'ābad* (to cultivate) and *somer* (to care), that constitute the vocation in Genesis 2:15 suggestively point to the interconnected nature of the love of God, neighbor, and earth. In addition to translating as "to cultivate" or "to till," *'ābad* can also translate as "to serve." The work of cultivation, then, is imbued with an ethos of service. As Davis writes, *'ābad* connotes "*working for* the garden soil, serving its needs."[26] Even more notably, within the biblical corpus, *'ābad* is interpreted in terms of service most frequently when describing the proper human posture toward God; the human person is meant to serve (*'ābad*) God. The use of *'ābad* in Genesis 2:15 unites these usages: the human person serves God through serving the needs of the soil and all that comes from the soil. Similarly, *somer* translates not only as "to care" but also as "to keep" and "to observe." As Davis points out, in scripture "to keep," is associated with the human person's responsibility to both God and neighbor.[27] Similarly, "observe" is used varyingly in reference to observing the "dictates of justice" (Hos 12:7; Is 56:1), "the rhythms of nature" (Jer 8:7) and "the ordinances of God" (Ex 31:13).[28] The multiple valences of *somer* capture the multiple dimensions of the praxis of *homo hortulanus*.

The vocation of gardener corresponds to the end for which God creates the human person. God calls the human to a tripartite form of love precisely because God creates the human person to live in communion with God, neighbor, and earth. The threefold sense of intimacy, for which God creates the human, is conveyed in a number of ways within the second creation narrative. As I just noted, the human is intimately related to the soil and therefore appears as kin to the other living creatures of the garden. Moreover, the human is tasked by God with the responsibility of naming these living creatures (thereby, carrying

---

[24]This etymological link is preserved in the English "human" and "humus."

[25]In *Laudato Si'*, Pope Francis preserves this dual sense of love in applying the vocation of Genesis 2:15 to "the garden of the world." See *Laudato Si'*, no. 57.

[26]Davis, *Scripture, Culture, Agriculture*, 29. Davis does distance herself from Hiebert when Hiebert argues that the earth in Genesis 2 can be understood as sovereign. Davis finds that the evidence is clear that within the Primeval History only God is viewed as sovereign (29–30). See also Hiebert, "Human Vocation," 140.

[27]Davis, Scripture, Culture, Agriculture, 30.

[28]Ibid.

out the obligation to observe creation carefully).[29] After sexual differentiation, Adam exclaims, "This one, at last, is bone of my bone and flesh of my flesh" (Gen 2:23)—an exclamation of deep affinity.[30] Moreover, Adam and Eve stand naked and unashamed before each other, hiding nothing from each other. The primordial couple, likewise, stands before God in this manner, walking with God in the cool of the evening. By serving and observing the soil and all that comes from the soil, the human sustains the threefold communion for which it was created. Thus, the cultural life and the political ecology of the garden—informed as they are by an ethos of service, care, and careful observation—correspond to the wisdom of God. Thus human culture and its political ecology continue to organize the garden rightly.[31] Abiding in the wisdom of God, the praxis of *homo hortulanus* is itself a sacrament of integral ecology.

Among the connotations of the vocation of gardener, perhaps most striking is the manner in which it elucidates an implicit praxic *imago Dei* anthropology within this second creation narrative. Recall that, in the second chapter of Genesis, God is the one who plants the garden. God is the one who initially works with the soil, organizing it in accordance with God's wisdom so that creation might flourish. Within the second creation narrative, God is depicted as Gardener.[32]

---

[29]Although some have argued that Adam's act of naming the animals constitutes an act of imperiousness on the part of the human, this is not so. See, for example, George W. Ramsey, "Is Name-Giving an Act of Domination in Genesis 2:23 and Elsewhere?" *CBQ* 50 (1988): 24–35; Mark G. Brett, "Earthing the Human in Genesis 1–3," in *The Earth Story in Genesis*, ed. Norman C, Habel and Shirley Wurst (Sheffield: Sheffield Academic Press; Cleveland, Ohio: Pilgrim, 2000), 2:81; Eric D. Meyer's analysis "Gregory of Nyssa on Language, Naming God's Creatures, and the Desire of the Discursive Animal" in *Genesis and Christian Theology*, ed. Nathan MacDonald et al. (Grand Rapids, MI: Eerdmans, 2012), 103–16; Claus Westermann, *Genesis 1–11* (Minneapolis: Augsburg, 1985), 228. The qualitative dimension of this act of naming should be controlled by Genesis 2:15. Here, the person names that which is to be served and cared for.

[30]Although it is true that the primordial woman is formed out of the rib of the primordial human and not out of the earth itself, this should not be interpreted as creating an opposition between the woman and the soil. After all, the rib itself is composed of soil. The call to care for the soil and all that comes from the soil, should be interpreted as including the woman as both an object and agent of care. Rejecting any interpretation of this passage that would suggest a subordinate or derivative status of the woman to the man, I affirm Phyllis Trible's view that the rib signifies "solidarity and equality" between human sexes. See Phyllis Trible, "Eve and Adam: Genesis 2–3 Re-read," *Andover Newton Quarterly* 13, no. 4 (1973): 253. Along these same lines, the vocation of gardener should be ascribed to all human persons regardless of their sex. Moreover, especially in view of the patriarchal and misogynist character of so much of the Christian imagination, the earth should not be coded "female" in contemporary interpretations of this text.

[31]Although commentators often associate the advent of culture in Genesis with Cain's founding of the city, this is incorrect. As Brown observes, human culture in the second creation account is initially identified with the work of cultivating and caring. See Brown, *Ethos of the Cosmos*, 134. Indeed, the entirety of Ellen Davis's *Scripture, Culture, Agriculture* proceeds from the view that care for the soil is fundamental to biblical understandings of culture.

[32]Walter Brueggemann alludes to this at various points in his commentary on Genesis. See Brueggemann, *Genesis*, 49 and 51. See also William P. Brown, "The Gardener and the Groundling," *Journal for Preachers* 32, no. 3 (2009): 33–37.

Thus, in setting the human person to the task of cultivating and caring for creation, God calls humanity to inhabit God's own image. For the human person, to cultivate and care, to serve and observe, the soil and all that comes from the soil is not simply to serve God, it is also to conform to God's very image. *Homo hortulanus is imago Dei*.[33] According to the narrative logic of Genesis's second account of creation, the human person comes to inhabit the image of God most fully through properly responding to God's call to love the soil and all that comes from the soil, thereby enfleshing God's wisdom in the world.[34]

Genesis 3: The Fall—Breaking of the Bonds of Communion

If Genesis 2 describes an idyllic situation in which all things are ordered by, and hold together in accordance with, the wisdom of God, then Genesis 3 narrates the manner in which things fall apart when humanity eschews God's wisdom. In order to grasp the theological implications of "the fall," it is necessary to return to the garden's geo-ethical landscape and consider the tree of knowledge of good and evil, which, as noted above, is ostensibly located very near the tree of life at the garden's center. When we encounter the tree of knowledge in Genesis 3, it is the object of a discussion between Eve and the serpent, who is described as the "most cunning of all the wild animals" (Gen 3:1). The serpent entices the woman to eat the fruit of the tree of knowledge, which appears as "good for food," "pleasing to the eyes," and "good for gaining wisdom" (Gen 3:6). Moreover, the serpent asserts that by eating the fruit, the humans "will be like gods, who know good and evil" (Gen 3:5).

---

[33]Along these lines, N. T. Wright remarks, "The notion of the 'image' doesn't refer to a particular spiritual endowment, a secret 'property' that humans possess somewhere in their spiritual makeup, something that might be found by a scientific observation of humans as opposed to chimps. The image is a *vocation*, a calling. It is the call to be *an angled mirror*, reflecting God's wise order into the world and reflecting the praises of all creation back to the Creator." N. T. Wright, "Excursus," in John H. Walton, *The Lost World of Adam and Eve* (Downers Grove, IL: InterVarsity, 2015), 175.

[34]It can be noted, here, that the implicit description of *imago Dei* in Genesis 2 accommodates the underdetermined and pliable character of humanity that David Kelsey, Kathryn Tanner, and Ian McFarland all stress in their recent constructive work on the image. See David Kelsey, *Eccentric Existence: A Theological Anthropology,* 2 vols. (Louisville, KY: Westminster John Knox, 2009); Kathryn Tanner, *Christ the Key* (New York: Cambridge University Press, 2010); and Ian McFarland, *The Divine Image: Envisioning the Invisible God* (Minneapolis: Fortress, 2005). Here, *imago* need not be tied to a strong ontological account of the human person but, rather, connects most obviously to the dynamism of human praxis. Here, *imago Dei* appears as much as a call to holiness as it does an essence. However, the coordinates of this call are more determined at the outset of the Bible than the aforementioned authors seem to allow. In Genesis 2, holiness, and thus *imago*, is expressed through loving communion with God, neighbor, and earth. (It is important to emphasize that the implicit image-of-God anthropology in Genesis 2:15 is not inherently closed off to strong ontological accounts.) I should also note that, in keeping with the concerns of the three aforementioned authors, the conception of *imago Dei* has a strong Christological grounding, which I discuss in Chapter 4.

Given that we have already identified the tree of life with the wisdom of God, it is striking that the human now perceives the tree of knowledge as conducive to attaining wisdom. Precisely what type of wisdom does the tree of knowledge of good and evil provide? Here the meaning of the expression "knowledge of good and evil" provides a basic insight. The expression is a merism; it uses two contrasting terms in order to refer to an entirety. Thus, the knowledge of good and evil implies "the knowledge of all things." Within the spectrum of comprehensive knowledge, however, Claus Westermann suggests that the practical dimension of knowledge is highlighted here. In other words, the serpent tempts the primordial woman with knowledge that allows one to manipulate the whole of reality in order to become a success.[35] Brown echoes Westermann's view more forcefully, writing that the knowledge offered by the latter tree is "eminently instrumental in nature, a knowledge of means for attaining desired ends, the requisite know-how for mastering life. The tree represents a form of intellectual capital that can function in self-serving ways, depending upon the aim of the wielder of wisdom."[36] The promise of the knowledge of all things, then, carries with it the implicit prospect of the mastery of all things.

Taken by itself, apart from the semiotic field of Genesis 2–3, the tree of knowledge is not intrinsically evil. The knowledge of all things, after all, can provide an avenue toward flourishing.[37] However, the context in which the tree of knowledge appears in this narrative does not allow for abstract suppositions.[38] This is because the alluring promises of the tree of knowledge must always be considered together with the prohibition that God places against eating it. Within the narrative logic of Genesis 2–3, grasping at the fruit of the tree of knowledge necessarily represents a rebellion against God. Monika Hellwig captures the significance of the primordial couple's action poignantly, observing that by grasping at and internalizing the fruit of the tree of knowledge, they echo "the refrain from Lucifer: I will not serve; I will exist as a god in my own right."[39] Hellwig's observation is telling. In Genesis 2, God places the human

---

[35]Westermann, *Genesis*, 241.

[36]Brown, Ethos of the Cosmos, 155.

[37]As could "sustainable development" in the contemporary global context.

[38]The wisdom literature of the Bible typically exalts wisdom in an uncritical manner (similar, for example, to the manner in which contemporary political discourse exalts the concept of "sustainable development"). In Genesis 2–3, however, the author describes two trees (that of "life" and that of "knowledge"), each of which could be identified ostensibly with God's wisdom. The addition of the second tree, *the tree of knowledge*, into the narrative of Genesis "bifurcates wisdom to suit the dramatic development of the story, and in so doing introduces a critical, indeed polemical, dimension not found in the wisdom literature" (Brown, *Ethos of the Cosmos*, 155). In other words, in Genesis 2–3, the tree of knowledge functions as a symbol for false wisdom, wisdom that appears to be from God and conducive to life but rather appears this way only in a deceptive light and, in fact, leads to death, suffering, and bondage. By juxtaposing the two trees, the author of Genesis 2–3 provides a framework for ideology critique.

[39]Monika K. Hellwig, *Understanding Catholicism* (New York: Paulist, 2002), 48.

the serpent is a liar

person in the garden to serve God through caring for the soil and all that comes from the soil. Now the primordial couple grasps at knowledge of good and evil, thereby rejecting the vocation of gardener. They will not serve the soil and all that comes from the soil; instead, *in their own image* "like the gods," they will be served. The knowledge of good and evil appears, therefore, as an *inversion* of the wisdom offered through the tree of life. It is true that the tree of knowledge grants the ability to know good from evil, but this access is always already predicated on the disordering of perception and desire so that those who eat of it will "call evil good and good evil" (Is 5:20).[40]

In effect, the "wisdom" of the tree of knowledge reflects the serpent's own guile.[41] Commentators frequently note that the Hebrew word used to describe the serpent as cunning (*erum*) closely approximates the word describing the nakedness ('*ārûm*) of the woman and man.[42] Thus, the narrator of Genesis utilizes a poetic play on words to draw attention to the manner in which the cunning serpent preys on the innocent vulnerability of the human person. Often overlooked, however, is how the reference to the serpent's cunningness also approximates the "shrewdness" ascribed to pharaoh at the beginning of the Exodus narrative—a pharaoh whose cunning knowledge informs a political ecology of oppression, domination, and de-creation.[43] The destructiveness of pharaoh's shrewdness, then, is anticipated canonically, in the effects of the primordial couple's decision to grasp at the fruit of the tree of knowledge and internalize the serpent's cunningness.

As we have seen, prior to the fall, the primordial couple exists in intimate communion with God, one another, and the earth (a threefold communion sustained through responding positively to the vocation of gardener). Now, however, these relationships become warped and disordered. After internalizing the knowledge of domination, the couple hides from God, and they cover themselves in shame of being seen by each other (2:7, 2:9). Abusive power comes to characterize human relationships (2:16). Furthermore, the earth itself is now cursed so that human toil upon the land must increase (2:17–19). Thus, the fullness of communion described in Genesis 2 cedes to a tripartite alienation. The political ecology predicated on God's wisdom is fractured—displaced, at least in part, by a disordered political ecology, a new geo-ethical

---

[40]The verse in its entirety reads, "Woe to those who call evil good and good evil, who put darkness for light and light for darkness, who put bitter for sweet and sweet for bitter." On this passage, see McConville's perceptive commentary in *Being Human in God's World*, 39–43.

[41]Tellingly, the serpent is frequently identified with wisdom in ancient Near Eastern mythologies. See Karen Randolph Joines, *Serpent Symbolism in the Old Testament* (Haddonfield, NJ: Haddonfield House, 1974), 21–26. Again, however, in this narrative the serpent functions to convey false wisdom.

[42]See Richard J. Clifford and Roland E. Murphy, "Genesis," in *The New Jerome Biblical Commentary*, ed. Raymond E. Brown et al. (Englewood Cliffs, NJ: Prentice Hall, 1990), 12.

[43]Brown is one who does make this connection. See Brown, *Ethos of the Cosmos*, 203.

terrain, organized around a cunning knowledge and in service to a disordered form of self-love.[44]

So far, this analysis of the tree of life and the tree of knowledge has highlighted the ways in which the two trees stand in diametrical opposition to one another. The tree of life, identified with the wisdom of God, sustains the love of God, neighbor, and earth, and informs the proper organization of creation through a praxis of service and care. In contradistinction, the tree of knowledge represents the rejection of God's wisdom, elevates a disordered form of the love of self, and informs a praxis of destructive de-creation predicated on the refusal to serve. On the one hand, there is a sense in which these dichotomies must be upheld. On the other hand, however, the relationship between the tree of life and the tree of knowledge cannot be reduced to simple opposition.

Reinhold Niebuhr opines that, within historical reality, there is "no possibility of drawing a sharp line between the will-to-live and the will-to-power."[45] Translated into the symbolic language of Genesis 2–3, Niebuhr's dictum posits a degree of similarity between the garden's two named trees. The ambiguous relationship between the two trees is acknowledged in the world of the text itself. Recall that, within the garden, the trees of life and knowledge appear quite close to each other. Indeed, when the serpent presents the tree of knowledge to the primordial woman, we are told that it is this tree (and not the tree of life) that is located at the center of the garden (Gen 3:3). Far from being at opposite ends of the geo-ethical landscape of the garden, one can presume the two trees are nearly touching. Within the semiotic field of the second creation narrative in Genesis, then, one is able to detect an intuition that would inform the Christian imagination for subsequent centuries and millennia: that which can rightly be named as evil can approximate that which is good; just as Lucifer comes as a bearer of light, the tree of knowledge appears preciously close to the tree of life. The close proximity between the ways of good and evil, then, necessitates the careful discernment of what one would name as wise and good.[46]

If the physical nearness of the two trees complicates the oppositional character of their relationship, so too does the human person's ability to perceive rightly. For centuries, readers of Genesis have puzzled over a point to which I have just alluded. It is strange that after the narrator describes the tree of life

---

[44]Here, I wish to avoid characterizing all forms of self-love as disordered. Such characterizations of self-love can serve to underwrite the internalization of the identity of nonperson. There is a difference between humility and shame/degradation, just as there is a difference between acknowledging one's own dignity (as it is imbued by God) and pride.

[45]Reinhold Niebuhr, *Moral Man and Immoral Society: A Study in Ethics and Politics* (Louisville, KY: Westminster John Knox, 2013), 42.

[46]Along these lines, Brown writes, "Partaking the fruit in violation of the interdiction may suggest a lack of discernment, as might be confirmed in the proverb: 'Desire without knowledge is not good, and one who moves too hurriedly misses the way' (Prov 19:2 NRSV)." Brown, *Ethos of the Cosmos*, 156.

[handwritten: perspective matters; how we order ourselves]

at the center of the garden, we find that in the very next chapter the primordial woman is tempted by the tree of knowledge at the garden's center. While it is appealing for modern exegetes simply to dismiss this contradiction simply as an error in redaction, Joseph Blenkinsopp posits a different approach for making sense of this incongruity between Genesis 2 and 3. In Genesis 3, the tree of knowledge is described at existing at the center of the garden because the narrator invites the reader to enter into the primordial woman's perspective of the garden's ethical terrain.[47] From the woman's perspective, bedazzled as she was by the cunning serpent, it appears that it is the tree of knowledge that rightly orders the garden. From this vantage point, the fruit of the tree of knowledge appears pleasing and desirable. Thus, it is not simply the spatial closeness of the two trees that results in confusion, but also the warped desires informing the human person's perception.[48] The distorted perception of the primordial couple not only leads to the misperception of wisdom, it is also tied to a misunderstanding of what it means to be divine. As it was already noted, this is the prospect with which the serpent tempts the primordial woman. "You certainly will not die!" the serpent tells Eve; "God knows well that when you eat of it your eyes will be opened and you will be like gods" (Gen 3:5). There is a certain truthfulness to the serpent's assertion: the tree of knowledge presents the primordial couple with the prospect of exaltation—with having their name glorified like God's own name (see also Gen 11:4).[49] Indeed, the validity of the serpent's claim is confirmed by God later in the narrative (Gen 3:22). Nevertheless, on a deeper level, the serpent is revealed to be a liar. In tempting the woman, the serpent implicitly suggests that God finds the prospect of human divinization undesirable. Eve takes this as fact. However, this is simply not the case. From the beginning of the second creation account, God has called the human person to be "like God" through serving and caring for the soil and all that comes from it. God, the Gardener, calls humanity to abide in God's own image and to live in accordance with God's wisdom. When the serpent tempts Eve with the fruit of the tree of knowledge, she is, in truth, already "like God."[50]

[handwritten margin note: humans are already like God]

The narrative of the fall, then, is shot through with tragic irony. In grasping at a conception of divinity defined foremost in terms of power and aggran-

[handwritten: are we obscuring something important from one POV?]

---

[47] See Joseph Blenkinsopp's comment in *Creation, Un-Creation, De-Creation: A Discursive Commentary on Genesis 1–11* (New York: T&T Clark, 2011), 76.

[48] Blenkinsopp's reading, therefore, coheres well with the traditional Augustinian view that "the evil will preceded the evil act." See Augustine, *City of God*, XIV.13.

[49] As Westermann observes, "The promise 'to be like God' is not something over and above knowledge, but describes [knowledge] and all that it is capable of. It is concerned with a divine and unbridled ability to master one's existence." Westermann, *Genesis 1–11*, 248. In this narrative, the human person attains an approximation of this status. However, it is a status informed by a perverse understanding of the nature of God.

[50] She already exists in a tripartite communion that is secured through service and care.

dizement—a conception of divinity that is both alluring and grotesque—the primordial couple disfigures *imago Dei* and becomes markedly less like God.[51] By internalizing the shrewdness associated with the serpent (and the pharaoh of Exodus), the couple displaces the wisdom of God. This displacement occurs not only within the hearts of the couple, but within the world as well. The logic of the fruit of the tree of knowledge, as we have observed, now comes to order the culture and political ecology of the world; the peaceable communion that defined the *shalom* of the garden cedes to a harshness.

God's response to the transgression of the primordial couple is also important. There is judgment and punishment of the couple's pride and lust for domination. The couple is cast out of the garden, and the experience of shame supplants their innocence. Significantly, however, God's final act before sending Adam and Eve into the world outside of the garden is one of protection. God makes "garments of skin" (Gen 3:21) for the couple. God's action should be understood as an act of divine care—God, after all, remains Gardener. In a world now disfigured by self-seeking shrewdness, a form of knowledge that seeks to dominate the soil and all that comes from the soil, the nakedness of the primordial couple is no longer tenable. Their nakedness must be covered over for their own protection. Here, however, the ambiguity between the logics of the trees of life and knowledge is further heightened. Recall that, after eating the fruit, the first act of Adam and Eve was to cover themselves in an attempt to hide their shame and guilt. Their act, it follows, is the product of their decision to internalize the fruit of the tree of knowledge. God's act, which is identical in form, accords with the fruit of the tree of life. Within the context of a sinful political ecology, God makes a wise provision for the primordial couple. Indeed, God's act of clothing Adam and Eve anticipates other allowances on the part of God, as God shepherds a rebellious creation toward the fullness of life[52] (see Gen 9:3). In the post-lapsarian world, the indistinctness characterizing the relationship between the tree of life and the tree of knowledge is intensified.[53] This is especially sobering, given the manner in which the presence of sin now orders the human intellect and will. Nonetheless, God's act of clothing the primordial couple should be interpreted as a sign of hope. Despite the primordial couple's rebellion against the wisdom of God, God does not abandon humanity to death.

human should act the same

---

[51]Related to this point, see McConville's discussion of *imago* in *Being Human in God's World*, 39–43.

[52]For example, after the flood, God permits Noah to eat meat (Gen 9:1–4).

[53]Michael James Williams argues that deception subsequently takes on a morally ambiguous role in Genesis. The righteousness or unrighteousness of deception is tied to whether the deceit restores or disrupts *shalom*. See Michael James Williams, *Deception in Genesis: An Investigation into the Morality of a Unique Biblical Phenomenon* (New York: Peter Lang, 2001), esp. 221–26.

Cain and Abel

The hopeful note introduced at the end of Genesis 3 is carried into the beginning of the story of Cain and Abel (the sons of Adam and Eve). At the beginning of the story, Cain is described as a "cultivator" (*'ābad*) of the soil and Abel as a "keeper" (*somer*) of flocks (Gen 4:2). Commenters often place the distinct tasks associated with the brothers in juxtaposition, suggesting that these designations recall the ancient societal tension between agrarians and nomadic shepherds, thereby anticipating the outbreak of violence between Cain and Abel.[54] Although there is certainly an element of truth in this interpretation, it overlooks a more fundamental point: the vocation that God gives to humanity in Genesis 2 remains in place after the fall. Despite the introduction of sin into the story of creation, the generation after Adam and Eve continues to cultivate and care for creation. The human person, though wounded by sin, continues to make manifest something of God's image. Likewise, the possibility of intimacy between God, neighbor, and earth continues to be sustained. Regrettably, this hopefulness serves to heighten the tragic elements of the Cain and Abel narrative.

As the story develops, Cain and Abel bring their distinct offerings before God. God finds that only the offering of Abel, the younger brother, is acceptable. Cain, the firstborn son, would have expected to be favored. Indeed, Cain's privileged status within the world is underscored by the meaning of his brother's name. In Hebrew, Abel (*Hevel*) means, "vapor," "nothingness," or "meaninglessness."[55] In the eyes of the world, then, Abel appears as a nonperson.[56] The elder brother cannot reconcile himself with God's decision to opt for the one of no account. Cain, we are told, becomes "long in the face," a phrase signifying alienation.[57] He then lures his younger brother "out to the field" (Gen 4:8), the site of Cain's vocational work as gardener, and kills Abel.

In Cain's actions, humanity's rejection of the call to serve and care intensifies. Whereas the primordial couple's pride gives rise to a lust for domination, here Cain's pride and lust result in murder. As we observed in Chapter 2 with Pope Francis, the amplification of the disordering power of sin in the Cain and Abel narrative is threefold in its dimensionality. Cain not only kills his brother; he is also cursed from the ground and driven away from both the soil

---

[54]See interpreter's comment on Genesis 4:2 at http://www.usccb.org.

[55]Larry Rasmussen, *Earth-Honoring Faith: Religious Ethics in a New Key* (Oxford: Oxford University Press, 2013), 205.

[56]Gutiérrez alludes to this in *TL*, xxvii. Abel's status in the world can also be understood as the reason for God's partiality toward the younger brother. God exercises a preferential option for the poor. On this point, see *GoL*, 115–17. See also Johanna W. H. Van Wijk-Bos, *Making the Wise Simple: The Torah in Christian Faith and Practice* (Grand Rapids, MI: Eerdmans, 2005), 86–90.

[57]Westermann, *Genesis 1–11*, 297.

reseub ws wcastr of gardener

and the presence of God. The hopeful note that was present at the beginning of the story now rests. Not only has Cain killed his brother, but the vocation of "gardener"—precariously present at the outset of the story—now appears lost to humanity. Abel, the one who "cares" and "keeps," is murdered. Cain, the one who "serves" and "cultivates," flees from God and the soil in shame and fear. Significantly, the last mention of Cain notes that, having traveled "east of Eden," he "became founder of a city" (Gen 4:17). Therefore, the "city-builder" functions as a counter-symbol to that of "gardener." Whereas the vocation of gardener signifies God's call to inhabit *imago Dei* through serving and caring for the soil and all that comes from the soil, city-builder, as it appears here, denotes the grotesque inversion of *imago* through the human person's desire to dominate creation and displace God.[58]

It is especially noteworthy that the Hebrew for "Cain" translates as both "metal worker" and, perhaps even more tellingly, as "spear."[59] In Cain's actions, we find the realized antithesis of the prophet Isaiah's much-cited vision of salvation. As Isaiah prophesies, "They will beat their swords into plowshares and their spears into pruning hooks. One nation will not raise the sword against another, nor shall they train for war again" (Is 2:4). Cain begins Genesis 4 by employing the tools of cultivation and care—the plowshare and pruning hook—and inhabiting the vocation of gardener. However, by the conclusion of the narrative, Cain, the metalworker, has beaten the tools of the gardener into the weapons of domination. Reshaped by Cain's own disordered desire, the plowshare and pruning hook become the sword and spear of the city-builder.[60] The city, therefore, materializes as an important symbol in its own right. If city-builder symbolizes the human person's rejection of the vocation of gardener, then "city" symbolizes the social or structural embodiment of this rejection. The city, as it first appears in scripture, reflects the destructive character and desire of Cain. Thus it emerges as a disordered system of political ecology

---

[58]The counter-symbol of city-builder, when taken together with the symbol of gardener, provides the foundation for a reading of salvation history that accounts for the ambiguous character of human creativity and labor. In scripture, human beings are called to actively work with creation from the beginning. This labor is a good and, indeed, sacred task. However, sin disorders the quality of human labor, often setting it at cross-purposes to God's desires. Thus, the creative acts of humanity are always ambiguous and subject to the disordering power of sin.

[59]See Westermann, *Genesis 1–11*, 289. For the sake of transparency Westermann observes that no one translates it in this manner, but that does not seem to be a value judgment on his part. In light of the reading of salvation history developed here, identifying Cain with "spear" and "metal-worker" is both appropriate and theologically fruitful.

[60]This process of devolution from Adam to Cain continues in the genealogy that immediately follows the Cain and Abel narrative (Gen 4:17–26). There, for example, Tubal-Cain becomes "the ancestor of all who forge instruments of bronze and iron" (4:22), and hostility and retribution among humanity is said to grow exponentially (4:24). Notably, though, in the midst of this genealogy of devolution, Seth is born to Adam and Eve. Thus, according to the lineage, the sin of Cain does not appear to shape uniformly the human condition.

organized around the de-creational principles of the tree of knowledge.[61]

At this point, it is necessary to make explicit a point that, until this juncture, I have only implied. The symbols of gardener, city-builder, and city, as I am developing them here, should be interpreted dynamically and not in a strict literalistic sense. In other words, gardener need not denote the actual work of gardening or a narrowly defined agrarian lifestyle. Instead, the symbol identifies the human person whose fundamental disposition is toward serving and caring for creation in accordance with the will of God, and who makes this disposition manifest through praxis. This is *homo hortulanus*.[62] Likewise, city-builder does not refer to an urban planner, as it were, but rather it refers to the human person whose praxis is ordered by an overweening love of self that makes manifest within the world a contempt for the soil and all that comes from the soil.[63] Finally, on these same terms, the symbol of city should not be equated with urban space per se but more broadly with systems or subsystems of human civilization (understood in terms of political ecology).[64]

DE-CREATION, RE-CREATION, COVENANT, AND THE PEOPLE OF GOD

The initial narrative sequence of Genesis can be summarized in the following manner. God brings a good creation into existence out of the chaotic abyss, ordering the world in accord with God's wisdom, and creating the human person for communion with God, neighbor, and earth. In accordance with this purpose, God gives the human the vocation of gardener, calling the human to cooperate with God's wisdom in preserving the threefold sense of communion for which the human was created. The human rejects the vocation of gardener, refusing to

---

[61]Even here, the city should not be construed as wholly opposed or completely antithetical to God and God's wisdom. In Genesis it is the chaotic abyss of total de-creation that appears as a contradistinction to God and God's purposes. As is the case with Cain, insofar as the city participates in being, it reflects something of God's goodness, however fleetingly or distortedly. I am in agreement, then, with Walter Wink's judgment of "the powers" (i.e., city). Wink finds the powers are good, the powers are fallen, the powers will be redeemed. See Wink, *Engaging the Powers*, 65–86.

[62]*Homo hortulanus* can be placed in juxtaposition to more familiar anthropological constructs such as *homo faber* and *homo economicus*. Whereas Marx construes the human person as "the maker" and liberal economic theory conceives of the person as a narrowly self-interested agent intent upon rationally optimizing his or her well-being, *homo hortulanus* defines the human in terms of serving and caring for the soil and all that comes from the soil.

[63]After all, an engineer could use his or her expertise and skill for the service and care of the world, as could a lawyer or baker. By way of contrast, a farmer could employ his or her knowledge toward the exhaustion of the land and the abuse of creation and inhabit the role of city-builder.

[64]Here, one might note that for Augustine the cities of God and "man" are described in terms of *civitas* and not *urbs*.

serve and care. In so doing, the human community introduces the disordering and fragmenting power of sin into the world. As the distortive and de-creational effects of sin amplify, the human person flees both God and soil, and builds a city that, in large part, stands against God's intention for creation. The human person, then, moves from cooperating with God's wisdom and imaging God to embracing a shrewdness that distorts and ultimately inverts *imago Dei*, while threatening creation itself. These themes are echoed in remarkable fashion in the second narrative cycle of Genesis (Gen 5–11, the second half of the book's primordial history).

The second cycle, constituted primarily by the stories of the Flood (Gen 6–9) and the Tower of Babel (Gen 11), serves to underscore the basic character of both God and the world, highlighting the steadfast righteousness of God and the intransigence of sin in history. As the story of the flood begins, we find the presence of sin in the generations following Cain has become so amplified that God regrets bringing creation into existence and moves to eradicate the world through flood. As the narrative unfolds, God calls on Noah to build an Ark in order to preserve a remnant of creation from the flood, so that the earth might ultimately flourish once again. With the flood, the world is reduced to a state of primordial chaos, recalling the opening verses of the book of Genesis (compare 1:2 and 7:11). bringing back chaos to the world cm

As the chaotic waters recede, a new creation emerges. Within the context of be this new creation, the narrator depicts Noah as a "new Adam." Noah is described Orders as a "man of the soil" (Gen 9:20), thereby recalling both Adam's name and again the vocation of gardener. The narrative then reinforces the vocational parallel. After God enters into covenant with Noah and with creation, Noah plants a vineyard (Gen 9:20). Thus, Noah appears in contradistinction to Cain who fled from the soil and God. Noah, a "righteous man" (Gen 6:9), images God's own righteousness in caring for creation. Initially, within the postdiluvian world, humanity reinhabits, at least partially, *homo hortulanus*; the possibility of a semblance of the threefold intimacy has been reopened.[65]

Nevertheless, within the story of Noah, the hopeful prospect of a new creation and a new humanity are quickly met with an echo of the fall. Noah, the new gardener, becomes drunk off the fruits of his labor, removes his clothing, and falls asleep in his tent, only to be discovered by his son Ham. As Timothy Stone observes, the events that ensue closely mirror the tragedy in Genesis 3. "Ham, seeing the nakedness of his father, shares his discovery with his brothers, as Eve shared the fruit with Adam. Like God covering Adam and Eve, the brothers cover the nakedness of their father. Awaking from his wine, Noah knew, as Adam and Eve knew their nakedness, what Ham had done. This results in a

---

[65]Again, this intimacy is at its best a simulacrum of what God intended. The new creation is not the idyllic garden. Now animals fear the human, who is no longer vegetarian.

the proun is original?

not God's image

divided family and a curse on Ham."[66] The promise of a new creation and the fulfillment of the vocation of gardener are once again derailed by the growing power of sin in the world. Indeed, in the second narrative cycle of Genesis, humanity's inability to respond faithfully to God's call soon culminates in the formation of another city—Babel.[67]

The construction of Babel in Genesis 11 echoes Cain's founding of the city in Genesis 4. Babel, whose very name evokes the Babylonian empire, is a city in Cain's own image. At the outset of the Babel narrative, the builders deign to "make a name" for themselves by constructing "a city and a tower with its top in the sky" (Gen 11:4). As commentators frequently note, within the biblical imagination, the heavens are most properly the province of God. Thus, like Adam and Eve grasping at the fruit of knowledge of good and evil, the builders embark on a program of self-divinization. Rather than serve, and thereby image, God, the builders will become "like God." Similarly, the construction of the city's tower also indicates the builders' repudiation of the soil. Recalling Cain's flight from the earth, the ascension of the builders distances them precisely from that for which God calls humanity to serve and care.[68]

The refusal of the builders to serve is heightened by the subtle associations of their project with that of the pharaoh of Exodus. The initial phrase spoken by the builders, "Come let us . . . ." is identical to the first words uttered by pharaoh as he ushers in his exploitative and repressive projects in Egypt. Likewise, the materials that the builders employ—mortar and brick—match those used in service of pharaoh. Given the character of pharaoh's projects in Exodus, these linkages intimate that the political ecology of Babel is organized not only by Babel's refusal to serve neighbor and earth but also its desire to dominate both.[69] Thus, the arc of the second narrative cycle of creation mirrors that of the first. Both cycles begin with humanity employing the tools of the gardener and culminate with the establishment of a fallen city, whose very existence is predicated on the sword and spear. The parallels between the first and second

---

[66]Timothy J. Stone, "Joseph in the Likeness of Adam: Narrative Echoes of the Fall," in *Genesis and Christian Theology*, 63–64.

[67]Thus, the two narrative cycles of primordial history unfold in the following parallel manner: Abyss→ Creation→Vocation→"Fall"→City.

[68]On this point see Ellen von Wolde, "The Earth Story as Presented by the Tower of Babel Narrative," in *The Earth Story in Genesis*, ed. Norman C. Habel and Shirley Wurst (Sheffield: Sheffield Academic, 2000), 150–51.

[69]Gustavo Gutiérrez finds that the "one language" of Babel—characteristic of the city that is frequently remarked upon by commentators—is itself a product of oppression. As he avers, "The single language is not . . . the expression of an idyllic unity of humankind, nor must it be an ideal yearned for; instead, it must be seen as the imposition of an empire. Such a language facilitates centralized power and the political yoke." For Gutiérrez, the one voice with which the builders speak is realized through drowning out the "cries of the poor" and rendering mute all those who would stand against the aims of the builders. The unity of Babel is achieved through the silencing of "the other."

narrative cycles of Genesis's primordial history underline an essential insight: while God desires the world to flourish in accordance with God's wisdom, humanity continually embraces a shrewdness that fractures peace and threatens the life of the world.

THE PEOPLE OF GOD
AND THE VOCATION OF GARDENER

Of course, the builders of Babel are unable to sustain their project of distorted divinization. Instead, at the conclusion of the narrative, God reduces their work to rubble and scatters the inhabitants of the city throughout the earth while confusing their tongues.[70] Nonetheless, God remains faithful to the covenant with Noah. Despite the appearance of Babel, a rebellious city aimed at organizing the "whole world" in accord with its own purposes (Gen 11:1), God does not return creation to the abyss. Rather, divine judgment is limited to the city (the "global system," not the earth). God continues to work to redeem creation. Now, however, the obstinacy of sin in the world leads God to take a new tack.

With primordial history (Gen 1–11) serving as the backdrop, the story of Genesis now tightens its focus, turning, in its remaining chapters (Gen 12–50) to consider God's dealings with a particular people. This people, represented by Abraham, Sarah, and their descendants, enters into covenant with God. They commit themselves to trust in God and live in accordance with God's wisdom. Likewise, God commits to bless them and, through them, the world. Brueggemann describes this shift in the scope of the Genesis story, as well as the import of God's call to Abraham and Sarah, writing: "The one who calls the worlds into being now makes a second call. This call is specific. Its object is identifiable in history. . . . The purpose of the call is to fashion an alternative community in creation gone awry, to embody in human history the power of the blessing."[71] Thus Brueggemann concludes, "The call to Sarah and Abraham has to do not simply with the forming of Israel but with the re-forming of creation, the transforming of the nations."[72] Within the symbolic framework of Genesis, then, the people of God are called to inhabit the vocation of gardener; they are covenanted with God to actively presence *imago Dei* in the world so that all of creation might ultimately flourish in accordance with God's wisdom.

The association of the people of God with the vocation of gardener is presented initially by way of contrast. After dispersing the inhabitants of Babel,

---

[70]Gutiérrez finds in God's action a blessing for those silenced by Babel's singular language. See "Theological Language: The Fullness of Silence," *DoP,* 186–208.

[71]Brueggemann, *Genesis*, 105.

[72]Ibid.

God speaks to Abraham:

[handwritten: has Gods permission to build]

[handwritten margin: God is a builder here]

> Go from your country and your kindred and your father's house to the land that I will show you. I will make of you a great nation, and I will bless you, and make your name great, so that you will be a blessing. I will bless those who bless you, and the one who curses you I will curse; and in you all the families of the earth shall be blessed. Abram went as the Lord directed him. (Gen 12:1–4)

[handwritten margin: tree of knowledge tied to instrumented reason]

Abraham is immediately juxtaposed to the city-builders of Babel. Abraham exhibits an openness to God's call that is not present in the actions of the builders who excluded God from their project. Accordingly, where the builders were intent to secure themselves in one place, Abraham leaves behind his home, trusting in divine providence.[73] Ultimately, where the builders were determined to make a name for themselves (in accordance with the fruit of the tree of knowledge), Abraham allows God to make his name great (in accordance with the fruit of the tree of life). Thus, Abraham is defined in contradistinction to those who would counter the human vocation. Dahlberg observes that the narratives of Abraham, Sarah, and their descendants in Genesis record a gradual reordering of creation through their ongoing relationship to God.[74]

[handwritten between lines: Sin of pride become god-like]

[handwritten margin: how intrinsically is sin the intent matters]

Nonetheless, the faithfulness of the people of God is halting, and their reordering of creation is far from linear. In the stories of "the patriarchs," the people of God appear as susceptible to the power of sin as the world from which they are called to live in contrast.[75] As with Noah and his sons, the fall and its effects echo throughout the lives of God's people in Genesis. This continued resonance is evidenced, for example, in Abraham and Sarah's dealings with Hagar. When Abraham and Sarah become doubtful that God will bestow the blessing upon them, they seek to acquire the blessing for themselves (in effect, seeking to make a name for themselves). Sarah gives Abraham her servant Hagar to impregnate so that Abraham might secure his future lineage. Grasping at security and exaltation in a manner that recalls the story of the fall, Abraham uses Hagar as an instrument, and they produce a son, Ishmael.[76] As in Genesis 3, however, things fall apart. Sarah becomes wracked with jealousy at Ishmael's birth and effectively drives Hagar and her son to the wilderness, presumably to die. In this episode Abraham and Sarah invert the praxis of gardener, reducing Hagar

---

[73]Note the parallel here with Augustine's reading of Cain and Abel in *City of God.*

[74]Dahlberg, "On Recognizing the Unity of Genesis," 362.

[75]"Contrast," here should not be reified or overextended. As noted above, the difference between the wisdom of God and the cunningness of the serpent can at times appear as a polarity and at other times be proximate to the point of enmeshment. This fact does not signal relativism. Rather, it underscores the need for careful and ongoing discernment in light of the word of God.

[76]On this point, see Stone, "Joseph in the Likeness of Adam," 64–65.

to the status of nonperson—an object of *libido dominandi*, whose body and labor can be cast aside at the whim of the couple.[77] God, in contrast, attends to the marginalized and vulnerable Hagar and Ishmael, working to sustain their lives even while remaining faithful to the covenant.[78]

The tenuous and fluid relationship between God's people and *homo hortulanus* continues to be elucidated in the subsequent narratives of the patriarchs. The prosperity of Abraham's son, Isaac, leads him into conflict with the Philistines so that he is cast off of his land. He later quarrels with neighbors over the rights to well water.[79] More striking is the "trickster" character of Isaac's son, Jacob. At one point, Jacob is described as a "moral man" (Gen 25:27).[80] However, he is also depicted in ways that recall the serpent in the garden—he grasps at his brother's heel (Gen 25:26)[81] and is identified as a "smooth man" (Gen 27:11).[82] Through deception, he steals his father's blessing from his brother Esau. Jacob's duplicitous procurement of blessing entrenches a violent sibling rivalry between him and Esau, and threatens to estrange him from the land. As with Abraham's embodiment of faithfulness, the realization of Jacob's moral uprightness requires a process of conversion, one that only partially repairs the damage that results from his deceitfulness.[83]

The stories of Abraham, Isaac, and Jacob paint ambiguous portraits of the character of God's people. In a world disordered by sin, which distorts and impairs humanity's love of God, earth, and neighbor, the people of God are called to renew creation through inhabiting *imago Dei*. The people of God's inhabitation of *homo hortulanus* is intended "to repair the world," healing human relationships with God, neighbor, and earth. For this purpose, they are

---

[77]On the other hand, Abraham and Sarah later "welcome the stranger" into their household (Gen 18), in stark contrast to Sodom and Gomorrah's exploitation of vulnerable sojourners (Gen 19). On this point, see Wes Howard-Brook, *"Come Out, My People!": God's Call out of Empire in the Bible and Beyond* (Maryknoll, NY: Orbis Books, 2010), 58–65. The difference between Abraham and Sarah's actions in these two stories underscores their real but fraught faithfulness to their covenant with God.

[78]Delores Williams's profound theological-ethical reflection on the figures of Hagar and Ishmael, of course, casts into sharp relief the limits of the liberationist paradigm. See Delores Williams, *Sisters in the Wilderness: The Challenge of Womanist God-Talk* (Maryknoll, NY: Orbis Books, 1993), 187–203. Liberation theology (inclusive of eco-liberationist discourse) must be mindful of the limits of human agency and respectful of the ways in which the sin of the world can undercut the agential power of those who cry out for a more humane world. At the same time, and informed by an awareness of its own limitations, liberation theology must continue to denounce the sin of the world and announce the coming of another.

[79]Underscoring the connection between neighbor and earth, it is only when Abimelech, the king of the Philistines, seeks out Isaac to reconcile with him, that Isaac's own well begins to produce water (Gen 26:12–32).

[80]See Brown's translation, *Ethos of the Cosmos*, 195.

[81]Compare with Genesis 3:15.

[82]See Brown's translation, *Ethos of the Cosmos*, 196.

[83]Ibid., 195–200.

covenanted to God. Nonetheless, the effects of sin resound in the lives of God's people. Their witness to the ways of God's wisdom is a halting struggle. They experience and are often agents of estrangement from God, neighbor, and earth. The fall and its effects resound through their collective story evidenced by various attempts at procuring their own exaltation, the strife between siblings, and their continued alienation from the land.

JOSEPH THE RIGHTEOUS, THE VOCATION OF GARDENER, AND THE FATE OF THE CITY

Against the background of both the faith and failure of God's people, the final narrative in Genesis is of particular importance with regard to the fate of *imago Dei* and the vocation of gardener. This narrative centers on the figure of Joseph, Jacob's youngest son, who is sold into slavery by his brothers and later imprisoned in Egypt, only to rise to prominence within pharaoh's court. Joseph's status within the book of Genesis in unique. Unlike his forebears, Joseph does not grasp at power, nor does a lust for domination control his action. Rather than attempting to make a name for himself, Joseph steadfastly abides in the wisdom of God and faithfully enacts the praxis of the gardener. Through Joseph's faithfulness, God works to repair the damage wrought by sin in the world, thereby reconciling humanity, in an anticipatory manner to God, neighbor, and earth. Joseph's wise actions, therefore, represent a proleptic reversal of Adam's folly. In order to understand Joseph in this manner, I consider three elements of the narrative: Joseph's encounter with Potiphar's wife, Joseph's relationship with his brothers, and Joseph's land reforms during the famine in Egypt.

Joseph, Potiphar, and Potiphar's Wife

As noted, the narrative of "the fall" resounds throughout the book of Genesis. In the Joseph story, one detects an echo of the fall in the scene detailing Joseph's life within the house of Potiphar. This scene provides a hermeneutical key to understanding the character and actions of Joseph.

After Joseph's brothers sell him into slavery, he is taken to Egypt and purchased by Potiphar, the chief steward of pharaoh. We are told that "the Lord was with Joseph" (Gen 39:2), and he quickly gains Potiphar's favor and rises to prominence within the Egyptian's household. Potiphar places his entire household under Joseph's oversight, withholding only sexual relations with his wife from Joseph (Gen 39:9). This setting formally resembles that of Genesis 2. In the garden of Eden—the *oikos* of God—Adam is the servant appointed by God to attend to the affairs of the garden so that creation might continue to flourish. Within that context, God withholds one thing from Adam, instructing the primordial human not to eat the fruit of the tree of knowledge. Joseph, then, is like Adam. Both are the chief servants within their master's respective households, and both have a single stricture placed upon them.[84]

Within the Joseph narrative, Joseph's situation quickly becomes complicated. Potiphar's wife, struck by Joseph's physical beauty, begins to make sexual advances toward him. Joseph, however, rebuffs these advances, saying to her: "How . . . could I commit so great a wrong and thus stand condemned before God?" (Gen 39:9). Later, Potiphar's wife intensifies her attempts to seduce Joseph, grasping him by the sleeve of his robe, and saying to him "Lie with me!" (39:12).[85] At this, Joseph flees, as Potiphar's wife pulls off his robe, leaving him naked. Subsequently, Potiphar's wife accuses Joseph of attempting to rape her, and he is taken and imprisoned within an Egyptian jail, presumably left to die.[86]

The initial parallels between Adam and Joseph serve to highlight the profound difference between their dispositions and actions. Whereas Adam's will is seized by pride and a lust for domination, leading him to transgress the limits placed on him by God, Joseph, whose concern is to remain faithful to God, adopts a posture of restraint.[87] The contrast between Adam and Joseph is emphasized in the shifting appearances of these two figures. Whereas Adam goes from naked to clothed after eating of the fruit, Joseph—in resisting the temptation to partake in the "forbidden food"—goes from clothed to naked.[88] In this case, Joseph's nakedness recalls the prelapsarian innocence of Adam. As Timothy Stone comments, "Like Adam, Joseph is tempted, loses his position, and is judged; unlike Adam, Joseph does not yield to the temptation and is innocent of wrong." Thus, Stone concludes: "Joseph is *like* Adam and the others in fall stories in Genesis, yet he overcomes their folly."[89]

Joseph is faithful to God

---

[84]See Stone, "Joseph in the Likeness of Adam," 66. "Food" often acted as a euphemism for sexual relations. Thus Joseph is tempted with a forbidden food.

[85]The manner in which Genesis frequently depicts women as beguiling temptresses—a depiction that, in part, has deformed the Christian imagination in patriarchal and misogynistic ways—is obviously problematic. In interpreting the story of Joseph and Potiphar's wife, it is better to associate Potiphar's wife with "imperial power" than with "woman." As Brueggemann observes, the lust of Potiphar's wife "suggests the characteristic imperial attempt to generate security in manipulative ways. The ones who have royal power are tempted to imagine they are beyond the reach either of the Torah or of common sense (wisdom)." See Brueggemann, *Genesis*, 314.

[86]It is profoundly unfortunate that a scene describing a false accusation of sexual assault plays as prominent a role as it does within the Joseph narrative. While we must deal with the text as it is, we should not take this report to be representative of reports of assault in history. Within the world of the text, it is better to interpret this false accusation in light of the power differential between Potiphar's wife and Joseph. Here, Joseph is actually the more vulnerable of the two figures.

[87]One can also note, here, that love of God is bound up with love of neighbor. Joseph's transgression against God would have also entailed a transgression against both Potiphar and Potiphar's wife.

[88]Stone, "Joseph in the Likeness of Adam," 66.

[89]Ibid., 67.

The story of Joseph and Potiphar's wife suggests that, unlike Adam, Noah, or even Abraham, Joseph remains steadfast in his faithfulness to God. Within the symbolic logic of Genesis, Joseph is uniquely disassociated with the shrewdness of the tree of knowledge and, by implication, uniquely allied with the tree of life, the wisdom of God, and the vocation of gardener.[90] In light of this, and given the interconnectedness between the loves of God, neighbor, and earth, it is reasonable to expect that Joseph's faithfulness to God would effectively promote the healing of the human/neighbor and human/earth relationships. Indeed, in all of the Joseph narrative God is working through Joseph's faithfulness to reverse the effects of the fall, reconciling humanity to itself and to the earth. The former is made especially clear in Joseph's dealings with his brothers.

Joseph and His Brothers

The narrative thread of Joseph's relationship to his brothers interweaves the entirety of Genesis 37–50, providing the longest arc of any story in Genesis.[91] The story begins by noting the hatred and resentment that Joseph's brothers bear toward him for being favored by their father, Jacob, despite Joseph's status as the youngest son. This animosity leads the brothers (with the exception of Reuben) to plot to murder their favored sibling. When Joseph approaches his brothers while they are tending to their sheep, the brothers seize Joseph, strip him of his robe, and throw him into a pit to die.[92] Subsequently, the brothers sit down and eat as Joseph languishes in the pit before them. The act of eating underscores the malice that Joseph's brothers bear toward him. As Gary Anderson observes, "In the Psalter, to eat and drink in the presence of the demise of another is to put oneself in the role of the 'enemy.'"[93]

Nonetheless, providence intervenes on Joseph's behalf. A caravan of traders passes by the brothers as they eat, and, at the behest of Judah, the brothers decide to profit by selling Joseph into slavery rather than allowing him to perish in the pit. The traders take Joseph to Egypt where he is purchased by Potiphar. After selling Joseph to the traders, the brothers send word to Jacob that Joseph has been killed by a wild animal. From the outset the theme of sinful and fratricidal

---

[90]W. Lee Humphreys argues that, in Genesis, Joseph is presented as the ideal "wise courtier." See Humphreys, *Joseph and His Family: A Literary Study* (Columbia: University of South Carolina, 1988), 139–51. Read canonically, the figure of Joseph is consonant with that of the Tree of Life.

[91]Brueggemann finds that Joseph's negotiations with his brothers parallel his negotiations with the power of empire. See Brueggemann, *Genesis*, 297.

[92]Gary Andersen points out that the details included by the narrator regarding the well—that it was deep and without water—offer a clear indicator that the brothers intend for Joseph to die in the pit. See Gary A. Anderson, "Joseph and the Passion of Our Lord," in *The Art of Reading Scripture*, ed. Ellen F. Davis and Richard B. Hays (Grand Rapids, MI: Eerdmans, 2003), 209.

[93]Ibid.

enmity hangs over the narrative of Joseph. Whereas the story of Potiphar's wife recalls the fall in Genesis 3, the actions of Joseph's brothers recall Cain's murder of Abel in Genesis 4. As with the fall, the violence of Cain continues to resound throughout the book of Genesis.

I have already observed that Joseph, after initially flourishing within Potiphar's house, is, for a second time lowered into a pit of death—he is unjustly imprisoned in pharaoh's jail. Once more, however, Joseph is liberated from death. When pharaoh hears of Joseph's adeptness at interpreting dreams, he calls for Joseph to be brought before him. Joseph's interpretation of pharaoh's dream, in which Joseph warns of a coming famine, impresses the ruler. Soon, pharaoh tasks Joseph with overseeing the affairs of Egypt as it prepares to face the looming famine. Whereas, in the vignette of Potiphar and his wife, Joseph was second only to Potiphar in overseeing the courtier's household, now Joseph is second only to pharaoh in overseeing the governance of the entire Egyptian nation.[94] *increasing his role*

In his role as Egypt's administrator, Joseph once again encounters his brothers. At this point, nine years have passed since Joseph ascended within pharaoh's court. The brothers, who are suffering the effects of the famine, sojourn to Egypt in order to buy food from pharaoh. The brothers appear before Joseph but do not recognize him. Joseph, who identifies his murderous brethren immediately, does not divulge his identity. Instead, Joseph sets out a number of tests for his brothers, aimed at eliciting conversion on the part of his brothers. These tests culminate in Judah offering himself as a slave to Joseph in exchange for the freedom of their brother Benjamin who Joseph has claimed as a servant for himself. This marks a striking reversal.

Judah, the brother who first recommends selling Joseph into slavery now offers himself as a slave to liberate his brother. In short, then, Joseph's wise dealings with his brothers lead to a reversal of their fratricidal hatred.

This reversal is further underscored in Joseph's final interactions with his brothers in the book of Genesis. As the narrative draws to its conclusion, Jacob dies. The brothers, who at this point are aware of Joseph's true identity, begin to worry. "Suppose Joseph has been nursing a grudge against us," they say, "and now most certainly will pay us back in full for all the wrong we did him!" (Gen 50:15). The brothers go to Joseph fearfully, asking for forgiveness, and offering themselves to Joseph as servants (Gen 50:17–18). The same brothers who at the outset of the story had rebelled against God and neighbor now offer to serve the figure in Genesis who conforms most fully to God's wisdom. Joseph's response to his brothers' plea is noteworthy, "Do not fear," Joseph replies. "Can

Joseph is image of
restoration of vocation from sin

---

[94]Stone thus finds that the episode in Potiphar's house foreshadows Joseph's experience in Pharaoh's house. See Stone, "Joseph in the Likeness of Adam," 68.

I take the place of God?"[95] Unlike Adam, the builders of Babel, and Abraham in his relationship with Hagar, Joseph does not grasp at "becoming like God." In a manner that is consistent with the depiction of Joseph in the narrative of Potiphar's wife, Joseph is revealed as the one who, in Genesis, most fully inhabits *imago Dei*. In this instance Joseph's righteousness takes the form of forgiveness as Joseph pardons his brothers for their sin against him. Anderson highlights the significance of this final act of Joseph, by emphasizing the fact that the brothers were right to expect punishment from Joseph. He writes, "The brothers' hatred and envy of Joseph is crucial to the story as a whole . . . the beneficence of Joseph, his providing for his family, and overlooking the sin of his brothers, loses its gravitas if it is not calibrated against the *expectation of retributive justice*."[96] The "violence of Cain," inflicted on Joseph at the beginning of the narrative, is finally overcome, not with retribution, but with Joseph's restraint, which leaves open the possibility of reestablishing the *shalom* of intimacy.[97] Whereas Cain's fratricidal enmity (an enmity that, like the fall, echoes throughout the book of Genesis) rends the bonds of fraternal communion, Joseph's steadfast inhabitation of *imago Dei* (the vocation of gardener) restores the possibility of communion.

Joseph's Land Reforms

The restoration of intimacy between the sons of Jacob bears witness to the manner in which the wisdom of God, through Joseph, begins to reverse the effects of the fall. Within the Joseph narrative, the reversal of the fall's effects is observable not only with regard to the transformation of the human/neighbor relationship (i.e., Joseph and his brothers) but also with regard to the transformation of the human/earth relationship. This latter transformation, which also represents a form of reconciliation, can be discerned in the land reforms Joseph undertakes during the famine that plagues Egypt and the surrounding lands. This claim is controversial. Scholars are often highly critical of Joseph's reforms, discerning within these reforms a shrewdness on Joseph's part that more closely approximates the cunning of the serpent than the wisdom of God.

As the land reform narrative (Gen 47:13–26) begins, the famine that Joseph

---

[95]Joseph's rhetorical question, then, is particularly poignant. Joseph, abiding within the limits appropriate to God's wisdom, does not attempt to take the place of God as Adam and the builders before him. As Stone writes, "In sum, Joseph resists temptation, living under the authority of God by ruling *for* him [*sic*]—not *instead* of him [*sic*]" (ibid., 70, italics are Stone's). Nonetheless, if Joseph so chose, he could utilize political power to take, in effect, the place of God. The danger of a distortive self-divinization accompanies all manifestations of power.

[96]Gary A. Anderson, Christian Doctrine and the Old Testament: Theology in the Service of Exegesis (Grand Rapids, MI: Baker, 2017), 88.

[97]Again, this is not the "cheap grace" of reconciliation without conversion. Joseph has carefully observed that a metanoia has taken place within the hearts and actions of his brothers.

predicted has overtaken Egypt and Canaan, and the land languishes. In the midst of this crisis, "the Egyptians" come to Joseph, crying out to him for grain so that they might eat. In return for grain, Joseph demands that the Egyptians give their livestock to pharaoh. The following year, the Egyptians, now in corpse-like condition, approach Joseph once more. Claiming that they are unable to hide anything from Joseph, the Egyptians again cry out to him, only this time they ask for seed, so "that we may survive and not perish, and that our land may not turn into a waste" (Gen 47:19). The Egyptians then offer all of their lands as well their bodies in servitude to pharaoh.[98] Joseph accepts this offer, acquiring for pharaoh the lands of the Egyptians and the Egyptians themselves. Joseph gives them seed for "sowing" the land and requires the Egyptians to double the tax to pharaoh that they had previously paid. The Egyptians' last proclamation is one of praise: "You have saved our lives!" (Gen 47:25).

For obvious reasons, this narrative troubles interpreters who might otherwise be inclined to look favorably upon Joseph. Miguel De La Torre, for example, finds these lines "disturbing, for they provide a portrait of the Most High's servant heartlessly appropriating all of the land's resources for the privileged few at the expense of the many."[99] Sharing De La Torre's position, J. Gerald Janzen concludes a scathing critique of Joseph's reforms by observing that "long before there arose a new king over Egypt who knew not Joseph (Exod. 1:8), there arose a new Joseph over Egypt who had all too successfully forgotten his painful past, and in so doing had forgotten also the old Joseph."[100] The "old Joseph" was, of course, the faithful and righteous Joseph. Along similar lines, Leon Kass views Joseph's land reforms as the cruel act of a technocrat in the service of a despot. Thus, according to Kass, "Joseph's sagacity is technical and managerial, not moral and political. He is long on forethought and planning but short on understanding the souls of men. Shrewd about things, but dumb about the human heart."[101] It appears, therefore, that within the book of

---

[98]Notably, the Hebrew term used to describe the Egyptian status at the conclusion of the land reforms is the derivative of *'ābad*. This is commonly translated in terms of slavery. The NAB translation is typical: "Take us and our land in exchange for food, and we will become Pharaoh's slaves and our land his property" (47:19). The Hebrew, however, *'ābad* can be translated as either "slave" or "servant." As Carol Meyers writes, "Biblical Hebrew does not have a vocabulary that accounts for the different kinds and conditions of servitude that we recognize in the language of various genres of biblical literature, and the specific kind of labor must generally be discerned from context." See Carol Meyers, *Exodus* (New York: Cambridge University Press, 2005), 35. At any rate, the reference to *'ābad* followed immediately by reference to seed and care for the soil recalls Genesis 1–2, a point I develop further below.

[99]Miguel De La Torre, *Genesis: Belief: A Theological Interpretation* (Louisville, KY: Westminster, 2011), 328.

[100]J. Gerald Janzen, *Genesis 12–50: Abraham and All of the Families of the Earth* (Grand Rapids, MI: Eerdmans, 1993), 182.

[101]Leon R. Kass, *The Beginning of Wisdom: Reading Genesis* (Chicago: University of Chicago Press, 2007), 633–34.

Genesis even the figure of Joseph is seduced by the shrewdness of the serpent. Nonetheless, it is my contention that these appraisals of Joseph's reforms, though understandable, miss the mark.

A number of interrelated points can be raised in advancing a defense of Joseph's land reforms. First, it must be acknowledged that within the biblical imagination, "Egypt," like Babel before it, is paradigmatic of the fallen "city"— that is, the domination system. On this same account, then, "the Egyptians" can be associated typologically with the builders of Babel, those who have made a name for themselves by refusing to serve and, instead, dominating the soil and all that comes from the soil. "Egypt," is not a neutral background against which the morality play of Joseph's land reforms is set. To the contrary, Egypt symbolically represents the corporate rejection of God's wisdom and the organization of a political ecology around the tree of knowledge of good and evil—a political ecology of domination. It is against this background Joseph's actions must be judged.[102]

Second, the famine itself witnesses to the disordered character of Egypt's political ecology.[103] Within the complex character of the biblical imagination, famine is associated with divine judgment against human action.[104] The description of the land as "languishing" at the outset of the famine in the Joseph narrative recalls the opening chapters of Genesis when the soil is cursed because of humanity's refusal to serve. In view of these connections, the descent into famine testifies against the political ecology that Egypt imposes on the world. Westermann, for example, finds that Joseph's initial pronouncement of the coming famine functions "unmistakably" as a "prophetic proclamation of woe."[105] This is telling because such proclamations are intended to give voice to divine judgment. Along these lines, Brueggemann argues that the whole of the initial exchange between pharaoh and Joseph delegitimizes the power of the empire and reveals its impotency in the face of God's action.[106] Indeed, Brueggemann finds that the threat of famine anticipates the plagues in Exodus.

Third, it should be observed that in the course of Joseph's reforms, the effect

---

[102] Against this point, Theodore Hiebert argues that "the image of Egypt in the Joseph traditions is overwhelmingly positive. Above all, Egypt is recognized as the savior of Israel whose very existence was threatened by famine (45:5–8; 50:20–21)" (Theodore Hiebert, "Genesis," in *Theological Bible Commentary*, ed. Gail R. O'Day and David L. Petersen [Louisville, KY: Westminster John Knox, 2009], 24). While this is true, Egypt only comes to function as a refuge under Joseph's directive, which represents a radical reversal of the established order. See also the point that immediately follows, regarding the function of Joseph's warning to pharaoh. Joseph's prophetic interpretation of pharaoh's dream implicitly casts Egypt in a negative light.

[103] Brown finds that, in Genesis, Egypt is understood as "an inversion of Eden." See Brown, *Ethos of the Cosmos*, 192.

[104] See J. A. Motyer and F. F. Bruce, "Famine," in *New Bible Dictionary*, ed. J. D. Douglas (Downers Grove, IL: Intervarsity Press, 1996), 364.

[105] Claus Westermann, *Genesis 37–50* (Minneapolis: Augsburg, 1986), 91.

[106] See Brueggemann, *Genesis*, 325–35.

of the curse on the land is reversed. As just noted, at the beginning of the land reform narrative the land is languishing and the life of the world is threatened. The direness of the situation appears equal to that of the primordial flood in the Noah narrative.[107] However, by the close of the narrative, the soil once again becomes generative and the life of the world is preserved as a result of Joseph's wise actions.[108] As Brueggemann observes, "The narrative contrasts the futility of Egyptian technique and Joseph's capacity to turn the earth to life-giving possibility. Before Joseph (vv. 1–8), there is imperial death. After Joseph (vv. 46–57), there is life."[109]

The criticisms of Joseph's reforms, of course, do not focus on his dealings with the soil as such, but rather on his interactions with "the Egyptians." As we have seen, Joseph allows this group to be reduced by the famine to a position of servitude and, subsequently, appropriates their land, placing them and their land under pharaoh's control. It is these actions that critics find troubling. However, these appraisals of Joseph's actions are based on readings that do not fully attend to the power dynamics at play in the scene. When these power dynamics are brought to the fore, a remarkably different understanding of Joseph's actions emerge.

In negatively evaluating the tactics that Joseph employs with the Egyptians, critics are consistent in conceiving of "the Egyptians" as powerless victims facing the dual threats of famine and imperial coercion. However, as I have already noted, it is doubtful that "the Egyptians" should be understood in these terms. Rather, "the Egyptians" refer to those who have *benefited* from the coercive power of the Egyptian empire—they are the proud, those who refuse to serve. The cry of the Egyptians, then, is remarkable. Suffering the effect of God's judgment upon Egypt's fallen political ecology, a political ecology that they have been complicit in preserving, the Egyptians now assume the position of supplicants. *a deserved punishment?*

More striking still, is the final part of the Egyptians' second request to Joseph, "only give us seed, that we may survive and not perish, and that our land may not turn into a waste." The Egyptians—the "builders," as it were—beg Joseph for seed so that they might come to inhabit the vocation of gardener. The people most emblematic of humanity's refusal to serve, now offer themselves as servants, requesting seed so that the land (which is intended by God to be a garden) does not become a wasteland. Joseph's struggle with the Egyptians in the midst of divine judgment elicits a profound conversion on the part of the builders, those who had dominated the soil and all that comes from the soil now

fulfilling God's vocation

---

[107]See Dahlberg, "On Recognizing the Unity of Genesis," 364.
[108]See Eric Lowenthal, *The Joseph Narrative in Genesis* (New York: Ktav, 1973), 127.
[109]Brueggemann, *Genesis*, 329.

inhabit the vocation of gardener.[110] Far from acting as a cruel tyrant, Joseph uses the authority that has been granted him in the service of God's wisdom, allowing creation to flourish once more. At the conclusion of the narrative the Egyptians themselves acknowledge this, proclaiming to Joseph, "You have saved our lives!"[111]

While inducing metanoia on the part of the Egyptians, Joseph's actions also sustain the lives of those inhabiting the lands surrounding Egypt. The verse immediately following the land reform narrative observes that "Israel" comes to flourish under Joseph's wise shepherding. Although Kass judges this negatively as Joseph working to "take care of his own," it is better to interpret this as evidence that Joseph has not only humbled those who had exalted themselves but also exalted the lowly.[112] Joseph's actions, rather than being associated with those of a cruel tyrant, in fact, recall both Mary's Magnificat prayer in the gospel of Luke and the Beatitudes in both Matthew and Luke's gospels (see Chapter 4). Thus Joseph's actions at the conclusion of the book of Genesis align well with the vocation of gardener first introduced in the opening chapters of the book. Dahlberg notes that in Joseph "we see that he does on a grand scale what Adam was created to do but did not back in the beginning."[113] Under Joseph's guidance, the world is being repaired.

Perhaps the strongest argument against the interpretation of Joseph's land reforms, is that the Egyptians do not give themselves or their lands to YHWH but to pharaoh. Thus, Joseph dismantles the Egyptian oligarchy only to consolidate power even more absolutely under pharaoh. Although this is undoubtedly true, it is essential to acknowledge that this pharaoh stands as an antitype to the pharaoh of Exodus. The pharaoh that Joseph encounters is one who fears God. If Joseph's initial warning to pharaoh of the oncoming famine functions as a prophetic "Woe to you!" then it must be admitted that the pharaoh of

---

[110]Thomas Brodie captures the relationship between Genesis 47 and Genesis 2 well: "The concept of land is central to Genesis, and Joseph's acquisition of the land is part of a much larger pattern about possessing the land and serving it. The idea of serving (*'ābad*) the ground (*adama*) or land first appears in Genesis as something very positive, in the Garden of Eden (Gen. 2:5, 15). So, when Joseph acquires the ground (*adama*) and induces the people into being servants (*ebed*; 47:19;21), his action has two levels of meaning. At one level it is a subjection to servitude. At another, it is a recovery of an aspect of the primordial human relationship to the ground." Thomas Brodie, *Genesis as Dialogue: A Literary, Historical, and Theological Commentary* (Oxford: Oxford University Press, 2001), 399. While Brodie connects Genesis 47 to Genesis 2, the specific reference to "seed" suggests that Genesis 1 might also be in view of the redactor.

[111]The proclamation of the Egyptians is consonant with the author's use of *nahal* in 47:17. When Joseph acquires their livestock, he then "shepherds" (*nahal*) them through the year. This verb has a life-giving connotation that, indeed, evokes the God of life throughout scripture (see Ex 15:13; Ps 23:2, 31:3; and Is 40:11, 49:10).

[112]Eric Lowenthal finds that Joseph's reforms function specifically to weaken the powerful while uplifting the poor. See Lowenthal, *Joseph Narrative in Genesis*, 124–27.

[113]Dahlberg, "On Recognizing the Unity of Genesis," 364.

Genesis responds rightly. This pharaoh displays nothing of the imperial hubris or hardness of heart that one might expect of the ruler of Egypt.[114] Instead, he elevates Joseph, who at that point is the archetypal "nonperson," to oversee the ordering of pharaoh's *oikos*. Thus, the pharaoh of the Joseph narrative bears a stronger likeness to the king of Nineveh—the king who hears Jonah's warning and calls on his people to repent—than to his counterpart in Exodus. Although it is true that this appraisal of pharaoh's character does little to appease the way in which Joseph's consolidation of power offends contemporary democratic sensibilities, Joseph's actions should not be judged by these sensibilities in any straightforward manner. Instead, within the narrative logic of Genesis, the fundamental point of Joseph's consolidation of power is that the political ecology of Egypt is now organized by one who fears God.[115] This is good news for both the earth and the poor.[116]

Nonetheless, Joseph should not be entirely acquitted with regard to his interplay with pharaoh and the Egyptians. Audre Lorde's oft-cited assertion appears particularly pertinent here. "The master's tools," writes Lorde, "will never dismantle the master's house. They may allow us temporarily to beat him at his own game, but they will never enable us to bring about genuine change."[117] Joseph's discerning actions induce the Egyptians to take up the tools of the gardener, thereby dramatically reshaping Egypt's political ecology. However, this inducement is underwritten by Joseph's own access to the coercive power of pharaoh. Joseph dramatically reorganizes the master's house, but to do so he utilizes the sword and spear of imperial power.[118] Thus, while the *oikos* of Egypt is reorganized, its foundation remains intact. To use another familiar

[114]Consider the contrast between pharaoh's reaction to Joseph and the response of the princes in Zedekiah's court to Jeremiah's warning. Whereas Joseph is elevated, Jeremiah is thrown into a pit (Jer 38:1–6).

[115]Lindsay Wilson finds that "there are good grounds to believe that the acquisition of all the land is a way of bringing it all under the wise administration of Joseph." See Lindsay Wilson, *Joseph Wise and Otherwise: The Intersection of Wisdom and Covenant in Genesis 37–50* (Waynesboro, GA: Paternoster, 2004), 194.

[116]Without transgressing into unwarranted eisigesis, we can note that there is nothing particularly problematic with pharaoh doubling the taxes of the gardeners. Of course, this increased revenue might be used for the purposes of self-aggrandizement. However, it might also be employed to attend to the welfare of Egypt's most vulnerable. Our knowledge of the pharaoh of Exodus should not inform our presumptions of the pharaoh of Genesis.

[117]Audre Lorde, "The Master's Tools Will Never Dismantle the Master's House," in *Sister Outsider: Essays and Speeches* (Berkeley, CA: Crossing, 2007), 110–14. It bears noting that Lorde originally coins this phrase in criticizing monolithic approaches to feminism.

[118]It is telling that Joseph states that he has "acquired" the land and the bodies of the Egyptians for pharaoh. "Acquire" is another of the meanings associated with Cain's name, thus bearing a negative connotation. However, more positively, the term also suggests "redemption." The tensive ambiguity of these two associations should be maintained. Joseph has redeemed the people, returning them to the vocation of gardener, to a closer approximation of *imago Dei*. However, he has done so through the wise use of a coercive power that can be repurposed in accordance with an ethos of domination, which is precisely what occurs at the beginning of Exodus.

biblical metaphor, Joseph places new wine into an old wineskin. Moreover, the narrative tells us that Joseph and the Hebrews remain in pharaoh's house; flourishing though they may within the *oikos* of a pharaoh who knows Joseph, the well-being of the people of God is left in a precarious position. None of this invalidates the wisdom of Joseph's reforms. If a tree is to be judged by its fruit, the final proclamation of the Egyptians links Joseph with the tree at Eden's true center—"You have saved our lives!" However, the critical observations do qualify the absolute righteousness of Joseph's reforms while also bounding them temporally.[119] Joseph "has beaten Egypt at its own game," but, as one finds in Exodus, this victory is fleeting.

Nonetheless, Joseph's actions to preserve the life of a world threatened by famine continue the trope of Joseph as an antitype of Adam. In Potiphar's house, when Joseph is tempted by the power of lust to transgress the boundaries of his position, he exercises an ethic of limitation and remains faithful to God. Faced with the temptation to exact revenge on his murderous brothers, Joseph, instead, induces their conversion and reconciles with them. Likewise, after receiving the authority to oversee the affairs of Egypt, Joseph does not utilize his power for self-aggrandizement but rather to induce the conversion of the Egyptians, shepherding them through a process that transforms their collective identity from city-builder to gardener. From a Christian perspective, then, the figure of Joseph bears a far greater resemblance to the final Adam—Jesus Christ, the wisdom of God—than he does to the first Adam.[120]

If Joseph represents the human person redeemed in a proleptic and partial manner, then the same is true of Egypt in a corporate sense. At the conclusion of Genesis, Egypt comes to represent the partially and tenuously redeemed city. Whereas Enoch (the city of Cain) and Babel epitomize the city ordered in accordance with the cunningness proper to the tree of knowledge, a shrewdness that is always already in the service of the lust for domination, Egypt emerges as the "city" organized in accordance with the wisdom of God, a wisdom bound to the humility and restraint of Joseph. In harmonizing the political ecology of Egypt with God's wisdom, Joseph transforms Egypt into a "garden city." The new Egypt is a city that serves and cares for the soil and all that comes from the soil. Although the hybrid symbol of the city-that-is-garden is only implicitly defined at the end of Genesis, it becomes more fully demarcated as the story of salvation develops within the biblical canon. Indeed, as we shall see, the city-that-is-garden becomes an essential symbol for the salvation of the world. As Genesis draws to its conclusion, Egypt, somewhat startlingly, represents a sign of hope at what the wisdom of God can effect in and for the world.

---

[119]The former qualification does not suggest that this connotes a separation from God's wisdom. As we have seen, YHWH in fact makes concessions, working with creation as it is.

[120]See Anderson, "Joseph and the Passion of Our Lord," 198–215.

CONCLUSION

In this chapter, we have observed that the book of Genesis elucidates a coherent politico-ecological theology developed throughout the book as a whole. In accordance with divine wisdom, God creates a good and beautiful creation. Likewise, God creates the human person and calls the person to live in a threefold communion with God, neighbor, and earth. In order to sustain these bonds of communion, God calls the human person to live in accordance with the wisdom of God through serving and caring for the garden of the world. When the primordial couple transgresses the boundaries of their vocation, refusing to serve and care, they unleash the de-creational power of sin into the world. Sin, at least partially, sets the human person against God's purposes and ultimately threatens the life of the world. In order to repair the world, God makes a covenant with a particular people, calling that people to abide by God's wisdom so as to inhabit the vocation of gardener and participate in the redemption of the world. In Genesis, Joseph bears the fullest witness to the redeeming power of God's wisdom and thus works to reverse the ruptures of communion initiated by Adam. Thus, as we observed with Dahlberg at the outset of this chapter, the book of Genesis ultimately discloses a unified (or at the very least, a unifiable) theological vision.

The theological vision internal to the book of Genesis is, in itself, a great theological achievement with profound implications for Christian praxis in the contemporary world. However, it is important to recall the partial validity of von Rad's initial claim. The theology of Genesis is best understood in relationship to the subsequent books of scripture. In light of this, it is important to explore the ways in which the politico-ecological theology of the book of Genesis informs an interpretation of the broader contours of salvation history as they are mediated through scripture. Thus, in Chapter 4, I turn to interpret the biblical themes of exodus and promise in light of the theology of Genesis.

Chapter 4

The Jubilee of Liberation

The biblical testimony affirming the interrelated character of the love of God, neighbor, and earth is not unique to the book of Genesis. Rather, this testimony permeates the broader biblical witness, informing key narratives, figures, and symbols of the canon. Therefore, scripture both invites and supports a politico-ecological interpretation of salvation history. In this chapter, I develop such an interpretation in an explicitly eco-liberationist key, drawing on and extending the theological interpretation of Genesis articulated in Chapter 3. The argument of this chapter is straightforward: The themes of salvation history (e.g., exodus, promise, and the reign of God) elucidate the ways in which God labors to liberate the soil and all that comes from the soil from the destructive sway of sin, while restoring humanity to the vocation of gardener, and establishing a political ecology of communion centered on the wisdom of God. I begin by considering the exodus, examining the political ecology of Egypt and the significance of the plagues, the manna, the covenant, and the law. I then move to examine the politico-ecological implications of Jerusalem, the prophets, the reign of God, and the New Jerusalem. In so doing, I show that interrelated options for the earth and the poor are intrinsic to the canon's story of salvation and are rooted in a faithful response to God's saving work.

EXODUS AND THE POLITICAL ECOLOGY
OF SIN AND SALVATION

At the outset of the book of Exodus, we find that after Joseph's death, "a new king who knew nothing of Joseph" rises to power in Egypt (Ex 1:8).[1] When

---

[1]The phrase "knew nothing of" suggests antipathy more than mere unknowing. As Cornelis

viewed against the backdrop of Genesis, this description of the new pharaoh is as powerful as it is succinct. As Terence Fretheim observes, the figure of Joseph is "more than a reference to the individual; he is the one in and through whom God has preserved the people alive."[2] As we have seen, Joseph's role in preserving life owes to his steadfast commitment to abide in God's wisdom and, thus, his inhabitation of the vocation of gardener. In Genesis, Joseph is the fullest expression of *imago Dei*. Thus, the assertion that pharaoh knows nothing of Joseph implies that this new king knows neither God nor God's wisdom. The new pharaoh is ignorant of the vocation of gardener.[3]

Pharaoh's first pronouncement in Exodus confirms his ignorance. Observing the manner in which the Hebrews continue to flourish within Egypt, he becomes fearful and exclaims, "Come, let us deal shrewdly with them to stop their increase" (Ex 1:10).[4] As we noted in Chapter 3, this pronouncement identifies the new king both with the cunning serpent and the builders of Babel, all of whom wish to displace God and invert the ways of the Gardener.[5] At the outset of Exodus, then, pharaoh announces that he will abide by the de-creational knowledge that stands in opposition to the ways of *homo hortulanus* and disorders the tripartite communion that God intends for the human person. Pharaoh, as one who is willfully ignorant of the vocation to cultivate and care for creation, embraces the work of domination. Once more, the *libido dominandi* of "the builders" transforms the plowshares and pruning hooks of the gardener into the weapons of oppression.

The political ecology of Egypt quickly comes to reflect the new pharaoh's specific forms of ignorance, knowledge, and desire. Whereas, under the guidance of Joseph, Egypt's political ecology functions to "feed the entire world" and

---

Houtman notes, the Targum Onqelos understands the new king as one "who invalidated the decrees of Joseph," and "the Targum . . . finds that this king 'refused to know about Joseph and did not walk according to his laws.'" Houtman finds that the phrase suggests that pharaoh "did not want to have anything to do with" Joseph. See Cornelis Houtman, *Exodus*, vol. 1, trans. Johan Rebel and Sierd Woudstra (Kampen: Kok, 1993), 235–36.

[2]Terence E. Fretheim, *Exodus* (Louisville, KY: Westminster John Knox, 2010), 27.

[3]Just as Abraham's initial description in Genesis 12 places him in juxtaposition to the city-builders of Babel, here, pharaoh's initial description juxtaposes him to the city-redeemer Joseph.

[4]Exodus 1:7 notes that the Hebrews were "fruitful and multiplying," obviously recalling God's command to humanity in Genesis 1:28. Thus, pharaoh's will is demonstrated to run contrary to that of God's. This is not to suggest that, today, we should read Genesis 1:28 uncritically or ignore concerns regarding overpopulation. Rather, it is merely to point out that in "the world of the text" pharaoh is immediately placed in opposition to God.

[5]While one must acknowledge that the word "shrewd" is used to describe Joseph in Genesis, it cannot be the case that this descriptor links the two together. After all, it just has been made clear that pharaoh knows nothing of Joseph. Rather, the link between pharaoh and Joseph is better understood as analogous to the link between the tree of life and the tree of knowledge. The "wisdom" with which pharaoh and the tree of knowledge are associated is one that, from a certain standpoint, can appear as if it were God's own wisdom (that which is associated with the tree of life and Joseph); however, it ultimately leads to death.

ignorance of the earth and poor

allows the soil to regain its health, pharaoh's dictates undo Joseph's work. The new king's policies propagate injustice and ecological catastrophe throughout the lands of the empire. The city of the gardener devolves into the image of the cities of Enoch and Babel.

The injustices fostered by pharaoh are manifold. As Gutiérrez observes, "repression (Exod. 1:10–11), alienated work (5:6–14), humiliations (1:13–14), [and] enforced birth control policy (1:15–22)" come to define the experience of the Hebrews in the "land of slavery."[6] Ellen Davis captures well the totality of the ills denoted by Gutiérrez: "The Deuteronomist aptly names Egypt 'the Iron Furnace' (Deut. 4:20), for it is the biblical archetype of the industrial society: burning, ceaseless in its demand for slave labor (the cheapest fuel of the ancient industrial machines), consuming until it is itself consumed."[7] Along these lines, Davis finds that Egypt's storehouses, which stood as a sign of life and abundance under Joseph, become a symbol of death under the new king.[8] They are now edifices that house an unsustainable abundance, harvested through the sacrifice of a people.[9]

Subjugated to pharaoh's system of domination, the oppressed Hebrews cry out to God, who hears and responds: "I have witnessed the affliction of my people in Egypt and have heard their cry against their taskmasters, so I know well what they are suffering" (Ex 3:7). Moved by the cry of the poor, God confronts pharaoh with the enormities of pharaoh's project.[10] In accord with God's response, the earth itself testifies against the political ecology of the iron furnace. The calamities that strike Egypt bear witness to its disordered character.[11] On this point, William Brown finds that the blood-filled Nile symbolizes

punishment for sin

---

[6]Gustavo Gutiérrez, *A Theology of Liberation*, Eng. trans. (Maryknoll, NY: Orbis Books, 1973), 88 (hereinafter *TL*).

[7]Ellen F. Davis, *Scripture, Culture, and Agriculture: An Agrarian Reading of the Bible* (New York: Cambridge University Press, 2009), 69. With regard to the notion that the storehouses function as a sign of life under Joseph, see Bruce T. Dahlberg, "On Recognizing the Unity of Genesis," *Theology Digest* 24 (1976): 364.

[8]See her discussion on this point in Davis, *Scripture, Culture, Agriculture*, 75–79.

[9]Of note here is Gustavo Gutiérrez, *The God of Life*, Eng. trans. (Maryknoll, NY: Orbis Books, 1991), 48–64 (hereinafter *GoL*).

[10]Reflecting on the political character of salvation with specific reference to Exodus, Gutiérrez asserts that the exodus "is a political action. It is the breaking away from a situation of despoliation and misery and the beginning of the construction of a just and comradely society. It is the suppression of disorder and the creation of a new order." See *TL*, 88.

[11]Fretheim: "H. H. Schmid and others have shown that in Israel and the ancient Near East, the just ordering of society—reflected in its laws—was brought into close relationship with the sphere of creation. A breach of those laws was considered a breach of the order of creation with dire consequences on all aspects of the world order, not least the sphere of nature. One must speak of a symbiotic relationship of ethical order and cosmic order. This understanding of the created order undergirds the plague cycle in Exodus." See Terence E. Fretheim, *God and World and the Old Testament: A Relational Theology of Creation* (Nashville: Abingdon, 2005), 115. Later Fretheim continues, "God sees to the moral order of things, enabling the working out of the effects of Pharaoh's sinfulness. Such judgments are not imposed on the situation from without but grow out of

God using the earth to express pain and anger

God and creation

dirtying the earth, making it milieu

"Egypt's moral ruin. . . . The Nile's blood testifies to the structural violence wrought upon Israel in the same way that the blood-soaked ground was a stark testimony to Cain's crime (Gen. 4:10)."[12] The signs and wonders that befall Egypt correspond, in negative terms, to God's creative work in the first creation account of Genesis. In Genesis, in accordance with divine wisdom, God calls light into existence; brings order to the water and land; creates the living creatures to flourish within the water, upon the land, and in the air; and commands the humans to be fruitful and multiply. In Exodus, pharaoh's shrewd- *the* ness results in the calamities that bring darkness, threaten life within the water, *opposite —* upon the land, and in the air; and culminate in a plague that visits death upon *the* the children of Egypt.[13] As Fretheim finds, "The collective image presented is *of* that the entire created order is caught up in this struggle. . . . Pharaoh's antilife *God* measures against God's creation have unleashed chaotic effects that threaten the very creation that God intended."[14] In Exodus, as in Genesis, the destructive effects of sin bear a distinctly politico-ecological character. Accordingly, the cries of both the earth and the poor serve to unmask and judge the hubris and ignorance of pharaoh's project. *injustice to the earth and poor*

will result in punishment

The People of God, Pharaoh, and YHWH *rhyme is always in sins*

Amid the struggle between the creational power of God and the de-creational power of sin, the story of Exodus centers on a question that drives the entire narrative: Who will the people of God serve? This key question is surfaced implicitly early in Exodus when the narrator describes pharaoh's program of subjugating the Hebrew people (Ex 1:13–14). As Fretheim translates these verses:

> So they made the people *serve* with rigor, and made their lives bitter with backbreaking *service* in mortar and brick, and with every kind of *service* in the field; with every kind of *service* they made them *serve* with rigor.[15]

In this crucial passage, various forms of the verb *'ābad* are utilized five times. This use—indeed, overuse—of the term highlights the centrality of the issue of service within the Exodus narrative.[16]

---

and have an intrinsic relationship to the sinful (or good) deed" (ibid., 121). This harmonizes with the Yahwist anthropology of the human person as one who is meant for threefold communion.

[12]William P. Brown, *The Ethos of the Cosmos: The Genesis of Moral Imagination in the Bible* (Grand Rapids, MI: Wm. B. Eerdmans, 1999), 204.

[13]Carol Meyers notes many of these parallels. See Carol Meyers, *Exodus* (New York: Cambridge University Press, 2005), 79.

[14]Fretheim, *God and World*, 119.

[15]Fretheim, *Exodus*, 30. Emphasis is Fretheim's.

[16]In total, Fretheim counts ninety-seven instances in which a form of *'ābad* is used in Exodus.

As I observed in Chapter 3, the significance of *'ābad* has its roots in Genesis 2:15, where its use is foundational to the conception of both the human vocation and *imago Dei* in the second creation account. The use of *'ābad* at the beginning of Exodus should be understood in light of Genesis 2. At the opening of Exodus, the people of God have been conscripted into a situation deeply at odds with the vocation that God intends for the human person. Here God's people are forced to serve the designs of pharaoh. Their service perpetuates Egypt's political ecology of de-creation. In light of this, the question of who the people of God will serve can be further specified: Will the people of God serve the overseer of the iron furnace or the God of the garden city? Will God's people allow themselves to be conformed to the likeness of the Gardener, or will their praxis support the image the city-builder par excellence?[17] An initial and hopeful response to these queries comes from the Hebrew midwives, Shiphrah and Puah. When pharaoh declares that these women must kill every Hebrew male newborn, the women resist, engaging in civil disobedience by claiming that the strength of the Hebrew women make it impossible for them to carry out pharaoh's orders.[18] Likewise, when Moses's mother gives birth to him, she defies pharaoh's orders and, instead, places her child in a basket, which she sends down the Nile.[19] These actions have the effect of preserving life while resisting pharaoh's idolatrous decrees.

Nevertheless, on the whole, the people of God appear much more ambivalent than the three aforementioned Hebrew women with regard to the issue of whom they would serve. In general, the Hebrews are resistant to challenging the Egyptian structures of power. This is, of course, understandable. As James Scott has shown, within historical reality subjugated communities rarely confront oppressive power regimes directly; such a tack can be unwise, leaving the community exposed to violent reprisals. Thus, when the people of God are located within the structural boundaries of Egyptian authority, announcing their commitment to serve God is a particularly fraught declaration. Indeed, within pharaoh's "city," prudence may dictate subtler arts of resistance than outright rebellion.[20]

[handwritten margin note: forced to break her relationship with God]

---

[17]Gutiérrez would frame the questions in this manner: Will Israel serve the God of Life or the Idols of Death? See *GoL*, 49.

[18]Meyers, *Exodus*, 37. See also William H. C. Propp, *The Anchor Bible: Exodus 1–18*, vol. 2 (New York: Doubleday, 1999), 142.

[19]The basket is discovered by pharaoh's own daughter, who raises Moses as her own son. As numerous scholars have noted, the Hebrew word used for "basket" (*tēbâ*) appears in only one other place in the Bible. In the story of flood in Genesis, *tēbâ* refers to Noah's ark. See Meyers, *Exodus*, 43. Just as Noah's cooperation with God allowed for the emergence of a new creation, the women's resistance to pharaoh's proscriptions set in motion a similar process of re-creation.

[20]See James Scott, *Domination and the Arts of Resistance: Hidden Transcripts* (New Haven, CT: Yale University Press, 1992). Scott's analysis aligns well with the sense in Genesis that the cunning of the vulnerable coheres with the wisdom of God.

[handwritten: nondescript]

More striking, however, is that the Hebrews' reticence to serve God continues even after God has liberated them from the structures of Egypt's politico-ecological system. Indeed, once God shepherds the people through the abyss of the sea and into a new creation,[21] the people quickly begin to "grumble," longing for their life of servitude to pharaoh: "If only we had died at the LORD's hand in the land of Egypt, as we sat by our kettles of meat and ate our fill of bread! But you have led us into this wilderness to make this whole assembly die of famine!" (Ex 16:3). Their complaints indicate that although God has delivered them outside the boundaries of pharaoh's physical control, the people of God are subject to a hardness of heart similar to that of pharaoh's. God's people have internalized something of "the sickness of Egypt," carrying it with them into the wilderness.[22] To use Gutiérrez's terminology, it appears that the Hebrew people had come to accept the validity of their identity as "nonpersons"—an identity upon which the exaltation of Egypt's diseased political ecology depended. In accordance with this acceptance, the people desire the safety of subjugation to pharaoh over the precariousness of the wilderness and dependency on God (a dependency that the unstable character of the wilderness necessitates). *[handwritten: they want the easy way out to be in/out idea]*

The wilderness, then, not only marks a break from the socio-structural realities of Egypt; it also inaugurates a period of cultural and psychological reformation as God reshapes the collective imagination and desire of the people in accordance with God's wisdom (and in opposition to pharaoh's shrewdness).[23] As Gutiérrez puts it, the wandering in the wilderness encompasses a "gradual pedagogy of successes and failures . . . necessary for the Jewish people to become aware of the roots of the liberation to which they were called."[24] For the people of God to enter truly into the new creation to which God calls them, God would have to form them into a new humanity—a human form in which their desire to serve God is made manifest in the care for the poor and the earth. This process of reformation is evidenced in both the narratives of the manna and the giving of the law tied to the covenant.

[handwritten: their renewal must be done in nature]

---

[21]As Gutiérrez notes, "The 'waters of the great abyss' are those which enveloped the world and from which creation arose, but they are also the Red Sea which the Jews crossed to begin the Exodus. Creation and liberation from Egypt are but one salvific act" (*TL*, 88).

[22]The phrase comes from Davis's translation of Exodus 15:26. See Davis, *Scripture, Culture, Agriculture*, 68.

[23]As Norbert Lohfink writes, "Now the narrative of the events in Egypt is finished. It was a story of a sick society in which human beings were enslaved and exploited, where those in positions of authority did not listen to YHWH's voice, and where, as a result, plague after plague erupted—a society that must ultimately sink down into sickness and death. Now there begins . . . the story that can be told about the proper society, the one in which people do listen to YHWH's voice and in which, as a result, no diseases break out; where, instead, is realized what the prophets have promised as the salvation that YHWH will create . . . a healthy, living people." Norbert Lohfink, "'I am Yahweh, your Physician' (Exodus 15:26)," in *Theology of the Pentateuch: Themes of the Priestly Narrative and Deuteronomy* (Minneapolis: Fortress, 1994), 93.

[24]*TL*, 88.

Manna, Covenant, and Law: Recovering Imago Dei

In the wilderness, the manna comes as both a gift and a test from God. As Davis observes, "It is given on certain conditions and thus is meant to reveal whether Israel 'will walk by [God's] teaching or not' (16:4)."[25] This act of eating, she maintains, "constitutes the litmus test of Israel's separation from the culture and mind-set of Egypt." The most basic point of separation is clear: where the culture of the iron furnace gives rise to unceasing production and consumption resulting in the exhaustion of the poor and the earth, the culture of the gardener is one that cultivates trust in God and a corresponding praxis of restraint, allowing rest for the soil and all that comes from it.[26] "In the manna economy," Davis notes, "Israel is called upon to engage in two concrete practices of restraint, namely, eschewing excess and keeping Sabbath."[27]

The manna economy also orients the people of God toward identification with those who would be most susceptible to exploitation in society. As Davis writes, "The narrative clearly identifies their work in the wilderness as 'gleaning' . . . gleaners were the most vulnerable and often the most desperate participants in the ancient food economy."[28] Thus, she finds that "as the Israelites begin their journey to the land they will possess, they are put in the position of the most dependent members of the society they themselves will form."[29] The culture that the people of God are called to cultivate—and the politico-ecological structures that spring forth from this culture—grow out of the people's concrete experience of identification with those who are most at risk of being marginalized and exploited within "the city." The experience of cultural/psychological liberation, then, challenges the people of God to re-imagine and reconfigure their relationships with God, the poor, and the earth.

The pedagogy of the wilderness, initiated with the manna, reaches its zenith in God's covenant with the Hebrew people and the bestowal of the law. As Gutiérrez avers, it is the covenant that "gives full meaning to the liberation from Egypt; one makes no sense without the other."[30] For Gutiérrez, liberation and covenant are two dimensions of God's saving action in history. The covenant binds the people irrevocably to the liberating God who labors to deliver humanity and redeem creation. The covenant itself is witnessed by the bestowal

---

[25]Davis, *Scripture, Culture, Agriculture*, 70.

[26]Both Davis and Brown juxtapose the act of eating manna to Adam and Eve's transgressive act of eating in the garden. See Davis, *Scripture, Culture, Agriculture*, 78; and Brown, *Ethos of the Cosmos*, 206. Whereas, through the transgression in the garden, the primordial couple internalizes the shrewdness of the serpent, the people of God, through the practice of restraint, come to know God's wisdom.

[27]Davis, *Scripture, Culture, Agriculture*, 74.

[28]Ibid.

[29]Ibid., 75.

[30]*TL*, 89.

"Man" becomes the ideal

of the law (exemplified in the Decalogue), which prescribes the shape of the Hebrews' servanthood to God. As with the manna, the law reorders the collective intellect and will of the people of God away from the sickness of Egypt (characterized by distortions of hubristic self-love and the internalization of the identity of nonperson) and toward the life-giving health of the Gardener.

In his consideration of the Decalogue, Walter Brueggemann distinguishes three principles fundamental to the law. First, the Decalogue affirms that God alone is to be worshipped and served—"a viable alternative to Egyptian slavery requires *a Holy God who, as a critical principle, deabsolutizes every other claimant to ultimate power.*"[31] Second, it seeks to ensure the health of human community "by *setting limits to the acquisitive capacity of members of the community*—the capacity to seize and confiscate by power or by cunning what is necessary to the life of the neighbor."[32] Here the quality of restraint, affirmed in the manna narratives, is codified. While Brueggemann emphasizes the law's prohibition against the use of manipulative or coercive power as a means of acquiring possession or status, the prohibition functions at a deeper level to order human desire. As René Girard observes, human desire is formed, in a fundamental way, through a process of *mimesis*. This process *reson-* bonds human persons together in a communion of shared identity. However, *mual* if unchecked, mimetic desire can also produce violent rivalries that rend the *mech* bonds of communion. Thus, Girard finds that the Decalogue's proscription *res* against unchecked acquisition functions to preserve the neighborly bond of communion.[33] The ordering of desire within a mode of restraint leads directly into the third principle of the law (also seen in the manna narratives), the command to keep Sabbath.[34] Notably, Brueggemann observes that the command to keep Sabbath in the book of Exodus is linked closely with rest for creation, whereas, in Deuteronomy, Sabbath is connected more closely with rest for slaves. For Brueggemann, "The juxtaposition of *creation* (Exod 20:8–11) and *rest for slaves* (Deut 5:12–15) nicely articulates Israel's characteristic way of

community is not inherently bad, it is bad when sin is at work in of community

[31]Walter Brueggemann, *Theology of the Old Testament: Testimony, Dispute, Advocacy* (Minneapolis: Fortress, 2005), 184.

[32]Ibid., 185.

[33]René Girard, *I See Satan Fall Like Lightning* (Maryknoll, NY: Orbis Books, 2001), esp. 7–48. For a Girardian reading of scripture, see also Gil Bailie, *Violence Unveiled: Humanity at the Crossroads* (New York: Crossroad, 1996). It should also be noted that the proscription against unchecked acquisition unquestionably is intended to preserve the integrity of creation itself. Likewise, this proscription is intimately tied to Brueggemann's first principle of the Decalogue, regarding God's holy transcendence and the call to worship God alone. God, as a critical principle, de-absolutizes each of the human person's mimetically formed desires, thereby providing a transcendent background against which they must be judged. The upshot, here, is that we can again discern the interrelated character of the love of God, neighbor, and earth.

[34]Patrick Miller argues that the Sabbath is the organizing principle of the Decalogue and key to understanding Deuteronomic theology as a whole. See Patrick Miller, "The Human Sabbath: A Study in Deuteronomic Theology," *Princeton Theological Seminary Bulletin* 6 (1985): 81–97.

linking cosmic and concrete social realities."[35] In other words, the love for neighbor and earth are inextricably bound together within the logic of the law. In Exodus, liberation takes the form of deliverance from the structures, culture-ideologies, and theological claims of the iron furnace. This integral liberation is brought to fruition in the covenant with God and the commitment to hear and respond to the cries of the earth and the poor. The re-formation of the people of God within the wilderness reorients them to the vocation of gardener, the call to serve and preserve the garden of the world. The people of God, in passing through the abyss and into the wilderness are called to reinhabit *imago Dei*, serving God in a manner that recalls Joseph at the end of Genesis. If, then, as Brueggemann argues, the whole of the biblical witness is saturated with the grammar of exodus, then it is not too much to affirm that the biblical witness, as a whole, constitutes good news for the poor and the earth. This view is confirmed through the biblical motif of promise.[36]

PROMISE AND THE POLITICAL ECOLOGY OF SIN AND SALVATION

As we have seen, liberation from pharaoh's reign does not culminate in the exaltation of an indeterminate freedom for the people of God. The people of God are not delivered from the politico-ecological formations of Egypt so that they may now "be like God" and subjugate the soil and all that comes from it to the brutalities of their own will. Rather, God liberates the Hebrews in order that they might serve God and, in so doing, learn to care for the soil and all that comes from it in accordance with God's work of liberation and redemption. The exodus opens the people of God to hope for a future lived in communion with God, a future in which the world is healed from the power of sin so that the whole of creation might flourish and find rest.[37]

---

[35]Brueggemann, *Theology of the Old Testament*, 185. Emphasis is Brueggemann's.

[36]Ibid., 178.

[37]The intractable difficulty for any liberationist interpretation of Exodus is the horrific violence that the Hebrew people inflict on the Canaanites on entering into "the promised land." The Hebrew people's attempts to annihilate the Canaanites can and has been used throughout history to justify wars of conquest, genocidal activity, and the demonization of "the other" (on this point, see George E. Tinker, *American Indian Liberation: A Theology of Sovereignty* [Maryknoll, NY: Orbis Books, 2008], 131–32). I make no attempt to justify what I find to be unjustifiable. In my view, these passages stand as a warning to and as testimony against any program or regime that would *identify* itself with the ways of the Gardener in order to justify its violence or oppressive practices. These passages cry out in warning against any sense of triumphalism present within a Christian eco-liberationist praxis and demand repentance. These cries must also serve to interrupt the grand narrative that I am developing in this chapter and in Chapter 3, calling into question the ways in which they perhaps too easily cohere.

The Political Ecology of Jerusalem

In reflecting on the history of salvation, Gutiérrez cites the work of Georges Casalis, observing that in the midst of the exodus from Egypt, "the hope of the people of God is not to return to the mythological primitive garden, to regain paradise lost, but to march forward towards a new city, a human and comradely city whose heart is Christ."[38] The hope for salvation, then, is symbolized by the transformation of the city itself—the redemption of the fallen political ecologies of the world. The promise of salvation takes the iconic form of Jerusalem, the city of God's peace. Nonetheless, Casalis's distinctly Christian understanding of the icon of Jerusalem (a "city whose heart is Christ") recalls strikingly the primordial garden of Genesis. As I observed in Chapter 3, it is Christ—the tree of life—who is planted at the heart of the garden, ordering the garden's geo-ethical landscape in accordance with God's wisdom. Thus, Casalis's description of the promise, symbolized in the city centered on Christ, points toward the fulfillment of the city of the gardener (a city that was partially, if all too fleetingly, realized in Egypt under Joseph's guidance). Jerusalem, then, is the symbol of the political ecology of salvation, the symbol of integral ecology.

The icon of Jerusalem stands largely in opposition to the symbolic cities of Enoch, Babel, and the Egypt of Exodus (Egypt under the rule of a pharaoh who "knows nothing of Joseph"). As we have seen, the political ecologies of "the builders" are founded on the refusal to serve, constructed through the exploitation of the earth and the poor, and sustained by the sword and the spear. In contrast, the foundation of the city of God is prepared in the wilderness, where the desires of God's people are reoriented toward the service of God, and where an ethic of restraint and concern for the most vulnerable is instilled in the hearts of the people. Correspondingly, the tools of this city are the plowshare and the pruning hook—the instruments of service and care—fashioned in accordance with God's wisdom. Unsurprisingly, then, the political ecology of Jerusalem is envisioned in terms that differ starkly from the image of the dominative city. As Davis argues, whereas the latter is understood in terms of the iron furnace, devouring its hinterland until the city consumes itself, the city of God is envisioned as a "mother city"[39]—a city whose blessings flow outward

---

[38]Cited in *TL*, 89.

[39]The gendered language is, of course, highly problematic and cannot be accepted uncritically. Particularly concerning is the manner in which the image of a nursing mother sustaining the world can reinforce patriarchal notions of women as self-emptying/auto-annihilating givers who exist to be exploited. Catherine Keller's reflection on the nascent colonial imagination of Cristóbal Colón captures this problem well. She notes that, informed by the geography of his time, Colón thought the world to be shaped like a woman's breast. In 1492, he believed that he had arrived at the earth's paradisal nipple. As Keller observes, "This is no casual analogy but the basis for serious cartography. The continent looms as . . . the mother breast ready to suckle death-ridden, depressed Europe into its rebirth. . . . Gaia's nipple arises in the sterility of the all-male world of

sue of Wse

from its core so as to sustain and renew the hinterlands.[40] Jerusalem, then, is meant to nourish both the marginalized loci inhabited by the poor (including the very bodies of the poor) and the wilderness that lies beyond direct human cultivation. The mother city is the city of the gardener—the city that serves and cares for the garden of the world.[41]

assumes
everybody
carry
for
all

Of course, within the story of salvation, the promise of peaceable communion, symbolized by Jerusalem, does not emerge as an inevitability. Instead, it is tied to the covenantal faithfulness of the people of God and their commitment to cultivate and care for the soil and all that comes from it, in accordance with divine wisdom. Like the manna, the promised land appears as both a gift and a task. *has to be earned* The people of God are called to make manifest the political ecology of the garden city in the promised land.[42] With this in view, it is worth exploring more fully the manner in which the observance of Sabbath (along with the closely related observance of jubilee) is meant to inform the eco-social formations of Jerusalem.

Above, I considered the significance of the Sabbath laws in both the books of Exodus and Deuteronomy, noting their political ecological ramifications. However, among Sabbath prescriptions in the Old Testament, it is those in Leviticus, dealing with the year of Sabbath rest, that perhaps best capture how this practice is meant to sustain communion with God, neighbor, and earth. The description of Sabbath in Leviticus reads,

> For six years you may sow your field, and for six years prune your vineyard, gathering in their produce. But during the seventh year the land shall have a Sabbath of complete rest, a Sabbath for the Lord, when you

to worship God

---

the conqueror, promising not relationship but suckle" (Catherine Keller, *Apocalypse Now and Then: A Feminist Guide to the End of the World* [Minneapolis: Fortress Press, 1996], 157). It is vital, therefore, to keep in mind that, with the symbol of "mother-city," it is the would-be center of power that divests itself of its dominative presumptuousness so as to serve as a blessing to the world, *not* the marginalized spaces that are perennially threatened with the prospect of annihilation.

[40]The city-hinterland dialectic refers primarily to power differentials within the system of political ecology and not primarily to an urban-agricultural divide. As Davis writes, the divide "that would have been widely and keenly felt was not between village and city as such but rather between the general populace and the very small ruling stratum that controlled the royal and administrative cities. That cleavage is reflected in such antiurban traditions as are found in the Bible" (Davis, *Scripture, Culture, Agriculture*, 159). With this in mind, it is also possible to clarify the proper analogue for conceiving of this biblical dialectic in contemporary politico-ecological terms. The city-hinterland dialectic finds its proper referent in the core-periphery dialectic utilized within present-day sociological analysis. The "city" runs parallel to the "core" where politico-ecological power is concentrated. The "hinterland" corresponds to the "periphery," with both representing spaces where such power exists only in comparatively diminished forms.

[41]As Davis finds, "The whole world is Zion's hinterland" (*Scripture, Culture, Agriculture*, 165).

[42]Brueggemann describes the land as a "temptation" and "threat" in addition to a "gift" and "task," in *The Land: Place as Gift, Challenge and Promise in Biblical Faith* (Minneapolis, MN: Fortress Press, 1977), 43–65.

[handwritten: give the earth a rest]

may neither sow your field nor prune your vineyard. The aftergrowth of
your harvest you shall not reap, nor shall you pick the grapes of your
untrimmed vines. It shall be a year of rest for the land. While the land
has its Sabbath, all its produce will be food to eat for you yourself and
for your male and female slave, for your laborer and the tenant who live
with you, and likewise for your livestock and for the wild animals on
your land. (Lev 25:3–7)

[handwritten: caring for all, fulfilling the three components of love]

This biblical text envisions three essential functions of the practice of Sabbath. First, it allows the land rest, thereby preserving the land, at least in part,
from human abuse. Second, as in the wilderness, the Sabbath command returns the people of God to the position of gleaner. This designation displaces
socio-hierarchical patterns of consumption and wealth accumulation with an
egalitarian mode of distribution. It also consigns the whole of the people to an
explicit position of dependence on God, and engenders an ethos of solidarity
with the vulnerable. Finally, the command to keep Sabbath in Leviticus calls
the community to enact peaceable relationships with the land's wild animals
(creatures who would typically be seen as threatening and inimical to the community's social order). Taken as a whole, the observance of Sabbath described
in Leviticus calls the people of God to bear witness, in an anticipatory manner,
to the tripartite communion of peace that originally characterized the garden
of Eden (even reconciling the domesticated world with the wilderness).[43] In
effect, Sabbath rest guards against the temptation to transform the plowshares
and pruning hooks of Jerusalem (see Lev 25:3 above) into the swords and
spears of domination. "Sabbath," as Brueggemann writes, "is a voice of gift
in a frantic coercive self-securing world."[44]

Significantly, the description of Sabbath observance in Leviticus is followed
immediately by the prescriptions for the jubilee year. The jubilee, the "Sabbath
of Sabbaths,"[45] constitutes the culminating moment of every seven Sabbath
cycles.[46] This year of liberation, is marked by four forms of "release": the land
is once more allowed to rest; financial debts are forgiven; servants and slaves
are set free; and ancestral land rights are restored.[47] Following the work of Sam-
son Raphael Hirsch, Ephraim Radner argues that, when taken together, these
forms of release are best understood as a practice of homecoming, "a returning
to the source of all things who distributes them, a restoration to God's own true

[handwritten: both land and poor heard]

---

[43]See Margaret Barker, "The Time Is Fulfilled: Jesus and the Jubilee," *Scottish Journal of Theology* 53, no. 1 (2000): 24.

[44]Brueggemann, *Land*, 59.

[45]Barker, "Time Is Fulfilled," 24.

[46]There is some controversy as to whether the jubilee was intended to occur every 49 or 50 years. The possible variance is inconsequential to this analysis.

[47]See Sharon Ringe, *Luke* (Louisville, KY: Westminster John Knox, 1995), 68–69.

purpose."[48] The theology of Leviticus proclaims that the land is God's (Lev 25:23). Here the soil and all that comes from it are returned to God so that the patterns of politico-ecological distortion that accumulate over time might be surrendered to God. The jubilee, then, re-centers the city's political life on the tree of life. Again, however, the jubilee should not be construed in terms of some sort of attempt at a reentry into Eden. As Radner posits, the homecoming anticipated in the Jubilee, is not a *reditus* but an *anakephalaiōsis*.[49] That is to say, rather than a *return* to the primordial garden, the Jubilee *recapitulates*—it gathers together—all of that which is created good (Gen 1:1–2:3) on earth and throughout history and centers it, once more, on God. In this way, to recall Casalis's view, the practice of jubilee ensures that Jerusalem, in its pilgrimage through history, continues to exist as a comradely city whose heart is divine wisdom. Here, though, the love of neighbor and the love of God that Casalis takes to be constitutive of the "comradely city" are interlinked with the love of earth.

The Prophets and the Promise

Of course, in the history of salvation, Jerusalem fails to live up to both its mandate and moniker. This is well attested to within the biblical witness. Rather than functioning as a city of peace that bestows blessings on the hinterland in accordance with God's wisdom, the people of God turn away from their covenant with God.[50] In so doing, the "faithful city" breaks collectively from the vocation of gardener. Its political ecology of righteousness and peace devolves into one that ties heavy burdens on the poor (e.g., Mic 3:1–12) and exhausts the earth (2 Chron 36:21). In short, the city of the gardener comes to resemble the city of the builders; the wisdom of God at the heart of the mother city is displaced by the cunning knowledge of the serpent. In effect, Jerusalem "forgets Joseph."

It is within the general context of the people of God's forgetfulness and neglect of the covenant that the role of the prophets comes into sharpest relief. The prophets consistently respond to the cry of the poor by calling on the kings and the elite classes of their communities to amend practices that exploit "the orphan" and "the widow" (Is 1:17).[51] Recent studies of the prophets have begun to explore the manner in which the cry of the earth also shapes the prophetic imagination.[52] In this regard, Davis offers a helpful summary of the ecological

---

[48]Ephraim Radner, *Leviticus* (Grand Rapids, MI: Brazos, 2008), 266.

[49]Ibid., 265.

[50]See Brueggemann, *Land*, 85–100.

[51]On the prophets' concern for the vulnerable, see for example, *GoL*, 48–91. See also Brueggemann, *The Prophetic Imagination*, 2nd ed. (Minneapolis, Fortress, 2001), 39–58.

[52]See Davis, *Scripture, Culture, Agriculture*, 120–38; Ellen Davis, *Biblical Prophecy: Perspec-*

sensibilities governing prophetic insight. Consonant with the politico-ecological narration of salvation history that we have advanced thus far, Davis finds that, for the prophets:[53]

1. There exists an essential three-way relationship among God, humanity, and creation. (84)
2. Human and nonhuman creations together are "the poor and vulnerable"; they suffer together, and both stand in need of deliverance. (89)
3. God feels pain and anger when the earth and its creatures suffer. (93)[54]
4. The suffering of the earth itself is a primary index of the brokenness in the human relationship with God. (96)
5. The earth and its nonhuman inhabitants serve as divinely appointed witnesses to and agents of judgment. (100)
6. God already intends a restored or "new" creation. (104)

The role of the prophet, then, is to challenge the people of God to hear and respond to the cries of the earth and the poor. The prophets continuously confront the people of God, calling them to inhabit more fully *homo hortulanus*.

The principles outlined by Davis are found throughout the prophetic literature. In Jeremiah, for example, an oracle announces that the health of the earth is threatened by the people's violation of the covenant.[55] Here the Lord is presented as the true fertility God, and when Jerusalem fails to care for the poor, the specter of drought appears (Jer 5:20–28). Jeremiah describes the effects of sin in a manner that echoes the de-creational character of the "plagues" that beset Egypt in the book of Exodus. Jeremiah cries out,

> I have seen the earth, and here, [it is] wildness and waste . . .
> and [I look] to the heavens—and their light is gone.
> I have seen the mountains, and here, they are wavering,
> And all the hills palpitate.
> I have seen, and here, there is no human being,
> And all the birds of the heavens have fled.
> I have seen, and here, the garden-land is now the wasteland,

---

tives for Christian Theology, Discipleship, and Ministry (Louisville, KY: Westminster John Knox, 2014), esp. 83–142; and Hilary Marlow, *Biblical Prophets and Contemporary Environmental Ethics: Re-Reading Amos, Hosea, and First Isaiah* (Oxford: Oxford University Press, 2009).

[53]See Ellen Davis, *Biblical Prophecy: Perspectives for Christian Theology, Discipleship and Ministry* (Louisville, KY: Westminster John Knox, 2014), 83–108. The specific page number for each statement in the list is in parentheses.

[54]I would interpret "God's pain" metaphorically, so as to respect the doctrine of divine impassibility.

[55]See Norman C. Habel, *The Land Is Mine: Six Biblical Land Ideologies* (Minneapolis: Fortress, 1995), 75–96.

>   and all its cities are pulled down,
>   because of YHWH, because of his hot anger. (Jer 4:23–26)[56]

Moreover, Jeremiah announces that the earth itself mourns the people of God's unfaithfulness (Jer 12:4), implicitly affirming the agential capacity of the soil.

Elsewhere, Micah denounces the rulers of the houses of Jacob and Israel, proclaiming that they have turned Jerusalem into a city built with blood and injustice (Mic 3:10).[57] In response, Micah proclaims that because of this Jerusalem will be plowed (Mic 3:12). Enclosed in Micah's image is both a warning and a message of hope. The admonition is obvious: if Jerusalem persists in its ways, the city will fall.[58] However, the image of God plowing the city of blood suggestively recalls Genesis 2–4. In Micah, God is once more depicted as a Gardener plowing the land. Daniel Smith-Christopher finds that, in this passage, God is returning the soil to its original purpose and re-leasing it to those who would attune themselves to God's ways. On this point, Smith-Christopher cites Gary Stansell's view: "for Micah the Judean peasants will again care for the land. . . . The Judean peasants will have their expropriated land restored to them; hence it is with them, whom Micah calls 'my people,' that any future existence is to be found."[59] Here one finds the prophet's hope for a restored creation, a vision which is good news for both the earth and the poor.

Micah's proclamation of the renewal of creation is consonant with his and Isaiah's vision of a time when the swords and spears of the city-builders are transformed into the plowshares and pruning hooks of the gardener (Is 2:4; Mic 4:3), which I wrote about in Chapter 3. This vision, as noted in Chapter 3, augurs the restoration of the human vocation and the healing of *imago Dei* throughout the nations of the world. The image of humanity re-forming its swords and spears into plowshares and pruning hooks, therefore, foresees a time when the love of God, neighbor, and earth are properly cultivated and preserved.

This is also true of Isaiah's second famous image of communion: the peaceable kingdom (Is 11:1–9). In this oft-cited passage, the prophet speaks of a time when God's justice reigns over the land so that the poor and afflicted are

---

[56]This translation is Davis's. See Davis, *Scripture, Culture, Agriculture*, 10.

[57]This description recalls the founding of Enoch by Cain, the original shedder of human blood.

[58]Again, translating this worldview into the present day requires nuance. Fundamentally, the biblical worldview, here, points to how the health of the earth is inextricably tied to the health of the human communities that abide on the earth. However, this worldview can also be used to suggest that those who suffer the consequences of environmental disaster are somehow to blame for their plight. Any hermeneutic that would interpret historical disasters in this manner must be looked upon with deep suspicion and wholly condemned if it functions to scapegoat the victims of injustice, be it environmental injustice or otherwise. In terms of biblical worldviews, the theology of Job and Psalm 44 must interrupt the theology of Psalm 1.

[59]Daniel L. Smith-Christopher, *Micah: A Commentary* (Louisville, KY: Westminster John Knox, 2015), 125.

a+ peace; no violence

cared for. The prophet then describes, in striking terms, the peaceable character of this reign: the lion will lie down with the lamb, the leopard with the young goat; the cow and the bear will graze together; the human child will play with the viper and rest with the adder. At this time, "the earth shall be filled with knowledge of the Lord, as water covers the sea" (Is 11:9).

The language of the oracle of the peaceable kingdom is so familiar that its significance is often simply assumed. However, the meaning of this oracle is complex and worth dwelling on. This vision of communion is polyvalent, suggesting three dimensions in which the peace that God intends shall be realized. First, Isaiah 11:1–9 points to a time when the nations of the world will be reconciled with one another. This interpretation becomes apparent when the passage is read in light of Isaiah 13:14, in which the various nations of the earth are symbolically identified with specific animals (e.g., "a hunted gazelle" and "sheep without a shepherd"). In view of this identification, the communion experienced between the lion and the lamb connotes an end to the violence experienced between warring nations.

Second, a plain reading of the text suggests that the prophet's description of the peaceable relationships between the predatory animals and their prey looks toward a time when the violence that afflicts creation is put to rest. On this interpretation, Isaiah foretells the reestablishment of the harmony associated with the paradisal garden. The groaning of creation, under the curse of sin, will be no more. A third reading of the peaceable kingdom is closely related to the second but elucidates a particular dimension of the peace made manifest in creation. As Richard Bauckham points out, in Isaiah's prophecy each of the predatory animals (e.g., lion, bear, and adder) is wild, belonging to the wilderness, while each of the vulnerable animals is domesticated. In light of this, the vision of peace in 11:1–9 describes a time when the wilderness is reconciled with the domesticated regions of the world.[60] This understanding of reconciliation, recalls, then, Leviticus's description of Sabbath as a time when the human, the domesticated animal, and the wild animals will all coexist peaceably as gleaners upon the earth.[61] The three interpretations of the oracle of the peaceable kingdom suggest distinct dimensions of the intimate communion to which God calls creation, once again indicating the politico-ecological character of the promise of salvation.

---

[60]That the expectation is controlled by the prevalent perception of enmity between the human world and the dangerous wild animals is shown by the fact that there is no mention of peace between the predatory wild animals and the wild animals . . . that they usually hunt and kill, but only of peace between the predatory wild animals and the domestic animals which they sometimes attack" (Bauckham, *Living with Other Creatures,* 125).

[61]It can be said that in order for *homo hortulanus* to resist the temptation of transforming the plowshare and pruning hook into the sword and spear, the person must rest, occupying the position of gleaner and cultivating the practice of restraint.

love of God is linked to love of neighbor

JESUS AND THE PROMISE

As we have seen, at a fundamental level, the theme of promise refers to the hope for the restoration of communion with God, neighbor, and earth. Within the Jewish imagination, the reestablishment of this tripartite communion is tied to a precise place, a specific land on which the people of God are called by God to enact the political ecology of the gardener. Thus, in the time of exile, hope for the restoration of communion is especially bound up with hope for restoration to the promised land, so that God's people might, once again (and more fully), live in accordance with God's wisdom in that place. Within this worldview, hope for communion with God, neighbor, and earth is identified with the land of the covenant.

The Christian conception of promise departs in a notable way from the traditional Jewish notion. The Christian tradition affirms that the promise of salvation and redemption are fulfilled through the person of Jesus in a unique, unrepeatable, unsurpassable, and irreversible manner. Thus, as W. D. Davies argues, within the Christian imagination, the "holiness of the Person" comes to substitute for the "holiness of place."[62] In effect, the Jewish focus on the promised land is displaced within the Christian imagination by the latter's emphasis on the person of Jesus Christ. As Davies argues, Christianity has "Christified holy place."[63] Since Jesus Christ is the fulfillment of the promise, it is the relationship of the human person or community to Christ that sanctifies a place. Thus, in a certain sense, all space becomes homogeneous within the Christian worldview.[64] That is to say, all space appears potentially as "promised space," space that can be transformed in Christ through the work of the Holy Spirit.

The historical effects of the substitution of the holiness of place with the holiness of person within the Christian imagination have been manifold. One result that Davies notes is the tendency of this imagination to spiritualize holiness.[65] Since, for Christians, the practice of the love of God is not intrinsically bound up with the love of a specific place (and the politico-ecological relationship that constitute that place), the love of God is especially vulnerable to abstraction from historical reality. In effect, the spiritualization of holiness allows one to

all of earth might be transformed to be a promised land

---

[62]W. D. Davies, *The Gospel and the Land: Early Christianity and Jewish Territorial Doctrine* (Berkeley: University of California Press, 1974), 368.

[63]Ibid.

[64]Here it is vital to recall and affirm Jennings's critique of the manner in which place has been homogenized under the gaze and praxis of the colonial imagination. Cf. Chapter 3, note 15. The homogeneity that I refer to here, in following Davies, does not conform to the sense that is the object of Jennings's critique. Rather, it simply acknowledges that all places are potentially equally graced. This "homogeneity," however, must be cultivated in a manner that allows for a unity-in-diversity to emerge.

[65]Davies, *Gospel and the Land*, 367.

conceive of the love of God as decoupled from love of neighbor and love of earth. Within this spiritualizing mode of conceptualization, the promise comes to be understood solely in terms of communion with God (through Christ); on this account communion with neighbor and earth appear as marginal or even unrelated to the promise.

Of course, as I observed in Chapter 1, it is precisely the spiritualist temptation to abstract the practice of Christian holiness from historical reality that Gutiér-rez and other liberationists argue against. In a Christological key, liberation theology seeks to overcome distorted spiritualist worldviews by emphasizing Jesus's prophetic inauguration of the reign of God within his own sociohistorical context.[66] On liberationist interpretation, then, Christified space bears witness in history to the social and ethical character (i.e., the preferential option for the poor) of God's reign.

The challenge for a Christian eco-liberationist reading of salvation history is to elucidate the manner in which the promise of salvation and redemption, fulfilled in Christ, not only binds together love of God and neighbor but also love of earth. In other words, an eco-liberationist interpretation of Christ as the fulfillment of the promise must demonstrate that the threefold communion with God, neighbor, and earth properly constitutes Christified space. In order to do so, we must begin to conceive of the incarnation and Jesus's proclamation of God's reign in politico-ecological terms. This task, however, brings with it distinct dif-ficulties. Whereas liberationist interpretations of scripture can draw on a wealth of material from the gospels that makes apparent the preferential option for the poor within the reign of God inaugurated by Jesus, evidence for a preferential option for the earth is more elusive. Davies, for one, is doubtful that the land was of particular concern to Jesus, noting that specific references to the land appear in only four instances in the gospels.[67] Following Davies's observation, we can note that when Jesus speaks to his disciples about the relationship between the love of God and neighbor, he does not broach the subject of the love of earth (Lk 10:27). Thus, as Bauckham observes, "From a cursory reading of the Gospels, it would not be difficult to get the impression that the Kingdom is about the rela-tion between God and humans, and has nothing to do with the rest of creation."[68]

The Political Ecology of God's Reign

Bauckham, however, argues that a close reading of the gospels (particularly when read canonically) can locate concern for the human/earth relationship

---

[66]See *TL*, 97–105, and *GoL*, 65–140. See also Jon Sobrino, *Jesus the Liberator: A Historical-Theological Reading of Jesus of Nazareth* (Maryknoll, NY: Orbis Books, 1993).

[67]Davies, *Gospel and the Land*, 355–65.

[68]Bauckham, *The Bible and Ecology: Rediscovering the Community of Creation* (Waco, TX: Baylor University, 2010), 164.

at the heart of Jesus's mission. As Bauckham points out, the gospels suggest that Jesus presupposed the "rich creation theology of the Hebrew Bible, which taught, not only that God created all things, but also that God cares generously and tenderly for all his creatures . . . not only for humans."[69] Most important, Bauckham develops this insight with regard to Jesus's proclamation of God's reign. As Bauckham notes, within the Old Testament, it is the book of Psalms that describes God's reign in greatest detail. The reign of God is envisioned in terms consonant with the threefold sense of relatedness (God, neighbor, and earth) that has been foregrounded in this reading of salvation history. As Bauckham writes,

> In the Psalms, the kingship and rule of God are closely related to creation. It is as Creator that God rules his whole creation (Ps. 103:19–22). His rule is over all that he has made, human and otherwise (Pss. 95:4–5 and 96:11–13), and it is expressed in caring responsibility for all creatures (Ps. 145). All non-human creatures acclaim his rule now (Pss. 103:19–22 and 148) and all nations must come to do so in the future (Ps. 97:1), for God is coming to judge the world, that is, both to condemn and to save (Pss. 96:13 and 98:9). His own people Israel's role is to declare his kingship to the nations (Pss 96:3 and 10; 145:10–12). When God does come to judge and to rule, all creation will rejoice at his advent (Pss. 96:11–12 and 98:7–8).[70]

In short, the reign of God as described in the Psalms is ecotheopolitical in character. Bauckham interprets the aim of Jesus's inauguration of God's reign accordingly. Jesus's mission is "the renewal of the whole of creation in accordance with God's perfect will for it."[71] The significance of this argument is that it places the renewal of creation (as opposed to simply the renewal of human/ divine or human/neighbor relationships) at the center of Jesus's mission to proclaim, enact, and embody God's reign. In inaugurating the reign of God, Jesus ushers in the renewal of the creation—the restoration of communion between the human person and God, neighbor, and earth. To affirm that Jesus proclaims, enacts, and embodies the reign of God, then, is to affirm that Jesus's mission is to restore the tripartite communion sustained by the vocation of gardener. With these points in mind, it is possible to draw out some of the politico-ecological implications and presuppositions of the gospels, which become apparent early on in their narratives.

The gospels describe the world at the time of Jesus's birth, in terms antithetical to Isaiah's vision of restoration. Far from a period in which knowledge

---

[69]Ibid., 164–65.
[70]Ibid., 165.
[71]Ibid., 166.

of God fills the earth (Is 11:9), Luke testifies that Jesus is born into an epoch in which the Roman Empire, through census, is enrolling "the whole world" to serve the logic of Caesar (Lk 2:1).[72] Thus, the world is filled and ordered with and according to the knowledge of the Roman Empire, an empire that, throughout much of the New Testament witness, is conceived of in a manner that aligns it with "the builders" of Egypt and Babylon. In this world there appears to be no room for Christified space, no place for the wisdom of God.[73]

The tension between the wisdom of God and the ways of the world at the time of Jesus's birth is captured vividly in John's gospel. In the prologue to the fourth gospel, John identifies Jesus as God's creative Word, the one through whom all things are made (Jn 1:1–3). With the birth of Jesus, the Word is incarnated in a world that "[does] not know him" (Jn 1:10).[74] As Richard Hays writes, "The prologue of John's Gospel is best understood as a midrash on Genesis I, a midrash that links the idea of a preexistent creative divine *logos* to the motif of divine Wisdom seeking a home in the world (e.g., Sir 24:3–8)."[75] The fourth gospel, then, identifies Jesus with both the Word and Wisdom of God.[76] "In contrast, however, to those earlier Jewish traditions that identify the earthly presence of Wisdom among the people of Israel or in Israel's law," Hays continues, "John insists that *Logos*/Wisdom found only rejection in the world, even among God's own people."[77] Thus, the gospels present the coming of Christ as a moment pregnant with eschatological significance. A world that appears conscripted to serve the designs of "the builders" is now confronted by the incarnation of God's wisdom—the one who enfleshes the true logic of the *kosmos*. Jesus, the "human one" (Jn 19:5) who would serve and care for the world in accordance with the logic of love (Jn 3:16), confronts a world

the physical embodiment

---

[72]That the world is being conscripted to serve Caesar is implied by the reference to the census itself. Consider Walter Brueggemann's comment on David's census in 2 Samuel. Brueggemann writes, "The census . . . is a sin." It "serves to enhance royal, bureaucratic oppressive power." See Walter Brueggemann, *First and Second Samuel* (Louisville, KY: John Knox, 1990), 351–52.

[73]Thomas Merton has commented on the apocalyptic character of this setting. See Thomas Merton, "The Time of the End Is the Time of No Room," in *Raids on the Unspeakable* (New York: New Directions, 1964), 65–78.

[74]The situation, therefore, bears a resemblance to that at the outset of Exodus, where a pharaoh arose who "knew nothing of Joseph."

[75]Richard Hays, *Echoes of Scripture in the Gospels* (Waco, TX: Baylor University Press, 2016), 310.

[76]Elisabeth Schüssler Fiorenza argues that a Sophia Christology is embedded in the fourth gospel but is overshadowed by John's identification of Jesus with the Word. See Elisabeth Schüssler Fiorenza, *Jesus: Miriam's Child, Sophia's Prophet: Critical Issues in Feminist Christology* (New York: Continuum, 1994), 150–54. Along these lines, see also Elizabeth A. Johnson, *She Who Is: The Mystery of God in Feminist Theological Discourse* (New York: Crossroad, 1992), 96–99. Denis Edwards makes an argument similar to that of Hays while following the work of Raymond Brown. See Denis Edwards, *Jesus the Wisdom of God: An Ecological Theology* (Maryknoll, NY: Orbis Books, 1995), 42–43.

[77]Hays, *Echoes of Scripture,* 310.

vocation of gardener

system that subjugates the soil and all that comes from the soil, in order to exalt itself.[78] To describe the situation in Johannine terminology (once again recalling the language of Genesis 1), the light of God's wisdom enters into the world to confront the anti-creational forces of darkness (Jn 1:5).[79]

This confrontation portends a dramatic transformation of the world, one that is signaled early in Luke's gospel, in the canticle of Mary. There in a prayer that anticipates the mission of her soon-to-be-born child, Mary recalls the ways in which God has overthrown the powers of the world throughout history, proclaiming:

> The Mighty One has done great things for me,
> and holy is his name.
> His mercy is from age to age
> to those who fear him.
> He has shown might with his arm,
> dispersed the arrogant of mind and heart.
> He has thrown down the rulers from their thrones
> but lifted up the lowly.
> The hungry he has filled with good things;
> the rich he has sent away empty.
> He has helped Israel his servant,
> remembering his mercy,
> according to his promise to our fathers,
> to Abraham and to his descendants forever. (Lk 1:49–55)

cannot see the poor

restoration of Israel

Brueggemann describes Mary's hymn as "the poetry of inversion."[80] He remarks, "Quite clearly this is a vision of land-loss by the graspers of land and land-receipt by those who bear promises but lack power."[81] Thus, into a world in which there appears to be no room for her, a world that is seemingly wholly numbered and organized by the reasoning of the iron furnace, Sophia, the wisdom of God, becomes flesh so that a new political ecology might be inaugurated.

---

[78]N. T. Wright argues that the whole of the gospel of John narrates a story of re-creation, with Jesus portrayed as the final Adam. See N. T. Wright, *The Resurrection of the Son of God* (Minneapolis: Fortress Press, 2003), 669, 440. I follow some of Wright's argument in more detail below. On the character of "the city of men," see Augustine's judgment of Rome and Cain, *City of God*, XV.4–7.

[79]See the discussion of the signs and wonders in Exodus above. In Mark's gospel, Jesus's presence is depicted in similarly conflictual terms. Jesus comes as a robber who binds the "strong man" occupying a house (Mk 3:27). See Ched Myers, *Binding the Strong Man: A Political Reading of Mark's Story of Jesus* (Maryknoll, NY: Orbis Books, 2003), 164–67. In an eco-liberationist key, we might construe this "house" (*oikos*) in terms of land's political ecology (*oikologia*).

[80]Brueggemann, *Land*, 161.

[81]Ibid.

The Inauguration of Sabbath Peace

The prospect of creation's renewal through the inauguration of God's reign is intimated at the beginning of Mark's gospel through its description of Jesus's experience in the wilderness. As the passage reads,

> [Jesus] was in the wilderness forty days, tempted by Satan;
> and he was with the wild animals;
> and the angels ministered to him. (Mk 1:13)[82]

a close relationship w/ God in nature

Mark's dual reference to "wilderness" and "forty days" recalls the wilderness experience of the Hebrews during their exodus from the structures and sickness of Egypt. The re-formation of the people of God in the wilderness, as I have already observed, is part of a broader narrative of re-creation within the book of Exodus.[83] Thus, Mark's succinct description of Jesus's experience in the wilderness associates Jesus with the advent of a new creation. This advent is further attested to by the gospel's description of the relationship between Jesus and the wild animals.

Located between the figures of Satan and the angels, the status of the wild animals in relation to Jesus appears somewhat ambiguous in Mark's description. Whereas Satan is unquestionably an enemy who must be resisted and the angels are unequivocally friendly creatures who care for Jesus, we find that Jesus is simply "with" the wild animals. Bauckham maintains that in order to clarify Jesus's relationship to these animals, three points are vital to keep in mind. First, generally speaking within the biblical imagination, wild animals are viewed primarily as a threat to human well-being. Second, the danger these animals pose to human flourishing was thought to be a result of sin and humanity's expulsion from the garden. Third, the descriptor "with" suggests a positive relational quality. With regard to this last point, Bauckham writes, "The expression 'to be with someone' frequently has, in Mark's usage (3:14; 5:18; 14:67; cf. 4:36) and elsewhere, the sense of close, friendly association."[84] Thus, within a scene that anticipates the renewal of creation by recalling the wilderness experience of exodus, Mark describes Jesus entering into amiable relationship with elements of creation that would have been understood predominantly in hostile terms. Given this setting, Jesus's presence among the wild animals signals the initial in-breaking of peace between the human one

---

[82] This is Richard Bauckham's translation. See Bauckham, *Living with Other Creatures: Green Exegesis and Theology* (Waco, TX: Baylor University, 2011), 75.

[83] The reference to "forty days" specifically recalls Moses's forty-day encounter with God on Mount Sinai (Ex 34:28). See Daniel J. Harrington, "The Gospel according to Mark," in *The New Jerome Biblical Commentary* (Englewood Cliffs, NJ: Prentice-Hall, 1968), 599.

[84] Bauckham, *Living with Other Creatures*, 76.

and the earth's wild animals. The human one's experience in the wilderness, then, initiates an inversion of the ways in which the power of sin has come to shape the human/earth relationship.[85] As Bauckham argues, "Jesus goes into the wilderness, the realm outside of human habitation, in order to establish his messianic relationship with the non-human creatures."[86]

Jesus's experience with the wild animals recalls two interrelated moments that have already surfaced in our exploration of the theme of promise. Most obviously, his mode of communing with the wild animals recollects Isaiah's prophecy of the peaceable kingdom, which envisions not only reconciliation among the nations but also peace between the world's domesticated places and its wilderness regions. Relatedly, Jesus's experience in the wilderness recalls the Sabbath prescription in Leviticus, which mandates that both domesticated and wild animals are to glean food from the fallow fields, (presumably) alongside their human counterparts. As one who is dependent on God in the wilderness, Jesus takes his place beside the wild animals as a gleaner upon the land while beginning to effect the in-breaking of a new political ecology—that of God's reign. *Jesus is function of just unrians*

The Proclamation of Jubilee

Jesus's mode of relating to the wild animals anticipates the reestablishment of the city of the gardener, a "city" whose center extends blessings on the hinterland. As I have observed, at the time of Jesus's birth, the world has been made to serve the logic of the iron furnace and its de-creational power. Jesus's peaceable presence among the wild animals, then, anticipates the transformation of the city (the politico-ecological system) that organizes the spaces of the world. J. W. Rogerson and John Vincent posit that Jesus's inauguration of God's reign can be understood as the call to construct an alternative city.[87] In a manner anticipated by Joseph in the book of Genesis, Jesus labors to reorganize the political ecology of his time and place so that it would conform to the logic of the tree of life. In committing himself to this task, Jesus proclaims Jubilee—the proclamation at the heart of his mission.

Both Luke's and Matthew's gospels connect the inception of Jesus's ministry

---

[85]As Bauckham argues, "Mark's image of Jesus with the animals provides a biblical symbol of the human possibility of living fraternally with other living creatures. Like all aspects of Jesus's inauguration of the Kingdom of God, its fullness will be realized only in the eschatological future, but it can be significantly anticipated in the present by respecting wild animals and preserving their habitat." See Bauckham, *Bible and Ecology*, 128–29.

[86]Bauckham, *Living with Other Creatures*, 76.

[87]See J. W. Rogerson and John Vincent, *The City in Biblical Perspective* (London: Equinox, 2009), 52–81. Along liberationist lines, Rogerson and Vincent construe the city primarily in terms of a social "community." Nonetheless, as I argue below, their description remains apt for describing the eco-social community begun by Jesus.

to the announcement of Jubilee.[88] This connection is most explicit in Luke. As told there, Jesus enters into the synagogue at Nazareth and proclaims Isaiah 61:1–2 to the assembly. These verses, with their reference to the "year acceptable to the Lord," are well known for describing the coming of a year of Jubilee, referring to the prescription originally found in Leviticus. The passage, which the gospel of Luke modifies slightly from its original form, reads

> The Spirit of the Lord is upon me,
> because he has anointed me
> to bring glad tidings to the poor.
> He has sent me to proclaim liberty to captives
> and recovery of sight to the blind,
> to let the oppressed go free, *a year of rest*
> and to proclaim a year acceptable to the Lord. (Lk 4:18–19)[89]

In concluding his reading of the scroll of Isaiah, Jesus proclaims to the assembly, "Today this scripture passage is fulfilled in your hearing" (Lk 4:21). In effect, Jesus tells those assembled in the synagogue that he has come to inaugurate "a year acceptable to the Lord." In proclaiming Jubilee, Jesus announces that the reign of God is being made manifest. *restoration of the relation—*

In her study of this passage in Luke, Sharon Ringe elucidates a number of *who* points that are worth reflecting on here.[90] First, in announcing Jubilee, Jesus *with* makes clear that his mission will be characterized by justice and liberation for *God* those who are poor and oppressed. In agreement with traditional liberationist interpretation, Ringe writes, "'the poor' are linked to such other persons as those who are blind, maimed, or lame—suffering from both physical ailments and social ostracism—and to those who are captives or in prison, to encompass all persons who are oppressed." Jesus's ministry is not aimed only at sustaining the poor who are suffering but also in effecting "substantive changes in *different types of poor*

---

[88]Dale Allison argues that the presentation of the beatitudes, found in both Matthew and Luke, allude to or draw on Isaiah 61:1–2. Allison further observes that in Matthew 11:1–6, Jesus is identified as Isaiah's eschatological prophet, the one in whom the oracle is fulfilled. See Dale Allison, *The Sermon on the Mount: Inspiring the Moral Imagination* (New York: Crossroad, 1999), 15–16. On these points, see also Ben Witherington III, *Matthew* (Macon: Smyth & Helwys, 2006), 118–23.

[89]Luke modifies the passage by omitting the phrase, "and a day of vindication by our God." Gutiérrez argues that Luke's reason for making this modification is that the phrase is suggestive of violence toward gentiles, which Jesus rejects. See *GoL*, 7–8.

[90]See Sharon H. Ringe, *Jesus, Liberation, and the Biblical Jubilee: Images for Ethics and Christology* (Philadelphia: Fortress, 1985), 91–98. In addition to the issues that I surface here, Ringe also discusses the eschatological significance of Jubilee. With regard to the implications of Jesus's proclamation of jubilee, see also André Trocmé, *Jesus and the Nonviolent Revolution*, ed. Charles E. Moore (Maryknoll, NY: Orbis Books, 2004), esp. 13–41; Paul Hertig, "The Jubilee Mission of Jesus in the Gospel of Luke: Reversal of Fortunes," *Missiology: An International Review* 26, no.2 (1998): 167–79.

bessumfy juir hues

people's circumstances, such that they enjoy the chance for a new beginning."[91] Jubilee—the practice of God's reign—transforms dehumanizing social realities, so that persons and communities might live more humanely.[92]

Second, in reflecting further on the significance of the term "liberty," which she translates "release," Ringe argues that the term affirms the ultimate sovereignty of God. The release from bondage, she argues, is not only from empirical forms of debt or captivity but from idolatrous and self-apotheosizing ideologies that refuse to serve God. Importantly, Ringe notes, "Jubilee images of God as sovereign also suggest that to speak of God's sovereignty is to speak of the primacy of God over all creation."[93] Ringe's claim can be helpfully extended by Radner's comment discussed above. The Jubilee is intended as a return of all things to God so that they might be organized and used in accordance with God's wisdom and, thereby, be restored to their true purpose. Captivity, as is by now clear, describes not only the condition of human persons and communities living under the yoke of sin and injustice, but that of creation as a whole. As the theology of Leviticus makes plain, the sovereignty of God is made manifest in God's reign over the soil and all that comes from the soil: "The land is mine!" the Lord proclaims. Thus, the release required by Jubilee calls for the earth to be liberated from political ecologies of domination so that the soil and all that comes from it might be returned to the political ecology of the Gardener.[94] The proclamation of Jubilee, then, is a call to make manifest the preferential option for the earth (a point to which I return in the section below).

Finally, Ringe observes that Luke depicts Jesus as the "herald of the jubilee."[95] The patterns and promises of "a year acceptable to the Lord" are realized in the person and praxis of Jesus, the one who inaugurates and embodies God's reign. Thus, what is affirmed with regard to Jesus's relationship to God's reign is also true of Jesus's relationship to the Jubilee: Jesus is the sacrament of Jubilee.[96] Again recalling Radner's observations, Jesus appears

---

[91]Ringe, *Jesus, Liberation, and the Biblical Jubilee*, 93–94.

[92]Ringe also argues that the liberation called for by Jesus requires not only the forgiveness of debts but the forgiveness of sin. For this reason, those who suffer injustice are called to forgive their oppressors so that all might live more freely in this world. Ringe correctly underscores that the practice of forgiveness must be linked to the practice of justice. See ibid., 94–95. For a careful study of the place of forgiveness and reconciliation within liberation theology, see O. Ernesto Valiente, *Liberation through Reconciliation: Jon Sobrino's Christological Spirituality* (New York: Fordham University Press, 2016), esp. 154–91.

[93]Ringe, *Jesus, Liberation, and the Biblical Jubilee*, 96.

[94]In support of this point, see Trocmé, *Jesus and the Nonviolent Revolution*, 28–29.

[95]Ringe, *Jesus, Liberation, and the Biblical Jubilee*, 97.

[96]On the identification of Jesus with Jubilee, see Christopher R. Bruno, *Jesus Is Our Jubilee . . . But How?: The OT Background and Lukan Fulfillment of the Ethics of Jubilee, JETS: Journal of the Evangelical Theological Society* 53, no. 1 (2010): 81–101. See also Matthew Philipp Whelan, "Jesus Is the Jubilee: A Theological Reflection on the Pontifical Council for Justice and Peace's *toward a Better Distribution of Land*," *Journal of Moral Theology* 6, no. 2 (2017): 204–29.

as the "head" under and through which creation is gathered and organized (recapitulated) according to the principles of Jubilee. In light of what I have just argued with regard to the Jubilee, to identify Jesus with the Jubilee is to affirm that Christified space is space that is organized not only by the option for the poor but the option for the earth as well.

Meekness, Obedience, and the New Adam: Jesus Christ the Gardener

If Jesus comes to transform the political ecology of the world through announcing Jubilee and inaugurating the reign of God, he expresses the vision of this transformation vividly in his articulation of the beatitudes. As Dale Allison observes, the beatitudes allude and draw on Isaiah's jubilee oracle.[97] Unsurprisingly, then, the beatitudes, which are key to understanding the character of the reign of God,[98] are akin to the poetry of inversion found in Mary's canticle. They describe a situation of politico-ecological reversal and reorientation—a time when mourners are comforted and "those who hunger and thirst for righteousness" are satisfied. The beatitudes articulate the vision of a time when the garden of the world is no longer numbered by the logic of the domination system but organized in accordance with the wisdom of God. Although each of the beatitudes expresses hope that God will renew the face of the earth, the most pertinent of these annunciations to the present analysis is one that is unique to the gospel of Matthew: "blessed are the meek, for they shall inherit the earth."

The meaning of "meek" (*praus*) has been the object of enduring discussion throughout centuries of biblical interpretation.[99] Gutiérrez, citing Romano Guardini, describes meekness not as "weakness" but rather as "strength become mild."[100] Meekness, then, does not suggest resignation or timidity in the face of injustice. Rather, it connotes something of a sense of active nonviolence.[101] Hays interprets meekness in Matthew's gospel as indicating "humility" and "gentleness."[102] Meekness, then, stands in contradistinction, not to confronta-

---

[97]Allison, *Sermon on the Mount*, 15–16.

[98]See Brackley, *Divine Revolution: Salvation and Liberation in Catholic Thought* (Maryknoll, NY: Orbis, 1996), 126–27.

[99]For an in-depth examination of the reception history of the beatitudes, see Rebekah Eklund, *Happy Are the Hungry: The Beatitudes through the Ages* (working title, forthcoming with Eerdmans, 2019). The Matthean insertion appears to be a reference to Psalm 37:11, which the NAB translates, "the poor will inherit the earth." The broader context of Psalm 37 describes a situation of reversal consonant with the canticle of Mary.

[100]Gutiérrez, *GoL*, 122.

[101]See both Warren Carter, *Matthew and the Margins: A Socio-Political and Religious Reading* (London: T&T Clark, 2000), 132–33, and Michael H. Crosby, *Spirituality of the Beatitudes: Matthew's Vison for the Church in an Unjust World*, rev. ed. (Maryknoll, NY: Orbis Books, 2005), 81–99.

[102]Hays, *Echoes of Scripture in the Gospels*, 153.

tionality, but rather to pride and the lust for domination. This contrast recalls the dichotomies initially surfaced in Chapter 3 between the gardener, whose praxis of serving and protecting is informed by the wisdom of God, and the city-builder, whose praxis of domination is informed by the shrewdness of the serpent. Thus, it is fitting that, as Allison suggests, the inheritance of the earth by the meek can be understood as a recovery of "the dominion of what Adam and Eve lost."[103] Jesus's proclamation that the meek shall inherit the earth intimates that the political ecology proper to the garden will be restored and that the earth will be filled with knowledge of God's will. Thus the reign of God appears not only as good news for the meek but for the earth as well. No longer will the proud and violent reign over the soil and all that comes from the soil.[104] Instead, in a manner that recalls Isaiah's vision of peace, the humble—those whose tools are the plowshare and the pruning hook—shall come to organize the political ecology of the earth.

The gospel of Matthew describes Jesus as meek (Mt 11:29, 21:5), thereby identifying him as the template for recovering the patterns of communion lost by humanity through sin.[105] Matthew's presentation of Jesus in this manner is consistent with an underlying pattern found in the four gospels, throughout which Jesus is depicted as one who is wholly obedient to the will of God. Indeed, early Christian theologians drew on the depictions of Jesus in the gospels in order to emphasize the obediential character of Jesus and present him as an antitype to Adam.[106] Whereas Adam disobeys the stricture against consuming the knowledge of good and evil (thus refusing to serve God, neighbor, and

---

[103]Allison, *Sermon on the Mount*, 48.

[104]As I have observed, in Luke's gospel the "reign of the builders" is alluded to in the narrative of the Roman imperial census. In Matthew's gospel, the presence of this reign is initially described in the narrative of the massacre of the innocents when Herod, Caesar's vassal, orders the slaughter of the male children of Bethlehem under the age of two, in an effort to have Jesus killed and protect the regnant regime. Here, however, Matthew's narrative also points to the inability of the regime to enroll the entire world. After all, it is precisely because of Herod's ignorance of Jesus's location that the king commits mass murder. On this point, see Carter, *Matthew and the Margins*, 86.

[105]In Matthew 11:28–29, Jesus proclaims, "Come to me, all you who labor and are burdened, and I will give you rest. Take my yoke upon you and learn from me, for I am meek and humble of heart; and you will find rest for yourselves." Here, then, Jesus appears as the typological model of meekness. It is also worth noting Jesus's offer of rest to those who labor and are burdened. Scholars have argued that in this passage Jesus is comparing his way to the legalism of the Pharisees (see Benedict T. Viviano, "The Gospel according to Matthew," in *The New Jerome Biblical Commentary*, 653). While this may be true, "labor" and "burden" also call to mind the plight of the Hebrews in Egypt (Ex 1:14; 5:7–18), and "rest" certainly refers to the practice of Sabbath. Here, then, Jesus's proclamation can fruitfully be read in relation to Exodus. Jesus brings the offer of Sabbath rest to those crushed by the iniquitous demands of the iron furnace. Notably, Patrick Miller argues that is precisely in light of the context of Exodus 5:7–18 that the practice of Sabbath must be understood. See Miller, "Human Sabbath," 87–88.

[106]See Brandon Crowe, *The Final Adam A Theology of the Obedient Life of Jesus in the Gospels* (Grand Rapids, MI: Baker Academic, 2017). As Crowe maintains, through his obedience, "Jesus was accomplishing salvation throughout his life" (17).

earth), Jesus remains obedient to God's will and the call to serve and care for the garden of the world. Accordingly, Jesus's humility moves him to confront and denounce the forces of the "anti-reign"—the forces that devour the earth and crush the poor—even at the consequence of suffering an unjust death on the cross.[107] The cross, then, viewed in light of both Jesus's proclamation of God's reign and his subsequent resurrection, unmasks the depraved logic organizing the domination system and thereby surfaces the character of God's true wisdom.

Through his obedience, Jesus is revealed as the fulfillment of that which is anticipated in Genesis by Joseph. Jesus not only remains faithful to the wisdom of God but, in fact, is the wisdom of God made flesh. Jesus is the "final Adam" through whom God restores and brings to fulfillment that which was lost through Adam. Thus, the Christ event—Jesus's life, death, and resurrection—liberates the world from the power of sin and restores the communion that God originally intends for the human and for creation. Within the gospels, this view is intimated in dramatic fashion in the first resurrection account in the gospel of John.

From an eco-liberationist perspective, the most significant allusion in the gospels to Jesus as a type of Adam is found in the first resurrection account in the fourth gospel, which it may be noted, traffics in allusive rhetoric.[108] Recall that the creation theology of Genesis is central to John's portrayal of Jesus. Jesus is God's creative Word/Wisdom made flesh. With this in mind, the fourth gospel's initial account of the resurrection is illuminative, particularly when it is read in light of the foregoing interpretation of salvation history.

John's account of the resurrection begins when Mary Magdalene sets out to visit Jesus's tomb on "the first day of the week . . . while it was still dark." The two descriptors that John initially uses to frame the resurrection account are notable. The references to both darkness and the first day recall the creation narrative of Genesis 1:1–2:3. These descriptors, particularly when coupled as they are in John's gospel, evoke God's initial creative act in Genesis: calling light into existence amid the primordial darkness on the first day of creation. Notably, in the fourth gospel, Jesus is identified with "the light" (Jn 1:5; 8:12). This

---

[107]James Cone, for one, makes the connection between humility (before God) and confrontation within history. Cone argues that in a world that is substantially organized by the logics of white supremacy, black people can "serve" white people by confronting the latter with realities of antiblack racism. See James Cone, *God of the Oppressed* (Maryknoll, NY: Orbis Books, 2010), 137–38. For a nuanced overview of Cone's thought, see Andrew Prevot, *Thinking Prayer: Theology and Spirituality amid the Crises of Modernity* (Notre Dame, IN: University of Notre Dame Press, 2014), 280–325.

[108]Hays writes, "John is the master of the carefully framed, luminous image that shines brilliantly against a dark canvas and lingers in the imagination. . . . John's manner of alluding [to the Old Testament] does not depend upon the citation of chains of words and phrases; instead it relies upon evoking images and figures from Israel's scripture." Hays, *Echoes of Scripture*, 284. Emphasis is Hays's.

is relevant because in John's resurrection account Mary Magdalene sojourns from the primordial abyss of darkness to her encounter with the creative and re-creative light revealed fully in the resurrected Christ. The fourth gospel, thus, narrates the resurrection as the in-breaking of God's new creation. As N. T. Wright argues, "The resurrection matters for John because he is, at his very heart, a theologian of creation. The Word, who was always to be the point at which creator and creation came together in one, is now, in the resurrection the point at which creator and *new* creation are likewise one."[109] To borrow from the imagery of the synoptic gospels, the resurrection marks the definitive in-breaking of the political ecology of Jubilee—the new creation.

The re-creational themes of the first resurrection narrative in John provide the context for discerning the meaning of Mary Magdalene's initial encounter with the resurrected Christ. In this encounter the gospel's use of creation imagery shifts from Genesis's first account of creation, to its second—the tomb in which the body of Jesus had been laid is located in a garden.[110] While Mary weeps at the empty tomb, believing that Jesus's body has been taken, she encounters the resurrected Jesus but does not recognize him. When she first sees him, she takes him to be "the gardener" (Jn 20:15) and asks if he has taken the Lord's body away. That Mary misidentifies Jesus should be understood as an instance of John's well-known use of irony.[111] As Wright opines, Mary "makes the right kind of mistake."[112] In other words, without understanding it in the moment, Mary's identification of Jesus with the gardener is correct. Jesus, in fact, is *the*

---

[109]Wright, *Resurrection*, 667.

[110]This is implied by Mary Magdalene's confusion over the resurrected Jesus's identity (Jn 20:15). With regard to the garden setting, Samuel Wells writes, "This is the first day of the week, and this is a man and a woman in a garden. There could hardly be three more explicit references to the creation story in Genesis." Samuel Wells, *Power and Passion: Six Characters in Search of Resurrection* (Grand Rapids, MI: Zondervan, 2007), 177. In his monumental treatment of the fourth gospel, Edward Klink also emphasizes the relationship between Adam and Christ with regard to the renewal of creation in John. See Edward W. Klink III, *John* (Grand Rapids, MI: Zondervan, 2016), 823–86.

[111]Raymond Brown summarizes John's use of irony thus: "A particular combination of twofold meaning and misunderstanding is found when the opponents of Jesus make statements about him that are derogatory, sarcastic, incredulous, or, at least, inadequate in the sense that they intend. However, by way of irony these statements are often true or more meaningful in a sense that the speakers do not realize." See Raymond Brown, *An Introduction to the New Testament* (New York: Doubleday, 1997), 336. See also Paul D. Duke, *Irony in the Fourth Gospel* (Atlanta: John Knox Press, 1985). For his part, Brown rejects the notion that John's gospel alludes to the garden in Genesis 2–3. Brown's view is based on the fact that the word John uses for garden does not correspond to the word used to describe the garden of Eden in the Septuagint. Brown's judgment, however, appears overly determined by his strict historical-critical methodology, which has proven vital yet limited for theological interpretation. For an appreciative critique of Brown's approach, see Robert F. Leavitt and Francis Schüssler Fiorenza's discussion "Raymond Brown and Paul Ricoeur on the Surplus of Meaning," in *Life in Abundance: Studies of John's Gospel in Tribute to Raymond E. Brown*, ed. John Donahue (Collegeville, MN: Liturgical Press, 2005), 207–37.

[112]N. T. Wright, *Twelve Months of Sundays—Year A* (London, UK: SPCK, 2002), 54–55.

gardener; he is *homo hortulanus*, the fulfillment of the human vocation and the fullness of the image of God.[113] In John's gospel, then, the final creation is ushered in by the final Adam—the resurrected Christ.[114]

It is worth pausing here to reflect on the significance of John's resurrection account. In the gospel of John, we find an implicit New Adam Christology that corresponds to the implicit *imago Dei* anthropology of Genesis 2–3. In Genesis 2–3, God creates the human person to serve and care for the soil and all that comes from the soil. In serving and caring in this manner, the human person abides by the wisdom of God and comes to image God most deeply. This call and response "hold together" creation, allowing the human person to live in communion with God, neighbor, and earth. Sin, made manifest in humanity's refusal to serve, disorders *imago Dei*, disorganizes creation, fragmenting it and destroying communion. In John's gospel, Jesus—God's wisdom made flesh—is revealed as the sacrament of God's reign and the fulfillment of the human vocation. As such, Christ is *homo hortulanus*, the fullness of *imago Dei*. Accordingly, Jesus is revealed as the Word that reorganizes creation in accordance with God's desire. In the resurrection, the creational power of Sophia definitively overcomes the de-creational forces unleashed on the world through the refusal to serve and the advent of the domination system. Here we have the gospels' most striking intimation that Christified space represents good news for both the poor and the earth.

NEW ADAM, NEW CREATION, NEW JERUSALEM

The foregoing interpretation of the Johannine resurrection narrative coheres well with Paul's eschatological vision of redemption. As I passingly observed in Chapters 2 and 3, Paul's theological vision is cosmic in scope. For Paul, God brings all of creation into existence through Christ, and all of creation continues to hold together in Christ (Col 1:15–20). In his letter to the Romans, Paul emphasizes the Spirit's work in the redemption of creation:

---

[113]To this point, John Suggit writes, "Indeed he was! Adam was put in the garden of Eden to maintain it and care for it (Gn 2:15). He failed to do so, but Jesus is the second Adam, the true human being, as 19:5 (*idou ho anthrōpos*) ought to be understood. Jesus was there clothed in the glorious purple robe which (according to a Targum) Adam lost through sin." See John Suggit, "Jesus as Gardener: Atonement in the Fourth Gospel as Re-creation," *Neotestamentica* 33, no.1 (1999): 167.

[114]Wells posits, "John is offering us a new Adam and Eve, putting right the fatal error of the fall and describing the nature of the new creation. This is quite simply a new creation story. It is as grand as that. Humanity fell again in Gethsemane when the disciples scattered and hid, just as it had fallen in Eden, when the man and woman hid. But here it is, three days later, restored, redeemed, transformed." Wells, *Power and Passion*, 177–78.

> Creation awaits with eager expectation the revelation of the children of
> God; for creation was made subject to futility, not of its own accord but
> because of the one who subjected it, in hope that creation itself would be
> set free from slavery to corruption and share in the glorious freedom of
> the children of God. We know that all creation is groaning in labor pains
> even until now. (Rom 8:19–22)

God's adoption of humanity in Christ, through the work of the Spirit (Rom 8:
14–17), ultimately points to a time when all of creation will be liberated from the
power of sin. For Paul, as for John, the resurrection inaugurates the beginning
of the final epoch of history in which all of creation is brought to fulfillment in
God. Paul's claim that all of creation awaits "the revelation of the children of
God" also calls to mind the notion that, in God's reign, the meek shall inherit
the earth. However, I need not explore further Paul's thought, which has been
discussed at length elsewhere.[115] Instead, I wish to elaborate the connections
between the fourth gospel's account of the resurrection and the vision elucidated in the final text of the Johannine corpus, the book of Revelation. There,
the eschatological implications of John's presentation of the resurrection are
developed in explicitly politico-ecological terms.

In Revelation, John of Patmos articulates his vision of God's eschatological
victory over the forces of sin, domination, and death, forces that continue to
appear regnant over creation in the time subsequent to Jesus's death and resurrection. These forces are personified in the city of Babylon, which symbolizes
the Roman Empire and whose name simultaneously recalls the political ecologies of the builders (most obviously that of the Babylonian empire) who have
stood in opposition to the wisdom of the Gardener throughout history.[116] God's
victory over the forces of death is signified by the destruction of Babylon, the
establishment of the New Jerusalem, and the renewal of the earth. In effect, John

---

[115]For example, see David G. Horrell, Cherryl Hunt, and Christopher Southgate, *Greening
Paul: Rereading the Apostle in a Time of Ecological Crisis* (Waco, TX: Baylor University Press,
2010), 63–85.

[116]Catherine Keller is critical of the binary-oppositional rhetoric operative throughout the book
of Revelation and the manner in which this rhetoric can inform praxis. On these points she writes,
"We wish for messianic solutions and end up doing nothing, for we get locked into a particularly
apocalyptic either/or logic—if we can't save the world, then to hell with it. Either salvation or
damnation." Keller, *Apocalypse Now and Then*, 14. To be clear, I share Keller's concern. Throughout scripture, however, the language of prophecy is frequently characterized with a dichotomous
logic that functions to unveil the ways in which sinfulness has organized the political ecology
of the world. Rather than ignore this logic or otherwise marginalize the prophetic witness, it is
better in my view to allow the language of the prophetic speak, but also be interrupted by, what
Gutiérrez terms "the language of contemplation." The language of contemplation emphasizes
the hiddenness of God, the ambiguities of history, and the opaqueness of our own desires. This
language, therefore, functions to qualify the binary logic that, when unchecked, can feed both
fanaticism and fatalism.

of Patmos foresees the fulfillment of the new creation begun in the Incarnation and Resurrection of the final Adam.

THE CONTRASTING POLITICAL ECOLOGIES OF REVELATION AND THE VICTORY OF GOD

The description of Babylon and its fall are depicted in Revelation 17–19. There John indicates that Babylon, the "great city," is founded on murder (Rev 18:24) and obfuscation (Rev 17:4).[117] In accordance with this judgment, the seer presents the political ecology of Babylon as the quintessential "iron furnace"—devouring both the poor and the earth. Key to this depiction of Babylon is John's inclusion of a list of cargo describing the goods extracted from the periphery of the empire and brought to the empire's center, Rome:

> The merchants of the earth will weep and mourn for her, because there will be no more markets for their cargo: their cargo of gold, silver, precious stones, and pearls; fine linen, purple silk, and scarlet cloth; fragrant wood of every kind, all articles of ivory and all articles of the most expensive wood, bronze, iron, and marble; cinnamon, spice, incense, myrrh, and frankincense; wine, olive oil, fine flour, and wheat; cattle and sheep, horses and chariots, and slaves, that is, human beings (*psychas anthrōpōn*). (Rev 18:11–13)

Although the list of cargo is obviously similar to a register found in the book of Ezekiel (Ezek 13:9), Bauckham argues that a key to understanding the significance of the list lies in the fact that "most of the items were among the most expensive of Rome's imports."[118] The list, he observes, "features especially the luxury items which fed the vulgarly extravagant tastes of the rich."[119] This is evidenced by the verse in Revelation that immediately follows the inventory of goods, where John writes of Babylon, "The ripe fruit which your soul craves has gone from you, and all your luxuries and your glittering prizes are lost to you, never to be found again" (Rev 18:14).[120] Bauckham argues, "The first line evokes Rome's addiction to consumption, while the two words chosen

consumerism; how consumers [handwritten annotation]

---

[117]For a helpful presentation of the characteristics of Babylon and the contrasting characteristics of the New Jerusalem, see Wes Howard-Brook and Anthony Gwyther, *Unveiling Empire: Reading Revelation Then and Now* (Maryknoll, NY: Orbis Books, 2000), 160.

[118]Richard Bauckham, *The Climax of Prophecy: Studies on the Book of Revelation* (London: T&T Clark, 2000), 366.

[119]Ibid. Along these lines, David Aune observes that Roman elite could spend the equivalent of US$5–6 million on a citron wine table. Aune, *Revelation*, Word Biblical Commentary, vol. 52 (New York: Zondervan Academic, 2017), 1000.

[120]Translation is Bauckham's. See Bauckham, *Climax of Prophecy*, 368.

for the merchandise in the second line suggest both the self-indulgent opulence and the ostentatious display of Roman extravagance."[121] This, in part, explains why the kings, merchants, and mariners of the world weep and mourn over the destruction of Babylon (Rev 18:9–19). These three powerful classes despair at the loss of their source of wealth and power, the source through which they had made a name for themselves (Gen 11:4).

Critical assessments of Roman opulence were prevalent at the time John authored the book of Revelation. Laments by moralists over the loss of traditional Roman virtues such as austerity and simplicity proliferated in the decadent reign of Domitian. However, Bauckham observes John's prophecy differs from the jeremiads of the moralists in an essential way. Whereas the moralists were concerned with the loss of idealized Roman cultural values, John's critical view of Rome's economy focuses on the manner in which this economic system was predicated on the exploitation of the conquered peoples at the periphery of the empire. As Bauckham comments, "John saw Rome's wealth as her [*sic*] profit from her [*sic*] empire, enjoyed at the expense of the peoples of the empire."[122] Bauckham finds that John's positioning of slaves at the end of the list is not just intended as a condemnation of slavery but also functions as "a comment on the whole list of cargoes. It suggests the inhuman brutality, the contempt for human life, on which the whole of Rome's prosperity and luxury rests."[123] This view is further emphasized by Clarice Martin, who observes that John's description of the slaves as "human beings" (*psychas anthrōpōn*) contrasts with the common Roman characterization of slaves as "bodies" (*sōmata*). Martin finds Revelation's use of *pyschas anthrōpōn* to be "one of the most emphatic critiques of Roman ideology in Revelation"—it asserts that Rome "is an empire that enslaves human souls."[124] In other words, according to John's vision, Babylon's exalted status is predicated on its relegation of the human being—the image of God—to the status of nonperson.

The cargo list points not only to Babylon's self-aggrandizing exploitation of the poor but also to its exhaustion of the earth.[125] Bauckham rightly underscores

---

[121]Ibid. Davis also shares this judgment. See Davis, *Biblical Prophecy*, 130.

[122]Bauckham, *Climax of Prophecy*, 368–69.

[123]Ibid., 370. See Clarice Martin, "Polishing the Unclouded Mirror: A Womanist Reading of Revelation 18:13," in *From Every People and Nation: The Book of Revelation in Intercultural Perspective*, ed. David Rhoads (Minneapolis: Fortress, 2005), 100. Similarly, Bauckham concludes, "The wealth Rome squanders on luxuries from all over the world was obtained by conquest, plunder and taxation of the provinces. Rome lives well at her subjects' expense" (*Climax of Prophecy*, 370).

[124]Martin, "Polishing the Unclouded Mirror," 100.

[125]According to Rossing, "The Babylon vision offers a prophetic critique of environmental injustice—including global deforestation and ecological imperialism" ("River of Life in God's New Jerusalem: An Ecological Vision for Earth's Future," in Rosemary Radford Ruether and Dieter Hessel, eds., *Christianity and Ecology* [Cambridge, MA: Harvard University Center for World Religions, 1998], 206).

the luxurious character of many of the items on the cargo register, but Wes Howard-Brook and Anthony Gwyther observe that not all of the items would have been considered lavish. In taking into account the presence of the non-luxury items, Howard-Brook and Gwyther conclude: "Rather than portraying a city that extracted simply *luxury goods* from the entire earth, the list depicts Babylon as appropriating *everything* from the entire earth."[126] The political ecology of Babylon, then, appears as a manifestation of anti-jubilee. Whereas with the jubilee, all of creation is released from use, returned to its source, and allowed rest, Babylon's political ecology continuously lays claim to the whole of creation, conscripting creation to serve Babylon's idolatrous system.[127] The fall of this city, then, makes manifest a judgment pronounced earlier in Revelation. In overthrowing Babylon, God "destroy[s] those who destroy the earth" (Rev 11:8). The dominative political ecology of "the great city," whose manner of organizing the world gives rise to the cries of the earth and the poor, is undone by God's liberating action.[128] The destruction of Babylon marks a final exodus from the order imposed by the iron furnace.

The defeat of the political ecology of the anti-reign, however, is only one dimension of God's final salvific act. Babylon's fall is indissolubly bound to the fulfillment of the political ecology of God's reign—the new Jerusalem. As Brian Blount writes, "Theologically speaking, the judgement of Babylon/Rome *is* the realization of the salvific city that is the new Jerusalem. Figuratively, they happen together; they are the same climactic moment because they are different sides of the same apocalyptic act."[129]

The realization of the new Jerusalem is not only tied to the eschatological fall of Babylon, it is also bound up with the final renewal of creation (Rev 21).[130] "Contrary to current popular apocalyptic thinking," Barbara Rossing observes, "there is no 'rapture' in the Book of Revelation, no vision of people snatched from the earth. Instead, God is 'raptured' down to Earth to take up

---

[126]Howard-Brook and Gwyther, *Unveiling Empire*, 173 (emphasis is theirs).

[127]Of note here is Rossing's discussion of the ways in which the rhetoric of Revelation is related to historical descriptions of deforestation under Roman directives ("River of Life," 211).

[128]On the lament of the earth and poor in response to reign of Babylon, see Rossing's discussion of Revelation's use of *ouai*, which she translates as "alas." Rossing, "Alas for Earth! Lament and Resistance in Revelation 12," in *The Earth Story in the New Testament*, ed. Norman C. Habel and Vicky Balabanski (Cleveland: Pilgrim, 2002), 181–84.

[129]Blount, *Revelation*, 384.

[130]Within the new creation, John of Patmos finds that "the sea is no more." Here, Keller finds the supreme exemplification of the Christian imagination's *tehomophobia*—the chaotic sea is erased. However, as both Rossing and Davis argue, "the sea" in Revelation is symbolic of the extractive economy of Rome, which relied on the sea for its trade. Accordingly, they interpret the erasure of the sea as the erasure of imperial political ecologies of domination within God's new creation. See Rossing, "River of Life," 212–13; Davis, *Biblical Prophecy*, 133–42. See also Bauckham, *Climax of Prophecy*, 374.

residence and 'tent' (*skene*, *skenoō* with us."[131] The establishment of the new Jerusalem, then, symbolizes the final organization of creation in accordance with the wisdom of God. John symbolically intimates the sapiential structure of the eschatological city by describing it as cubic in form. As Harry Maier writes, this form "represents right Earth-divine relationship, even as oriental mythology associated quadrate cities with divinely arranged order."[132] Thus, the shape of the new Jerusalem recalls the geo-ethical character of the garden of Eden, which, as observed in Chapter 3, is organized in accordance with the Tree of Life. The new Jerusalem is the eschatological fulfillment of the city of the gardener; a political ecology arranged in accordance with the mind and will of Christ—the final Adam.

The character of the eschatological city is underscored by its further description, which recalls the garden imagery of the canon and signifies creation's ultimate renewal and fulfillment. As John of Patmos writes:

> Then the angel showed me the river of life-giving water, sparkling like crystal, flowing from the throne of God and of the Lamb down the middle of its street. On either side of the river grew the tree of life that produces fruit twelve times a year, once each month; the leaves of the trees serve as medicine for the nations. Nothing accursed will be found there anymore. (Rev 22:1–3)

Here John depicts the new Jerusalem in unmistakably Edenic terms.[133] Most striking is the manner in which this description marks the final transformation of the effects of the Fall. Recall, that in grasping and internalizing the fruit of the knowledge of good and evil, human life becomes alienated from the tripartite communion for which it was created. Sin disorders the human person's relationship to God, neighbor, and earth. As a result of sin, the earth itself is cursed. In the climactic moment of Revelation, God reconciles with creation, reigning fully over the world, and restoring God's communion with humanity.

---

[131]Rossing, "River of Life," 214. Similarly Blount writes, "John's intended creation, though new, will not be completely discontinuous from the one that went before it. When God declares at Rev 21:5 that God will make all things new, it is important to note precisely what the language intends. God is taking what is old and transforming it. Out of the destruction that occurs in the various plagues and battles for creation, God will weave God's new thing. The old will remain a constituent part of the new, but it will be fiercely transfigured." He continues, "John's vision . . . redeems the earth as a part of God's *good* creation and as the locus of God's grand re-creation. A witness for God and the Lamb does not dream of escaping the world. A witness for God and the Lamb works with God to transform the world" (*Revelation*, 376–77).

[132]Harry O. Maier, "There's a New World Coming! Reading the Apocalypse in the Shadow of the Canadian Rockies," in *The Earth Story in the New Testament*, 178.

[133]Of interest here is Micah Kiel's analysis of how the new Jerusalem is depicted in illuminated manuscripts within the Christian tradition. See Micah Kiel, *Apocalyptic Ecology: The Book of Revelation, the Earth, and the Future* (Collegeville, MN: Liturgical Press, 2017), 89–110.

Likewise, the enmity plaguing the nations, who age after age lived and died by the sword and spear, is healed through the medicinal power of God's wisdom, thereby reestablishing communion between neighbors. Finally, the curse borne by the soil, as a result of sin and as a signifier of humanity's alienation from creation, is undone. The human person's communion with creation is restored; nothing is accursed within creation renewed.

Perhaps most notable in John's depiction of the New Jerusalem, is the presence of its two named trees, recalling the two named trees of the garden of Eden. In the New Jerusalem, however, the alienating power of the tree of knowledge has been eclipsed, replaced by the tree of life, which is planted on both sides of the river. Thus all things are organized in accordance with God's wisdom. The city itself is redeemed and reconciled with creation.

In light of the eschatological liberation and reconciliation of the soil and all that comes from the soil, it is appropriate that in an earlier vision in the book of Revelation, John sees four creatures (lion, ox, human, and eagle) as representatives of the whole of creation praising God's holiness (Rev 4:6–10).[134] Further still, John sees that, on hearing the praise of creation, the people of God fall down in reverence and proclaim

> Worthy are you, Lord our God,
> to receive glory and honor and power,
> for you created all things;
> because of your will they came to be and were created. (Rev 4:11)

In the book of Revelation, God, the creator of all things, is also the liberator and redeemer of all things. The political ecology that God intended from the beginning—a political ecology that has been witnessed to through the ages by those abiding in God's wisdom, and is eschatologically initiated through the person of Jesus Christ—is brought to its fulfillment. This is the shape of the Christian hope of salvation.

CONCLUSION

In Part II of this text, I have argued that the reign of God is the political ecology of the Gardener—the political ecology of the God who calls the human person to cultivate and care for the soil and all that comes from the soil in

---

[134]Bauckham observes that the book of Revelation subtly reworks the imagery of Ezekiel. In Ezekiel, the human person stands above the other creatures while praising God. In Revelation, the human stands at the same level as the other creatures, suggesting a common dignity and vocation among all of creation. See Bauckham, *Living with Other Creatures*, 163–84.

accordance with divine wisdom. When humanity rejects its vocation, refusing to preserve the threefold communion for which it was created, the power of sin encroaches on all of creation. Driven by a desire to dominate rather than serve, humanity establishes its own false and exploitative political ecologies of domination. God confronts these realities, responding to the cries of the earth and the poor by liberating God's people from bondage so that they might rein-habit *homo hortulanus*, the image of God, and become a blessing for creation. Through the law and the prophets, God continuously labors to orient God's people toward the ways of the gardener and to save and redeem creation from the power of sin. God's definitive act of salvation is accomplished through the incarnation and resurrection of Jesus Christ—the wisdom of God made flesh, the final Adam, the fullness of *homo hortulanus*. It is through Jesus Christ that God's eschatological reign shall break into the world, liberating creation from the bondage of sin and establishing the final communion of God's peace.

Throughout Part II of this text, it has been my presupposition that this politico-ecological interpretation of salvation history, with its inflection on the liberating character of God's grace at work in the world, is vital to inform-ing the theological imagination of the ecclesial community as it confronts the contemporary global context. The initial task of Part III is to substantiate this presupposition by scrutinizing the structures and processes of the globalization project, so as to demonstrate the ways in which this project constitutes a "false ecology." The subsequent task of Part III is to operationalize the foregoing inter-pretation of salvation history, utilizing it both to judge the globalization project and to inform a vision of Christian praxis within the context of this project.

Part III

Christian Praxis
in a Globalizing World

In a pivotal passage in the gospel of Matthew, Jesus asks his disciples, "Who do you say that I am?" To this query, Simon Peter responds, "You are the Messiah, the Son of the Living God" (Mt 16:15–16). In Part II of this text, I argued that, when placed on the broad landscape of the canon and salvation history, one can interpret Simon Peter's response as signifying Jesus's fulfillment of the human vocation. On this same account, Jesus is *homo hortulanus,* the fullest expression of the image of God, God's wisdom made flesh. Jesus is the one who saves the world—that is, the soil and all that comes from the soil—from the anti-creational and dominative power of sin.

In Part III of this text, I consider the practical ecclesial implications of the foregoing proclamation of Jesus's identity. Part III explores what it means for the community of faith to live out its call to be a sacrament of salvation in the world, when salvation is understood as liberation from sin and the restoration of communion between the human person and God, neighbor, and earth. The final part of this book, then, explores what shape Christian discipleship might take within a world marked by a global politico-ecological emergency. In order to carry out this task, it is necessary to gain a clearer understanding of the world and the particular ways in which it has been organized by the dynamics of sin. Accordingly, Chapter 5 scrutinizes the ways in which the world has been shaped by the globalization project and its antecedents. Subsequently, Chapter 6 advances a number of judgments upon the politico-ecological formations of the world—judgments made in light of the foregoing interpretation of the word of God—and considers how the ecclesial community might begin to respond to the world in light of the Word.

Chapter 5

Making and Sustaining
the Planetary Emergency

In the introduction to this book, I observed that atmospheric scientists maintain that the world has moved into a new geological epoch, commonly termed the Anthropocene. In this era, human beings have become the primary driver of biophysical change at a planetary level. I also noted that, within the Anthropocene, the neoliberal globalization project functions as the dominant force organizing the political ecology of the planet. The globalization project, then, plays a major role not only in shaping the world's socioeconomic patterns but also in directing planetary biophysical transformation. The contemporary planetary emergency of ecological degradation and social inequity poses a crisis of legitimacy for the globalization project. It is vital, therefore, to understand the relationship between this emergency and the globalization project. However, to do so, a broad historical perspective is needed.

The roots of the present-day context lie in the decades and centuries leading up to the advent of both the globalization project and the Anthropocene.[1] As Richard Tucker writes, "The controversy over 'globalization' and its social and environmental costs is a relatively new debate, but the phenomenon itself has a five-hundred-year history, the history of intercontinental trade networks."[2] The rise of the Anthropocene, as well as the era's characteristic features, must

---

[1] For a helpful overview of recent literature on global change discourses, see Robin M. Leichenko and Karen L. O'Brien, *Environmental Change and Globalization: Double Exposures* (New York: Oxford University Press, 2008), 13–41.

[2] Richard P. Tucker, *Insatiable Appetite: The United States and the Ecological Degradation of the Tropical World*, concise rev. ed. (Lanham, MD: Rowman & Littlefield, 2007), 221. Tucker is referring here to the emergence of the European colonial project that began with Cristóbal Colón's contact with the Arawak on the island now known as Hispaniola. To be clear, the history of intercontinental trade networks predates this encounter by millennia.

be understood in relation to not only the globalization project but also the colonial project and the development project that preceded it. Put succinctly, it is necessary to comprehend the contemporary planetary emergency in relation to what Enrique Dussel terms "the system of 500 years" (henceforth, "the 500-year project").[3]

In this chapter, I demonstrate how the Anthropocene and the politico-ecological emergency endemic to it are the products of recurring colonial and neocolonial systems of domination. I also argue that this broadly construed paradigm of exploitation continues to characterize the present-day situation even as the language of sustainable development and ecological modernization suggests that the globalization project can attend to the cries of the earth and the poor and redress the wounds of colonial plunder. My aim is not to provide an historical survey of the 500-year project. Rather, by analyzing key concepts and historical events, I endeavor to surface the general dynamics of politico-ecological exploitation at play in the colonial project and its later iterations—dynamics that have been produced and reproduced over the past five centuries while exploiting the earth and the poor in profoundly interlinked ways. In organizing my argument, I expand on the analysis in *Laudato Si'* (hereafter, *LS*) by focusing on four key terms raised in the encyclical: (1) the emergence of the "technocratic paradigm"; (2) the "ecological debt" that the global north owes to the global south; (3) the "false and superficial" political ecology that characterizes the globalization project; and (4) the "culture of consumerism" that organizes the value systems of the globalization project today.

if capitalism were not the dominant economic system, would globalization be at the level it is today or even exist?

THE TECHNOCRATIC PARADIGM
WITHIN THE 500-YEAR PROJECT

Recall that when Pope Francis traces the history of the politico-ecological emergency, he locates its origin in the rise of what he terms the "technocratic paradigm."[4] As Francis describes it, "This paradigm exalts the concept of a subject who, using logical and rational procedures, progressively approaches and gains control over an external object" (no. 106). According to Francis, the subject, exalted by the technocratic paradigm, utilizes scientific forms of accounting to take possession of, master, and control the external objects encountered in the world. "It is as if," concludes the pope, commenting on the manner

---

[3]Enrique Dussel, *Ethics of Liberation in the Age of Globalization and Exclusion* (Durham, NC: Duke University Press, 2013), 39. Dussel borrows this term from Noam Chomsky, though it is unclear from where in Chomsky's writing.

[4]In Chapter 2, I considered the ideological character of the technocratic paradigm. Here I examine the manner in which this paradigm has served and continues to serve colonial and neocolonial interests in organizing the world over the course of the 500-year project.

in which the technocratic paradigm shapes the human person's encounter with the world, "the subject was to find itself in the presence of something formless, completely open to manipulation" (no. 106). objectification

The paradigm that the pope designates can, of course, be closely associated with the thought of Francis Bacon, the quintessential philosopher of the Enlightenment.[5] It was Bacon who advocated so ardently for an inductive form of reasoning aimed at subjecting the earth to increasingly pervasive forms of human control.[6] Nonetheless, in order to elucidate more clearly the politico-ecological implications of the technocratic paradigm—with the paradigm's proclivity to reduce the soil and all that comes from the soil to the status of a mere "it"[7]—it is necessary to look beyond Bacon, whose thought does not lend itself to charting the historical advance of this paradigm. Here the work of twentieth-century social theorist Karl Polanyi is particularly helpful. Polanyi's analysis of nineteenth- and twentieth-century society is chiefly concerned with the fate of both the human person and nature amid the rise of economistic technocracy. Polanyi's thought helps illuminate the relationship between the cries of the earth and the poor within the context of the technocratic paradigm.[8]

the domination over earth and people for Man's agenda

Market Society and the Technocratic Paradigm

In his classic work in political economy, *The Great Transformation*, Karl Polanyi argues that the pivotal event of the nineteenth and twentieth centuries was the rise of "market society."[9] Market society, as Polanyi describes it, represents a notable departure from the ways in which societies traditionally had organized themselves in relation to the marketplace. Traditionally, markets were "embedded" within the broader relational and moral-ethical fabric of society and culture.[10] Commenting on Polanyi's thought, Fred Block writes that the valua-

---

[5]Here one can also include René Descartes and his abstracting and universalizing method of philosophical inquiry. For a helpful critical analysis of Descartes's project and the form of modernity he inspired, see Stephen Toulmin, *Cosmopolis: The Hidden Agenda of Modernity* (Chicago: University of Chicago, 1992), esp. 1–88.

[6]See Francis Bacon, *The New Organon*, ed. Lisa Jardine and Michael Silverthorne (New York: Cambridge University Press, 2010). Carolyn Merchant provides an insightful ecofeminist critique of Bacon's language and methodology. See Carolyn Merchant, *The Death of Nature: Women, Ecology, and the Scientific Revolution* (San Francisco: HarperSanFrancisco, 1990).

[7]I am referring to Martin Buber's distinction between "I-Thou" and "I-It" relationships. Within an I-It relationship, the object that the person encounters is viewed merely in terms of its instrumental value. See Martin Buber, *I and Thou* (New York: Touchstone, 1970).

[8]For an initial analysis of the similarities between Polanyi's and Francis's thought, see Gregory Baum's paper, "Tracing the Affinity between the Social Thought of Karl Polanyi and Pope Francis," www.concordia.ca.

[9]Karl Polanyi, *The Great Transformation: The Political and Economic Origins of Our Time* (Boston: Beacon, 2001), esp. 35–135.

[10]Ibid.

[handwritten: pushing the boundaries]

tions of markets were constrained and subjugated to the often conflicting values and priorities of "politics, religion, and social relations."[11] The rise of market society, which accompanies the advent of economic liberalism in the nineteenth century, overturns this order. Within market societies, the market is "disembedded" from the broader relational matrices of society and nature, subsuming the latter matrices into itself. As Polanyi explains, within a market society, society runs "as an adjunct to the market. Instead of economy being embedded in social regulations, social relations are embedded in the economic system."[12] Thus the purported "self-regulating" market becomes the solitary mechanism for structuring society while value becomes identifiable with price.[13] Within a market society, all the elements of society and nature are reduced to commodity forms that can be organized instrumentally to maximize profit.[14] Market society, therefore, is effectively the politico-ecological expression of "the technocratic paradigm."

Although the movement toward liberal market societies has the effect of accelerating the rates of economic growth, Polanyi argues that the structures and dynamics of this society are ultimately untenable and unsustainable. This is because market societies attempt to commodify elements of life that, in fact, are not commodities, namely labor and land.[15] "Labor," Polanyi posits, "is only another name for a human activity which goes with life itself, which in its turn is not produced for sale but for entirely different reasons, nor can that activity be detached from the rest of life, be stored or mobilized." By the same account, he avers, "Land is only another name for nature, which is not produced by man [*sic*]."[16] In attempting to reduce human life and nature to commodity forms, market society threatens to disintegrate the social and ecological fabric of life, baldly subjecting this fabric to the vagaries and extreme fluctuations of pricing. In effect, when left unchecked, the dynamics of market society sanction an unrelenting politico-ecological violence that threatens the soil and all that comes from it. Here it is worth citing Polanyi at length:

> To allow the market mechanism to be sole director of the fate of human
> beings and their natural environment . . . would result in the demolition

[handwritten: increases precariousness]

---

[11]Fred Block, introduction to Polanyi, *Great Transformation*, xxiv.

[12]Polanyi, *Great Transformation*, 60.

[13]For Polanyi, as Matthew Watson argues, embeddedness "is the social control of economic relations through institutional means, where a link can be drawn between embeddedness and the social obligation to act in a morally dutiful manner. Insofar as 'the market' imposes purely functional character traits on individuals, the moral dimension of economic activity is increasingly dissolved." Matthew Watson, *Foundations of International Political Economy* (New York: Palgrave, 2005), 153.

[14]Polanyi, *Great Transformation*, 71.

[15]Ibid., 76. Polanyi also identifies money as a "fictitious commodity." However, for the purposes of the argument of this chapter, I focus solely on the categories of land and labor.

[16]Ibid., 75.

the market only benefits rich white men in the long run [handwritten annotation]

of society. For the alleged commodity "labor power" cannot be shoved about, used indiscriminately, or even left unused, without affecting also the human individual who happens to be the bearer of this peculiar commodity. In disposing of a man's [*sic*] labor power the system would, incidentally, dispose of the physical, psychological, and moral entity "man" attached to that tag. Robbed of the protective covering of cultural institutions, human beings would perish from the effects of social exposure; they would die as the victims of acute social dislocation through vice, perversion, crime, and starvation. Nature would be reduced to its elements, neighborhoods and landscapes defiled, rivers polluted . . . the power to produce food and raw materials destroyed.[17] *land and labor being abused and exploited until it can no longer provide* [handwritten annotation]

Polanyi's concern regarding the politico-ecological violence that market societies inflict can be further clarified when understood in relation to the thought of twentieth-century economist Joseph Schumpeter. Schumpeter argues that capitalist systems are fundamentally evolutionary in character. As such, these dynamic systems spur continuous economic growth and unrelenting social change through technological innovation, which, in turn, impels social transformation. Thus, in organizing the world, capitalist market economies catalyze and sustain an ongoing process of "creative destruction." Schumpeter writes that this is a "process of industrial mutation that incessantly revolutionizes the economic structure from within, incessantly destroying the old one, incessantly creating a new one."[18] The dynamism of capitalist market economies, which incentivize innovation with profit, continuously destroys and reorganizes the world through the unending production of novelty. *raising the market to the needs of Man* [handwritten annotation]

Undeniably, the process of creative destruction that Schumpeter describes has played a key role in spurring economic growth and introducing myriad innovations into the world over the course of the 500-year project. However, within market society, the politico-ecological formations of human life are now subjected to the unmitigated and unrelenting process of this destructive creativity in ways that are both brutal and unsustainable. In commoditizing labor and land for profit, market societies "incessantly destroy" the inherited conditions of social and ecological health.

In view of the brutality of the market society's reductionisms, Polanyi argues that this way of organizing the world ultimately cannot be sustained. He writes that although labor and land markets are vital to a market economy, "no society could stand the effects of such a system of crude fictions even for the shortest stretch of time unless its human and natural substance as well

---

[17]Ibid., 76.

[18]Joseph Schumpeter, *Capitalism, Socialism, and Democracy*, 2nd ed. (Floyd, VA: Wilder, 2012), 95.

as its business organization was protected against the ravages of this satanic mill."[19] In light of this view, Polanyi posits his famous conceptualization of "the double movement."[20] This concept describes how the movement to disembed the market from society by technocrats is met by a countermovement aimed at re-embedding the market into a broader socio-ecological matrix. For Polanyi, the second half of the double movement is a societal reflex aimed at protecting the society from the destruction wrought by a disembedded market.[21] Block describes this reflex thus: "As the consequences of unrestrained markets become apparent, people resist; they refuse to act like lemmings marching over a cliff to their own destruction."[22]

Polanyi finds that it is society's desperate response to protect itself from the ravages of market society that fuels the rise of fascist governments in Europe—regimes that ascended to power on the platform of protecting national interests and restoring some mythical past greatness. He maintains that "the victory of fascism was made practically unavoidable by [economic liberalism's] obstruction of any reform involving planning, regulation, or control."[23] Toward the end of this chapter, I return to this final point made by Polanyi, in order to consider its implications for the contemporary moment in global history.

The Technocratic Paradigm and the Extractive Zone

When human life and the earth itself are reduced to commodity forms, they become acutely vulnerable to various forms of abuse and exploitation. Thus, Polanyi's construal of market society and the liberal economistic push toward this form of politico-ecological organization helps explain the advent and progression of the planetary politico-ecological emergency and the relationship between this emergency and the technocratic paradigm. Nonetheless, the accounts of Polanyi and *Laudato Si'*, at least as I have presented them thus far, fail to attend adequately to a critical dimension of the advent of the planetary emergency, specifically, the emergency's relationship to the history and legacy of colonialism within the 500-year project. James Cone helpfully brings this relationship to the fore. Reflecting on the connections between the exploitation of the earth and the poor, Cone writes, "The logic that led to slavery and segregation in the Americas, colonization and Apartheid in Africa, and the rule of white supremacy throughout the world" likewise produces the destruction

---

[19]Polanyi, *Great Transformation*, 76–77.

[20]Ibid., 136–40.

[21]The reflex-character of the second dimension of the double movement should be emphasized. For Polanyi, it is the "free-market" that is, in fact, planned and regulated, whereas the movement toward re-embedding is unplanned. See ibid., 141–57.

[22]Fred Block, introduction to *Great Transformation*, xxv.

[23]Polanyi, *Great Transformation*, 265.

of the earth and biotic life. "It is a mechanistic and instrumental logic," writes Cone, "that defines everything and everybody in terms of their contribution to the development and defense of white world supremacy."[24]

Cone's evaluation makes clear that it is not enough to discuss in the abstract the rise of the instrumentalist logic characteristic of the technocratic paradigm. Nor is it adequate to link the commodification of land and labor to the histori-cal development of market society if one's focus is limited to the global north. Rather, one must scrutinize the instrumental logic that characterizes the tech-nocratic paradigm and the push toward market society in view of the manner in which that logic has been employed in the service of racist regimes of colonial plunder throughout the 500-year project. Only by broadening the scope of in-quiry in this manner, in order to focus on the relationship between the core and peripheries of colonial and neocolonial politico-ecological systems—that is to say, between the zones of accumulation and enjoyment and the zones of extrac-tion and degradation—can one begin to give a proper account of the historical roots of the contemporary planetary emergency.[25] It is necessary, therefore, to return to the theme of "plunder"—initially broached in Chapter 1—in order to account for its relationship to the rise of the technocratic paradigm.

Macarena Gómez-Barris locates the phenomenon of plunder—the theft of the soil and all that comes from the soil—within the long historical develop-ment of "extractive capitalism."[26] According to Gómez-Barris, extractive capitalism denotes "an economic system that engages in thefts, borrowing, and forced removals, violently reorganizing social life as well as the land by thieving resources from Indigenous and Afro-descendent territories."[27] Orga-nized in accordance with the logic of this system, the world's political ecology "continually perpetuates dramatic social and economic inequalities that delimit Indigenous sovereignty and national autonomy."[28]

The present-day system of extractive capitalism, a system intrinsic to the globalization project, has its origins in the colonial project. Along these lines,

---

[24]James Cone, "Whose Earth Is It Anyway?" *Cross Currents* 50 (Spring/Summer 2000): 36.

[25]The concepts of "core" and "periphery" originate in Immanuel Wallerstein's theorization of the world system, which develops an account of the ways in which the modern capitalist system has functioned to organize the world into regions of accumulation and skilled labor (the core) and regions of extraction and unskilled labor (the periphery). World-systems theory has been criticized for providing an overly economistic account of history and social change and for giv-ing an inadequate account of the role of culture in history and society. Although I agree with these critiques, Wallerstein's basic descriptors of core and periphery continue to be useful when analyzing the shape and dynamics of the 500-year project. For a helpful introduction to world-systems theory, see Immanuel Wallerstein, *World-Systems Analysis: An Introduction* (Durham, NC: Duke University Press, 2004).

[26]Macarena Gómez-Barris, *The Extractive Zone: Social Ecologies and Decolonial Perspectives* (Durham, NC: Duke University Press, 2017).

[27]Ibid., xvii.

[28]Ibid., xviii.

and echoing Cone's view, Gómez-Barris observes that the current system "was installed by colonial capitalism in the 1500s [converting] natural resources such as silver, water, timber, rubber, and petroleum into global commodities." Thus, for Gómez-Barris, "extractivism references colonial capitalism and its afterlives: extending from its sixteenth-century emergence until the present day, and including the recent forty-year neoliberal privatization and deregulation process, as well as the rise and fall of the progressive states." Extractivism, then, is a vital and ongoing dynamic of the 500-year project.[29] It is within the space of what Gómez-Barris terms "the extractive zone" that one finds the true character of the technocratic paradigm most clearly exposed. The extractive zone, Gómez-Barris posits, discloses most fully *"the violence that capitalism does to reduce, constrain, and convert life into commodities."*[30] In other words, it is precisely at the peripheries of the 500-year project—within the extractive zones—that the conditions of the market society are most fully realized.

Gomez-Barris's description of the extractive zone serves both to underscore Polanyi's analysis of the destructive character of market society and to surface a key shortcoming in his analysis. As I have observed, for Polanyi, economic liberalization is oriented toward reducing human life and the natural world into the commodity forms of labor and land that can then be organized by the market system. However, according to his theorization, market societies cannot be fully realized or sustained because human persons resist the reductive processes that would, at least functionally, commodify the ecological web of human life. More to the point, for Polanyi, human communities resist the implementation of the market society by employing their political agency in efforts to reorganize the system. However, in advancing this theory of the "double movement," Polanyi presumes that those resisting the rise of a market society would occupy the position of "citizen" within that society—that is to say, Polanyi takes for granted that the movement to resist the market society would be constituted by persons whose economic and political rights were recognized by the governing authority.

Within the peripheral zones of extractive economies, however, the human persons whose lives are reduced to commodity forms by the plunderers are not afforded the status of "citizen." Instead, these persons are relegated to the position of "subject." As Ellora Derenoncourt defines the latter, subjects are those "whose economic and political lives are hemmed in by coercive, undemocratic institutions, with no due-process rights, susceptible to coercive labor practices, and a distinct lack of opportunities to accumulate wealth."[31] Relegated to the

---

[29] Ibid., xvi.
[30] Ibid., xix.
[31] Ellora Derenoncourt, "The Historical Origins of Global Inequality," in *After Piketty: The*

status of subject, which can be taken as the functional equivalent of Gutiér-rez's epithet "nonperson," persons within extractive zones lack the requisite political power to enact and sustain the second, countervailing, dimension of the "double movement" that Polanyi takes to be inevitable.[32] As a result, the conditions for a market society are most fully instantiated in zones of extraction that are peripheral to the core regions of the system.[33] Human life, and all of its ecological dimensions, are most readily reduced to the commodity forms of land and labor within zones of extraction. Indeed, it is the reduction of the earth and human life at the periphery to the commodities of land and labor that maximizes the processes of extraction both in terms of efficiency and volume, thereby orienting history toward the advent of the Anthropocene.

Extracting Land and Labor from the "Hinterland" into the "City"

Highlighting the vampire-like character of the 500-year project, Eduardo Galeano remarks that the function of this project has been to reduce Latin America to a "region of open veins." Expounding on this point, he writes, "Everything, from the discovery until our times, has always been transmuted into European—or later United States—capital, and as such has accumulated in distant centers of power." Galeano goes on to emphasize this view in a manner that resonates with Polanyi's critique of market society. "*Everything: the soil, its fruits and its mineral-rich depths, the people and their capacity to work and to consume, natural resources and human resources*" has been transmuted

---

Agenda for Economics and Inequality, ed. Heather Boushey et al. (Cambridge, MA: Harvard University Press, 2017), 492. In making the distinction between citizen and subject, Derenoncourt borrows loosely from Mamhood Mamdani's *Citizen and Subject: Contemporary Africa and the Legacy of Late Colonialism* (Princeton, NJ: Princeton University Press, 1996). In his text, Mamdani's primary concern is to surface the colonial roots of the power structures in present-day Africa, giving special attention to the manner in which these structures continue to be character-ized by an urban (citizen)/rural (subject) divide.

[32] In both distinguishing between "citizen" and "subject" and in noting the comparatively circumscribed political power of the latter, in no way do I suggest that those relegated to the latter designation are without agency or the means to resist the processes of commoditization and extraction. As it has been well documented, human persons subjected to various systems of domination subvert these systems in myriad life-affirming ways. Nonetheless, the agency of exploited and marginalized human persons within sites of extraction does not dissolve the often vast differentials of power that characterize these historical realities. It is precisely these power differentials that must be attended to in order to comprehend the historical development of both the 500-year project and the global politico-ecological crisis that grew with it.

[33] To be clear, the argument here is not that the colonial project, or even the extractive zones therein, functioned to constitute a market society per se (this would have to involve an exami-nation of the ways in which markets functioned within the colonial project or within zones of extraction, which is beyond the scope of this study). Instead, my more modest claim, is that the politico-ecological realities of the extractive zone create the condition for the possibility of a market society to be realized.

into commodities.[34] Likewise, "production methods and class structure have been successively determined from outside for each area by meshing it into the universal gearbox of capitalism."[35] Here Galeano, the poet-turned-historian, captures the essence of the technocratic paradigm placed at the service of extractive colonial and neocolonial regimes.

As Galeano indicates, the endeavor to transmute Latin America—its people and its soil—into capital began with contact in 1492. This point is evidenced in the writings of Cristóbal Colón, who describes his first encounters with the land of Hispaniola in a letter to King Ferdinand and Queen Isabella of Spain: "The gold is most excellent, and he who fills his coffers with it will be able to do whatever he likes in the world."[36] Colón assures his royal financiers that the Arawak people indigenous to the island, could easily be conquered for the Spanish crown: "With fifty men you will have them all in subjection, and be able to do anything you want with them."[37] Here, Colón's early statements evidence the rudiments of what Bartolomé de Las Casas, the fifteenth-century Dominican friar, would label the "two feet" of the Spanish incursion: war and enslavement in the service of regimes of plunder.[38]

The processes of colonial extraction were first formalized with the creation of the Spanish *encomienda* system; Colón played a critical role in organizing this system.[39] Following Spanish wars of domination, the establishment of this system granted Spanish invaders legal authority over the soil and indigenous inhabitants of Latin America, at least from a European perspective. Some of the earliest moments of the *encomienda* system's governance of the "process of transmutation" are chronicled in the historiographies of Las Casas. In a well-known passage from his *Historia de los Indios*, Las Casas describes the manner in which indigenous labor was exploited in order to extract precious minerals from the earth:

> Mountains are turned over from bottom to top and top to bottom a thousand times; [the workers] dig, split rocks, move stones, and carry the earth

---

[34]Eduardo Galeano, *Open Veins of Latin America: Five Centuries of the Pillage of a Continent* (New York: Monthly Review Press, 1997), 3. Italics are mine.

[35]Ibid.

[36]Cristóbal Colón, *Textos y documentos completos de viajes, cartas, y memorials*, ed. Consuelo Varela (Madrid: Alianza, 1989), 327.

[37]Ibid., 33.

[38]On this point see *LC*, 99. For Gutiérrez's analysis of Las Casas's thought in relation to the first entry, see *LC*, Parts II and III. For Gutiérrez's account of Las Casas's thought in relation to the second entry, see *LC*, Parts IV and V.

[39]Colón himself granted the first *encomienda* on Hispaniola to a fellow Spaniard in 1499. See Lynne Guitar, "Encomienda System," in *The Historical Encyclopedia of World Slavery*, vol. 1, ed. Junius P. Rodriguez (Santa Barbara: ABC-CLIO, 1997), 250.

on their backs to wash it in the rivers, and those who wash gold stay in the water all the time with their waists bent so constantly it breaks their bodies; and when the mines take on water, the worst task of all is to take the water from below with washtubs and throw it outside.[40]

The forced labor of indigenous persons was unceasing. When enslaved persons failed to meet the quotas of goods that the *encomenderos* demanded as tribute, they faced torture and death—practices that would be repeated and refined over the course of the history of colonial and neocolonial extraction.[41]

The Spanish plunder of Latin America helped underwrite the expansion of war on the European continent. As Kenneth Pomeranz notes, the gold and silver taken from the so-called New World, "financed numerous wars, including Spain's nearly successful assaults on the emerging core economies of northwest Europe."[42] At the same time, the influx of precious metals into Spain and other parts of Europe also funded the expansion and diversification of the processes of extraction at the peripheries of the colonial system so that a wider array of raw materials could be appropriated to serve the aims of the architects of the colonial project. Likewise, as Pomeranz observes, the plunder of silver and gold was eventually utilized to cover "much of the cost of procuring slaves for the Americas."[43] One can begin to discern the vicious cycle of extraction that developed within the transcontinental political ecology of the colonial project. The conscription of land into the service of the colonizing powers served to finance the conscription of labor, which thereby allowed for the development of a more expansive and comprehensive exploitation of land by these same powers.

In embodying the early efforts of colonizers to bring their programs of extraction under formal control, the *encomienda* system of colonial Spain anticipated the rise of elaborate systems of monocrop plantation farming. These systems increased economic profit for the colonizers, not only by converting the lands of Latin America to fields for "cash crops" but also by streamlining the processes of extraction. Monocrop farming allowed for efficiency gains in the planting, harvesting, packaging, and transporting of the earth's commodities. As Pomeranz writes, the "concentration on one or two exports in most plantation areas greatly facilitated a crucial improvement in trade itself. Transatlantic shipping costs fell roughly 50 percent during the eighteenth century, even without sub-

---

[40]Bartolomé de Las Casas, *Historia de las Indias*, vol. 2, ed. André Saint-Lu (Caracas: Biblioteca Ayacucho, 1986), 57.

[41]On the development of torture, see Edward Baptist's account of the "pushing system" discussed below.

[42]Kenneth Pomeranz, *The Great Divergence: Europe, China, and the Making of the Modern World Economy* (Princeton, NJ: Princeton University Press, 2000), 270.

[43]Ibid., 271. As Pomeranz observes, European traders exchanged silver for Asian commodities, which were then used to finance the purchase of enslaved human persons.

stantial technological change."[44] Monocrop-agricultural systems thus helped to optimize the processes of extraction, with this optimization facilitating greater accumulations of wealth within the core regions of the colonial project.

Monocrop farming, as is well known, deleteriously affects ecosystems in numerous ways. To give but one illustration, Tucker, noting the effects of sugar plantations in the Caribbean, writes, "In many locations primary forest was cleared expressly so as to plant cane. In other instances, cane displaced previous field crops and pastures." Tucker notes that sugar cane displaced a multitude of vegetation and animal life. He concludes by observing that "in many locations the higher slopes above the cane fields were gradually stripped of timber for boiling the raw cane juice and cooking the workers' food."[45] In short, Tucker describes the ways in which the earth was pressed to exhaustion in the ongoing effort to convert the soils at the periphery of the colonial project into commodities.

The rise of cash crop agriculture within the emerging colonial project brought patterns of politico-ecological destruction under the sway of technocratic logic. However, these exploitative patterns began as the colonizers first unleashed their ravenous desire upon the world they had invaded. As Willie James Jennings observes, rather than attending to the nuances and differences of the ecosystems that structured the natural world of Latin America, Spanish invaders imposed their own image on these systems from the outset.[46] In so doing, they dramatically reorganized the indigenous landscapes while also unsettling the human communities. An early and infamous example of this imposition was the introduction of domesticated ungulates (e.g., sheep and pigs) to the Mezquital Valley of present-day Mexico. Ungulates devastated the landscape. Elinor Melville observes that, as a result of the introduction of these animals, "the once fertile flatlands were covered in a dense growth of mesquite-dominated desert scrub, the high, steep-sided hills were treeless, and the piedmont was eroded and gullied."[47] Sheep grazing undid traditional agricultural patterns, resulting "in the formation of a new and far less hospitable landscape within which the indigenous populations were marginalized

---

[44]Ibid., 267.

[45]Tucker, *Insatiable Appetite*, 7–8. For a nuanced analysis of the relationship between land and labor in the *zona de mata* in Brazil up through the twentieth century, see Thomas D. Rogers, *The Deepest Wounds: A Labor and Environmental History of Sugar in Northeast Brazil* (Chapel Hill: University of North Carolina Press, 2010). Rogers is less interested in the exogenous forces driving the rise of monocrop agriculture in Brazil. However, his analysis highlights well the intertwined relationship between humans and the land they cultivate.

[46]This is a point emphasized by Willie James Jennings in *The Christian Imagination: Theology and the Origins of Race* (New Haven, CT: Yale University Press, 2010), 65–118.

[47]Elinor G. K. Melville, *A Plague of Sheep: Environmental Consequences of the Conquest of Mexico* (New York: Cambridge University Press, 1997), 39.

and alienated, their traditional resources degraded or lost, and their access to the means of production restricted."[48] The imposition of ungulates, then, did not simply have a deleterious effect on the indigenous ecosystems but on the people as well. As Melville states, "Sheep did not simply replace men . . . although that was the final outcome; rather, they displaced them—ate them, as the saying goes."[49]

The politico-ecological devastation wrought by the ignorant and careless introduction of ungulates, foreshadowed the rationalized patterns of destruction that have continued to play out in history down through the present-day. If "sheep ate men," then extractive monocultures devoured entire cultures, societies, and ecosystems in order to fund the exaltation of the European core within the colonial project.[50] The common thread between the introduction of ungulates and the technocratic systems of extraction is that both signal the remaking of the world in the image of the colonizers. From the outset of the 500-year project, the earth's politico-ecology was organized to conform to the desires of the colonizer.

The general pattern of exploitation that emerged during the early decades of the colonial project can be summarized in the following manner. The impulse toward extraction and domination, fueled by what Las Casas would name as an idolatrous greed and desire for glory, initially manifested itself in rather desultory expressions of imposition.[51] However, these exploitative impulses quickly came to conform progressively to "rational" patterns of control endemic to the emerging technocratic paradigm, which systematically reduced the earth to the commodity form of land at the peripheries of the system. This land was organized, with increasing precision, in accordance with the fundamental aim of the colonial project—extracting the resources and wealth of the earth and concentrating them in European and, later, North American centers of power.

The reduction of the earth to the extractable commodity of "land" at the peripheries of the colonial project was vital to the rise of European dominance at the beginning of the 500-year project. Pomeranz argues that Europe's ap-

---

[48]Ibid., 40.

[49]Ibid., 39.

[50]For a broad critical account of this phenomenon, see Galeano, *Open Veins of Latin America*, 59–133. I should note here that the colonial exploitation of the earth at the periphery did result in the production of wealth within the periphery as well. However, this wealth production itself tended to be acutely asymmetrically distributed. Examining the extraction ratio of preindustrial societies, Branko Milanovic finds that the majority of European colonial regimes "pushed 'the art of exploitation' to the extreme." Moreover, he finds that these regimes created some of the most economically unequal geographical zones the world has ever known and, in so doing, established patterns of unjust political ecology that would be repeated over the centuries. See Branko Milanovic, *The Haves and the Have Nots* (New York: Basic, 2011), 198–202.

[51]See Gutiérrez, *Las Casas*, 420–43.

propriation of land at the peripheries of the project was a key driver of what he famously terms "the great divergence" between the European colonial powers and the rest of the world at the dawn of modernity. To give a striking example of Europe's insatiable appetite and desperate need for colonized land, Pomeranz finds that by 1830, Britain, through its imports of cotton, sugar, and timber, utilized somewhere between 25 and 30 million acres of land outside of its national borders.[52] Britain's appropriation of these "ghost acres," as Pomeranz terms them, is particularly notable because, within its geographical boundaries, Britain had only 17 million arable acres. Thus, in order to sustain its unprecedented levels of economic growth, the British empire required 45 to 75 percent more land than could be accounted for within the boundaries of its nation-state. As Pomeranz's argument makes plain, the rise of the European core depended on highly refined patterns of plunder.

Slavery, Racism, and Technocratic Paradigm

The technocratic paradigm functioned as the organizing rationale for the plunder of the earth at the periphery of the colonial project. This paradigm was also employed increasingly in efforts to reduce human life to labor within these zones of extraction. This is most clearly evidenced in the development of the system of chattel slavery within the colonial project, a system that played an indispensable role in sustaining the project in the fifteenth century and beyond.[53] Here I shift my argument to focus on innovations to the slave system in the nineteenth-century United States. However, before turning to consider the ways in which the colonial project's system of human enslavement was continually brought under ever more comprehensive forms of "rational control," it is important to comment on the emergence of anti-black and anti-brown racism within the nascent colonial project.

Ibram Kendi observes that it is a commonly held view that hateful and ignorant prejudices on the part of some group of human persons are what give rise to racist ideologies and that these ideologies, in turn, produce systems of racial exploitation and domination. However, in his masterly study of the emergence of

---

[52]Pomeranz, *Great Divergence*, 276.

[53]In his foundational account of the relationship between capitalism and slavery, Eric Williams develops the two-part thesis that chattel slavery was vital in financing the industrial revolution in England and that, subsequently, industrialization rendered the slave system obsolete, while continuing to exploit labor power along racist lines. See Eric Williams, *Capitalism and Slavery* (Chapel Hill: University of North Carolina Press, 1944). There has been a recent renewal of historiography on themes related to Williams's thesis. See, for example, *Slavery's Capitalism: A New History of American Economic Development*, ed. Sven Beckert and Seth Rockman (Philadelphia: University of Pennsylvania Press, 2016).

racist concepts in the United States, Kendi argues that this manner of construal inverts, more often than not, the actual historical development of racialized human exploitation. In reality, the implementation of exploitative practices and policies, laid down along racial lines, gives rise to racist ideologies that thereby produces hateful ignorance. To this effect, Kendi writes, "Racist ideas usually did *not* dictate the decisions of the most powerful . . . when they instituted, defended, and tolerated discriminatory policies that affected millions of Black lives." Rather, he argues, "Racially discriminatory policies have usually sprung from economic, political, and cultural self-interests."[54] For Kendi, it is the social power arrangements that exploited black and brown human persons that created the impetus for constructing anti-black racist ideologies.[55]

With regard to the advent of systems of human enslavement within the colonial project, Kendi's argument helps explain how the processes of extractive colonialism catalyzed the emergence of anti-black and anti-brown racist ideologies that have plagued modernity unceasingly ever since. The extraction of wealth and natural resources from the lands at the colonized periphery required a massive expenditure of labor power, particularly within the preindustrial context of the early colonial era. Within that context, the labor of enslaved human persons became the privileged manner of organizing labor in the service of plunder. When the peoples indigenous to Latin America proved to be a greater cost than benefit for the demonic demands of slavery, because of their vulnerability to European disease, the architects behind Europe's systems of plunder turned to the continent of Africa to procure the labor power required for the processes of extraction. It is this turn that gives rise to the colonial-project's anti-black racist ideologies, which attempted to justify the already incipient system of human enslavement needed to optimize the plunder of the Americas.

As the foregoing argument has already indicated, slave labor was utilized from the earliest moments of the colonial project. The underlying reason that the architects of extractive colonialism came to implement systems of slavery lies, in great part, in the degree of control over labor power that these systems afforded enslavers. As Edward Baptist points out, the seeds of this conception of the enslaved human as "labor" is evident in Aristotle's description of a slave as an "instrument . . . a living tool." As Baptist writes, Aristotle's description gave "formal recognition to the idea that the slave was the master's . . . will

---

[54]Ibram X. Kendi, *Stamped from the Beginning: The Definitive History of Racist Ideas in America* (New York: Nation, 2016), 9–10.

[55]Using the terminology developed in Chapter 2, it should be noted that Kendi's interpretation of history suggests that the socio-structural level of historical reality is the catalyst for shaping the cultural/psychological formations of society. At the same time, it is clear that for Kendi both of these dimensions of historical reality mutually condition the other.

embodied."[56] Within the dominant Western imaginary, the enslaved human was a tool for labor directed by the enslaver's desire.

Aristotle's description was closely reflected in the language that enslavers in the United States came to use in referring to enslaved human persons. Whereas enslavers in the United States initially described enslaved humans as "heads," by the early 1800s "hands" became the dominant denotation. This shift in language is telling. "Hand," Baptist writes, "was the ideal form of the commodity 'slave,' just as white crystals are the ideal commodity form of 'sugarcane.' Each person for sale was a commodity: alienable, easily sold, and in important ways, rendered effectively identical for white entrepreneurs' direct manipulation."[57] In short, the referent "hand" communicates the Aristotelian view that an enslaved human is an "'instrument' of the enslaver, 'a living tool'"—market society and the technocrat's ideal human person (at least with respect to production).[58] For the architects of the colonial project, the enslaved human person came to be viewed fundamentally as a tool for extraction. As Achille Mbembe observes in noting the connection between the rise of anti-black racist ideologies and the rise of chattel slavery, "To produce Blackness is to produce a social link of subjection and a *body of extraction* . . . a body from which great effort is made to extract maximum profit."[59] The degree of control that the slave system offered enslavers allowed them to procure longer working hours and higher productivity from enslaved humans at lower costs. Human enslavement, "legitimized" through racist ideologies, made the processes of extraction more efficient and thus more lucrative.

To be clear, the system of slavery was never wholly successful in reducing enslaved human persons to the category of "labor." As is well attested to in the twentieth-century literature on the experiences of enslaved human persons, resistance to the radically dehumanizing system of slavery abounded.[60] This resistance took numerous forms, from attempts at escape and outright insurrection to less dramatic practices such as surreptitious work slowdowns, sabotage (e.g., inserting rocks into bales of cotton) and the uncountable small acts that

---

[56] Edward E. Baptist, *The Half Has Never Been Told: Slavery and the Making of American Capitalism* (New York: Basic, 2014), 101. To be clear, the institution of slavery in Aristotle's time was distinct from that of chattel slavery in the modern United States. Indeed, the modern-day term "slave" came to be derived from "Slav" (as in a person of Slavic origin) well after Aristotle. Nonetheless, Baptist's citation of Aristotle here is apt in describing the intention of enslavers and the institution of chattel slavery.

[57] Ibid.

[58] Baptist argues that an important rationale driving the enslavers' fragmentation of enslaved families was that such fragmentation would render the enslaved individual more malleable to enforced labor. See ibid., 106.

[59] Achille Mbembe, *Critique of Black Reason* (Durham, NC: Duke University Press, 2017), 18. Italics are Mbembe's.

[60] This is a point that Baptist emphasizes at various points in *The Half Has Never Been Told*.

constitute the formation of humane communities of mutual care within a hor-rifically degrading context.[61] In myriad ways, enslaved human persons, despite the intentions of the enslavers, never allowed themselves to be reduced to the epithet of "hand."

However, it is precisely because of the various forms of resistance offered by enslaved human persons that the architects of colonial slavery sought to establish increasingly comprehensive systems of control with the intention of reducing the human person, as much as possible, to a tool for performing the process of extraction.[62] As Caitlin Rosenthal observes, "[Enslaved persons] seeking spaces for themselves faced complex and often quantitative informa-tion systems that knit together violence, fear, and social terror."[63] In order to appreciate more fully the courageousness of their resistance, it is necessary "to comprehend the system [against which] enslaved people sought to survive."[64] As Rosenthal argues, the system of colonial slavery increasingly came to utilize the accounting logic and instrumental manipulation inherent in the technocratic paradigm in efforts to control more fully the labor power of enslaved human persons and spur increases in their efficiency and overall productivity.

This is most strikingly evident in the modifications to the system of slavery in the United States in response to the invention of the cotton gin in 1793. For the burgeoning colonial project, the invention of the cotton gin marked a decisive moment. The gin permitted cotton producers to clean as much cotton as they could grow and harvest, allowing for the possibility of dramatically increasing the world's supply of refined cotton—a prospect that, if fulfilled, stood to transform much of the world's economy. However, in order to realize this possibility, it was necessary to increase the amount of cotton grown in the United States. After all, the gin could only clean cotton that first had been planted, grown, and picked. At the turn of the nineteenth century, these latter endeavors still relied wholly on the labor power of enslaved human persons. Thus, in order to fulfill the tantalizing promise of the cotton gin, enslavers needed to generate increasing rates of productivity from the humans they saw

---

[61]See, for example, John W. Blassingame, *The Slave Community: Plantation Life in the Ante-bellum South* (New York: Oxford University Press, 1979), and Stephanie M. H. Camp, *Closer to Freedom: Enslaved Women and Everyday Resistance in the Plantation South* (Chapel Hill: University of North Carolina Press, 2004).

[62]On this point Caitlin Rosenthal writes, "Control and resistance are not opposites. Control does not reflect a lack of resistance, nor does it in any way signal consent. To offer an adequate account of chattel slavery, historians need to acknowledge the vitality of slave culture without romanticizing it or overstating its scope. What enslaved people accomplished was remarkable but also dramatically circumscribed by systems of violence and surveillance. To understand the significance of moments of resistance, we need to comprehend the system that enslaved people sought to survive." Caitlin Rosenthal, *Accounting for Slavery: Masters and Management* (Cambridge, MA: Harvard University Press, 2018), 194.

[63]Ibid.
[64]Ibid.

as "hands." It was this predicament that led to the inception of "the pushing system"—a system of social engineering that revolutionized cotton production.

The pushing system combined innovations in surveillance, violence, and streamlined labor in order to boost the productivity of enslaved humans in an effort to fulfill the promise of the cotton gin. Fieldworkers were now placed under constant oversight and forced to work the land from sunrise "until it was too dark to tell cotton from weed."[65] Midday meals were eliminated. The work on the plantation became almost entirely uniform. Within the pushing system, nearly all enslaved human persons were given the identical tasks of planting, weeding, and picking seemingly unending and indistinguishable rows of cotton. Only a small number of enfeebled persons were left in the shelters to prepare the night's ration for the enslaved humans forced to work the fields.

Careful records were kept of each enslaved person's productivity. When these human persons failed to meet their individualized daily quota of production, enslavers would torture them with violence that night, if not sooner. "The key feature that distinguishes [torture] from mere sadistic behavior," writes Baptist, "is supposedly that torture aims to extract 'truth.'" He continues, noting that the torture of enslaved human persons did, in fact, divulge a truth: "The maximum poundage that a man, woman, or child could pick." Once this datum was ascertained, "The torturer then challenged the enslaved person's reason once again, to force the creation of an even greater capacity to pick. . . . This was why many planters and overseers whipped even—or, perhaps especially—their fastest pickers."[66] Enslavers, then, "rationally" calibrated torture in order to maximize increases in productivity.

Indeed, the accounting practices adopted by enslavers certified that their ways of optimizing labor achieved their desired ends. "The soft power of quantification complemented the driving force of the whip," writes Rosenthal. "Systematic accounting practices thrived on slave plantations not despite the chattel principle but because of it. . . . Through accounting, human figures became figures on paper, and human beings appeared as no more than hands."[67] Here, then, one finds on display the full barbarity of the technocratic paradigm and the commodification of human life in the service of extractive colonialism.

The innovations of enslavers did, in fact, bring about the outcomes they had desired. The effect of the widespread adoption of the pushing system across plantations in the United States catalyzed a remarkable burst of efficiency and output. Whereas at the beginning of the nineteenth century, enslavers commonly figured that one enslaved human could work five acres of land, by the

---

[65] Baptist, *Half Has Never Been Told*, 118.

[66] Ibid., 139–40

[67] Caitlin Rosenthal, "Slavery's Scientific Management: Masters and Managers," in *Slavery's Capitalism: A New History of American Economic Development*, ed. Beckert and Rockman, 86.

midpoint of that century that estimate had doubled to ten acres.[68] At the same time, enslaved fieldworkers became even more efficient at working the land allotted to them so that over roughly this same period the mean daily pounds of cotton harvested by an enslaved human person nearly quadrupled.[69]

The implementation of the pushing system and the gains in productivity that the system extracted from the labor power of enslaved human persons provided a vital economic boon to the growing US and world economies. This boon resounded throughout these economic systems in multiple ways. "Lower real cotton prices," Baptist writes, "passed on gains in the form of capital reinvested in more efficient factory equipment, higher wages for the new industrial working class, and revenue for factory owners, enslavers, and governments."[70] Moreover, the stability of Britain's nascent textile-based industrialization system relied on the expansion of US cotton production, so that "all of the accelerating curves of growth, would have been short-circuited if embryo industries had run out of cotton fiber."[71] The resources that the ghost acres of the colonial project afforded the nations at the core of the project would have been insufficient to produce the great divergence between core and periphery had the lives of enslaved human persons not also been largely reduced to labor within the zones of extraction. As it was, eventually, much of the world came to clothe itself in fabric made from cotton picked by "hands" in the United States, reaping benefit from that which it had not sown.

We are now at a point where we can better grasp the historical truth of Cone's statement. From its inception, the 500-year project functioned to create and sustain the otherwise untenable conditions of a market society at the periphery of the system. The aim of the project was to reduce the earth and human life at the periphery to the commodities of land and labor for the purpose of optimizing the extraction of wealth and power from the periphery and concentrating it in the colonial project's core regions. These processes of extraction, governed by the instrumental logic intrinsic to the technocratic paradigm, initiated a centuries-long process of ecological degradation and socioeconomic exploitation. At the same time, these processes of exploitation gave rise to racist anti-black and anti-brown ideologies that attempted to legitimize the already coalescing patterns of exploitation constituting the white European colonial project. These racist ideologies remain prominent factors in the organization of the world's political ecology today, shaping, among other things, labor markets and the distribution of pollution on local and global scales.[72]

---

[68] Baptist, *Half Has Never Been Told*, 117.

[69] Ibid., 126–27.

[70] Ibid., 128.

[71] Ibid., 82.

[72] On race and class, see Etienne Balibar and Immanuel Wallerstein, *Race, Nation, Class: Ambiguous Identities* (London: Verso, 1991), 29–36. On global environmental justice issues,

The reduction of the earth to land within the 500-year project also set the course for the transgression of multiple planetary boundaries, as defined by Johan Rockström. The conversion of the diverse arable terrains of the earth into land for monocrop agriculture, a prominent feature of extractivism, has become a dominant method of land management within the 500-year project. At the planetary level, this practice has driven "land-system change" to a point where there is increasing risk that the human transformation of the land will transgress its "safe operating" threshold. Moreover, the human transformation of land now constitutes one of the primary drivers of the sixth great extinction, thereby threatening the requisite biodiversity for a healthy biosphere.[73] Extractive land policies have also provided the pattern for the subsequent extraction of fossil fuels, charting the course for the current climate-change emergency.

In a different vein, Rosenthal argues that modern technocratic systems of accounting and labor control grew out of, at least in part, the techniques and schemes developed by enslavers to maximize the exploitation of labor power. Today, these modern systems of control, when coupled with both technological advances and the impulse toward the ever-greater accumulation of wealth, now propel a phenomenon of social acceleration in which time is increasingly compressed and organized for the purpose of extracting labor from workers.[74] Operating in accordance with the logic of the technocratic paradigm, contemporary technologies and management strategies conspire, in increasingly pervasive ways, to reduce human life to practices of incessant production and consumption.[75]

Finally, extractive colonialism established structures of global inequality and patterns of exploitation that have been reproduced institutionally over the last five centuries. Whereas the plunder of both land and labor initially spurred the "great divergence" between the global north and the global south, the institutionally mandated maintenance of the patterns of plunder has sustained the divergence throughout the 500-year project. Thus, to recall Gómez-Barris's

---

see David Naguib Pellow, *Resisting Global Toxics: Transnational Movements for Environmental Justice* (Cambridge, MA: MIT Press, 2007).

[73] A potentially catastrophic example of the rise in species extinctions can be observed in the populations of insect communities. In their review of the recent literature, Francisco Sánchez-Bayo and Kris A. G. Wyckhus find that approximately 40 percent of insect species are now facing extinction. Land transformation is among the key causes of the phenomenon. See Francisco Sánchez-Bayo and Kris A. G. Wyckhus, "Worldwide Decline of Entomofauna: A Review of Its Drivers," *Conservation Biology* 232 (2019): 8–27.

[74] See Harmut Rosa, *Social Acceleration: A New Theory of Modernity* (New York: Columbia University Press, 2013), 151–94.

[75] To be clear, I do not wish to suggest an equivalence between the horrors of slavery and the generalized texture of modern life. Any such equivalence must be vehemently rejected. My point here is simply to note that the management and accounting practices developed by enslavers have been adapted into contemporary management techniques, which, in themselves, work to reduce human life to the commodity of labor.

phrase, "the after lives" of extractive colonialism continue to live on. I now turn to consider more fully the exploitative patterns of technocratic extractivism.

ECOLOGICAL DEBT AND UNEQUAL EXCHANGE

how can reparations be made?

As I noted in Chapter 2, Pope Francis asserts in *Laudato Si'* that a "true 'ecological debt' exists, particularly between the global north and south." This debt, the pope observes, has accrued due to "the disproportionate use of natural resources by certain countries over long periods of time" (no. 51). Francis's judgment is consonant with the foregoing argument of this chapter. Here, then, I move to consider more deeply the nature of this debt and the dynamics through which it has been sustained over the centuries.

The early colonial plunder of the periphery by the core, as we have seen, created an initial "endowment" that allowed the core to exalt itself. However, this initial endowment was not self-sustaining. Derenoncourt notes that because of the inevitable economic shocks that occur throughout the course of history, endowments, if left alone, inevitably shrink until their benefit becomes negligible.[76] She emphasizes the importance of socio-political institutions in maintaining and expanding endowments throughout the subsequent years and centuries. Institutions are able to organize the political ecology of the world in ways that allow them to "maintain the disparity" established by the initial endowment.[77] In other words, institutional agency, when serving the self-interests of established powers, facilitates retrenchment and even the expansion of inequality over the course of history, even in the face of economic shocks.[78] Thus Derenoncourt concludes that "while initial endowments matter for global inequality in the short and medium run, in the long run only the effect of institutions remains."[79]

disparity
must
exist
for the
core
to
maintain
and
therefore
their
wealth

---

[76]Derenoncourt, "Historical Origins of Global Inequality," 491–511.

[77]See George Kennan's comment in Chapter 1 asserting that "*Our real task in the coming period is to devise a pattern of relationships which will permit us to maintain this position of disparity without positive detriment to our national security. . . . We need not deceive ourselves that we can afford today the luxury of altruism and world-benefaction*" (Chapter 1, note 89).

[78]Naomi Klein's work suggests that economic shocks can even be utilized to expand inequality when harnessed by entrenched powers. See Naomi Klein, *The Shock Doctrine: The Rise of Disaster Capitalism* (New York: Picador, 2007).

[79]Derenoncourt, "Historical Origins of Global Inequality," 494. It should be noted that Derenoncourt is not concerned with ecological debt specifically but economic inequality in general. As an example of the way institutions are capable of retrenchment, she cites the manner in which the outcome of the US Civil War erased the South's largest endowment of capital when it ended slavery. Despite this enormous shock to the Southern economy, enslavers were able to hold onto power and wealth in the subsequent decades. Of course, institutions have a tendency to reproduce the inherited status quo—"extractive institutions cast long shadows," writes Derenoncourt. In making this observation, she follows the findings of Daron Acemoglu,

Derenoncourt's argument is important because it suggests that the ecological debt owed to the global south is not simply an artifact from the receding past, but rather a dynamic phenomenon that has been maintained continually over the course of the 500-year project. Something of the character of this dynamic is captured by Stephen Bunker and Paul Ciccantell, who write that, in competing for trade dominance, the nations in the core regions of the 500-year project constantly "developed new and more powerful technologies, financial institutions, and state systems domestically" aimed at sustaining the processes of extraction. "Abroad, [core nations] reorganized raw materials markets and transport systems in ways that complemented their domestic innovations and made them more powerful."[80] Thus, once the core nations of the global north established their dominance through the early processes of colonial extraction, they quickly set about the protracted task of innovating and modifying the ways in which they organized the political ecology of the earth. Core nations employed their initial coerced endowment of power/capital in the service of protecting and expanding their grasp on the resources of the world. In *Laudato Si'*, Francis points to the ongoing character of this dynamic when he affirms that the ecological debt not only has deep historical roots but is also connected to continuing "commercial imbalances" (no. 51) in trade. Here, the pope refers to what scholars commonly refer to as the phenomenon of "ecologically unequal exchange."[81]

Following Andrew Jorgenson, ecologically unequal exchange can be defined as the production and maintenance of "asymmetrical power relationships between more-developed / more-powerful and less-developed / less-powerful countries, wherein the former gain disproportionate advantages at the expense of the latter through patterns of trade and other related structural characteristics."[82]

Simon Johnson, and James Robinson, "The Colonial Origins of Comparative Development: An Empirical Investigation," *American Economic Review* 91, no. 5 (2001): 1369–1401. The authors argue that weak institutions tend to perdure in regions where extractive colonialism first became entrenched. The perennial weakness of civic, political, and economic institutions within these regions has left them persistently vulnerable to continued programs of extraction. Derenoncourt, for example, observes that the regions where extractive colonialism first entrenched itself during the 500-year project have tended to lag behind other regions of the world in developing reliable systems of income tax. This is notable because income tax is vital to generating the necessary revenue for sustaining institutions capable of fostering and protecting regional interests and well-being. Thus, initial deficits, both in terms of endowments and institutional health, have tended to be reproduced over time.

[80]Stephen G. Bunker and Paul S. Ciccantell, *Globalization and the Race for Resources* (Baltimore: Johns Hopkins University Press, 2005), 224.

[81]For a helpful overview of this discourse, see Alf Hornborg and Joan Martinez-Alier, eds., "Ecologically Unequal Exchange and Ecological Debt," *Journal of Political Ecology* 23 (2016): 328–491.

[82]Andrew K. Jorgenson, "The Sociology of Ecologically Unequal Exchange, Foreign Investment Dependence and Environmental Load Displacement: Summary of the Literature and Implications for Sustainability," *Journal of Political Ecology* 23 (2016): 335.

the periphery can never extract from the core

The "disproportionate advantages" that the world's powerful countries gain include the ability to extract resources from the periphery and deposit wastes within the periphery at favorable rates of exchange. Thus, the advantages and disadvantages of ecologically unequal exchange present themselves in terms of both economic productivity and ecological health. As a result, the commercial imbalances that characterize ecologically unequal exchange sustain the plunder of both land and labor at the periphery by the powers of the global north.

As is evident in Jorgenson's definition, ecologically unequal exchange results from the sustained exploitation of the political and economic power differentials existing between the countries at the core and periphery of the project. This difference in power is emphasized by Joan Martinez-Alier, who observes that the concept of ecologically unequal exchange aims to highlight *"the poverty and the lack of political power* [of the periphery]."[83] The concept elucidates the periphery's "lack of alternative options, in terms of exporting other renewable goods with lower local impacts, or in terms of internalizing the externalities in the price of exports."[84] For Martinez-Alier, the historical phenomenon of ecologically unequal exchange is predicated on various forms of economic and political coercion. The phenomenon, then, testifies to the truth of Thucydides's observation regarding the illusory character of freedom within the broader political realm—"the strong do what they will" while "the weak suffer what they must."[85] Indeed, Jorgenson and Brett Clark argue that the positive correlation between high economic development and strong military power suggests that coercive military intervention always lurks as a threat to ensure that the terms of ecologically unequal exchange remain intact.[86]

the periphery is underpaid only by the core

Whereas the work of Jorgenson, Clark, and Martinez-Alier surfaces the asymmetrical power dynamics at play in perpetuating the phenomenon of ecologically unequal exchange, Alf Hornborg's analysis of this phenomenon helps clarify what is lost and gained in the exchange. As Hornborg argues, the ongoing plunder of the global south by the north can be construed fundamentally as the systematic transfer of productive energy from the former to the latter. The social metabolisms of the countries that make up the global north require

---

[83]Joan Martinez-Alier, "The Ecological Debt," *Kurswecshel* 4 (2002): 6.

[84]Ibid. Italics are Martinez-Alier's. Importantly, she also observes that the recognition of unequal ecological exchange does not demand that one adopt a strict bioregional approach to trade. It does, however, demand a better accounting of externalities in addition to responding to asymmetries of power.

[85]Thucydides, *Peloponnesian War* (Letchworth: Temple, 1914), 394.

[86]In their analysis, Jorgenson and Clark find that "more economically developed and militarily powerful nations are able to secure and maintain favorable terms of trade, allowing them to overutilize global environmental space, which suppresses the domestic consumption levels of many less-developed countries." See Andrew K. Jorgenson and Brett Clark, "The Economy, Military, and Ecologically Unequal Relationships in Comparative Perspective: A Panel Study of the Ecological Footprints of Nations, 1975–2000," *Social Problems* 56 (2009): 642.

the core cannot function on its own

more energy than these countries can produce.[87] Thus, the countries of the global north continue to turn to the south to secure the requisite raw materials needed to sustain their "highly developed" social metabolisms. These materials are then transformed into energy, goods, and commodities that are sold on the market at a profit.

Hornborg's key insight is that there tends to be an inverse relationship between exchange value and the productive potential of the materials traded on the market. Thus, finished goods and products, commonly understood simply to have had "value added" to them, at the same time also have had their productive potential irrevocably diminished. The common (mis)perception of value creates a situation in which the resources extracted from the global south are perennially undervalued. Likewise, the standardization of these asymmetric transfers has created a situation in which, at the close of the twentieth century, "the United States' share of world energy is 25%, while 20% of the world's people do not have access to enough energy to successfully maintain their own body metabolism."[88]

According to Hornborg, throughout the history of the 500-year project, the phenomenon of ecological unequal exchange has been consistently obscured, at least from the vantage point of the core. This concealment is due, in part, to the spatial distances that exist between the sites of extraction/dumping and the sites of use/enjoyment, which make it difficult for humans to connect these phenomena to each other.[89] However, Hornborg argues that it is more than simply spatial distancing that secures this cover-up. Rather, the obfuscation of ecologically unequal exchange also relies on an ideological inversion present in the manner in which the dominant social imaginary of modernity looks upon industrial and technological machinery. As he posits, the modern subject tends to fetishize the power of industrial technologies and, in so doing, mistakenly perceives that machines are productive in themselves.[90] In other words, because modern subjects believe that their technologies are generative in a fundamental sense, they can ignore the flows of energy that are concentrated in the core and used to feed industrial technologies.

the armed of America are the American Dream

With regard to the fetishization of industrial technology, Hornborg draws a comparison between the manner in which modernity invests industrial technologies with a generative capacity and his telling of a familiar European

---

[87]See Alf Hornborg, *The Power of the Machine: Global Inequalities of Economy, Technology, and Environment* (Walnut Creek, CA: Alta Mira, 2001), 9–156, and Alf Hornborg, *Global Ecology and Unequal Exchange: Fetishism in a Zero-Sum World* (New York: Routledge, 2011), 6–26.

[88]Hornborg, *Power of the Machine*, 28.

[89]Andrew K. Jorgenson, "Global Social Change, Natural Resource Consumption, and Environmental Degradation," in *Global Social Change*, ed. Christopher Chase-Dunn and Salvatore Babones (Baltimore: Johns Hopkins University Press, 2006), 181–82.

[90]Hornborg argues that the modern subject invests power in machinery in a manner that is similar to the way premodern subjects invested power in their rulers (*Power of the Machine*, 1–11).

folktale of a tramp who makes soup out of a stone. He relates the folktale in the following manner,

✷ The tramp is reluctantly admitted into a kitchen, but the housewife has no intention of serving him any food. He pulls a stone out of his pocket, asking merely for a pot of water to boil some soup on it. The housewife is too intrigued to deny his request. After a while, stirring and carefully tasting the water, the tramp observes that it could do with some flour, as if this was the only missing ingredient. The housewife consents to offer him some. Then, one by one, he similarly manages to lure her to add the various other ingredients, until, finally, she is amazed to find a delicious soup *cooked on a stone.*[91]

As Hornborg comments, "The stone in the soup is the prototypical fetish. It *transfers our attention from the wider context to its imaginary center.*"[92] In his view, industrial machines perform the same function within modernity as the stone in the folktale. They turn a person's attention away from the broader context that allows the fetishized object to function. In the case of industrial machines, the broader context is made up of the global networks of resource extraction. When the systemic processes of extraction are submerged in one's account of contemporary historical reality, the industrial machines gain the appearance of being productive in and of themselves. This view, in turn, gives the impression that technological development can produce a "cornucopia" of benefits that can be extended globally. In effect, technological advancements become the key to attending to the problems posed by eco-social emergency.

The fundamental problem with this view of technological progress, argues Hornborg, is that machines have never been productive in and of themselves. Instead, they have always relied on greater inputs of productive energy than they are capable of putting out. At least in part, this is why industrializing England needed to have millions of ghost acres of productive land at its disposal. In facilitating development at the core of the colonial system, the machines

---

[91]Hornborg, *Power of the Machine*, 151. Emphasis is Hornborg's. A version of this story is commonly recounted in social justice circles. In this version of the story, various members of a community contribute ingredients to the stone soup despite the fact that each of these individual members does not have enough food to furnish a meal of her or his own. By the time that every member of the community contributes to the pot of soup, however, they find that through their contributions, they have produced a soup capable of feeding the entire community. This version of the parable, then, emphasizes the possibility of mutual flourishing through the just distribution of resources. Obviously, Hornborg's interpretation of the story produces a different moral.

[92]Ibid. Emphasis is Hornborg's. He also draws a parallel between the tendency within modernity to fetishize machines and the tendency within some premodern societies to fetishize emperors, revering these figures as gods capable of producing the goods necessary to sustain the well-being of that society. See ibid., 65–87, 131–53.

of industry relied on complex systems of extraction in order to maintain the social metabolisms of industrial societies. These processes of ecologically unequal exchange have been ongoing throughout the project of five hundred years, creating an asymmetrical push toward the Anthropocene, even as the asymmetries were variously legitimized, ignored, or covered-up.[93]

THE GLOBALIZATION PROJECT:
A FALSE AND SUPERFICIAL (POLITICAL) ECOLOGY

In Chapter 1, I observed that by the middle of the twentieth century, the colonial project had collapsed. In its place, Western powers, led by the United States, worked to organize the world around an emerging developmentalist paradigm. Thus, within twenty years of United States President Harry Truman's call for the United States to embark on a project of development, the United Nations proclaimed the 1960s as "the decade of development." Under the aegis of the development project, technological modernization would reproduce, so it was claimed, the socioeconomic conditions of the core within the periphery.

However, by the 1970s, two lines of criticism to the development project emerged, both of which can be understood in relation to the ongoing processes of ecologically unequal exchange. As noted in Chapter 1, critical popular movements throughout Latin America pushed back against the development paradigm, calling into question its effectiveness and noting that the project was intertwined with policies of US imperialism and extraction. To borrow Gutiérrez's phrase, in these movements, the cry of the poor "irrupted" into the hegemonic consciousness constructed by the neocolonial powers of the core.[94] This irruption called into question whether the development project was truly aimed at constructing a more equitable world.

At the same time, although coming from within the core itself, the "cry" of the earth also began to gain resonance, further calling into question the hegemonic presumptions of the core. A key inflection point for this second irruption was the publication of *The Limits to Growth* (hereinafter *LTG*) in 1972.[95] In *LTG*,

still
exploitative

---

[93]Edward Barbier argues that the global economy systemically underprices natural capital instead of facing the true costs of expanded resource use and heightened forms of ecological scarcity. The upshot of this underpricing, argues Barbier, is that future generations will have to contend with acute forms of ecological degradation and economic inequality. See Edward Barbier, *Nature and Wealth: Overcoming Environmental Scarcity and Inequality* (New York: Palgrave Macmillan, 2015), 123–64.

[94]*PPH*, 38.

[95]Donella Meadows et al., *The Limits to Growth: A Report for the Club of Rome's Project on the Predicament of Mankind* (New York: Universe Books, 1972). The global north's burgeoning ecological consciousness undoubtedly predates *The Limits to Growth* (hereinafter *LTG*). In many ways, Rachel Carson's *Silent Spring*, published a decade before *LTG*, served as the catalyzing

the research team headed by Donella Meadows and sponsored by the Club of Rome, postulated that economic growth, as it was presently constructed, was causing unsustainable damage to the biosphere. Startlingly, the team found that if planetary trends in "population, industrialization, pollution, food production, and resource depletion continue unchanged," then the thresholds of growth that the planet could bear would be surpassed by the close of the twenty-first century. This scenario would most likely result in "a rather sudden and uncontrollable decline in both population and industrial capacity."[96]

Importantly, *LTG* affirmed that this path toward the bleak planetary fate it warned against was not solidified. Rather, the path could be altered so that a future of general "ecological and economic stability" could be sustained into the extended future. The report, however, also cautioned that time was relatively short for undertaking the massive politico-ecological conversion required to avoid moving the world too far down a catastrophic path. If the current trajectory of the development project was maintained via a "business as usual" approach to growth, then the future of human civilization would be increasingly imperiled. Thus, whereas the "cry of the poor" foregrounded the problem of asymmetrical growth within the 500-year project, the "cry of the earth" called into question the project's orientation toward the unending expansion of affluence. Here, Meadows and her colleagues argued for an urgent shift away from the "business as usual" approach to structuring the world's political ecology. They advocated for the reorganization of the world's political ecology in response to the limitations of the earth's ecosystem while also working to establish a more equitable distribution of wealth in the present era. Although many of the findings from *LTG* were criticized and dismissed by economists and politicians, the report undeniably served as a catalyst for critical ecological discourse throughout the world.[97] As a result, it became increasingly clear throughout the 1970s that the ways in which human beings organized the world would have to respond not only to concerns about pervasive socioeconomic inequity but also to issues of ecological health.

The development project, however, would not have to justify itself before

---

text for the formation of the environmental movement in the north, at least in the United States. See Rachel Carson, *Silent Spring* (1962; New York: Houghton Mifflin, 2002). Nonetheless, *LTG* engendered an unprecedented amount of worldwide reaction. The Club of Rome's study also uniquely focused attention on the tensive relationship between economic and ecological health. *LTG* was released the year between the original publication of Gutiérrez's *Teologia de Liberacion* in 1971 and the release of its English translation *A Theology of Liberation* (Maryknoll, NY: Orbis Books) in 1973.

[96] Meadows et al., *LTG*, 23–24.

[97] See Peter Passell et al., "The Limits to Growth," https://www.nytimes.com. Forty years after *LTG*'s publication, Graham Turner has argued that the empirical evidence demonstrates that the trends in human global environmental impact are closely tracking *LTG*'s model of "business as usual." See Graham Turner, "Is Global Collapse Imminent?" MSSI, sustainable.unimelb.edu.au.

the twin demands of planetary equity and health. This is because during the same years in which environmental concern was building into a global force, the dynamics of the development project were giving way to those of the globalization project. Whereas the former project was characterized by "a strategy of national economic growth," the latter came to be defined by a growth strategy that reshaped the world's economic structures through the softening and elimination of national economic borders and trade protections—in short, the globalization project was defined by the tenets of neoliberalism.[98] The architects of the globalization project would have to maintain its legitimacy in the face of the burgeoning cries of the earth and the poor. It is here that the language of *sustainable development* rose to prominence in political and economic discourse as a way of justifying neoliberalism's organization of the world.

Legitimization or Obfuscation?

The concept of "sustainable development" became popularized by the United Nations report titled *Our Common Future* in 1987.[99] Also known as the "Brundtland Report," in reference to its primary author Gro Brundtland, the UN called for the document in response to the growing global concern that a complex politico-ecological emergency was forming. The report examines the possible conflicts between policies aimed at ensuring economic development and those intended to sustain the health of the biosphere. The report affirms that, in working to counter the crises of underdevelopment and ecological degradation, "painful choices have to be made."[100] In acknowledging this, the Brundtland Report calls for a turn toward "sustainable development," which it defines as a form of development meeting "the needs of the present without compromising the ability of future generations to meet their own needs."[101]

In confronting the fact that the world must face "painful choices," the Brundtland Report implicitly recognizes a tensive relationship between wealth production and ecological stability. In other words, the report seemingly indicates that

---

[98]Discussing the socio-structural dimensions of neoliberalism, Philip McMichael observes that economic liberalization "*downgrades* the social goals of national development, while *upgrading* participation in the world economy (tariff reduction, export promotion, financial deregulation, relaxation of foreign investment rules)." Philip McMichael, *Development and Social Change: A Global Perspective* (Los Angeles: Pine Forge, 2008), 158. Italics are McMichael's. More recently, Adam Kotsko has argued that the formations of neoliberalism extend well beyond the socio-structural, that they constitute a "cohesive moral order" built on constrained agency, competition, and conformity at every level of society. See Adam Kotsko, *Neoliberalism's Demons: On the Political Theology of Late Capital* (Stanford, CA: Stanford University Press, 2018), 89–96.

[99]Gro Harlem Brundtland, ed., *Our Common Future: The World Commission on Environment and Development*, http://www.un-documents.net.

[100]Ibid., no. 3.30.

[101]Ibid., no. 3.27.

a sustainable future, a future which secures the flourishing of humans and the earth, cannot simply be predicated on an uncritical program of economic growth. However, this view is undercut by the notably ambiguous definition attached to the central term in the document. The concept of "sustainable development" in the Brundtland Report is intentionally underdetermined; it is unclear precisely what constitutes the needs of the present and future. As Herman Daly writes, the meaning of the concept was left "sufficiently vague to allow for a broad consensus," in order to assure that the report would be accepted.[102] Although this may have been a politically astute move, the underdetermined meaning of the concept also meant that it was vulnerable to manipulation. Indeed, this is precisely David Harvey's concern when he notes that the language of sustainable development "can rather too easily be corrupted into yet another discursive representation of dominant forms of economic power. It can be appropriated by multinational corporations to legitimize a global grab to manage all of the world's resources."[103] According to Leslie Sklair, as a result of what was at stake, the concept of sustainable development came to be "seen as a prize that everyone involved in these arguments wanted to win" in the wake of the Brundtland Report.[104] The winner, of course, would determine the concept's *functional* definition.[105]

Commenting on the manner in which the ambiguity of the term leaves it prone to misappropriation by the hegemonic powers of the globalization project, Gilbert Rist observes that the concept of sustainable development can be construed in two notably different manners. From one perspective sustainable development can be interpreted as implying "a production level that can be borne by the ecosystem, and can therefore be kept up over the long term; reproduction capacity determines production volume, and 'sustainability' means that the process can be maintained only under certain externally given conditions."[106] In other words, from this perspective, the emphasis is placed on the need for production to respect the "planetary boundaries" of earth.[107]

From another perspective, however, sustainable development is interpreted in a manner that yields dramatically different results. As Rist notes, this latter perspective presupposes that economic growth is *necessary* for meeting the needs of the present and future. Therefore, priority is placed on sustaining

---

[102]Herman Daly, *Beyond Growth: The Economics of Sustainable Development* (Boston: Beacon, 1996), 2.

[103]David Harvey, "What's Green and Makes the Environment Go Round?" in *The Cultures of Globalization*, ed. Fredric Jameson and Masao Miyoshi (Durham, NC: Duke University Press, 1998), 343.

[104]Leslie Sklair, *The Transnational Capitalist Class* (Oxford: Blackwell, 2001), 200.

[105]Ibid.

[106]Ibid., 192.

[107]On the concept of planetary boundaries, see Johan Rockström et al., "A Safe Operating Space for Humanity," *Nature* 461 (2009): 472–75.

economic growth, and concern over the negative ecological impacts of growth is subordinated to the growth imperative.[108] On this interpretation of the term, "It is not the survival of the ecosystem which sets the limits of 'development,'" writes Rist, "but 'development' which determines the survival of societies."[109] Thus, he concludes: "The two interpretations are at once legitimate and contradictory, since two antinomic signifieds correspond to the same signifier."[110] In Rist's view, it is the definition of sustainable development that privileges the growth imperative that captures the functional meaning of sustainable development within the globalization project. He writes, "Even if the bait is alluring, there should be no illusion about what is going on. The thing that is meant to be sustained really is 'development', not the tolerance capacity of the ecosystem or of human societies."[111] Here, the prospect of harsh choices is deferred by the recommendation that a "business as usual" approach be adopted.

Sustainable Development and Hegemonic Power

An in-depth study of the issues surrounding Rist's position is beyond the scope of my argument here. Nonetheless, it is possible to point to a number of corresponding findings that help corroborate his claim that the concept of sustainable development has functioned predominantly as a structure of obfuscation. In his study of the World Bank, Michael Goldman observes that in recent decades, the bank has become the world's leading producer of environmental knowledge. Thus, the bank plays a pivotal role in shaping contemporary understandings of the relationship between human economies and the environment. It is of great importance, then, that Goldman finds the bank championed a

---

[108]Recall Karl Marx's observation of the fundamental character of capital. He writes that "a barrier to capital's advance appears [to it] as an accident which has to be conquered. . . . If capital increases from 100 to 1,000, the 1,000 is now the point of departure, from which the increase has to begin; the tenfold multiplication, by 1,000%, counts for nothing." See Karl Marx, *Grundrisse: Foundations of the Critique of Political Economy* (New York: Penguin, 1973), 143. John Bellamy Foster, Brett Clark, and Richard York observe that this characteristic poses difficulties for organizing a political ecology aimed at respecting the planetary boundaries of the earth. See John Bellamy Foster, Brett Clark, and Richard York, *The Ecological Rift: Capitalism's War on the Earth* (New York: Monthly Review, 2010), 13–49. It should be noted, as Michael Northcott correctively observes, Foster and his colleagues maintain an overly positive outlook on Marx as a foundation for political ecology. See Michael Northcott, *A Political Ecology of Climate Change* (Grand Rapids, MI: Eerdmans, 2013), 144–53.

[109]Gilbert Rist, *The History of Development: From Western Origins to Global Faith*, fourth edition (New York: Zed Books, 2014), 193.

[110]Ibid. Rist overdraws the contrast of these two definitions. The tolerance capacity of the earth or of any ecosystem is malleable. Thus, "development" can reshape ecological boundaries in various ways and degrees. More problematic, as I argue below, is the way in which the privileging of "sustained development" leads to the rise of a "win-win" ideology that obfuscates the potentially unsustainable stresses being placed on the earth.

[111]Ibid., 194. Left unstated in Rist's assertion is that this sustained growth continues to be asymmetric in nature.

specific view regarding this relationship. One of the bank's environmental unit economists aptly describes this view in an interview with Goldman: "When authors of *WDR* '92 [the highly influential 1992 *World Development Report* that featured the environment] were drafting the report, they called me asking for examples of 'win-win' strategies in my work. What could I say? None exists in that pure form; there are tradeoffs, not 'win-wins.' But they want to see a world of win-wins, based on articles of faith, not fact."[112]

The concept of "win-win strategies," when taken alone, suggests that growth can be positively correlated to the reduction of negative environmental impacts in an unambiguous manner. Although there are instances in which positive correlations occur, these instances remain far from clear-cut, as the economist interviewed by Goldman makes plain. It is problematic, therefore, that a "win-win ideology" seems to have eclipsed the Brundtland Report's acknowledgment that sustainable development would require "painful choices."[113] Instead of painful choices, the World Bank champions a concept of sustainable development that suppresses the reality of trade-offs and instead presents economic growth as an unambiguous (and, hence, unifying) good.[114] Goldman's study reveals a number of mechanisms built into the bank's structure that help ensure that the bank's employees conform to its ideology. Thus, Goldman concludes, the bank's production of environmental knowledge, "is less a process of discovery, creativity, and refutation than one of *manufacturing consent*."[115]

An experience that Herman Daly recounts from his time working in the Environmental Department of the World Bank serves to illustrate Goldman's findings.[116] Daly recounts a series of exchanges he had with peers while working on the publication of the World Bank's 1992 World Development Report.

---

[112]Michael Goldman, *Imperial Nature: The World Bank and the Struggle for Justice in the Age of Globalization* (New Haven, CT: Yale University Press, 2005), 128.

[113]I discuss below the prospect of decoupling economic growth from environmental impact. The promulgation of this "win-win" ideology is also closely associated with a theory claiming that as a region first develops economically, the environmental impacts of the economy within that region increase, but after a certain level of development is attained, the growth in negative environmental impacts flattens and then decreases. This theory is captured visually with the "environmental Kuznets curve" (EKC). This curve appears as an "inverted U" in which the vertical axis refers to environmental impact and the horizontal axis refers to economic growth. The theory associated with the EKC is controversial. Although there are some isolated cases where this phenomenon appears to have taken place, it is unclear as to whether the environmental impact decreased or whether these impacts were simply pushed onto other regions. There is also no evidence that the phenomenon described by the EKC is taking place at the global level. See Nebojsa Nakicenovic et al., "Global Commons in the Anthropocene: World Development on a Stable and Resilient Planet," *International Institute for Applied Systems Analysis* (2016): 10–12. www.jstor.org.

[114]Goldman's study goes on to analyze the ways in which various institutional mechanisms and pressures within the bank function to produce a single voice with regard to sustainable development discourse. See, ibid., 100–180.

[115]Goldman, *Imperial Nature*, 148–49.

[116]Daly, *Beyond Growth*, 6.

As Daly writes: "An early draft contained a diagram entitled 'The Relationship Between the Economy and the Environment.' It consisted of a square labeled 'economy,' with an arrow coming in labeled 'inputs' and an arrow going out labeled 'outputs'—nothing more." Daly took issue with the diagram, arguing that it failed to properly capture the relationship between the economy and the environment. Instead, Daly suggested that a box should be drawn around the existing diagram and that this box should then be labeled "environment." Daly wanted to emphasize that "the economy is a subsystem of the environment and depends upon the environment both as a source of raw material inputs and as a 'sink for waste outputs.'" According to Daly, the next draft did include the box around the initial diagram; however, the box was unlabeled. Daly again protested, arguing that by not labeling the box "environment," the box appeared to be simply ornamental and failed to accurately convey the relationship between the economy and the environment. "The next draft," Daly writes, "omitted the diagram altogether."[117] As Daly's narrative makes clear, within the discursive space of the bank, the prospect of painful choices is quite literally subject to erasure.

Perhaps even more problematic than the manner in which the World Bank controls the language of sustainable development within its own institution, however, is the way that this influence extends beyond its own walls. According to Goldman, "Besides being the world's main producer of concepts, data, analytic frameworks, and policies on the environment, the World Bank has also become the world's most powerful environmentalist, teaming up with prominent NGOs, scientific institutions, borrowing states, and Northern aid agencies."[118] These alliances, in which the bank always occupies the position of power, dampen the possibility of external critique or alternative visions. Goldman argues, "The Bank's form of environmental knowledge production has rapidly become hegemonic, disarming and absorbing many of its critics, expanding its terrain of influence, and effectively enlarging the scope and power of its neoliberal agenda."[119] On Goldman's account, then, it appears that the hegemonic moment has arrived, the dominant bloc controls the discourse of sustainability to such a degree that what qualifies as sustainable development goes unquestioned.[120]

---

[117]Similarly, in an interview with Goldman, Daly observes, "Since the Bank pushes the concept that affluence through development is good for the environment, it's not possible to make a peep about how this might not be true. A few of us tried to get that point across in *World Development Report, 1992* but they would not allow it—not even a couple of pages. We even tried to publish a 'minority opinion' as a separate document, with two Nobel Prize winners as main contributors, but the Bank's censors in External Affairs wouldn't accept it. The Bank is a tough place to discuss different ideas." Goldman, *Imperial Nature*, 143.

[118]Ibid., 180.

[119]Ibid.

[120]Goldman draws on Antonio Gramsci's conception of "hegemony," which describes a form of discursive (and hence, cultural-psychological) control, in which the dominant bloc "also pos[es] the questions around which the struggle rages." See Antonio Gramsci and Nathan Hoare,

[handwritten: supports capitalism]

To be clear, Goldman does not suggest "that the world is run by the World Bank president, but rather that the global political economy has at its core a set of elite power networks in whose reproduction the World Bank is deeply embedded."[121] The bank is but one node (albeit an important node) within a broader web of power that shapes the discourse of sustainable development in the contemporary world. It is helpful, therefore, to locate Goldman's investigation of the bank within a conceptual framework of this global network.

In his analysis of the globalization project, Sklair finds that the structures and dynamics of the system are ordered by what he terms the transnational capitalist class (TCC)—a class composed of globalizing corporate elites, elected officials, *[handwritten: also political]* and bureaucrats.[122] According to Sklair, the TCC has transformed the concept of sustainable development into "a major industry" while distancing this concept *[handwritten: commodification]* from discussions of the common good.[123] In so doing, the TCC successfully muted environmental movements that called into question the growth imperative of the global economy. Thus, concepts of sustainability that recognize the reality of "painful choices" have given way to theories that align sustainable *[handwritten: counterproductive]* development with hyperindustrialization.[124] Indeed, Sklair finds that by the 1990s a form of "'sustainable' global consumerist capitalism" came to dominate the discourse.[125] Its ethos is captured well by an environmental executive of a food distributor in Loblaw, Canada, who proclaims, "If we made a lot of money destroying this planet, we sure can make money cleaning it up."[126] Thus, the TCC has constructed a conception of sustainable development wholly in line with the "win-win ideology" that Goldman finds at the heart of the World Bank's faith. The degree to which the discourse of sustainable development has been co-opted by the TCC leaves Sklair suspicious that the "poacher" has become the "gamekeeper."[127] *[handwritten: manipulation of the whole system]*

The foregoing discussion raises questions as to whether the globalization project is effectively responding to the cry of the earth, and Branko Milanovic's analysis of globalization questions whether this project is attending adequately to the cry of the poor. Milanovic observes that discussions in economics are too often dominated by "Pollyannaish" conceptions of globalization that present

---

Selections from the Prison Notebooks of Antonio Gramsci (New York: International, 1971), 182.

[121]Ibid., 12.

[122]Sklair, *Transnational Capitalist Class*, 17–23.

[123]Sklair finds that Daly and Cobb's call for an economics of community, which they identified with sustainable development, "sank almost without trace," while sustainable development went on to dominate the world's collective imagination. Ibid., 200. See also Herman E. Daly and John B. Cobb, Jr., *For the Common Good: Redirecting the Economy Toward Community, the Environment, and a Sustainable Future* (Boston: Beacon, 1989).

[124]Ibid., 201.

[125]Ibid., 206.

[126]Ibid., 253n33.

[127]Sklair, *Transnational Capitalist Class*, 202.

the phenomenon as a purely benign force in history.[128] Milanovic notes that when mainstream economists examine the forces at work in the "first global-ization" (the period of liberal globalization from 1870 to 1914), they highlight increases in gross world product (GWP) and the free movement of labor while suppressing the ways in which the first globalization was intertwined with the social technologies of extraction, slavery, and other forms of colonial domina-tion in structuring the world. "The heyday of imperialism and colonialism," Milanovic writes, "is made to appear as the period of universal growth, and catch-up of poor countries."[129]

The inclination within economic history to present globalization as an unam-biguously benign force extends into the discipline's analyses of the neoliberal globalization project. Milanovic maintains that, at the turn of the twentieth century, mainstream economists displayed a tendency to manipulate empiri-cal evidence in order to present neoliberalism as a force for convergence—a force working unambiguously to reduce global economic inequality. In his own presentation of the empirical data, however, Milanovic finds that in the 1980s and '90s the globalization project was actually less successful at facili-tating economic convergence and overall poverty reduction than the economic programs and policies that preceded it in the decades before.[130] Perhaps most problematically, Milanovic notes that although economists would couch their celebrations of liberal and neoliberal globalization within carefully qualified statements in academic papers—qualifications that often severely undercut their celebratory assertions—politicians would appropriate the exalted affirmations made by economists without giving heed to the accompanying qualifications.[131] As a result, global elites consistently misrepresent globalization in simplisti-cally positive terms that elide from their narratives the realities of the victims of the globalization project.

Pope Francis shares the concerns and suspicions articulated by thinkers such as Rist, Sklair, and Milanovic. As we have seen, Francis is dubious that the globalization project can respond adequately to the politico-ecological di-mensions of the planetary emergency, calling the ecology of the globalization project a *"a false or superficial ecology which bolsters complacency and a cheerful recklessness"* (no. 59). In effect, Francis argues that the vision of the good life promoted by the globalization project is predicated on a cover-up that results in an evasion of the politico-ecological emergency in which we are now entrenched. This avoidance, writes Francis, "serves as a license to carrying on

---

[128]Branko Milanovic, "The Two Faces of Globalization: Against Globalization as We Know It," *World Development* 31, no. 4 (2003): 667–83.

[129]Ibid., 668.

[130]Ibid., 670–76.

[131]See, for example, Milavonic's discussion of the claim that the rich and poor gain "one for one" from trade liberalization (ibid, 667–68).

with our present lifestyles and models of production and consumption" (no. 59). As a result, the dynamics of the globalization project continue to work to suppress not only the cries of the earth and the poor, but also the prospect that painful choices will have to be made in order to respond adequately to these cries. Thus, within the globalization project's sustainable development regime, persons of privilege are encouraged "to feed their self-destructive vices: trying not to see them, trying not to acknowledge them, delaying the important decisions and pretending that nothing will happen" (*LS*, 59), as Francis warns us.[132]

UNCOVERING THE FALSE ECOLOGY
OF THE GLOBALIZATION PROJECT

The obfuscation structures that serve to legitimize the business as usual approach of the globalization project are manifold. Leaving aside both the outright lies of the climate-change denial industry and the failure of the globalization project to acknowledge the ecological debt that the global north owes the south, there are at least three ways in which the relationship between this project and the planetary emergency continues to be obscured in public discourse.[133] Here I consider the submergence of (1) the distinctions between "strong" and "weak" sustainability, (2) the limitations and ambiguities of technological efficiency with regard to sustainability, and (3) the connection between the globalization project's growth strategies and the destabilization of democracy.

Sustainable Development

Generic appeals to sustainable development within the public sphere mask the difference between the concepts of "weak sustainability" and "strong sustainability."[134] Advocates of weak sustainability argue that the exploitation of the planet's natural capital (i.e., the world's stocks of natural "resources") can be sustained so long as the depletion of natural capital is substituted by the production and accumulation of human capital that is of equal or greater

---

[132]On this point, Francis's assertion is consonant with Stephen Gardiner's view that the current attempts to attend to the climate-change emergency is plagued by pervasive moral corruption that indefinitely defers meaningful action. See Stephen Gardiner, *The Perfect Moral Storm: The Ethical Tragedy of Climate Change* (New York: Oxford, 2011), 301–97.

[133]On the connections between climate-change denial and big tobacco, see Naomi Oreskes and Eric M. Conway, *Merchants of Doubt: How a Handful of Scientists Obscured the Truth on Issues from Tobacco Smoke to Global Warming* (New York: Bloomsbury, 2011).

[134]For a comprehensive study of these two positions, see Eric Neumayer, *Weak versus Strong Sustainability: Exploring the Limits of Two Opposing Paradigms* (Northampton: Edward Elgar, 2013).

still wasting natural resources

value to the natural resources being spent down.[135] In other words, as long as the value of accumulated human capital equals or surpasses the lost value of depleted natural resources and degraded ecosystems, the economy is judged as "sustainable." Weak sustainability advocates make this claim based on the position that human capital is capable of funding technological innovations and "fixes" to the deleterious effects of ecological degradation.[136] A phrase from Marx and Engels can elucidate further the position of weak sustainability. For advocates of this position, the processes of capital accumulation not only "melt into air" the inherited politico-ecological patterns of relationship found in any given *oikos*; these processes also convey to human beings the power to reform the "air" into new inhabitable politico-ecological formations.[137] The gains in human capital grant society the power to continually remake the world, thereby sustaining the human endeavor. This is the logic of the contemporary globalization project. *← humans have no limitations*

Proponents of the strong sustainability paradigm are doubtful that the production of human capital can continually substitute for the loss of natural capital without severely affecting the vitality of the biosphere. Adherents of this view emphasize that some forms of ecological degradation are irreversible and that some forms of natural capital are nonreproducible. Likewise, strong sustainability advocates are dubious that human beings can adequately grasp (and thus properly price) the deleterious effects of ecological degradation. Thus strong sustainability advocates call for policies of limitation with regard to the exploitation of natural capital stocks.[138] They worry that while the processes of capital accumulation can "melt into air" the inherited politico-ecological formations of the *oikos*, those formations will be substituted with patterns less beautiful, resilient, and inhabitable for future generations. When presented with possible

---

[135]Ibid., 22–25.

[136]Ibid., 52–78. This view comes across in environmental economist Dieter Helm's undialectical celebration of human ingenuity. See Dieter Helm, *Natural Capital: Valuing the Planet* (New Haven, CT: Yale University Press, 2015), 240–41. Compare his technological optimism and buoyant outlook for the future of the Anthropocene with Kathryn Yusoff's analysis of the "age of man." See Kathryn Yusoff, *A Billion Black Anthropocenes or None* (Minneapolis: University of Minnesota Press, 2019), 23–64.

[137]Marx and Engels famously use this phrase in describing the effect that the birth of capitalist society had on the inherited value system and social patterns of the precapitalist period. They write, "All fixed, fast-frozen relations, with their train of ancient and venerable prejudices and opinions, are swept away, all new-formed ones become antiquated before they can ossify. All that is solid melts into air, all that is holy is profaned, and man [*sic*] is at last compelled to face with sober senses his real conditions of life, and his relations with his kind." Karl Marx and Friedrich Engels, "The Communist Manifesto," in *Manifesto: Three Classic Essays on How to Change the World*, intro. Armando Hart (New Melbourne: Ocean, 2005), 33. For weak sustainability advocates, capital accumulation can be leveraged to sweep away inherited ecological patterns and replace them with "improved" patterns of relating.

[138]Neumayer, *Weak versus Strong Sustainability*, 25–29. See also Neumayer's discussion of preserving natural capital amid uncertainty, 102–29.

not using up all natural resources

exchanges of natural and human capital, advocates of strong sustainability caution restraint, calling for an ethic rooted in practices of conservation.[139]

The disagreements between supporters of the strong and weak sustainability paradigms cannot be fully adjudicated here. However, it is worth noting that even advocates of weak sustainability are dubious that the globalization project's manner of organizing the world under the auspices of sustainable development is viable. Although the architects of the globalization project appeal to the language of sustainable development, the reality of the project fails to meet the standards of even the weak sustainability paradigm. *bad* *am ground* Prominent environmental economist Dieter Helm, for example, finds that the political ecology of the neoliberal globalization project fails to value the world's natural capital properly in two potentially catastrophic ways. First, the globalization project accounts incorrectly for the value of renewable resources. The tendency among economists and policymakers has been to assign negligible value to renewables precisely because they are self-renewing.[140] *encourages abuse* However, as Helm argues, this manner of pricing has created a situation in which human economies now threaten to exploit renewables in a manner that exceeds the ability of these resources to renew themselves. Since renewables are radically undervalued, they are, in effect, exploited as if they are worthless.[141] *no time period for renewal*

Second, Helm finds that the globalization project fails to invest the wealth extracted from the exploitation of nonrenewable resources properly. He argues that the extracted wealth should be conserved and invested in a "natural capital fund" aimed at ensuring that future generations would have the requisite capital to maintain a stable politico-ecological system. Instead of being saved and invested, however, this wealth is currently squandered at unsustainable rates for the sake of short-term satisfactions. Thus, Helm concludes that "we have been depleting this cornucopia [of nonrenewable resources] like children in a sweet shop. The stocks have been plundered, with little or no thought for future generations." This prodigal manner of spending obscures reality, according to Helm, creating the appearance that the situation is better than it truly is. "It is like selling the family silver and pretending to be wealthier as a result."[142] In *used to fund more exploitation via projects*

---

[139]Additionally, from a strong sustainability perspective, the weak sustainability paradigm appears perniciously anthropocentric in its outlook. Within this paradigm, the human person is not just the measure of all things but the totality of the measure as well. Along these lines, the weak sustainability paradigm encourages a way of seeing the world that continues to reduce the life of the world to the commodities of labor and land. Under the weak sustainability paradigm that informs the logic of the globalization project, the entire world in now conscripted to serve the global accumulation of capital with minimal regard to how these conscriptions affect local communities and places.

[140]To give an obvious example, oxygen-rich air, which is obviously indispensable to human life, has no economic value because of its abundance and natural renewability.

[141]Helm, *Natural Capital*, 242–43.

[142]Ibid., 243. One can note a limitation in Helm's analogy. In view of the history and ongoing

light of Helm's views, it appears that even by the measures of the weak sustainability paradigm, the politico-ecology of the globalization project is failing to meet the standards for a sustainable future.[143]

Ecological Modernization

As I have already observed, the architects of the globalization project have sought to justify the project's manner of organizing the world through appeals to "win-win" scenarios—scenarios in which economic growth can be positively correlated with increases in ecological health and stability. The language of ecological modernization becomes prominent in validating the globalization project's way of organizing the world. Central to the discourse of ecological modernization is the idea that, as the processes of production become increasingly efficient, economic growth can be sustained indefinitely. As Tim Jackson describes it, ecological modernization holds that human innovations will allow economic output to become "progressively less dependent on material through-put" so that "the economy can continue to grow without breaching ecological limits—or running out of resources."[144] In effect, economic growth can be separated—"decoupled"—from negative environmental impacts.

However, appeals to ecological modernization, at least in popular political discourse, commonly elide the distinction between "relative decoupling" and "absolute decoupling." Yet this distinction is crucial. As Jackson defines these terms, relative decoupling refers to "a decline in the ecological intensity per unit of economic output," whereas absolute decoupling describes the scenario in which "resource impacts decline in absolute terms."[145] As Jackson observes, it is absolute decoupling that "is essential if economic activity is to remain within ecological limits." For example, with regard to carbon emissions, it is not enough for technological innovation to produce machinery that emits less carbon per unit of economic growth. Instead, if we are to respect the planetary boundary of atmospheric carbon density, what is required are gains in efficiency that would allow the economy to continue to grow while simultaneously reducing *overall* global carbon emissions.[146]

---

processes of extractive colonial and neocolonial regimes, the great-grandfather of this family stole the silver that his prodigal descendant now pawns off for short-term pleasure.

[143]Consider that the 2005 *Millennium Ecosystem Assessment* report found that approximately 60 percent of the ecosystems they examined were being "degraded or used unsustainably." See the report, "Summary Findings," https://www.millenniumassessment.org.

[144]Tim Jackson, *Prosperity without Growth: Economics for a Finite Planet* (New York: Earthscan, 2009), 67. For a helpful introduction to ecological modernization discourse, see Arthur Mol, *Globalization and Environmental Reform: The Ecological Modernization of the Global Economy* (Cambridge, MA: MIT, 2001), 17–46.

[145]Jackson, *Prosperity without Growth*, 67.

[146]Ibid., 67–68. This reduction is what is required in order to meet the IPCC's stabilization

In Jackson's review of trends in the impact of economic growth on atmospheric carbon density, he finds evidence of a consistent increase in *relative* decoupling in recent decades. In other words, the global economy has been able to "do more with less" with regard to carbon throughputs. While this might be understood as a positive sign, Jackson also observes that the gains made in relative decoupling do not come close to approaching the levels needed to bring about the absolute decoupling required to keep human activity from transgressing the recommended atmospheric carbon-density threshold. Indeed, he finds that in order for the global economy to produce the requisite decoupling, the world would need "a completely different kind of economy from the one we have at the moment which drives itself forward by . . . emitting more and more carbon."[147] For this reason, Jackson is dubious that the earth can sustain the globalization project's business-as-usual economy. He finds that an approach solely reliant on technological fixes to compensate and eventually overcome the ecologically deleterious effects of economic growth is "grossly inadequate."[148]

Jackson's judgment is particularly sobering when one notes that his analysis focuses solely on the emergency of climate change. His evaluation does not consider the challenges that other planetary boundaries pose for continued economic growth. In other words, even if increases in efficiency are able to attend adequately to the climate change emergency, it remains unclear how gains in efficiency alone will allow the globalization project to respond to the other interrelated dimensions of the planetary emergency, such as the advent of the sixth great extinction and the continuing acidification of the world's oceans. In short, the difficulties with relying on gains in efficiency to respond adequately to the planetary emergency are even more pronounced than Jackson's analysis suggests.[149]

Given all of this, it is unsurprising that over the last four decades, many of the trends in the world's political ecology have prompted growing concern about the ecological health of the planet. Amid the crass denialism of

---

target of 450 ppm. With respect to carbon emissions, the overall reduction would need to be 50–85 percent by the year 2050.

[147]Ibid., 81–82.

[148]Ibid., 82. To be clear, Jackson does not reject the need for continued technological innovation. To the contrary, he maintains that both improvements in efficiency and other forms of ecological modernization are vital to an adequate response to the planetary emergency. However, he is clear that these endeavors must be carried out within the context of a break from the business as usual approach.

[149]With regard to decoupling, a further concern is the prospect of "the Jevons paradox" or "rebound effect," which holds that, within a capitalist system aimed at the goal of inexorable growth, gains in energy efficiency result in greater resource exploitation since profits are continually reinvested into production. See William Stanley Jevons, *The Coal Question: An Inquiry Concerning the Progress of the Nation, and the Probable Exhaustion of Our Coal Mines* (New York: Augustus M. Kelley, 1905), 152. For a helpful overview of this potential paradox, see Blake Alcott, "Jevons' Paradox," *Ecological Economics* 54, no. 1 (2005): 9–21.

the Trump Administration in the United States, the US federal government's "Fourth National Climate Assessment," released at the end of 2018, finds that anthropogenic climate change likely will lead to new and heightened risks for human health and life. These risks include increased water scarcity, rises in disease transmission, the suppression of economic growth, major disruptions of ecosystems, and lower agricultural yields. Notably, the report finds that impoverished communities and indigenous communities are likely to experience these deleterious effects in a disproportionately acute manner.[150] Equally concerning, the United Nations Intergovernmental Panel on Climate Change (IPCC) released its own report one month prior to the US report and warned that the world has roughly a decade to implement significant politico-ecological transformations if it hopes to mollify the destructive impacts of climate change.[151] It is prudent, therefore, to remain chary of the view that the globalization project is responding adequately to the cry of the earth.

Material Inequality and Democracy

In view of both the acceleration of global economic inequality at the end of the twentieth century and the staggering poverty that continues to afflict billions of persons throughout the world today, it is tempting for those who are critical of the globalization project's socioeconomic dynamics to proffer a wholesale rejection of the project, perhaps blithely (and out of context) echoing Francis's assertion that "this economy kills."[152] However, recent trends in the global reduction of poverty and inequality must give one pause. It is vital to acknowledge the evidence that points to marked improvements for the lives of the poorest in the world since the advent of the globalization project. Over the last four decades, extreme poverty has declined worldwide.[153] Moreover, after five centuries of growing divergences in wealth between the materially rich and poor regions of the world (divergences that had accelerated during much of the twentieth century) over the last two decades, global economic disparity has begun to decline.[154] This point must be acknowledged.

---

[150]See "Fourth National Climate Assessment, Volume II: Impacts, Risks, and Adaptation in the United States," https://nca2018.globalchange.gov/.

[151]See "Summary for Policymakers of IPCC Special Report on Global Warming of 1.5°C Approved by Governments," https://www.ipcc.ch.

[152]Pope Francis, *Evangelii Gaudium*, no. 53, http://w2.vatican.va.

[153]See, for example, Jeffrey Sachs, *The Age of Sustainable Development* (New York: Columbia University Press, 2015), 141. The reduction in poverty during this period is most pronounced in India and China.

[154]See Christoph Lakner and Branko Milanovic, "Global Income Distribution: From the Fall of the Berlin Wall to the Great Recession," World Bank Policy Research Working Paper 6719, documents.worldbank.org/curated/en/914431468162277879/pdf/WPS6719.pdf. Note that Lakner and Milanovic's famous "elephant graph," which depicts the compression of global economic

Nonetheless, there are reasons to remain dubious of the view that the globalization project is responding to the cry of the poor in a manner that is either morally sound or socially sustainable. For one, the prospects of eliminating poverty and decreasing inequality at the global level continue to demand rates of growth that, at the very least, appear to be both threatening to the vitality of the biosphere and threatened by the burgeoning ecological emergency. Beyond this concern, however, another recent trend in inequality needs to be considered closely. As I briefly noted in this book's introduction, during roughly the same time frame in which global economic inequality has shrunk between the global north and south, the economic gains of the hyper-wealthy have skyrocketed in a historically unprecedented manner. As Saskia Sassen writes, "There has been a 60 percent increase in the wealth of the top 1 percent globally in the past twenty years; at the top of that 1 percent, the richest '100 billionaires added $240 billion to their wealth in 2012—enough to end world poverty four times over.'"[155]

The explosion of wealth among global elites also has been accompanied by a notable dip in the relative economic well-being of the majority of populations within economically developed countries. The 2018 *World Inequality Report* finds that real income growth among the bottom 90 percent of the populations of the United States and Europe has been notably suppressed relative to that experienced at the periphery and among global elites. In effect, the distribution of economic growth has functioned to "squeeze out" the middle and lower classes within the perennial core regions of the 500-year project. These phenomena—the eruption of hyper-wealth, the reduction of global inequality, and the suppression of wealth among the working classes of the core—are interrelated, tied together by, among other factors, various forms of outsourcing that have been directed by the logic of neoliberalism. As Sassen argues, in the early decades of the twenty-first century, regions that traditionally have been sites of accumulation during the 500-year project are being transformed into sites of "expulsion"—sites from which wealth and the social stability that accompanies wealth are now expelled, directed in this manner by policies that are aimed to enrich further the global elite.[156]

The difficulty with current trends in global economic poverty and inequality between the north and south is not, of course, that they are diminishing. Rather, the problem lies in the staggering prosperity of the hyper-wealthy that is cotemporaneous with the hollowing out of wealth among the majority of the

---

inequality, appears on page 31 of the report.

[155]Saskia Sassen, *Expulsions: Brutality and Complexity in the Global Economy* (Cambridge, MA: Belknap Press of Harvard University Press, 2014).

[156]Ibid., esp. 1–54. In light of this phenomenon, even Jeffrey Sachs, one of the world's foremost advocates for globalization, has stated publicly that the globalization project needs to be rethought. See Sachs's interview on WBUR's *On Point*, "Economist Jeffrey Sachs on Globalization's Risks," https://www.wbur.org.

population within the core. These trends point to the fact that the globalization project is fundamentally oriented toward serving the interests of the elite and not in redressing histories of exploitation or responding to global inequality. Although these dynamics are troubling, they are also interconnected with another global trend threatening the world with increasing immediacy: the rise of authoritarianism.

To understand how the present-day dynamics of inequality and authoritarianism are related, it is illuminating to return to Polanyi's theory of the double movement. Recall that Polanyi believed both the rise of authoritarian regimes in Europe and the outbreak of the world wars in the twentieth century had their roots in the nineteenth-century utopian liberal economic dream of the market society. The liberal project of dis-embedding markets from their broader societal-relational matrices resulted in exposing the "citizens" of the global north to the brutalities of a market society. This exposure resulted in the reflexive action on the part of the global north's citizenry to protect themselves from the creative destruction of capitalism. To do so, these populations turned to strong men, who, we might add, stoked the closely allied sentiments of nationalism and white supremacy while inaugurating protectionist economic policies. These developments, in turn, seeded the soil for the outbreak of global war.

In light of Polanyi's theorization, recent geopolitical developments appear particularly concerning. Britain's embrace of Brexit, the ascendancy of Donald Trump to the presidency in the United States, and the demonstrable rise of fascist and white-nationalist sentiment across Europe and the United States—all are consonant with the protectionist reflex of the double movement. Although the causes of these phenomena are undoubtedly complex, one can begin to discern a global trend in which the utopian vision of neoliberal globalization is now replicating the social conditions brought about by liberalism at the turn of the twentieth century (the era of the "first globalization"). Milanovic, for one, worries that the growth of intranational wealth inequality within traditional core nation-states is funding the rise of racist nationalism and further securing oligarchical regimes within these spaces.[157] Along these lines, Robert Kuttner finds that the world has entered a moment in which the backlash against the neoliberal globalization project now threatens to overturn democratic institutions and their ideals throughout the world.[158] Polanyi's analysis appears disturbingly prescient once again.

Although Kuttner holds that the cataclysms of the twentieth century can be avoided in the twenty-first, he is not optimistic, arguing that in order to minimize the chance of a catastrophic outcome it is imperative to reduce intranational

---

[157]Branko Milanovic, *Global Inequality: A New Approach for the Age of Globalization* (Cambridge, MA: Belknap Press of Harvard University Press, 2016), 192–211.

[158]Robert Kuttner, *Can Democracy Survive Global Capitalism?* (New York: W.W. Norton, 2018).

economic inequality in the very near future. It is disconcerting, therefore, to consider Thomas Piketty's prognostication that domestic inequality is likely to continue to rise in the coming decades unless governmental policies are implemented to counteract this trend.[159] What is more, the *World Inequality Report 2018* suggests that if the trends in domestic inequality continue to hold to "a business as usual trajectory," these trends will outpace the gains in economic wealth made by the global south, leading once more to an increase in global inequality over the next thirty years.[160] Thus, even in light of the recent trend in global economic convergence, it appears dubious that the globalization project as it is currently structured can attend to the cry of the poor in a sustainable manner. Instead, neoliberal globalization appears poised to unleash the catastrophes of the twentieth century in the twenty-first century, amid a planetary context of unprecedented ecological instability.

THE CULTURE-IDEOLOGY OF CONSUMERISM: HOLDING TOGETHER THE UNSUSTAINABLE

In this chapter, I have posited that the spatial distance between sites of extraction and sites of enjoyment, the fetishization of technology, and the vacuous descriptions of sustainable development all conspire to distract from both the magnitude of the complex politico-ecological emergency the world now faces and the contemporary globalization project's inability to respond to the emergency.[161] To these dynamics of obfuscation, one final factor can be added: willful ignorance. As Kari Norgaard finds in her study of climate change denial, "We don't really want to know."[162] The embrace of ignorance, especially by persons of privilege within the world organized by the globalization project, should be unsurprising. After all, the scale of the emergency and the tragedies that it portends have the power to overwhelm the imagination. Nonetheless, the embrace of ignorance is not simply tied to a generic fear of facing the emergency, nor can it be reduced to a generalized social inertia, though both of

---

[159] As Piketty famously argues, this likelihood is because of the historical tendency of the rate of return on capital to outpace the rate of growth. See Piketty, *Capitalism in the Twenty-First Century* (Cambridge, MA: Harvard University, 2017), esp. part 2. Piketty is also concerned about the prospect of an "oligarchic divergence," in which the global elite ("the one percent"), leave behind the great majority of the world's population (ibid., 463–67).

[160] See the *World Inequality Report 2018*, part 5, https://wir2018.wid.world/part-5.html.

[161] Of course, the distraction and cover-up are especially effective in spaces of socioeconomic privilege, privilege that too often translates into epistemic poverty. See Sandra Harding, "Standpoint Epistemology (a Feminist Version): How Social Disadvantage Creates Epistemic Advantage," in *Social Theory & Sociology: The Classics and Beyond*, ed. Stephen P. Turner (Cambridge, MA: Blackwell, 1996), 146–60.

[162] Kari Marie Norgaard, "'We Don't Really Want to Know': Environmental Justice and Socially Organized Denial of Global Warming in Norway," *Organization & Environment* 19, no. 3 (2006): 347–70.

these are important factors. Instead, the phenomenon of willful ignorance also must be understood in relation to the specific existential threat that it provokes in the persons whose worldview and desires have been formed by the cultural mechanisms of consumerism. *market society*

As I observed in Chapter 2, *Laudato Si'* finds that the contemporary politico-ecological emergency is deeply intertwined with an emerging global "culture of consumerism," a culture that is promulgated by the globalization project. In explicating the encyclical's critique of consumerism, I turned to Sklair's theorization of the globalization project. Recall that, for Sklair, consumer culture, what he terms the "culture-ideology of consumerism," is directed by the architects of the project in an effort to form human desire in a manner that promotes the continuing expansion of the cycles of production and consumption. Accordingly, the culture-ideology of consumerism proclaims that the good life is found in the consumption of goods and that for human persons to be "fully alive" they must consume.[163] Consumer culture, then, functions to increase and accelerate the material pressures that human populations collectively place on the biosphere.

Moreover, the culture-ideology of consumerism also promulgates, in a particularly destructive manner, the instrumental logic intrinsic to the technocratic paradigm. As John Kavanaugh argues, consumer culture teaches the human person to reduce other humans to "commodity forms."[164] With regard to the character of human relationships, then, consumerism normalizes and exalts the transactional "I-it" relationship while marginalizing and denigrating the personal "I-thou" relationship. The culture-ideology of consumerism disciplines human desire in ways that vitiate the human person's capacity for intimacy and the ability to care. Human persons (as well as the rest of creation) are presented as things to be manipulated for one's own satisfaction. Thus, this culture-ideology not only celebrates unceasing consumption; it also encourages disordered versions of self-concern that blunt concern for both neighbor and earth.

Returning to Sklair's analysis, it is apparent that consumer culture works to construct a fictive persona of the ideal human. This fictive ideal can be termed "*homo consumens*."[165] The culture-ideology of consumerism celebrates *homo*

---

[163]Obviously, all biotic life must consume to sustain itself. This is not what Sklair has in mind. Rather, it is the consumption of luxury goods. See, for example, Leslie Sklair, "The Transnational Capitalist Class and the Discourse of Globalization," *Cambridge Review of International Affairs* 14, no. 1 (2000): 67–85.

[164]See John F. Kavanaugh, *Following Christ in a Consumer Society: The Spirituality of Cultural Resistance* (Maryknoll, NY: Orbis Books, 1991), esp. 54–115.

[165]Here I borrow a term coined by Erich Fromm. While *homo consumens* can be used to specify the fictive persona idealized within the culture-ideology of consumerism, it must be affirmed that Fromm's intention is not to exalt this construction of the subject but to demystify it. According to Fromm, although the images associated with *homo consumens* may appear glamorous, powerful, and intoxicating, this imagery masks deep insecurities, destructive narcissistic tendencies, and underlying anxieties. In short, Fromm finds that *homo consumens* is an infantilized subject whose

consumens as the supreme exemplification of the fullness of life and in so doing organizes human desire to aspire toward inhabiting this ideal. In light of this, the deepest reason that human persons willfully embrace ignorance in the face of the global politico-ecological emergency becomes apparent. This emergency throws into question the meaning of life for those persons whose desires correspond to the fictive ideal of the person-as-consumer. The reality of the politico-ecological emergency creates an identity crisis for persons inhabiting (or at least striving to inhabit) the image of *homo consumens*. In other words, the damage wrought upon the earth by the growing emergency functions to reveal as false and superficial the very shape of the lives of those who are formed by the regnant culture-ideology. Likewise, this damage unveils their accompanying vision of the good life as fraudulent. For this reason, among the others referred to above, human persons under the influence of the globalization project's cultural milieu willfully maintain their own ignorance of the emergency and its accompanying damage.[166]

Finally, before concluding this chapter it is important to take note briefly of how the culture-ideology of consumerism sustains the racist imaginaries endemic to the 500-year project. This culture-ideology exists in reciprocal relationship with the socio-structural realities of the globalization project. The architects and institutions of the globalization project actively promote the culture-ideology of consumerism and its accompanying idealized persona *homo consumens* while, in turn, the culture-ideology energizes the globalization project's dynamics of production and consumption in a manner that ensures the continued functioning of the project as a whole. In a very real sense, then, the Anthropocene, that is to say, the world currently organized by neoliberal globalization, is both *created for and holds together in homo consumens*. Given this, it is important to observe that *homo consumens* does not simply refer to the person-as-consumer in a wholly abstract manner; instead, this persona has been constructed historically along anti-black racist lines.

As James Davis observes, "The ways in which people thought and wrote about consumer society helped to maintain the concept of race and reproduce assumptions about white supremacy."[167] Within the culture-ideology of consumerism, Davis finds that whiteness "stand[s] tacitly for universal personhood."[168] Thus, the human person who is celebrated as most "fully alive"

---

freedom is reduced to the freedom to consume. See Erich Fromm, *The Revolution of Hope: Toward a Humanized Technology* (New York: AMHF, 2010), 48.

[166]It may also be that the language of willfulness needs to be at least somewhat qualified by the fact that the culture of consumerism increasingly promotes addictive patterns of consumption that diminish human freedom and enthrall persons to these patterns. Ignorance appears less willful on the part of the consumer and more the product of the engineering of desire.

[167]James Davis, *Commerce in Color: Race, Consumer Culture, and American Literature, 1893–1933* (Ann Arbor: University of Michigan Press, 2007), 12.

[168]Ibid., 28.

by the globalization project is, implicitly, *the white consumer*. The culture-ideology of consumerism, then, at least historically, not only fuels the global mechanisms of material exploitation; it also sustains the racist social imaginaries that emerged with the advent of the 500-year project.[169] By the same account, therefore, *homo consumens* should be interpreted as a neocolonial subject.

CONCLUSION

The 500-year project has driven the world into the throes of a planetary emergency that is unparalleled in human history. The project has done so by organizing the world through racist and extractive colonial and neocolonial regimes that both helped fuel the great divergence between the core and peripheral regions of the project and reduced life to the commodities of labor and land at the periphery. The 500-year project constructed anti-black and anti-brown racist ideologies that aimed to legitimize the destruction of life at the periphery. The divergences initially established by extractive colonialism have been maintained in various ways through the processes of ecologically unequal exchange, which have continued to unfurl throughout the history of the 500-year project. These processes have promulgated the exploitation of the soil and all that comes from the soil from the advent of the project up through the contemporary era, transitioning colonial regimes into extractive neocolonial regimes.

In recent decades, the globalization project has come to organize the world in accordance with the dictates of neoliberal ideology. The present-day globalization project maintains its legitimacy through appeals to sustainable development and ecological modernization. However, these appeals serve to obscure and cover over both the complexities of the emergency and the ways in which the project fails to attend to the emergency. At the same time, the globalization project also produces a global culture-ideology that shapes human desire in ways that sustain overconsumption, exploitation, and racist ideologies. As a result, the globalization project continues to maintain a business-as-usual approach to the ways in which it organizes the soil and all that comes from it. Today, the world is at risk, and time appears to be growing short.

---

[169]bell hooks, for example, argues that although consumer culture frequently transgresses traditional white-supremacist cultural boundaries, it does so by aiming to reduce the (non-white) Other to a fetishized object that can be consumed by the white person (especially male). See bell hooks, "Eating the Other: Desire and Resistance," in *Eating Culture*, ed. Ron Scapp and Brian Seitz (Albany: State University of New York Press, 1998), 181–200. Rather than helping create the conditions for intimacy, then, consumer culture tends to advance a form of cultural imperialism that encourages the white consumer to reenact the "imperialist, colonizing journey as narrative fantasy of power and desire." Thus, consumer culture is steeped in what Renato Rosaldo terms "imperialist nostalgia," which perversely longs for that which it has destroyed. See Renato Rosaldo, *Culture and Truth: The Remaking of Social Analysis* (Boston: Beacon, 1993), 69–74.

Chapter 6

Bearing Witness
to a Humane World

The myriad phenomena that constitute the globalization project and the broader 500-year project are more complex than any theory or number of theories can articulate. The intricate ways that these projects owe their existence to the legacy of extractive colonialism defy singular explanation. Likewise, the globalization project's relationship to the politico-ecological emergency resists comprehensive elucidation. No single study, much less one condensed into the chapter of a book (i.e., Chapter 5), could hope to offer an all-encompassing statement on these issues. In view of this, any judgment made on the contemporary globalization project is necessarily partial, incomplete, and open to revision.[1] The work of seeing and judging this project demands an ongoing commitment to engaging with new and differing insights and perspectives in order to reflect critically on the proper shape of Christian praxis in this world.[2] The need for continual reflection is true not only with regard to the ways communities of faith read the signs of the times but also with regard to the ways they interpret the word of God. *following since we're in the with God*

Despite the foregoing caveats, at this juncture it is possible to offer an initial appraisal of the signs of the times in light of the word of God; it is possible to

---

[1] This is true of any theological engagement with the social sciences. See Gustavo Gutiérrez, "Liberation and Development: A Challenge to Theology," in Gustavo Gutiérrez, *The Density of the Present: Selected Writings* (Maryknoll, NY: Orbis Books, 1999), esp. 128–35. (Hereinafter *DoP*.)

[2] I am referring, of course, to the Young Christian Workers' "See-Judge-Act" method of theological engagement, which was pioneered by Cardinal Cardijn and subsequently influenced liberationist theological method. For a helpful account of this method in relationship to Ignatian discernment, see Jim Sheppard, "'See, Judge, Act' and Ignatian Spirituality," *The Way* 56 (2017): 102–11.

judge the globalization project in light of revelation so as to begin to elucidate the shape that Christian praxis ought to take within the world formed by this project.[3] Accordingly, this chapter begins by proffering a critical assessment of the ways in which the political ecology of the 500-year project (inclusive of the colonial, development, and globalization projects) has organized and continues to organize the world. The chapter then shifts to consider the difficulties with formulating a proper response to the globalization project in light of both the dangers tied to utopian thought and the present-day lack of a clearly defined alternative to neoliberal globalization. Finally, the chapter concludes by advancing a threefold approach for developing an eco-liberationist praxis through embracing a prophetic-reformist way of negotiating the structures of the globalization project, cultivating an ecological spirituality of liberation, and recovering a radical expression of Sabbath observance.

THE GLOBALIZATION PROJECT:
JUDGMENT IN LIGHT OF THE WORD OF GOD

The 500-year project has borne witness to nearly unfathomable transformations in the way human life, as well as life in general, is organized on the planet. There are grounds on which many of these transformations can be judged in a positive light. The advent of modern medicine has eased suffering and saved countless human lives from untimely death. The exponential acceleration in global wealth production and technological innovation has delivered myriad persons from lives of misery. Likewise, the rise of democratic institutions, while often overstated, nonetheless has afforded multitudes of persons with greater degrees of political agency than had been available in preceding eras. At the same time, in recent decades concern for the dignity of the human person has featured prominently within segments of global political discourse. From certain vantage points, it may be possible to interpret the history of the 500-year project as a "history of emancipation."[4] To use the language of Christian

---

[3]One familiar with Gutiérrez's theology may detect a subtle difference between the way Gutiérrez defines liberationist theological method and my phrasing here. Gutiérrez famously defines theology as critical reflection on praxis (or Christian praxis) in light of the Word of God. In my phrasing, I emphasize that critical reflection can help construct and orient praxis. The distinction is a matter of emphasis. The task of judging the signs of the times in light of the Word of God (which this chapter undertakes) is implicitly critical reflection on praxis subjugated to the logic of the globalization project. Hence, this chapter also critically reflects on praxis in light of the word.

[4]With a critical eye toward this type of view, Johann Baptist Metz writes, "Who in our emancipatory society is seeing to those usually forgotten or repressed freedoms: the freedom to suffer another's suffering and to heed the prophetic call of the stranger's suffering?" See Johann Baptist Metz, *Faith in History and Society: Toward a Practical Fundamental Theology* (New York: Herder and Herder, 2007), 90 (hereinafter *FHS*).

revelation, from such a standpoint, it would appear that the project of modernity has been organized around the tree of life—leading to human flourishing in a manner never before seen. From this perspective, the fruits of this project appear "good" and "pleasing to the eye" (Gen 3:6).

It is not by accident, however, that in Genesis the tree of life appears almost entangled and readily confused with the tree of knowledge of good and evil. Evil can approximate good, and human judgment can be corrupted so that what is good is called evil and what is evil is affirmed as good. While the emancipatory dimensions of modernity should not be dismissed, they must not be allowed to cover up the ways in which these outcomes have been and continue to be entangled with de-humanizing and destructive ideologies (most prominently, anti-black racism and misogyny) and allied with mechanisms of domination and plunder. Indeed, from the standpoint foregrounded in Chapter 5, the political ecology of the 500-year project can be likened to "the iron furnace" of the biblical imagination. Like the cities of Cain and Babel in scripture, this ongoing project establishes and supports a political ecology that is both unjust and unsustainable. This project, incessantly and often brutally, has fractured the relationships of intimacy and communion that God desires for human beings.[5] Modernity's escape from "the Malthusian trap" was financed by plunder, enslavement, torture, the degradation and eradication of cultures, and the desecration and exhaustion of myriad ecosystems and life forms.[6] These realities and their legacies rarely have been adequately acknowledged or attended to by the societies and groups that have "made names for themselves" through the exaltation of instrumental reason and the processes of extraction and subjugation. Instead, in far too many places, these histories of suffering remain interred. To modify the biblical metaphor, the foundation of the contemporary globalization project lies, not on sand (Mt 7:24–27), but on a mass grave—an equally unstable ground for constructing an *oikos*.

Nonetheless, the globalization project propagates an aura of legitimacy today. It does so not only by covering over the histories of suffering on which it is built but also by obfuscating the ways in which it fails, or may be failing, to attend to the unfolding politico-ecological emergency. This ongoing cover-up and the associated dampening of the cries of the earth and the poor sustain various dynamics of domination throughout the political ecology of the global system. Now, even within the spaces traditionally occupied by "the builders" themselves, these dynamics are threatening to rupture the façade of what the builders have labeled "peace"—be it through the rise of white-supremacist

---

[5]In making this claim, it is important to acknowledge that while this project has impaired relationships of intimacy, there was never a "pristine" communion antedating the project itself. It is vital to avoid the "imperialist nostalgia" referenced in Chapter 5.

[6]See Edward E. Baptist, *The Half Has Never Been Told: Slavery and the Making of American Capitalism* (New York: Basic, 2014), 112.

authoritarianism, the development of conscripting technologies, or the eclipse of multiple planetary boundaries.[7] Today's pharaohs arise with the ecological signs of judgment already unfolding around them. Grasped from this perspective, the political ecology of the contemporary globalization project is better understood as organized around the tree of the knowledge of good and evil than the tree of life. As such, the fruits of this political ecology portend alienation, no matter how pleasing to the eye they may appear.

If the globalization project, like the iron furnace of "Egypt," is organized around the tree of knowledge, then it is also true that myriad peoples throughout the world have been led to serve the shrewd logic that defines this project. On the one hand, this subjugation is made apparent through their conscripted participation in the flows of material goods and capital that constitute the unsustainable structures of globalization. On the other hand, it is also evidenced by the manner in which the globalization project forms the identities and shapes the desires of those existing within its sphere of influence. This second point is witnessed to most fundamentally through the ways in which the persona of *homo consumens* is promulgated as the supreme exemplification of what it means to be human. The culture-ideology of consumerism, with its colonialist heritage, functions to disseminate "the sickness of Egypt" throughout the world, reshaping the cultural imaginations of communities and reforming the dispositions of the human persons who make up these communities, so that *homo consumens* is exalted as the person fully alive.[8] Within the ideological spaces that the globalization project organizes, *homo consumens* is celebrated as "the glory of God."

Moreover, the judgments leveled against the 500-year project should be extended to the Anthropocene itself. After all, it is the colonial and development project that spurred this geological epoch into existence, and it is the globalization project that now organizes it. The Anthropocene is best understood as the era of the 500-hundred year project. This geological era cannot be grasped apart from the legacies of racism, plunder, and the varied political ecologies of domination that have fueled its advent. Indeed, the generic character of the term "Anthropocene" (the age of the human person) itself performs a cover-up. The term conceals the fact that, in biblical-typological terms, the human form driving the in-breaking of this era is "the city-builder." In historical terminology, the "age of the human" is more aptly understood as the age of the neocolonial white-supremacist man, for, as Kathryn Yusoff observes, "Black and brown death is the precondition of every Anthropocene origin story, and the *grammar*

the wolf mem

---

[7] Of course, the economic, cultural, and ecological violence endemic to the "peace" of the builders long has been visible to those located at the margins of power.

[8] See Chapter 5.

and *graphia* of this geology compose a regime for producing contemporary subjects and subtending settler colonialism."[9]

The political ecology of the present-day world is in need of metanoia. Nonetheless, the danger of narrating the foregoing judgments in the manner I have just articulated is obvious. It runs the risk of presenting the world as wholly fallen and utterly irredeemable. Thus, without withdrawing these denunciations and without equivocating, these judgments must be contextualized in four ways so as to both avoid a "Manichean" rendering of the contemporary context and uphold the ambiguity that shapes every historical context.[10] The two points raised at the outset of the chapter can be reiterated here. First, the foregoing denunciations are themselves based on partial information and an evolving method of interpretation. Thus, they are necessarily open to further reflection. Second, the projects of modernity have produced innovations and creative endeavors that have alleviated suffering in myriad ways. This second point cannot be discarded. Organized as it is around the tree of knowledge, the globalization project continues to participate, however ambiguously, in the tree of life.[11] The desire to serve and the refusal to serve are not easily demarcated, at least in a totalizing manner.

Third, it is important to keep in mind that within the world, as well as throughout history, human communities have resisted the logics of exploitation and domination in myriad forms while witnessing to ways of living in generative relationship with the soil and all that comes from the soil—even during Caesar's census a stable in Bethlehem remains uncounted. Last, it must be acknowledged that the very character of biotic existence does not allow for an

---

[9]Kathryn Yusoff, *A Billion Black Anthropocenes or None* (Minneapolis: University of Minnesota Press, 2018), 66. Yusoff's judgments might also be extended to the dynamics of misogyny.

[10]In its common usage, "Manichean" refers to the third-century dualistic heresy postulated by "Mani." Here, I draw on Ignacio Ellacuría's liberal appropriation of the term. Ellacuría uses the term "Manichean" to refer to views that uncritically and absolutely identify the poor with goodness and the rich with evil. For Ellacuría, even as he steadfastly denounced the civilization of capital, this unnuanced position was to be rejected. See Ignacio Ellacuría, "The Crucified People: An Essay in Historical Soteriology," in *Ignacio Ellacuría: Essays in History, Liberation and Salvation*, ed. Michael E. Lee (Maryknoll, NY: Orbis Books, 2013), for his use of "Manichean"; and "Utopia and Prophecy in Latin America," in *Mysterium Liberationis: Fundamental Concepts of Liberation Theology*, ed. Ignacio Ellacuría and Jon Sobrino (Maryknoll, NY: Orbis Books, 1993), for his most focused discussion of the illnesses endemic to the civilization of capital.

[11]This is true not only of the socioeconomic structures that govern the globalization project's political ecology but also of its underlying ethos. As Albert Borgmann observes, "The desire to dominate does not just spring from a lust of power, but from sheer human imperialism. It is from the start connected with the aim of liberating humanity from disease, hunger, and toil, and of enriching life with learning, art, and athletics." See Albert Borgmann, *Technology and the Character of Contemporary Life: A Philosophical Inquiry* (Chicago: University of Chicago Press, 1984), 36. Of course, in addition to desacralizing nature, this ethos dehumanized uncountable numbers of human beings.

unambiguous praxis of "cultivation and care" to emerge.[12] Within an entropic world, shaped as it is by the second law of thermodynamics, death and loss are inescapable. Every act of cultivation and care on the part of the human person will be subject to its own ambiguities, its own sacrifices and diminishments.[13] Any politico-ecological formation will be both ambiguously dominative and generative. The establishment of the New Jerusalem is outside the reach of human agency; the full realization of the eschatological city lies beyond the bounds of history.

IDEOLOGY, UTOPIA, AND THE PRAXIS
OF THE GARDENER

Acknowledging that the New Jerusalem can never be fully manifested in history does not relieve communities of faith from the responsibility of bearing witness to the eschatological city's integral ecology. Nor does this acknowledgment render all historical projects equal in their manifestation of virtue and vice. As Gutiérrez maintains, the eschatological promise of God's reign continues to be "an intrahistorical reality" so that "the struggle for a just society is in its own right very much a part of salvation history."[14] Likewise, as Jon Sobrino emphasizes, the reign of God not only relativizes all social (i.e., politico-ecological) orders, it also provides a means of judging their adequacy.[15]

---

[12]Throughout this text, I have used the atmospheric conditions of the Holocene as a way to delineate the "ecological crisis." In other words, the ecological crisis is understood as the movement away from the conditions of the Holocene, a movement that portends catastrophic consequences for human societies. However, the appeal to the Holocene is ultimately a pragmatic appeal. The Holocene cannot be identified with "nature." Nor does that geological era provide an ultimate "ought." Rather, as Gerald McKenny finds, the defense of whatever one conceptualizes as nature must be tied to a defense of the good associated with that conceptualization: "The loss of nature brings with it the loss of certain goods that are dependent on nature or inextricable from it, and ultimately the defense of nature must take the form of an articulation and defense of those goods." Gerald McKenny, "Nature as Given, Nature as Guide, Nature as Natural Kinds: Return to Nature in the Ethics of Human Biotechnology," in *Without Nature: A New Condition for Theology*, ed. David Albertson and Cabell King (New York: Fordham University Press, 2010), 177. McKenny makes his point while discussing human nature; nonetheless, it holds for "nature" in a broader environmental sense as well.

[13]This is a point that Lisa Sideris implicitly surfaces in her critiques of Christian ecotheology. See Lisa H. Sideris, *Environmental Ethics, Ecological Theology, and Natural Selection* (New York: Columbia University Press, 2003), esp. chaps. 2 and 3.

[14]Gustavo Gutiérrez, *A Theology of Liberation: History, Politics, and Salvation*, Eng. trans. (Maryknoll, NY: Orbis Books, 1973), 96–97 (hereinafter *TL*).

[15]Sobrino writes, "The ideal of the Kingdom serves to measure, on principle, *how* much of the Kingdom there is in particular social developments. . . . The Kingdom of God certainly relativizes [social projects] but it also *grades* them, and this is supremely important." Jon Sobrino, *Jesus the Liberator: A Historical-Theological Reading of Jesus of Nazareth* (Maryknoll, NY: Orbis Books, 1993), 115. Emphases are Sobrino's.

From the perspective developed throughout this book, in the broadest sense this adequacy is measured by the manner in which humanity's historical projects hear and respond to the cries of the earth and the poor. On these accounts the globalization project's manner of organizing the world's political ecology cries out for conversion and is in need of redemption.

As the world moves toward the middle of the twenty-first century, the language and praxis of liberation remain as germane to the global context today as they were when Gutiérrez first called for "a radical break" from the development project in the early 1970s. The language of sustainable development in present-day discourse too often appears "synonymous with timid half-measures." Ths language consistently refers to strategies that are "ultimately counterproductive" to sustaining the life of the world. Thus the praxis of the gardener—the inhabitation of *imago Dei* through serving and caring for the soil and all that comes from it—demands a turning away from the political ecology of the globalization project.

The language of liberation serves to signify an incisive rejection of the harmful ways in which the world's global political ecology is organized. This language denounces the sinful dimensions of the globalization project's "false and superficial" political ecology and proclaims that the possibility of ad-equately responding to the cries of the earth and the poor demands conversion at the socio-structural, cultural/psychological, and theological levels of human experience. Today, a paradigm shift in how the globalization project organizes the world's political ecology is desperately needed if the Anthropocene is to resemble, in any appreciable way, the "age of the gardener." Along these lines, it is necessary to address the structural imbalances within the globalization project that undervalue natural capital and underinvest in the common good. Likewise, it is vital to confront and unmask the "win-win ideology" that governs the discourse of sustainable development and obfuscates the ways in which the globalization project is organized to serve the needs and concerns of a hyper-wealthy global elite. In view of the destructive legacies of the 500-year project with regard to extractivism and the production of anti-black racist ide-ologies, the age of the gardener would be constituted by a political ecology of reparations. This political ecology would not only work to repay the ecological debt that has accrued between the global north and south but also reject the cultural/psychological structures of white supremacy that continue to justify the phenomenon of plunder. In many respects, this work will require national and international coalitions and political movements, but much of it can also be enacted at local and regional levels. There is much to be done.

However, although the imminent need for conversion from the present-day status quo points to the ways in which the contemporary situation is consonant with the context out of which Gutiérrez wrote *A Theology of Liberation*, there is also an important manner in which the two situations differ. When Gutiérrez authored his earliest works, there was a sense in which a clear alternative to the status quo had emerged in the form of the democratic socialist movements of Latin America. As Ivan Petrella observes, "For Gutiérrez, socialism was the historical project that pertained to liberation; liberation [had] a specific political and economic content that could be envisioned and enacted within history."[16] Thus, the "radical break" that Gutiérrez called for was conceived as having both a clear point of departure and a clear point of arrival. (To be clear, I use "arrival" here in a qualified sense. Gutiérrez in no way identified socialism with the reign of God. He did not view socialism as the arrival of eschatological fulfillment. Rather, socialism functioned as a historically realizable point of arrival on an ongoing historical journey that demanded ongoing and new forms of liberating praxis.) Today, as I have argued, there is good reason to find that a paradigm shift away from the globalization project is necessary. However, unlike the Latin American context of the early 1970s, there is no clear landing point, even in a qualified sense, with regard to what type of historical project or projects should structure the world's political ecologies. Alternatives to the dominant global regime of neoliberal capitalism are either inchoate and fleeting or disturbingly authoritarian.

The difficulty that the contemporary situation presents for bearing witness to the integral ecology of God's reign can be further illuminated by considering the ways in which Gutiérrez reflects on the roles of ideology and utopia in *A Theology of Liberation*. As I alluded to in Chapter 1, Gutiérrez understands ideology primarily as a distorted way of interpreting the world—a manner of interpretation that, at its most extreme, inverts reality (so that good is called evil and evil good). In this sense, ideologies produce and maintain illusory interpretations of the world that do violence to historical reality.[17] Moreover, these illusory projections fund the maintenance of unjust systems of power, systems that, in truth, are in need of transformation. The call for conversion and its corresponding praxis of liberation require a utopian vision capable of both unmasking ideological claims (the act of denunciation) and providing a generative vision of the way the world ought to be organized (the act of annunciation). The utopian imagination, therefore, shapes and drives the transformative praxis of liberation.

However, the utopian imagination brings with it its own dangers and difficulties. Primarily, as Paul Ricoeur points out, this imagination runs the risk of devolving into a form of narcissistic daydreaming that engenders a flight from

---

[16]Ivan Petrella, *The Future of Liberation Theology: An Argument and Manifesto* (London: SCM, 2006), 81. As Petrella rightly underscores, this in no way suggests that Gutiérrez reduced integral liberation to the advent of socialist forms of government.

[17]As Gutiérrez writes, ideology "spontaneously fulfills a function of preservation of the established order" (*TL*, 137).

the world.[18] At its most extreme, the distorted utopian imagination can lead to the eclipse of praxis, when unrealizable goals become the object of paralyzing fantasy. There is a real sense, then, in which the utopian imagination can become just as much of a threat to the practical aims of liberation theology as the ideological imagination.

To be sure, Gutiérrez expresses an awareness of this danger of the utopian imagination. He acknowledges that the term "utopia" can signify a worldview characterized by "illusion," a "lack of realism," and "irrationality."[19] However, as he stresses, the proper function of utopia, which in theological terms can be properly identified with the eschatological realization of God's reign, is to define the telos to which historical projects can be oriented.[20] This orientation is practical, drawing these projects toward the manifestation of eu-topias—"good places"—within history.[21] If the utopian imagination fails to incarnate eu-topias within the world, then that imagination must be examined and revised. Gutiérrez writes, "Denunciation and annunciation can be achieved only *in* praxis. This is what we mean when we talk about a utopia which is the driving force of history and subversive of the existing order. If utopia does not lead to action in the present, it is an evasion of reality." At this point, he cites Ricoeur, asserting: "Utopia is deceiving when it is not concretely related to the possibilities offered to each era."[22] Therefore, according to Gutiérrez, a denunciation of the regnant system

> *will be authentic and profound only if it is made within the very act of creating more human living conditions.* . . . Utopia must necessarily lead to a commitment to support the emergence of a new social consciousness and new relationships among persons. Otherwise, the denunciation will remain at a purely verbal level and the annunciation will be only an illusion. *Authentic utopian thought postulates, enriches, and supplies*

---

[18]For Ricoeur, this negative mode of utopian thought is but one of three levels at which the utopian imagination is made manifest. The utopian imagination can also play a productive role in transforming history and in calling the legitimation schemes of established powers into question. As Ricoeur further demonstrates, the three levels at which the utopian imagination functions mirror (in contrasting ways) the ways in which ideology functions in the world. See Paul Ricoeur, *Lectures on Ideology and Utopia*, ed. George H. Taylor (New York: Columbia University Press, 1986). For a helpful summary of Ricoeur's schema, see Paul Ricoeur, "Ideology and Utopia," in *From Text to Action: Essays in Hermeneutics* (New York: Continuum, 2008), 300–316.

[19]Gutiérrez, *TL*, 135.

[20]Thus, Gutiérrez can write, "Although the Kingdom must not be confused with the establishment of a just society, this does not mean that it is indifferent to this society. . . . More profoundly, the announcement of the Kingdom reveals to society itself the aspiration for a just society and leads it to discover unsuspected dimensions and unexplored paths" (*TL*, 134–35).

[21]The distinction between u-topia (no place) and eu-topia (the good place) is Sobrino's. Nonetheless, the distinction serves to explicate Gutiérrez's own views on the utopian imagination.

[22]Gutiérrez, *TL*, 136.

new goals for political action, while at the same time it is verified by this action. Its fruitfulness depends upon this relationship.[23]

In sum, the validity of the utopian imagination—and thus, the legitimacy of the call for liberation—is substantiated through praxis. If this imagination does not produce meaningful transformations within historical reality, then it is tantamount to the ideological versions of reformism. Both are ultimately counterproductive, failing to respond to the planetary emergency.

Although the dangers of ideological distortions remain as ominous now as they were a half century ago, today the danger of distorted versions of utopia is more obviously present than when Gutiérrez authored his groundbreaking work. This is precisely because there is no clearly defined historical project to which a Christian eco-liberationist praxis can affirm as its orienting model in history. Thus there is a manifest danger that the utopian imagination will devolve into banal escapism within the contemporary era. The call for a radical break runs the risk of inciting the construction of proverbial "bridges to nowhere." Therefore, Christian praxis must embrace, in a qualified sense, the concrete work of reform in the service of more far-reaching paradigmatic transformation.

In numerous ways, the politico-ecological terrain of the globalization project cries out for an integral metanoia, and yet this break can only be accomplished through the difficult, halting, and often fragmentary work of incremental change.[24] In effect, communities of faith, or—to echo the scope of Francis's address in *Laudato Si'*—all persons living on earth, are called to participate simultaneously in two paradigms. Referring to Part II of this book, these paradigms can be described as the "Exodus paradigm" and the "Joseph paradigm." The Exodus paradigm foregrounds the call for a radical break, bringing to mind the flight of God's people outside of the formations of "the city" of Egypt and the passage into a new creation—a new political ecology. In contrast, the Joseph paradigm recalls the work of Joseph at the end of Genesis and underscores the need to work for change by transforming the extant structures even while working through and with those very structures that cry out for conversion.[25] Joseph, after all, remains thoroughly entrenched within the city itself. Yet in persisting in his faithfulness to God's wisdom, Joseph reshapes the fallen city into a new creation, thereby redeeming its political ecology. Thus, within the

[handwritten margin note: a pipe dream]

---

[23]Ibid. Emphases are mine.

[24]Expressions of reformism are not wholly alien to Gutiérrez's approach, even in his early work. In *A Theology of Liberation*, Gutiérrez notes that in the wilderness, the people experienced a *"gradual* pedagogy of successes and failures" (88, emphasis is mine).

[25]The Joseph paradigm also bears some affinity to Delores Williams's survival paradigm. Recall that Bruce Dahlberg likens Joseph's politico-ecological reforms to Noah's endeavor to build an ark. Timothy Gorringe likens the work of constructing ecologically sustainable and socially just communities to the work of ark building. See Timothy Gorringe, "On Building an Ark: The Global Emergency and the Limits of Moral Exhortation," *Studies in Christian Ethics* 24 (2011): 23–34.

space of the globalization project, the imitation of the final Adam—that is to say, the practice of Christian discipleship—finds models in both Joseph and Moses.

THE WAY OF THE GARDENER IN THE SPACE
OF THE GLOBALIZATION PROJECT

An eco-liberationist praxis that inhabits both the exodus and Joseph paradigms is, at least in its practical dimension, consonant with the type of prophetic pragmatism for which Willis Jenkins advocates. Jenkins follows Cornel West in defining this approach as one that "privileges 'emancipatory social experimentalism' in order to face collective experiences of disaster by working with inherited traditions to cultivate 'tragic action with revolutionary intent, usually reformist consequences, and always visionary outlook.'"[26] Three points from this definition can be underscored as a way of clarifying the character of eco-liberationist praxis within the contemporary global context. First, in reading the signs of the times, eco-liberationist method properly foregrounds the disastrous effects of the globalization project so as to surface the immediacy of the situation. Second, following this manner of interpreting the world, eco-liberationist praxis organizes with the intention of effecting paradigm shifts within the contemporary politico-ecological order so as to respond to the cries of the earth and the poor. Third, eco-liberationist praxis moves toward effecting the requisite shifts in political ecology by accepting and utilizing politico-ecological reforms in accordance with the prophetic-utopian vision that it continually cultivates. This approach, then, negotiates a path between the respective dangers of ideology and utopia by remaining steadfast in both the criticality of its diagnosis and orientation, and the practicality of its strategies.[27]

---

[26]Willis Jenkins, *The Future of Ethics: Sustainability, Social Justice, and Religious Creativity* (Washington, DC: Georgetown University Press, 2013), 9; and Cornel West, *The American Evasion of Philosophy: A Genealogy of Pragmatism* (Madison: University of Wisconsin Press, 1989), 214, 229. The position advanced throughout the argument of this book differs notably from Jenkins's position in the *Future of Ethics* in that Jenkins is dubious of turning to cosmology as a way of effecting practical-ethical transformations in the world. In contrast to beginning with cosmologies, Jenkins advocates a problem-based approach to ethics that foregrounds both the problems confronting the world and the responses already under way to the problem as the sites for moral reflection. In advocating for a problem-based approach, Jenkins places it seemingly in contradistinction to the cosmological approach (which in fact had characterized his previous book *Ecologies of Grace*). Although, for Jenkins, cosmological claims are allowable and potentially productive (see Jenkins, *The Future of Ethics*, esp. chap. 4), they are secondary within the ethical approach he recommends. My preference in this book is to conceive of the relationship between cosmology and practice as part of a hermeneutical circle in which both poles continually revise the other. Thus, although I agree with Jenkins's assertion "that the most interesting theological production is driven by confrontation with the most overwhelming problems" (Jenkins, *Future of Ethics*, 83), I simultaneously wish to emphasize that what constitutes a "problem" is itself always already delineated by various cultural, cosmological, and theological valuations.

[27]A productive reformist approach in fact has its roots in the formation of Latin American base

The work of Petrella helps elucidate a general path forward for organizing eco-liberationist praxis within contexts defined by the globalization project. Petrella critically observes that Latin American liberation theology has tended to view capitalism, and hence the world organized by the capitalist globalization project, in monolithic terms. He maintains that liberationists traditionally have gravitated toward interpretations of global capitalism that emphasize the "deep structure" of the system. Moreover, these interpretations present the system of global capitalism as having an essentialized nature that is unambiguously malignant.[28] According to Petrella, liberationist discourse tends to conceive of global capitalism as both unmalleable and irredeemable.

The tendency that Petrella identifies within liberation theology is problematic. As I have suggested, even with all of its failures, the aims and means of the globalization project remain ambiguous. However, the monolithic and Manichean view of capitalism that Petrella criticizes is especially problematic within a global context in which no clear or desirable alternative to capitalism is present. From such a perspective, within the contemporary context it appears not only that there is no obvious endpoint for liberationist praxis to move toward but also no apparent starting point to begin the work of social transformation. If the contemporary globalization project is both immutable and wholly disordered, then there is nothing within the project that can be transformed and oriented toward the good. In other words, in this totalizing view of capitalism there appears no foothold within the contemporary order upon which liberationist praxis might begin the arduous journey toward meaningful transformation. According to this way of seeing the world, the only option would appear to be resistance

---

ecclesial communities. On this point, see Petrella, *Future of Liberation Theology*, 56–60.

[28]Although Petrella's critique serves as an important caution against a general tendency within liberation theology, his argument is often inattentive to the ways in which early liberationist thought has been and can be dynamically traditioned to speak to varying contexts. Also, at times, Petrella extends his critique on spurious grounds. For example, following Jung Mo Sung, Petrella cites Gutiérrez's interpretation of the question of Caesar's coin in Matthew's gospel as an example of how Gutiérrez's theology had become detached from socio-critical analysis (see Petrella, *Future of Liberation Theology*, 81–82). The problem with this criticism is that, in *God of Life*, Gutiérrez is simply developing an interpretation of scripture that can then be placed into critical conversation with social analysis. To identify the Matthean narrative with a contemporary political program, as both Sung and Petrella seem to indicate is proper, is anachronistic at best. The fundamental problem with Petrella's (and Sung's) method is that he reduces the task of liberation theology to that of critical social analysis and, thereby, erases the task of critically reflecting on the word of God. Thus, on Petrella's account, any theology of liberation that troubles itself with reflecting on Christian revelation becomes unnecessarily disconnected from history. This is where his account errs. It is one thing to assert that liberation theology needs to recover its early impulse of working to advance concrete historical projects. It is quite another to assert that liberation theology should be reduced to the advancement of those projects. The latter is what Petrella ultimately (and wrongly in my view) argues for. This argument is made most baldly in Petrella, *Beyond Liberation Theology: A Polemic* (London, SCM, 2012); however, it is also present in chapter 2 of *The Future of Liberation Theology*.

Wosolvement of responsibility one effort

by way of withdrawal, waiting for the unsustainable system to collapse under its own weight.[29] As a result, Petrella observes, liberationist discourse that has allied itself with this manner of conceiving the regnant world order has tended to become disconnected from the construction of and engagement with historical projects that productively aim to transform the world. Instead, the discourse has become problematically overdetermined by advancing negative critiques of the dominant order. Once again, the danger that must be confronted here is the withdrawal from a praxis that makes manifest the preferential options for the earth and the poor.

In contrast to a totalizing and negative interpretation of capitalism, Petrella argues for the cultivation of a liberationist political imagination that acknowledges and foregrounds the various ways in which both capitalist systems and democratic governments can be revised and reorganized.[30] This political imagination requires that one "recognize the contingent nature of institutions." Instead of viewing the political ecology of neoliberalism as a uniform and immutable phenomenon, "the world should be seen as constructed from myriad tiny blocks that can be mixed, shifted and reconstituted for creating the world liberation theologians seek."[31] Against deep structuralist interpretations of the globalization project, Petrella emphasizes the conditional nature of social institutions, whose charters and missions rely on (often tenuous) political alliances that are capable of being reformed and transformed.[32] This political imagination, then, "relaxes the distinction between periods of stability and periods of transition or change to better recognize the existence of conflict at all periods." As a result of this recognition, liberationist praxis will prioritize "a type of change which is neither revolution (the wholesale change of one structure for another) nor reform (the humanization of the existing structure) but revolutionary reform."[33]

---

[29]In countering this view, Petrella calls for the cultivation of a more agile "institutional imagination." See Petrella, *Future of Liberation Theology*, 93–120.

[30]Ibid., 69–92, 121–43.

[31]Ibid., 111.

[32]Here Petrella's views are consonant with Sklair's conception of the global system (although Sklair is less open to the possibility of reforming capitalism than Petrella). It is important, however, to caution against dismissing the depth structure of global capitalism that has been formed over the long history of the 500-year project. Although Immanuel Wallerstein's account of the world system, for example, may be overdetermined by its structuralism and discounts the role that culture plays in shaping and maintaining global arrangements of power, to dismiss the existence of seemingly intractable structures that have calcified over time is to underestimate the difficulties in producing real and effective change in the world. For example, Petrella qualifiedly affirms the possibility of participatory democracy over a mere procedural approach to democratic governance (see Petrella, *Future of Liberation*, 46–68). However, participatory democratic practices are threatened more and more by the phenomenon of unrelenting social acceleration (itself a structural element of the globalization project), which siphons off the time needed to enact this form of democracy. Optimism at the prospect of transformation should be tempered by a sense of the tragic within history.

[33]Petrella, *Future of Liberation*, 108.

Of course, the ambiguity inherent in any type of reform project always threatens to undermine the integrity, criticality, and effectiveness of eco-liberationist praxis. Since there is no clear way of delineating strategies of revolutionary reform from those that constitute counterproductive reformism, there is always the risk that reformist projects devolve into the latter type. In response to this danger, the utility of "negative critiques" for shaping eco-liberationist praxis can be reasserted. In working to transform the political ecology of the globalization project, eco-liberationist discourse must continually return to the task of unmasking the ideological claims that legitimize the project. If reformist projects aim toward working with, abiding in, and enhancing "the peace of the city" (Is 29:7), then the prophetic corrective to reformism reminds the community that the city itself must repent and convert if the peace of the city is to be legitimate and sustainable.[34]

SUSTAINING AN ECOLOGICAL SPIRITUALITY OF LIBERATION: THE DISPOSITIONS OF THE GARDENER

An ecological theology of liberation must advance lines of critical questioning as a way of unmasking the machinations that legitimize inherited structures of domination so as to properly orient projects of prophetic reform. At the same time, eco-liberationist discourse must also nurture an ecological spirituality of liberation that rightly orders the desires of the human person within the sphere of the globalization project.[35] If the praxis of the gardener is to be

---

[34]Luke Bretherton offers a well-developed argument for reformist politics as appropriate to the life of faith. In so doing, he takes the above verse from Isaiah as his organizing theme. The danger with Bretherton's account and prescriptions, however, is that they underplay the manner in which the peace of the city in fact masks histories and structures of violence for which urgent repentance and conversion are necessary. Here, then, Jonah's encounter with the city of Nineveh may provide a more apt description of the manner in which communities of faith are to negotiate with the globalization project. These communities must work for the conversion of city that is moving headlong toward ruin. This difference can also be presented in terms of our cultural construction of time. In accordance with his prescription to seek the peace of the city, Bretherton advocates for the inhabitation of *ordinary time*—allowing this liturgical season to shape the Christian community's prayer and praxis. In contrast to this, as I develop immediately below, an eco-liberationist sensibility is informed more properly by the apocalyptic sense of time advocated for by Johannes Baptist Metz, for whom every moment is a gate through which God's transformative power and judgment break into history. It is better to understand ordinary time as always existing within apocalyptic time. To fail to do so is to risk organizing ordinary time in accordance with the apathy that characterizes what Metz calls evolutionistic time with its ersatz metaphysics of progress. For Bretherton's account of faithful responses to globalization, see Luke Bretherton, *Christianity and Contemporary Politics: The Conditions and Possibilities of Faithful Witness* (Malden, MA: Wiley-Blackwell, 2010), 175–209. For his account of ordinary time, see ibid., 192–99. For Metz's critique of evolutionistic time Metz, *FHS*, 156–65.

[35]Jon Sobrino helpfully describes Christian spirituality as a life that takes its orientation in the unfolding of history from Christ so as to commit itself "to the building of the reign of God" and

effectively discerned and sustained within history, the human person and his or her community must partake in an ongoing struggle for liberation from the cultural/psychological bondage to *homo consumens*. Here, the cultivation of three dispositions are vital to the process of liberating the human person from the cultural/psychological constraints of *homo consumens* and orienting the person toward the inhabitation of *homo hortulanus*. The first of these dispositions is an awareness and acceptance of guilt and the need for redemption in light of the history of suffering constitutive of the ongoing 500-year project.[36]

Johann Baptist Metz has stressed the need to structure human identity around the acknowledgment and acceptance of responsibility for the fate of history's victims.[37] Metz formulates this argument in response to his view that the subject of modernity (as well as its postmodern inheritors) has come to be characterized by a deep-seated fatalism. This fatalism seemingly absolves the human from the imperative to bear moral responsibility for the legacies of history and the ongoing formation of society. As a result of this perceived absolution, the person readily resigns himself or herself to "the cult of apathy" and "the apolitical life."[38] *must be held accountable*

Importantly, Metz finds that bondage to apathy relies in large part on covering up modernity's histories of suffering. Rather than acknowledge the voices of the victims of history, the history of modernity is projected fundamentally as one of progress—a history of emancipation. When history is interpreted in this manner, there is nothing within that functions to disturb the person, nothing that might call into question the ways in which the world is organized. Operating within an imaginary informed by this interpretation of history, the person can continue on in life, listlessly "sitting next to their fleshpots" (Ex 16:3) furnished by the architects of the globalization project.[39]

The acknowledgment of both guilt and the need for redemption, therefore,

---

to doing both "*what* Jesus did" and "*as* Jesus did." See Jon Sobrino, *Spirituality of Liberation: Toward Political Holiness* (Maryknoll, NY: Orbis Books, 1988), 7.

[36]My emphasis on guilt reflects especially my own social location within the globalization project as a white male of considerable privilege from the United States. Nonetheless, it remains true that all persons are called to make the preferential options for the poor and the earth, and thereby examine the ways in which their own desires might conform to the sinful logics of colonialist domination.

[37]This is not responsibility in an absolute sense, but rather, in a qualified sense that stresses both human sinfulness as a cause of suffering and the human capacity to enact moral agency in the world. For a helpful study of Metz's anthropology, see J. Matthew Ashley, *Interruptions: Mysticism, Politics, and Theology in the Work of Johann Baptist Metz* (Notre Dame, IN: University of Notre Dame, 1998).

[38]Metz, *FHS*, 157.

[39]"A history of emancipation without a history of redemption," Metz writes, ". . . reveals itself to be an abstract history of success, an abstract history of the victors—a halved history of freedom, so to speak, giving *homo emancipator* as the subject of history a perfect mechanism for justifying and exculpating himself" (*FHS*, 120).

serve as a galvanizing force in history, capable of fissuring the spell of modernity and the enthrallment of *homo consumens* to the logic of the technocratic paradigm. In turn, this fissuring creates and sustains the space in which a productive utopian imagination might emerge. As Metz writes, "Political imagination can avoid being absorbed once and for all into technological forces only if it holds on to that moral-religious imagination and power to resist that grow from the remembrance of the suffering that has piled up in history."[40] Remembrances of suffering, then, are *dangerous memories*, memories capable of interrupting the human person's comfort with the status quo. This subversive form of memory, Herbert Marcuse posits, "is a mode of dissociation from the given facts, a mode of 'mediation' which breaks, for short moments, the omnipresent power of the given facts."[41]

Whereas the architects of the Anthropocene glory in the advancement of their projects, the dangerous memories of the victims of history remind us that "every document of civilization is simultaneously a document of barbarity."[42] The memories of extraction and plunder, of enslaved humans, desolated ecosystems, massacres, war, and the unrelenting exhaustion of the soil and all that comes from the soil, serve to shatter the veneer of tranquility on the surface of the 500-year project. As Metz writes, "Remembering suffering compels us to look upon the public *theatrum mundi* not only from the perspective of the ones who have made it and arrived, but also from the vanquished and the victims."[43] Thus, where both the culture-ideology of consumerism and the promises of progress function to seduce the human person, in an attempt to return him or her to "the sleep of inhumanity," the dangerous memory of the suffering other rouses the person, imploring him or her to stay awake while continuing to hope in God.[44]

In stirring the person to consciousness, dangerous memories perform a twofold task. On the one hand, these memories painfully expose the need for the redemption of the world—a redemption whose fullness lies beyond the power of human capabilities.[45] Thus, dangerous memories continually provoke a turn-

---

[40]Ibid., 101.

[41]Quoted in ibid., 178.

[42]See Walter Benjamin, "Theses on the Philosophy of History," in *Illuminations*, ed. Hannah Arendt (Fontana/ Collins, 1973), 255–66.

[43]Metz, *FHS*, 102.

[44]On the "sleep of inhumanity," see Jon Sobrino, *The Principle of Mercy: Taking the Crucified People Down from Their Crosses* (Maryknoll, NY: Orbis Books, 1994), 1–14. For Metz the dangerous memory of the Christ event is not only one of suffering and death, but also one of hope in the resurrection. On the need to stay awake, see Ched Myers, *Who Will Roll Away the Stone? Discipleship Queries for First World Christians* (Maryknoll, NY: Orbis Books, 1999), 387–409.

[45]For Metz, this is especially true for memories of the dead and vanquished, those whose sufferings cannot be justified through the sublimations of history. Only God, "for whom not even the past is fixed," can redeem the lives of the vanquished. See Johann Baptist Metz, "Theology in the Struggle for History and Society," in *Expanding the View: Gustavo Gutiérrez and the Future of*

ing to God in both painful lament and eager expectation: "Come, Lord Jesus!" becomes the call of the Christian community, break into history and redeem creation![46] On the other hand, dangerous memories also summon the person to enter into solidarity with the victims of history (a turning toward neighbor and earth). Memories of suffering become "an orientation to action."[47] In rousing *homo consumens* from the sleep of inhumanity, dangerous memories of the domination of the soil and all that comes from it summon the person to live responsibly before the Gardener. The call "Come, Lord Jesus!" is inextricably bound up with Jesus's call, "Follow me!"[48] Thus, as Metz puts it, the aim of cultivating a memory of the history of suffering "is reducing the gap between the inhumanity that is all around us and the humanity that is possible for us."[49] Put in the terminology of this text, the awareness and acceptance of guilt and the need for redemption catalyzes and sustains a transformation of praxis that reduces the gap between *homo consumens* and *homo hortulanus*. This awareness and acceptance act as a refining fire, a fire through which the Spirit works to refashion humanity's instruments of domination into the plowshares and pruning hooks of solidarity. The acknowledgment of the depth of human guilt also serves to underscore that it is God who is the true subject of history and of salvation.

Gutiérrez's own reflections on the practical and political character of memory serve to further emphasize its capacity for catalyzing solidarity. "To remember," he writes, "is to have in mind, or care for, someone or something. One remembers in order to act. Without this, memory lacks meaning; it is limited to being a kind of intellectual gymnastics."[50] Importantly, Gutiérrez finds that the fundamental aim of remembering is to make God's memory our own; it is, in the Pauline language, to inhabit "the mind of Christ," a mind that, as I observed in Chapter 2, is characterized by "a very vivid and recent memory of . . . the most forgotten."[51] Here, as with Metz, memory functions not only to disrupt the cultural/psychological dimension of human life as it is sinfully constructed by the victors of history but also to impel the person to respond through metanoia and discipleship. Again, to place Gutiérrez's conception of memory within the framework of this text, to inhabit the mind of Christ is to enter into the mind of the Final Adam, the one who proclaims, inaugurates,

Jesus identifies w/ the poor

Liberation Theology, ed. Marc Ellis and Otto Maduro (Eugene, OR: Wipf and Stock, 2010), 98.

[46] Metz, *FHS*, 163.

[47] Ibid., 179.

[48] Ibid., 163.

[49] Ibid., 107–8.

[50] Gutiérrez, "Memory and Prophecy," in *The Option for the Poor in Christian Theology*, ed. Daniel Groody (Notre Dame, IN: University of Notre Dame Press, 2007), 19.

[51] Ibid. For Gutiérrez, the eucharistic liturgy summons the community of faith to make God's memory its own. Along these lines, but in conversation with Metz's political theology, see Bruce T. Morrill, *Anamnesis as Dangerous Memory: Political and Liturgical Theology in Dialogue* (Collegeville, MN: Liturgical Press, 2000).

and embodies the jubilee of God's reign.[52] The cultivation of an awareness and acceptance of guilt is requisite to hearing and responding to the cries of the earth and the poor, and to discern the ways of the gardener.

In his discussion of memory, Gutiérrez underscores the importance of cultivating not only dangerous memories constellated around the sufferings of those deemed nonpersons by the powers, but also joyous and hopeful memories that recall God's liberating works in history (liberating works which cannot be identified with Enlightenment conceptions of emancipation). Here Gutiérrez's emphasis surfaces a second key component of an ecological spirituality of liberation—the experience and cultivation of gratitude at the recognition of the goodness of God's work.

The disposition of gratitude derives from the experience of God's love for the world. On this point, I cite Gutiérrez at length:

> A spirituality of liberation must be filled with a living sense of *gratuitousness*. Communion with the Lord and with all humans is more than anything else a gift. Hence the universality and the radicalness of the liberation which it affords. This gift, far from being a call to passivity, demands a vigilant attitude. This is one of the most constant biblical themes: the encounter with the Lord presupposes attention, active disposition, work, fidelity to God's will, the good use of talents received. But the knowledge that at the root of our personal and community existence lies the gift of the self-communication of God, the grace of God's friendship, fill our life with gratitude.[53]

For Gutiérrez, the proleptic experiences of salvation—which I have defined as liberation from sin and communion with God, neighbor, and earth—function to shake the human person from both apathy and selfishness. Thus, as with guilt, gratitude interrupts the cultural/psychological constraints of *homo consumens*. Similarly, the experience of gratitude also grounds and sustains the call to conversion.[54] As James Nickoloff explains, capturing well the nuance of Gutiérrez's thought, "At bottom Gutiérrez believes that the free gift of God's love, made concrete above all in the gift of life, may awaken a sense of gratitude in the one who accepts it. Gratitude, however, does not stop at contemplating the gift; thankfulness gives rise to the desire to love in

---

[52]For his discussion of the jubilee, see Gutiérrez, "Memory and Prophecy," 22–23.

[53]Gutiérrez, *TL*, 118–19.

[54]Gutiérrez writes, "The free and gratuitous love of God, the heart of biblical revelation, is the model of action for the believer. It is the most important content of the memory that indicates the path for the community of Jesus's disciples, whose commitment is, precisely to be a sign of that love in history" (Gutiérrez, "Memory and Prophecy," 22).

return."[55] Thus, the experience of gratitude—informed by the recollection of God's love—is fundamental to the life of discipleship.

Throughout his writing, Gutiérrez emphasizes that gratitude is the human person's proper response to God, not only when remembering God's liberating work in history, but also when recalling and contemplating the gift of creation itself.[56] Particularly in this last regard, Gutiérrez's emphasis on gratitude is consonant with the positions delineated in *Laudato Si'*, where the interruptive capacity of gratitude is a key theme of Pope Francis's encyclical. For Francis, the gratitude that comes with perceiving creation as a gift shatters the technocratic gaze, which looks upon nature as simply "a problem to be solved."[57] Undercutting the technocratic worldview, the posture of gratitude helps the community of faith affirm that "the world is a joyful mystery to be contemplated with gladness and praise" (*LS*, 12).[58] This way of seeing, Francis intimates, has the capacity to liberate human desire from the compulsions of *homo consumens*. As I observed in Chapter 2, the cultivation of gratitude reorients the human person toward intimacy with creation. Indeed, as I noted there as well, it is the reception of the world in gratitude that properly grounds a praxis of service and care. Genuine gratitude, then, like the recognition of guilt, serves to reduce the gap between the inhumanity that defines the formations of the globalization project and the humaneness to which God calls the human person.

Both gratitude and the acknowledgment of guilt emanate from the disposition of humility and the cultivation of spiritual poverty, which signifies an openness to cooperating with the will of God. As should be clear by now, the disposition of humility is intrinsic to the vocation of gardener—a calling predicated

standard of Jesus

---

[55]James Nickoloff, *Gustavo Gutiérrez: Essential Writings*, ed. James B. Nickoloff (Minneapolis: Fortress, 1996), 149.

[56]For example, Gutiérrez writes, "Utility is not the primary reason for God's action; the creative breath of God is inspired by beauty and joy. Job is invited to sing with Yahweh the wonders of creation—without forgetting that the source of it all is the free and gratuitous love of God." See *OJ*, 75.

[57]As Metz observes elsewhere, "In a society that is pervasively determined by [scientific controlling knowledge], other ways in which human beings know and comport themselves—suffering, pain, mourning, but also *joy* and *play*—come into play only in a functional and derivative way. Their cognitive importance is largely underestimated" (Metz, *FHS*, 106, emphasis is mine).

[58]If the category of guilt is most properly related to justice, then the category of gratitude relates most closely to beauty. Whereas the acknowledgment of guilt cries out for reparation, the perception of beauty invites a response of protection and care for that which is. As Roberto Goizueta argues, beauty and justice should not be conceived of in isolation from each other. Rather, each participates in the other so as to properly order a liberationist spirituality and praxis. He argues that the difference in character between the praxis of beauty/justice and a purely instrumentalizing *poiesis* is akin to the difference between building a house and a home. See Roberto Goizueta, *Caminemos con Jesus: Toward a Hispanic/Latino Theology of Accompaniment* (Maryknoll, NY: Orbis Books, 1999). Goizueta's analogy is particularly striking for an ecological theology of liberation, given the etymological root of ecology (*oikos*). The praxis of beauty/justice (of which gratitude is a constitutive element) is requisite to the vocation of inhabiting the world as a home and resisting the horror of a totalizing regime of domination governed solely by instrumental reason.

only
imago
Dei

on the willingness to serve God through caring for neighbor and earth. Most fundamentally, the posture of humility reminds human persons that they are not God, and that they cannot be the author of their own (much less, the world's) redemption. By the same token, humility serves to relativize any claim that one can make with regard to inhabiting the mind of Christ and knowing the ways of the gardener. It affirms that the God who reveals Godself also remains hidden and unutterable (to say nothing here of the opaqueness of the world and even one's own intentions). Thus, the cultivation of humility de-absolutizes any praxis that the person would identify as the way of the gardener, calling that praxis into question and returning the person to the mystery of God.

In terms of praxis, humility also throws into constant question the validity of the community of faith's negotiations with "the city." This disposition, then, destabilizes reformist (or even revolutionary) politics, inviting the community to interrogate both the effectiveness of politics and the faithfulness of its witness. Here Gutiérrez's interpretation of the narrative of Mary and Martha's encounter with Jesus in Luke's gospel is instructive (Lk 10:38–42). In the Lukan story, Martha becomes ensnared by the demands of everyday life, with her tactics of service becoming something of an idol that must be followed obediently.[59] In contrast, Mary, in humility, turns to Jesus, thereby allowing God's wisdom to move her beyond herself and the routinized tactics of household maintenance. Here humility functions as an interruptive force that moves Mary beyond the logic of the accepted paradigm of her day. In a similar manner, the posture of humility must continually function to return the community of faith to the one who is *the way*, so as to discern more attentively the manners of inhabiting *imago Dei* within the ambiguous world of the globalization project. Humility awakens and reawakens the person's senses to the call of God and the vocation of gardener.

Taken together, the dispositions of humility, guilt, and gratitude help liberate the human person and the community of faith from the cultural/psychological bonds that define *homo consumens*, moving the person toward the freedom of the gardener. These dispositions help shift the character and content of praxis, spurring the community to continue to transform the weapons of the city into the tools of service and thereby inhabit more fully *homo hortulanus*. Likewise, what emerges from this (always ongoing!) process of cultural/psychological

---

[59]See Gutiérrez, *God of Life*, 169–70. It is notable that Gutiérrez, a liberation theologian, privileges Mary over Martha here. Within the Christian tradition, there is a long history of interpretation reflecting on the significance of each of these biblical figures and their relationship to each other. Traditionally, Mary is identified with contemplation and prayer and Martha with action. With Meister Eckhart, a line of thought emerges that reverses Jesus's verdict and affirms Martha as the one who most adequately fulfills the life of the Christian through her service. See *Meister Eckhart: The Essential Sermons, Commentaries, Treatises and Defenses*, ed. Edmund Colledge and Bernard McGinn (New York: Paulist, 1981), 177–81. That Gutiérrez valorizes the Marian option suggests that the contemplative life is of vital importance within his understanding of discipleship.

transformation is the emergence of a culture more properly attuned to the city that is the garden.

DISCIPLESHIP AND THE PRACTICE OF SABBATH

The cultivation of an ecological spirituality of liberation is necessary for maintaining a critical edge and liberating trajectory in the community's negotiations with the structures and dynamics of globalization project, to say nothing of an openness to God. Nonetheless, when adopted in a generalized manner, the dispositions of guilt, gratitude, and humility are likely insufficient for sustaining the liberationist impulse and utopian-prophetic vision requisite for effectively confronting the workings of this project. The unrelenting onslaught of the culture-ideology of consumerism, the experience of social acceleration, and other dynamics of globalization make it implausible that the person of community can maintain the life of the gardener amid the sickness of Egypt. Under the unremitting pressures of the globalization project, the interruptive and transformative task of Christian discipleship is likely to wear one down, with the result that the utopian imagination is likely to be dulled.[60] Thus it is not enough to name the coordinates for an ecological spirituality of liberation, even if those coordinates effectively orient the person toward the inhabitation of *imago Dei*. The commitment to imitating the way of the gardener must also be consistently and intentionally renewed. To renew the commitment, the transformative capacities of guilt, gratitude, and humility can be channeled through and accompanied by the observance of Sabbath.

As I noted in Chapter 4, the options for both the earth and the poor are constitutive of the observance of Sabbath, a practice that requires rest for the soil and all that comes from it. Here I add that Sabbath-keeping also undercuts the ideological homogenization of time and, instead, foregrounds the community's hope in the power of God to redeem history.[61] The observance of the holy day thus grounds the imminent expectation of the community of faith, continually reawakening the human person to the immediacy of the task of inhabiting more fully the *homo hortulanus* and witnessing to the New Jerusalem. This *day of rest*

---

[60] It is plausible that the cultural milieu of the globalization project will function to reduce the dispositions proper to the gardener to commodity forms, so that, rather than effecting a transformation of the person, these dispositions simply become items for consumption as part of a cathartic rite. Along these lines, see Vincent Miller's account of the ways in which consumer culture both accommodates and appropriates religious identity. See Vincent Miller, *Consuming Religion: Christian Faith and Practice in a Consumer Culture* (New York: Bloomsbury, 2003). See also Christian Smith and Melinda Lundquist Denton, *Soul Searching: The Religious and Spiritual Lives of American Teenagers* (New York: Oxford University Press, 2005), esp. 160–71.

[61] See, for example, Abraham Heschel, *The Sabbath* (New York: Farrar, Straus and Giroux, 2005), 94–101.

observance challenges the community to confront the dangers of complacency and fatigue that haunt and threaten to mute or overwhelm the strategies and tactics of prophetic reformism.

The observance of Sabbath becomes the temporal locus from which the life of discipleship (the cultivation of spiritual poverty and the praxis of solidarity) emanates. Karl Barth posits that the foundational principle of the practice of Sabbath is that of surrender to God (what Barth calls a "renouncing faith").[62] Within an eco-liberationist conceptual framework, the surrender required in observing Sabbath is one that renounces the ways of *homo consumens* and the prospect of service to the globalization project. It is in and through the practice of Sabbath that the need for a radical break from this project is reaffirmed and the commitment to the vocation of gardener is revivified and celebrated.[63] In the transfiguring moment of Sabbath the strategies and tactics of practical reform are explicitly relativized and judged incomplete.

Moreover, although the Sabbath is a distinct (and exalted) moment in the week, it also lays claim to all other moments of time. As Barth writes, the one "who has a self-renouncing faith on Sunday will have it also on a week-day."[64] Angela Carpenter develops this point, noting that the interruption and limit imposed by the Sabbath "function to constantly reiterate the comprehensive divine claim. All time belongs to God. . . . God claims all of time precisely so the whole of human life can be freedom for God and responsibility before God."[65] Therefore, the observance of the holy day continually challenges the community to maintain its prophetic edge in negotiating with the globalization project's ways of organizing creation.

DIMENSIONS OF SABBATH OBSERVANCE

In describing the character of Sabbath observance, five interrelated dimensions can be delineated: rest and restraint, mercy, protest, and solidarity; discern-

---

[62]Barth writes, "The Sabbath commandment demands the faith in God which brings about the renunciation of man, his renunciation of himself, of all that he thinks and wills and effects and achieves. It demands this renouncing faith not only as a general attitude, but also as a particular and temporal activity and inactivity of the Sabbath as distinguished from other days" (Karl Barth, *Church Dogmatics*, ed. Geoffrey W. Bromiley and T. F. Torrance [Edinburgh: T&T Clark, 1956–75], III.4, 59).

[63]To this effect, Barth writes that the ecclesial community "must not allow itself to become dull, nor its services dark and gloomy. It must be claimed by, and proclaim, the lordship of God in the kingdom of His dear Son rather than the lordship of the devil or capitalism or communism or human folly and wickedness in general. It must still see its responsibility toward its members and the world in the fact that when it is assembled there always sounds out the judging, attacking, critical, yet clear and unambiguous Yes of God to man" (ibid., 69).

[64]Ibid., 72.

[65]Angela Carpenter, "Exploitative Labor, Victimized Families, and the Promise of the Sabbath," *Journal of the Society of Christian Ethics* 38, no. 1 (2018): 87.

ment; convocation; and celebration. I begin by considering the dimension of rest and restraint. As I noted in Chapter 5, both the phenomenon of consumerism and the persona that it glorifies are predicated on the exaltation of a dazzling and unrestrained acquisitive desire within the cultural/psychological sphere of human existence. This acquisitive desire stands in stark contrast to the discipline of restraint that is at the heart of the practice of Sabbath.

Rest and Restraint

In the first place, then, Sabbath mandates an intentional and identifiable break from the culture-ideology of consumerism through the cultivation of restraint. Here, the practice of Sabbath challenges the human person and his or her community to reinhabit the posture of the gleaner so as to allow the soil and all that comes from the soil to rest. This posture, of course, may take any number of concrete expressions within the community's own context, and, to be sure, it is the community itself that must discern the practices of Sabbath rest that are proper to its specific situation. Nonetheless, a general principle of fasting can be suggested here. Most obviously, this principle suggests the exercise of restraint in shaping the manner in which the community eats during Sabbath.[66] Similarly, reinhabiting the posture of gleaner should shape the community's consumption of fuels and goods on the holy day, allowing the earth a greater possibility of rest. Likewise, within spaces governed by the logic of the globalization project, rest from addictive patterns of entertainment and practices that propel forward the phenomena of social acceleration are vital.[67]

Mercy, Protest, and Solidarity

While Sabbath-keeping is maintained through the disciplines of restraint and rest, the observance of the holy day cannot be reduced to these disciplines. In a world whose dominant political ecology unrelentingly exhausts the earth and the poor, the day of rest must also be a time to heal and tend to the needs of the afflicted (Mk 3:4). The observance of Sabbath requires a discipline of active solidarity and mercy. Accordingly, it is proper to undertake the works of mercy as a necessary element of Sabbath-keeping. Likewise, the solidaristic action

---

[66]For example, given both the environmental costs associated with the production of meat and the theological view that God's sanctioning of the human consumption of animal flesh is a concession made in view of the pervasiveness of sin, it is proper to practice vegetarianism or veganism during the Sabbath. In related fashion, Christopher Carter calls for the cultivation of "black veganism" among black Christian churches as a way of resisting and transforming racist neocolonial cultures. See Christopher Carter, *The Spirit of Soul Food: Race, Faith, and Food Justice* (Champaign: University of Illinois Press, forthcoming), see especially the section titled "Practice: Soul-full Eating."

[67]Here, then, the Sabbath becomes an instance of entering more fully into what Ellacuría terms the "civilization of poverty." See Ellacuría, "Utopia and Prophecy in Latin America," esp. 309–25.

proper to Sabbath-keeping invites public protest in the face of environmental injustice. If Sabbath is meant to witness to the gift of peace that emerges from the human person's communion with God, neighbor, and earth, then the absence of communion cries out to be met with acts of lament, confrontation, and protest on the Sabbath. Indeed, to cultivate the discipline of rest on the Sabbath while failing to tend to the disciplines of solidarity and mercy risks rendering rest a mere bourgeois expression of self-concerned leisure.

Discernment

If the practice of Sabbath is a time of self-renunciation before God, then it must also be a time of discernment. The observance of the holy day is meant to be constituted by reflection on the character of God's wisdom and the demands that Sophia places on the person who stands before the mystery of God. At the same time, the task of discernment must also be composed of careful study and analysis of the politico-ecological policies, programs, and ideologies that organize the world in all of its complexity. On this same account, Sabbath discernment can also involve the difficult work of listening to the cries as well as the hopes and joys of those relegated to the peripheries of the globalization project. Such analysis and listening is necessary for clarifying the shape of Christian witness to the cries of the earth and the poor within the concreteness of historical reality. In short, Sabbath is a time in which the ongoing task of reading the signs of the times in light of the word of God (in order to continually clarify the shape of Christian praxis) is given special attention.

Convocation

I have stressed throughout this text that the vocation of gardener is also a convocation—a calling together of the community of disciples to live in faithful solidarity with the world. Accordingly, the practice of Sabbath is a time in which the communal call to holiness is acknowledged as an imperative and put into practice.[68] The corporate nature of the call to keep Sabbath is worth underscoring here because, for the same reasons that the observance of Sabbath is vital to a Christian eco-spirituality of liberation, it is doubtful that the isolated human can sustain the observance of the holy day alone. The keeping of Sabbath requires the support, insights, and accountability of others committed to the task of discerning and incarnating the ways of the gardener. Indeed, the very act of gathering together in intimacy serves as a witness against the fragmenting

collectivism

---

[68]This is a point on which Barth is in basic agreement. See Barth, *Church Dogmatics*, III.4, 69–70.

and isolating mechanisms of consumer culture and social acceleration.[69] The task of rest, the works of mercy and environmental justice, and the practices of discernment are most likely to be sustained through the structures of a mutually supporting community of disciples and persons of goodwill. The responsibility of keeping Sabbath, then, is an invitation to recover the impulse that originally catalyzed the formation of the base ecclesial communities of Latin America that began to form in the wake of Medellín.[70]

Celebration

Finally, it must be added that all the dimensions of observing Sabbath surfaced here—rest and restraint, mercy and conflictive protest, discernment, and convocation—are meant to be undertaken as an act of celebration and joyful hope.[71] From a Christian perspective, the community is called to enter into the complex practice of Sabbath-keeping fundamentally as a witness to the Resurrection and a testament to the hope of God's power to break into history, bind the strong man, and transfigure a world that is organized (in varying degrees) by the power of sin (Mk 3:22–30). As Barth writes, emphasizing his claim, "*The minor interruption of our everyday by the weekly holy day corresponds to the great interruption of the everyday of world history by Easter Day*, no doubt only as a sign, but nevertheless as a concrete sign to which we must pay attention."[72] For the Christian community, then, the practice of Sabbath both emanates from and partially reflects the joyful hope of God's definitive victory over the power of sin.

The joy that catalyzes and sustains the witness of Sabbath is not only tied to the Resurrection and the eschatological hope from which it stems, but also to a hope for expressions of Jubilee in history. As I observed in Chapter 4, when considering the Levitical tradition, the practice of Sabbath culminates in the observance of Jubilee—an interruption of the regnant political ecology that is notably more substantial than that of Sabbath-keeping. In the contemporary politico-ecological context, organized as it is by the power of the globalization project, the hope for Jubilee looks with eager expectation for a paradigm shift in the political ecology of the world—a time when the soil and all that comes from the soil are released from the imposition of sinful extractivism, the one-dimensional logic of the technocratic paradigm, and the lust for domination channeled through the culture-ideology of consumerism. It is a time in which

---

[69]See Chapter 5.

[70]See Marcello de C. Azevedo "Base Ecclesial Communities," in *Mysterium Liberationis: Fundamental Concepts of Liberation Theology*, ed. Ignacio Ellacuría and Jon Sobrino (Maryknoll, NY: Orbis Books, 1993), 636–53.

[71]Cf. Barth, *Church Dogmatics*, III.4, 68–69.

[72]Ibid., III.4, 64–65.

the colonialist legacies of white supremacy, misogyny, and the degradation of the earth should be honestly confronted, denounced, and repented. Hope for the Jubilee, the in-breaking of God's reign, also looks to the day when the meek inherit the earth, the tools of innovation are used to serve the earth and the poor, and the wisdom of God stands as the organizing principle of the city. With these joyful hopes at its center, the praxis of Sabbath helps to ensure that prophetic reformism does not lapse into a counterproductivity that unwittingly fuels the political ecology of the iron furnace. Instead, in cooperation with the Spirit, Sabbath-keeping continues to engender hope and energize the in-breaking of a political ecology that resonates more deeply with the eschatological coming of the New Jerusalem. In this way, observance of the holy day not only serves as the axis for an ecological spirituality of liberation, but also helps to renew the critical edge to a praxis of prophetic reformism that seeks to transform the political ecology of the globalization project.

CONCLUSION

If the community of faith is to respond properly to its vocation to be a sacrament of salvation in the world, it must confront and unveil the complex ways in which the globalization project, in its lust for domination, works to subjugate the soil and all that comes from the soil to its own unjust and unsustainable ways. At the same time, the community must also respond in merciful solidarity to the places from which the cries of the earth and the cries of the poor emerge. These tasks, the tasks of discipleship, are complex and difficult. At its point of departure, a liberating praxis aimed at transforming the political ecology of the globalization project, even in modest ways, can designate no clear point of arrival. Moreover, the path that this praxis seeks is clouded in ambiguity. There is so much in the world to be denounced, so much to cultivate, so much to care for, and so much that might be redeemed. Into this whirlwind the community must sojourn, trusting that the wind itself is invigorated by the breath of life. Along this way of discipleship, the community is tasked with inhabiting more fully the image of God while discerning and resisting the false logics of the city, however alluring these logics might appear. Through the cultivation of humility, guilt, mourning, and gratitude, and through the recovery of observance of the Sabbath—all in the service of making manifest the preferential options for the earth and the poor that arises from faith in God—it is possible that a new creation might emerge, a historical transfiguration that anticipates the final transformation of all things.[73]

---

[73]Karl Rahner, for example, finds that the Christ-event initiates the divinization of the world itself. See Karl Rahner, "Dogmatic Questions on Easter," in *Theological Investigations*, vol.

As I observed earlier in this text, perhaps the most vivid allusion to Jesus as *homo hortulanus* (the one who properly reconciles God, neighbor, and earth) occurs in the first resurrection account of John's gospel. There, within a setting already framed by the creational language of Genesis, Mary identifies Jesus as "the gardener." This identification, as I have argued, serves as a foundational point for connecting theological anthropology and Christology within an eco-liberationist soteriological framework. Jesus, the incarnation of God's wisdom, liberates the world from the alienating power of sin so as to renew creation and restore communion between God, humanity, and earth.

In drawing this book to its conclusion, I observe here that the re-creational theme of the first resurrection account in John's gospel does not end with Mary's encounter with Jesus. Rather, this motif arises again in Jesus's initial appearance to the other disciples. In this appearance, I find that the anthropological-Christological symbolism of the fourth gospel is pressed in an ecclesiological direction. When Jesus encounters the disciples gathered in the closed room, the narrator notes that it is once again "the first day of the week." (Whatever fears, doubts, or terrors the community of disciples were experiencing in the wake of the crucifixion, they had gathered together nonetheless.) On seeing the community gathered together, Jesus breathes on them, saying, "Receive the Holy Spirit."[74] Here, Jesus re-forms the community of disciples into *homo hortulanus*. In taking up its vocation once more, the ecclesial community is called back to the task of cultivating and caring for the soil and all that comes from the soil, thereby participating in the liberating restoration of communion with God, neighbor, and earth. Participation in this work is nothing less than the practice of resurrection—the experience of and witness to the mystery of salvation at work in the world.

---

4 (New York: Seabury, 1974), 126. See also Denis Edwards's reflection on the significance of Rahner's eschatology for creation in *Ecology at the Heart of Faith: The Change of Heart That Leads to a New Way of Living on Earth* (Maryknoll, NY: Orbis Books, 2006), 86–94. I would add that the Rahnerian "grammar of fulfillment" (to use Brian Robinette's terminology) must be interrupted and complemented by varying grammars of reversal. On this last point, see Brian Robinette, *Grammars of Resurrection: A Christian Theology of Presence and Absence* (New York: Herder and Herder, 2009), esp. part II.

[74]As Sandra Schneiders observes, "The verb 'breathe' is a *hapax legomenon* in the New Testament and occurs substantively only twice in the Septuagint. In Genesis 2:7, God at the first creation breathes life into the earth-creature, and it becomes the first living human being. In Ezekiel 37:9–10, God commands the prophet to breathe upon the dry bones 'that they may live,' i.e., that the people Israel might be re-created. In this Easter scene, Jesus, in an act of New Creation, breathes the promised Spirit of the New Covenant into the community of his disciples." Sandra Schneiders, *Jesus Risen In Our Midst: Essays on the Resurrection in the Fourth Gospel* (Collegeville, MN: Liturgical Press, 2013), 49–50.

Epilogue

Ignacio Ellacuría famously describes those whom the world relegates to the status of nonpersons as a "crucified people"—a people who are unjustly condemned to death as a result of the ways in which sin has structured and continues to structure the world.[1] Like the story of "the judgment of nations" in Matthew's gospel, Ellacuría's designation functions to identify "the least of these" with Christ. Upon their bodies, the very body of Christ, this people bears the marks of "the sin of the world," the marks of crucifixion. With this identification in view, Ellacuría calls on communities of faith to enter into meditative prayer, imaginatively placing themselves before the crucified people at the foot of the cross.[2] In contemplating the unjust suffering of the crucified, Ellacuría instructs the communities of faith to make a colloquy, asking, "[W]hat have I done to crucify them? What am I doing in order to uncrucify them? What ought I do so that this people will be raised?"[3] This colloquy, for Ellacuría, serves as the point of departure for the life of Christian discipleship.

As I noted in the introduction, Bruno Latour writes that today nature is becoming recognized as a "marked" category.[4] Latour seeks to highlight the dynamic character of nature and the ways in which the formations of the natural order are inextricably bound to the cultural and social formations of the world. If nature is a *marked* category, defined as much by its historicity, contingency, and its myriad permutations, as it is by some universalized essence, then Latour's

---

[1]See Ignacio Ellacuría, "The Crucified People: An Essay in Historical Soteriology," in *Ignacio Ellacuría: Essays in History, Liberation and Salvation*, ed. Michael E. Lee (Maryknoll, NY: Orbis Books, 2013), 195–224.

[2]Here Ellacuría is historicizing the "Colloquy at the Foot of the Cross" in the first week of Ignatius's *Spiritual Exercises*. In this colloquy, Ignatius asks the retreatant to place himself or herself imaginatively at the foot of the cross and ask, "What have I done for Christ? What am I doing for Christ? What ought I to do for Christ?" See Ignatius of Loyola, *The Spiritual Exercises and Selected Works*, ed. George E. Ganss (Mahwah, NJ: Paulist Press, 1991), 138. For a helpful discussion of Ellacuría's interpretation of the *Spiritual Exercises*, see J. Matthew Ashley, "A Contemplative under the Standard of Christ: Ignacio Ellacuría's Interpretation of Ignatius of Loyola's Spiritual Exercises," *Spiritus* 10, no. 2 (2010): 192–204.

[3]Cited in Kevin Burke, *The Ground Beneath the Cross: The Theology of Ignacio Ellacuría* (Washington, DC: Georgetown University Press, 2000), 26.

[4]Bruno Latour, *The Politics of Nature: How to Bring the Sciences into Democracy* (Cambridge, MA: Harvard University Press, 2004), 48–49.

designation is apt for a reason that extends beyond his intention in utilizing the term. It is clear, today, that the natural world bears the marks of sin, the marks of crucifixion, as a result of the ways in which human persons have tread upon and organized the earth and its ecologies. Indeed, a point of emphasis through this book is that the effects of sin upon the nonperson are inextricably bound up with the effects of sin upon the earth. In effect, the crucified people are hung upon the tree of life, the tree of creation. In facing the crucified people, then, as Ellacuría exhorts, communities of faith must also face the earth, asking what we have done to crucify and what we must do to bear witness to the resurrection, to a new creation. With this in mind, it is appropriate to give the penultimate word to Gutiérrez, whose thought has shaped the argument of this book profoundly. Here, I quote him at length:

> We must be careful not to fall into intellectual self-satisfaction, into a kind of triumphalism of erudite and advanced "new" visions of Christianity. The only thing that is really new is to accept day by day the gift of the Spirit, who makes us love—in our concrete options to build a true human fellowship, in our historical initiatives to subvert an order of injustice—with the fullness with which Christ loved us. To paraphrase a well-known text of Pascal, we can say that all the political theologies, the theologies of hope, of revolution and of liberation, are not worth one act of genuine solidarity with exploited social classes. They are not worth one act of faith, love, and hope, committed—in one way or another—in active participation to liberate humankind from everything that dehumanizes it and prevents it from living according to the will of the Father.[5]

The cries of the earth and the poor demand that those who would follow Christ—the final Adam—commit more fully to transforming the swords and spears of domination into the plowshares and pruning hooks of the gardener, entering more deeply into solidarity with the soil and all that comes from it. One concrete action to this effect, continues to be worth more than any of the theologies seeking to justify that action.

---

[5]Gustavo Gutiérrez, *A Theology of Liberation: History, Politics, and Salvation*, Eng. trans. (Maryknoll, NY: Orbis Books, 1973), 174.

Index